THE MANCHUS AND THEIR ENTERPRISE

Yong Liang

THE MANCHUS AND THEIR ENTERPRISE

The Role of Language
and
Three Eighteenth Century Primers

EBERHARD KARLS
UNIVERSITÄT
TÜBINGEN

TÜBINGEN
LIBRARY PUBLISHING

Bibliografische Information der Deutschen Nationalbibliothek
Die Deutsche Nationalbibliothek verzeichnet diese Publikation in der Deutschen Nationalbibliografie, detaillierte bibliografische Daten sind im Internet über http://dnb.d-nb.de abrufbar.

Die Online-Version dieser Publikation ist auf dem Repositorium der Universität Tü-bingen frei verfügbar (Open Access).
http://hdl.handle.net/10900/123474
http://nbn-resolving.de/urn:nbn:de:bsz:21-dspace-1234747
http://dx.doi.org/10.15496/publikation-64838

Tübingen Library Publishing 2022
Universitätsbibliothek Tübingen
Wilhelmstraße 32
72074 Tübingen
druckdienste@ub.uni-tuebingen.de
https://tlp.uni-tuebingen.de

ISBN (Hard/Softcover): 978-3-946552-56-7
ISBN (PDF): 978-3-946552-57-4

Umschlaggestaltung: Susanne Schmid, Universitätsbibliothek Tübingen
Satz: Helena Nebel, Universitätsbibliothek Tübingen
Druck und Bindung: Open Publishing GmbH
Printed in Germany

Dedication

To Lars Peter Laamann, Hans Ulrich Vogel, Achim Mittag and George Bryan Souza, for their encouragement and fostering my personal and professional scholarly efforts in pursuing Manchu Studies. To Jie Deng and Lujia Liang for their relentless and tireless support for my efforts to engage in and complete this work.

Table of Contents

Acknowledgements

The translation of these Manchu primers was started in 2015, when I pursued an academic career at SOAS University of London under supervision of Professor Lars Perter Laamann, who offered me a chance to conduct a Manchu class of reading Manchu-language chronicles. Practice of teaching Manchu as a research language, in combination with my profession of teaching Chinese and English as Second Language Acquisition, has convinced me that it is necessary to introduce some comprehensible reading materials into the academia, by which scholars could master the Manchu language steadily for research purpose. The hypothesis of Comprehensible Input has been consistently tested in learning of second language, foreign language, heritage language, extinct language, etc., and its efficiency has also been confirmed by linguists across the globe. So does my Manchu classes in the University of Tübingen, where I am funded to pursue a PhD project in Manchu economy while teaching courses in fields of linguistics and history. A number of students have gradually acquired the Manchu language through guided reading of Manchu documents, which are easy to comprehend and apply into research.

I wish to thank my PhD supervisors, Hans Ulrich Vogel, Achim Mittag, and Lars Laamann for their support for my research and their encouragement towards my employment of Manchu-language chronicles to examine the history of the Manchus and their unification of China and the transcription, translation, and annotations of these primers. I want to thank Jie Deng for her efforts in revising my Manchu transliteration of these original manuscripts. I am also grateful to George Bryan Souza for his interest in this work and his guidance in the preparation of this manuscript for publication. Special thanks go to Keith Richardson for his detailed proofreading. Finally, I want to thank Tübingen Library Publishing for their interest in and for printing this work, which I hope will promote and stimulate further interest and work in Manchu Studies.

23/12/2021, Xi'an International Studies University

List of Pictures and Maps

Abbreviations

1. Kimeng: manju nikan gisun kamqiha manjurara fiyelen qingwen ki-meng bithe (jian manhan yu manzhou taohua qingwen qimeng 兼滿漢語滿洲套話清文啟蒙)
2. Oyonggo One: manju gisun i oyonggo jorin i bithe (qingwen zhiyao 清文指要)
3. Oyonggo Two: sirame banjihuha nikan hergen i kamqibuha manju gisun oyonggo jorin bithe (xubian jianhan qingwen zhiyao 續編兼漢清文指要)
4. In glossary and footnotes, man. indicates Manchu-language and chin. indicates Chinese-language.

Glossary

Academician of Grand Secretariat (*neige xueshi* 內閣學士)

Banner-men stationed in the capital (*jingqi* 京旗)

Banner-men stationed throughout the empire (*zhufang baqi* 駐防八旗)

Civil Examination System (*keju* 科舉)

Comprehensive History in Aid of Governance (man. *hafu buleku*; chin. *zizhitongjian* 資治通鑑)

An Important Agency (*yaoque* 要缺)

Assistant Grand Secretary (*xieban daxueshi* 協辦大學士)

Banner Commanders-in-Chief (*dutong* 都統)

1. Biographies of Qing History (*Qingshiliezhuan* 清史列傳)
2. Blue Feather (man. *lamun funggala*; chin. *lanling* 藍翎)
3. Bureau of Xi'an General (*xi'an jiangjunshu* 西安將軍署)
Chinese-Martial Banner-man (man. *ujen qooha*; chin. *hanjun* 漢軍)

Chinese-Martial Commander-in-chief of Bordered Yellow Banner (man. *kubuhe suwayan gvsai ujen qoohai ejen;* chin. *xianghuangqi hanjun dutong* 鑲黃旗漢軍都統)

Company (man. *niru*; chin. *niulu* 牛錄)

Company Commander (man. *nirui janggin*; chin. *zuoling* 佐領 or *niulu zhangjing* 牛錄章京)

Compendium of Materia Medica (*bencao gangmu* 本草綱目)

Councillor (man. *jargvqi;* chin. *zha'er guqi* 扎爾固齊)

Cultivated Talents (*xiucai* 秀才)

Director in Ministry of Rites (*libulangzhong* 禮部郎中)

Double-peak Hall (*Shuangfeng'ge* 雙峰閣)

Draft of Qing History (*Qingshigao* 清史稿)

Fiery Wine (*huojiu* 火酒)

First Candidate (man. *qohoho*; chin. *nizheng* 擬正)

Five-cloud Hall (*wuyun tang* 五雲堂)

General of Jilin (*jilin jiangjun* 吉林將軍)

Grand Councilor (*zaixiang* 宰相)

Grand Mentor of Heir Apparent (*taizi taifu* 太子太傅)

Grand Minister Consultant (*canzan dachen* 參贊大臣)

Grand Ministers (*dayuan* 大員)

Grand Secretary of the Eastern Hall (*dongge daxueshi* 東閣大學士)

Green Standards (*lüying* 綠營)

Hall for Advancement of Literature (*hongwen ge* 宏文閣)

Hall of Three Chinese-scholar Tree (*sanhuaitang* 三槐堂)

Imperial Guards (man. *hiya*; chin. *shiwei* 侍衛)

Imperial Household Department (*neiwufu* 內務府)

Inner Grand Ministers (*neidachen* 內大臣)

Inscription upon the Hall of Three Chinese-scholar Tree (*sanhuaitang ming* 三槐堂銘)

Investigating Censor (*yushi* 御史)

Jurchen (man. *nioiji* or *Juxen*; chin. *Nüzhi* 女直 or *Nüzhen* 女真)

One Hundred Chapters of Manchu Language (man. *tanggv meyen*; chin. *Qingwen baitiao* 清文百條)

Manchu Chinese Simultaneous Combinations (*manhanhebi* 滿漢合璧)

Manchu Vice Commander-in-chief of Bordered White Banner (man. *kubuhe xanggiyan gvsai manju meiren i janggin;* chin. *xiangbaiqi manzhou fudutong* 鑲白旗滿洲副都統)

Metropolitan Examination (*huishi* 會試)

Metropolitan Graduates (*jinshi* 進士)

Metropolitan Graduates in Translation (*fanyi jinshi* 翻譯進士)

Minister of the Court of Colonial Affairs (*lifanyuan shangshu* 理藩院尚書)

Mongol Reader-in-waiting of Grand Secretariat (*neige menggu shidu xueshi* 內閣蒙古侍讀學士)

Mongol Vice Commander-in-chief of Bordered Blue Banner (man. *kubuhe lamun gvsai monggo meiren i janggin;* chin. *xianglanqi menggu fudutong* 鑲藍旗蒙古副都統)

National language, riding and shooting (*guoyuqishe* 國語騎射)

National Library of China (*Guojia tushuguan* 國家圖書館)

Palace Examination (*dianshi* 殿試)

Permanent Chief of Study in Capital City (*Jingdu Yongkuizhai* 京都永魁齋)

Plain Yellow Banner (man. *gulu suwayan gvsa*; chin. *zhenghuangqi* 正黃旗)

Prefecture Examination (*yuanshi* 院試)

Provincial Education (Intendant *tidu xueyuan* 提督學院)

Provincial Examination (*xiangshi* 鄉試)

Provincial Graduate (*juren* 舉人)

Qing's Lexicographical Work (man. *manju gisun i buleku bithe;* chin. *qingwen jian* 清文鑒)

Rice Wine (*mijiu* 米酒)

Same Principle for Treating Small Pox and Herpes (*douzhen yiguan* 痘疹一貫)

Scholar (man. *baksi;* chin. *bakeshi* 巴克什)

Second Candidate (man. *adabuhangge*; chin. *nipei* 擬陪)

Secretary in Ministry of Rites (*libu zhushi* 禮部主事)

Sinicized (*hanhua* 漢化)

Six Ministries (*liubu* 六部)

State Language of the Qing Empire (man. *manju*; chin. *qingwen* 清文)

Superintendent Commander (man. *hontoho;* chin. *guanling* 管領)

Three Dukes (*sangong* 三公)

Three Eastern Provinces beyond Shanhai Pass (*guandong sansheng* 關東三省)

Three Highest Administrations (*sanfu* 三府)

Three Superior Banners (*shangsanqi* 上三旗)

Top Fifteen Shooters (man. *tofohon mangga*; chin. *shiwu shanshe* 十五善射)

Version of Preserved Print in Permanent Chief of Study(*yongkuizhai canban ban* 永魁齋藏板版)

Vice Minister in Ministry of War (*bingbu shilang* 兵部侍郎)

Vice Director in the Ministry of War (man. *qoohai jurgan i aisilakv hafan*; chin. *bingbu yuanwailang* 兵部員外郎)

Weak Rice Wine (man. *nitan nure*; chin. *bojiu* 薄酒)

INTRODUCTION

Preface

This book leads readers to observe various aspects of Manchu life in the High Qing era (1683-1839). Manchus were the banner-men who spoke their own language and practiced martial skills of riding and shooting. Besides these magnificent features, they also ate, drank, got married, laughed, cried and even became addicted to alcohol and gambling. Yet they were Manchu people in fundamental ways. To study the original Manchu society, one needs to look at historical relics or documents. These three Manchu primers were textbooks that were used by Manchu people to learn their first language since the early eighteenth century, in which researchers can find valuable texts for approaching the past. There are various versions that survived in the course of history. Since the early Qing time, Christian missionaries from Europe travelled to the Qing empire and studied the Manchu language for mission purposes. Three Manchu primers, *Kimeng, Oyonggo One* and *Two*, were their first choices. Accordingly, a few versions of these primers, the relevant translation and research documents were kept in Europe and later, purchased by some American libraries. Japanese and Korean scholars diligently studied Manchu as the Qing's official language, in comparison to the Chinese language, for better understanding their giant neighbor. Therefore, these three Manchu primers were also well reserved in Korea and Japan in form of compiling Asian or Chinese languages. There are at least seven major versions of *Oyonggo One* and *Two* that still exist in libraries or publishing firms across the globe, and the number of original documents could be dozens. Furthermore, modern Japanese scholars worked with their Chinese peers and published these three Manchu primers, separately, to help the academia access the original Manchu sources. Due to development of information technology, the original documents of these Manchu primers can also be traced on the Internet from time to time. Nevertheless, an English interpretation and translation of the original Manchu documents is in urgent need.

As basic textbooks for learning the Manchu language, *Kimeng, Oyonggo One* and *Two* were mainly used by the Manchu banner-men for maintaining their identity as the ruling elites in the Qing dynasty. The Eight-banner system indicates a separation between banner-men and commoners. Banner-men were military men who were the unification elites led by the Manchus. Manchu language was the lingua franca among the banner-men. Whether they were Manchu, Mongol or Chinese by origin, all banner-men spoke Manchu as their first language. Language is an identity. Manchu language represents a Manchu identity that signifies a Manchu unification in politics, economics, military superiority, territory and other cultural norms. Military superiority, maintained by the Manchus through shooting from stance and horseback, exemplifies the unification and dominance over the other peoples. Other Manchu customs, such as education, hunting and a frugal lifestyle, all designate a unique identity that is ethnic in essence, also politically as the ruling elite.

What is Manchu Language?

This book presents you with three Manchu primers, which were popular textbooks used in the High Qing era. Before we go to the details of these primers, we shall prepare ourselves with some basic concepts, such as, what is Manchu language?

The cradle-land of Manchu ethnic groups is conventionally considered as Three Eastern Provinces beyond the Shanhai Pass,[1] from which the Manchus expanded their rule into vast regions of Northeast, Central, South and Southeast Asia. Manchu language was the prime official language of the Qing dynasty (1636-1912), which was dominated by the unification elites, consisting of Manchus, Mongols and Han Chinese banner-men. Manchu language was a typical Tungusic language being spoken in the northeast regions of Asia, which covers modern China's Liaoning, Jilin and Heilongjiang provinces, and the far east area of Russia.

It is reasonable to assume that Manchu language is nearly identical with Jurchen language in aspect of speaking.Nurgaqi (1559-1626), the founder of the Later Jin (1616-1636), started his great enterprise in Hetu ala, which roughly is Jianzhou garrison in the Ming China and Xinbin[2] county in modern China.[3]The Jurchen language spoken by Nurgaqi could be a dialect among all the Jurchen-speaking regions. Nonetheless, Nurgaci and his son Hong Taji (1592-1643) gradually integrated the Jurchen-speaking tribes of Northeast Asia into one regime (see Map 1), and accordingly, their way of speaking Jurchen (whose name was officially changed to Manchu in 1635) could have played a major role of popularizing Manchu as the official language during the imperial unification.

---

[1] Guandong sansheng 關東三省

[2] Under modern China's administration, Xinbin 新賓 is a county, in which the Yongling Town (man. *hetu ala*; chin. *yongling zhen* 永陵鎮) was the birth place of Nurgaqi, the founder of Later Jin.

[3] Jianzhou 建州 was a garrison set up by the Ming central government to bridle (*jimi* 羈縻) the ethnic groups that were not yet converted to the Chinese culture. According to the Chinese administrative structure, this region is divided into three divisions: Jianzhou garrison (Jianzhou wei 建州衛), Jianzhou Left Garrison (Jianzhou zuowei 建州左衛) and Jianzhou Right Garrison (Jianzhou youwei 建州右衛).

Map 1: The Cradle of Manchus

The concept of Jurchen is identical to the Manchu term of Nioiji, a transliteration from Khitan concept of Lüzhen,[4] which later was changed to Nüzhi for evading the same words in the Khitan emperor's name Yelüzongzhen.[5] The corresponding pronunciation in the Manchu language is Juxen, by which the Jurchen people referred to themselves before 1635. Nüzhi or Nüzhen is an ethnic label that was universally recognized by both Jurchen, Mongol and Chinese people in Northeast Asia.[6] Nonetheless, the name of Manchu was gradually re-enforcedby the ruling

---

[4] Lüzhen 慮真，see Alexander Wylie (1855), Translation of the Ts'ing wan k'e mung, a Chinese Grammar of the Manchu Tartar Language with Introductory Notes on Manchu Literature, London Mission Press, Shanghai, p. iv.

[5] *Nüyhi* 女直 and *Yelüzongzhen* 耶律宗真, see *Dongyi kaolüe* 東夷考略 (Evidential Research upon the Eastern Barbarians) composed by Mao Ruizheng 茅瑞徵 (circa 1601), collected in *Qing ruguanqian shiliao xuanji yi* 清入關前史料選輯 1 (Compilation of Selected Historical Materials before the Qing Entered the Passes), vol. 1, compiled by Pan Zhe 潘喆 et al., edition Beijing: Zhongguo renmin daxue chubanshe, 1984, p. 47.

[6] In many regions of current mainland China, consonants *l* and *n* cannot be distinguished by dialect speakers. *Lüzhen* can also pronounce as Nüzhen.

26

elites and widely accepted by people since the early Qing time. Though Jurchen language is alike Manchu in aspect of speaking, Manchu script is alphabetical, being different than the Jurchen script that was created in reference to Chinese characters and Khitan writing system for matching the Jurchen pronunciations.[7]

In the twelfth century, the Jurchens successively developed two scripts, Large and Small, as their official language of the Jin dynasty (1115-1234). The Large Script is closer to the Chinese characters and the Small Script is similar to a syllabary, as Martin Soderblom Saarela suggested.[8] But both of them were gradually abandoned after 1234, when the dynasty fell into the Mongol rule. In 1403, Korean government departments held a meeting to discuss matters of recruiting Jurchen people into their administration:

> On the eighth day the Three Highest Administrations met to discuss the Jurchen matter.[9] The Emperor sent decrees to pacify the Jurchen leaders, such as Wuduli, Wuliangha and Wudiha, etc., requesting them to pay tribute. The Jurchens belonged to us in the first place, and thus the Three Highest Administrations met to discuss their matter. [However,] their official documents were written in Jurchen script, whose words cannot be understood. [Therefore,] some Jurchen people interpreted its meaning, and translated it for discussion.[10]

---

[7] *Jinshi,* Tuotuo et al, edition Beijing: Zhonghua shuju, 1975,p. 1684.

[8] Martin Soderblom Saarela (2015), *Manchu and the Study of Language in China (1607-1911),* PhD dissertation, Chieftainton University, New Jersey, p. 104.

[9] San fu 三府

[10]xinwei sanfu hui yi nüzhen shi. Huangdi chiyu nüzhen Wuduli, Wuliangha, Wudiha deng, zhaofu zhi,shi
xian'gong. nüzhen deng ben shuyu wo, gu sanfu hui yi, qi chiyu yong nüzhen shu, zi buke jie, shi nüzhen
shuo qi yi, yi zhi er yi. "辛未三府會議女真事。皇帝敕諭女真吾都里、兀良哈、兀狄哈等，招撫之、
使獻貢。女真等本屬于我，故三府會議，其敕諭用女真書，字不可解，使女真說其意，譯之而
議。" *Mingdai manmeng shiliao, lichaoshilu chao,* diyice, Wenhai chubanshe youxian gongsi yinxing,
Tokyo, 1953, p.139.

This event happened in the early Ming period, which is the first year of Yongle reign (1403), proving that the character-based Jurchen script was still functioning in the northeast frontier. However, another Korean source, dated in 1483, records that on the command of the Korean king, an official Li Shizuo held a banquet for eight Jurchen leaders who were about to leave the country.[11] Li asked if the Jurchen people in their garrisons could read Korean king's documents, and the Jurchens responded that people may not be able to read Korean documents, but many can read Mongol scripts.[12] This record shows that Jurchens were deeply influenced by the Mongol culture and even adopted their writing system for communication.

One hundred years later, a Jurchen leader Nurgaqi(1559-1626), who was honored as the first emperor of the Qing dynasty, ordered his officials to create a new script in 1599. The new writing system was modified on the basis of Mongol alphabet, and Tatatungya, a Uighur official who used its alphabet to write Mongol speech sounds created the traditional Mongol script.[13] Essentially, the Manchu script can find its roots in Turkish and Arabic writings. The "Manchu Veritable Records" says that:

> In the year of Light Yellow Pig [1599], ... in the second month, Taizu, the Wise Chieftain, wanted to change the Mongol writings into Manchu-language writing [system]. Erdeni, the scholar [baksi], and G'agai, the councillor [jargvqi], said, "[We have learned] the Mongol writings and therefore know [them]; how could [we] change the wrings that have come from the ancient time?" Thus, [they] declined. Taizu, the Wise Chieftain, said, "[When one] reads the Chinese country's writings, people who know the Chinese writings and people who don't all understand. [When one] reads the Mongol writings, people who don't know writings also understand. Our writings are written in Mongol

---

[11] Li Shizuo 李世佐
[12] Qingchu shiliao congkan diyi zhong, chaoxian lichao shilu zhong de nüzhen shiliao xuanbian, Wang Zhonghan jilu, edition Shenyang: Liaoning daxue chubanshe, 1978, pp. 134-135.
[13] *Yuanshi*, Song Lian et al., vol. 124, Liezhuan dishiyi, collected in *Chizaotang Sikuquanshu huiyao*, edition Taipei: Taiwan shijie shuju, 1985, p. 15.

words and [when one] reads them, our country people who do not know the [Mongol] writings could not understand. Why [is it] difficult to write our country's language? Besides, how could [one] say that the Mongol country's language is easy?" The councillor G'agai and the scholar Erdeni answered, "To write our country's language is certainly good. [But] we sincerely cannot change the writing [from Mongol to Manchu] and therefore [we] refused." Taizu, the Wise Chieftain, said, "Write the word 'a' and put 'ma' under it, isn't that 'ama' [father]? Write the word 'e' and put 'me' under it, isn't that 'eme' [mother]? That is all [I] think on my mind. You write and see [what happens] and that's it." Thus, [he] alone rejected speaking and reading in Mongol documents and changed [them] to the Manchu language. Since then, Taizu, the Wise Chieftain, created the Manchu script and disseminated [it] in the country. [14]

The above passage was composed in Hong Taiji's reign (r. 1627-1643), when the Manchu identity was just created and gradually accepted by Jurchen people. The Jurchen identity, which is *juxen* in Jurchen language, was officially changed into Manchu in 1635, when Hong Taiji commanded his people to stop using Jurchen but only Manchu.

On that day, the Khan said that originally our people's name is Manchu. Those ignorant people call us Juxen, Hada, Ula, Yehe

---

[14] soho ulgiyan aniya, … juwe biya de, Taizu sure beile manggo bithe be kvbulime manju gisun i araki seqi, erdeni baksi, g'agai jargvqi hendume, be monggoi bithe be taqiha dahame sambi dere, julegeqi jihe bithe be te adarame kvbulimbumbi seme marame gisureqi, Taizu sure beile hendume, nikan gurun i bithe be hvlaqi, nikan bithe sara niyalma sarkv niyalma gemu ulhimbi, monggo gurun i bithe be hvlaqi, bithe sarakv niyalma inu gemu ulhimbi kai, musei bithe be monggorome hvlaqi, musei gurun i bithe sarkv niyalma ulhirakv kai, musei gurun i gisun i araqi adarame mangga, enqu monggo gurun i gisun adarame ja seme henduqi, g'agai jargvqi, erdeni baksi jabume musei gurun i gisun i araqi sain mujangga, kvbulime arara be meni dolo bahanarakv ofi marambi dere, Taizu sure beile hendume, a sere hergen ara, a i fejile ma sindaqi, ama wako, e sere hergen ara, e i fejile me sindaqi eme waka, mini dolo gvnime wajiha, suwe arame tuwa ombi kai seme emhun marame monggorome hvlara bithe be manju gisun i kvbulihuha tereqi Taizu sure beile manju bithe be fukjin deribufi manju gurun de selgiyehe. See Qing shilu, diyijuan, Manzhou shilu, Zhonghua shuju, 1986, pp. 110-112.

29

and Hoifa. The Juxen people are the relatives of Sibe's Qoo mergen tribe, which has no concern with us. From now on, every person should address our people as Manchu, which is the previous title. Those who call us Juxen should be punished.[15]

Meng Sen argued that Jurchen tribes such as Hada, Ula, Yehe and Hoifa had been unified in Nurgaqi's reign, but in Hong Taiji's reign, the tribal people still used the old tribal titles for identification. Therefore, Hong Taiji's intended to eradicate these previous tribal names and unite all Jurchen people into the identity of Manchu.[16] Nonetheless, at the time, most people, including the Manchu supreme leader, still often referred to themselves as Jurchen when necessary. For instance, in 1636 Hong Taiji gave a speech to his family members, Chieftains and officials, urging them to follow the good example of the Shizong Emperor (r. 1161-1189),[17] and to maintain the Jurchen language as their unique weapon for ruling the Han Chinese people:

The Holy Khan said to people, "... Shi Zong Ulu later ascended to the Khan's throne, and long ago [he] had been afraid that the children would sink into the   Chinese customs. Repeatedly, [he warned that] forefathers' old customs should not be forgotten, [and they] should wear the Jurchen clothes, learn the Jurchen   language and practice shooting from stance and horseback from time to time, and   thus [he] said seriously, ..."[18]

This speech confirmed that Jurchen language is the same as Manchu language, and they are just different in respect of writing. A Qing histori-

---

15 tere inenggi, han hendume musei gurun i gebu daqi manju. hada, ula, yehe, hoifa kai. tere be ulhirakv niyalma juxen sembi. juxen serengge sibei qoo mergen i hvnqihin kai. tere muse de ai dalji. ereqi julesi yaya niyalma muse gurun i da manju sere gebu be hvla. juxen seme hvlaha de weile. See Manwen yuandang, Dijiuce, Feng Mingzhu zhubian, Guoli gugong bowuyuan, Taibei, 2005, p. 408.
[16] Meng Sen (1992), *Manzhou kaiguo shi,* Shanghai guji chubanshe, p. 10.
[17] man. *xizung*; chin. *shizong* 世宗
[18] enduringge han geren i baru hendume, ... xizung ulu han de isinjiha manggi, dade olhome doigon qi juse omosi be nikan i doro de dosirahv seme, dahvn dahvn i mafari fe doro be ume onggoro, nioi ji etuku be etu, nioi ji gisun be taqi, gabtara niyamniyara be erindari urebu seme jing henduhebi, ... See Dorgi yamun asaraha manju hergen i fe dangse (neige cangben manwen laodang), Wu Yuanfeng zhubian, Liaoning minzu chubanshe, pp. 8280-8283.

an Jiang Liangqi[19] (1723-1790) recorded the same event of creating Manchu script and said that in the second month of 1599, Nurgaqi ordered his officials to transform Mongol letters into the imperial language and to create Manchu script.[20] Up to this moment, this newborn script was widely accepted, even by the Han Chinese scholars, as the first language of the empire.

Manchu script is alphabetical. As Evelyn S. Rawski pointed out the Manchu alphabetic letters were borrowed from Mongol script, which derived from Uighur that had originated in Sogdian.[21] Furthermore, documents written in Manchu language represent the status of the Qing empire throughout the dynasty. In the following texts, one will see these primers highlight a core message of Manchu identity, which is the Qing language. In the Manchu perspective, the Qing language is identical with the Manchu language. The Original Manchu Archives, which were composed before the Manchu unification of China, also confirm that the concept of the Great Qing empire is Manchu in comparison with the Chinese-language official documents. For instance, Hong Taiji's Veritable Records, including its draft, says that the name of the state was established as Great Qing (man. *daiqing*. chin. *da qing*) on the eleventh day of the fourth month in 1636.[22] Nevertheless, the Manchu documents composed on the same day did not mention this great event, and six months later, on the thirteenth day of the tenth month, Hong Taiji proclaimed that the name of the state, or people, is Manchu,[23] as the state and people are the same entity in the Manchu language. Throughout the Qing era, the name of Manchu was identical with the Qing Empire, which is reflected in bilingual titles of numerous official documents, such as the *Qing's Lexicographical Work*.[24] So the Qing empire is the Manchu empire,

---

[19] Jiang Liangqi 蔣良騏

[20] *jihainian eryue, jiang menguzi zhiwei guoyu, chuangli manwen.* "己亥年二月，將蒙古字制爲國語，創立滿文。" See Jiang Liangqi (b. 1723-1790), *Donghualu*, Zhonghua shuju , Beijing, 1980, p. 4.

[21] Evelyn S. Rawski, "Presidential Address: Reenvisioning the Qing: The Significance of the Qing Period in Chinese History", *The Journal of Asian Studies*, 55.4: 829-850.

[22] *Taizong wen huangdi shilu*, excerpted from *Qingshilu*, vol. 2, edition Beijing: Zhonghua shuju, 1986, pp. 360-361.

[23] *Manwen yuandang*, dijiuce, p. 408.

[24] man. manju gisun i buleku bithe; chin. qingwen jian 清文鑒

which is also confirmed by Kiyohiko Sugiyama's research.[25] To maintain the empire, the Manchus need to hold onto their language as the foundation of their identity. To the modern academia, reading Manchu documents will enlarge scholars' vision to explore the profound cultural transformation in the central Eurasian continent.

Kimeng

Three Manchu primers are included in this book. The first one, *Kimeng*, is fully named as *manju nikan gisun kamqiha manjurara fiyelen qingwen kimeng bithe* (*jian manhan yu manzhou taohua qingwen qimeng* 兼滿漢語滿洲套話清文啟蒙), which means Manchu-Chinese language and Manchu conventional expressions--a book for illuminating the Qing language. From the title of the book, one should note that Manchu language is identified as the imperial language of the Qing empire,[26] which is separate from the other languages. The whole book is divided into four volumes with fifty-one sections, being written in Manchu and Chinese languages in the first place.

Regarding the physical appearance, this primer was created in forms of woodblock printing edition and bound with traditional thread, being designed with white blanks[27] preserved in top, bottom and inner margins. In the binding process, the mark for folding book pages is a single-straight line, which is called the Single-Fish Tail.[28] The periphery was framed with a bold line, paralleled by a thin line from inside. This printing style is named as the Four-Periphery-Single Side.[29] Each page is 21 centimeters high and 14 centimeters wide.

The author is Uge Xeoping,[30] whose life span stretched from the early reign of Kangxi, throughout Yongzheng, and to the early Qianlong time.

---

[25] Kihohiko Sugiyama (2015), *The Formation of the Qing Empire and the Eight Banner System*, the University of Nagoya Press, Nagoya.
[26] qingwen 清文
[27] baikou 白口
[28] danyuwei 單魚尾
[29] Sizhou danbian 四周雙邊
[30] Wuge Shouping 舞格壽平

The dates of his birth and death are not traceable so far, but his Kimeng was prefaced in 1730, thus we can estimate that his life expectancy could span from 1700 to 1760. On the front page of the original copy, there are two characters Changbai in front of Xeoping's name, which tells that the author must be an authentic Manchu person who conventionally believed his origin is the Long-white mountain in the northeast of Asia.[31]

Xeoping's friend, Cheng Mingyuan from Qiantang,[32] wrote the preface for the book, saying that the manuscript was written by Xeoping to teach his family children at home.[33] To facilitate young learners' understanding, the author put simple Chinese translation alongside the Manchu sentences.[34] This method is called "*neileme ulhiyen i ibebure*", which means "to make progress by gradual enlightenment" so that students can push forward their learning as the author intended.[35] In the beginning when teachers started to teach, as Cheng Mingyuan said, it would be fairly difficult for students to comprehend without such a comprehensible texts.[36] Thus, this book served as a training raft for young learners to cross a river and a shortcut to enter the door.[37]

This approach worked significantly as Cheng claimed that he eyewitnessed Xeoping's teaching, which helped young students, including the less capable ones, master basic skills of reading and writing within one month.[38] Moreover, the students spoke with decent pronunciation and wrote properly.[39] Given on that dramatic effect on learning, Cheng believed that this approach of teaching functioned like a miracle, which can correct mistakes in process of Manchu language teaching and start on the

---

[31] Changbaishan 長白山

[32] Qiantang Cheng Mingyuan 錢塘程明遠

[33] qing wen ki meng bithe serengge, mini guqu xeo ping xiyan xeng ni fisembume arafi, booi taqikv de taqibuhangge,

[34] ede sume sindaha nikan gisun, udu umesi muwa qinggiya biqibe,

[35] miqihiyan qi xumin de dosinara, goro yabure de hanqi qi deribure gvnin tebukebi,

[36] tere anggala tuktan yarhvdame taqibure de, enteke getuken iletu bithe waka oqi, inu sara ulhire de mangga ombi,

[37] ere yargian i ajigan taqire ursei suqungga doobure ada, duka dosimbure doko jugvn kai,

[38] bi kemuni siyan xeng ni erebe jafafi ajigan urse be taqibuha be tuwaqi, majige sureken ulhiqungga urse oqi, taqime biyalame baiburakv, uthai hvlame arame mutembi,

[39] sere anggala, jilgan mudan getuken bolgo, hergen i jijun tob tondo ojorakvngge akv,

right foundation from the beginning.[40] Therefore, for a long time Cheng asked Xeoping for permission to publish his manuscript for helping beginners learn Manchu language effectively,[41] which is also the purpose of this publication. But Xeoping did not agree to publish, on the ground that this book was designed for homeschooling and the Chinese annotations are not in a decent shape, so therefore scholars would ridicule it.[42]However, after Cheng's repeated request, finally Xeoping agreed to publish this primer.[43] His friend Cheng Mingyuan was able to obtain the manuscript for engraving and printing, which would greatly benefit the young learners.[44]

From the interactions between Cheng Mingyuan and Xeoping, it is reasonable to assume that both of them lived in the region of Qiantang, which is part of today's Hangzhou City. According to Mark C. Elliott's research, there was a Manchu city in the Zhejiang province of the time, which is Hangzhou garrison as provincial banner residence since 1645.[45] Because Cheng Mingyuan wrote the preface in both Manchu and Chinese languages, he must be a Chinese-martial banner-man[46] who kept his Chinese name and knew the Manchu language very well. Besides, Cheng also referred to himself as *"zo jung tang ni booi ejen"*, which means "the house owner/master of Behavior-Loyal Hall.*[47] The title of"booi ejen" literally means the master of household, which is a typical Manchu expression that indicates Cheng's identity under the Eight Banner system. Therefore, the two of them should be military men under the Eight Banner system: Cheng was a Chinese Martial and Xeoping was a Manchu. Cheng prefaced and revised the book. Besides, this book was also revised

---

[40] geli gung tusa be hvdun ojoro ferguwequke babi, fulehe be tob selgiyen be bolgo obure gvnin ambula bisire dade,
[41] bi aifini jise be gaifi folobufi, teniken taqire urse de durun tuwakv obuki seme baihade,
[42] siyan xeng ohakv henduhengge, ere bithe serengge, mini booi juse be taqihiyame, suhengge yooni buya qalgari gisun muwa albatu fiyan akvngge, folobuqi basuqun akv semeo sehe bihe,
[43] bi dahvn dahvn i hvsutuleme baire jakade,
[44] teni bahafi aqabume folobuha, ede ajigan taqire urse de, ainqi ambula niyeqequn tusa ojoro ba bidere,
[45]Mark C. Elliott (2001), *The Manchu Way: The Eight Banners and Ethnic Identity in Late Imperial China,* Stanford University Press, Stanford California, pp. 108-109.
[46] man. *ujen qooha*; chin. *hanjun* 漢軍
[47] zuozhongtang zhuren 作忠堂主人

by Peihe[48], whose name appeared after Cheng Mingyuan. The name of Peihe is phonetically similar to Xeoping, which must be a native Manchu name, too. Therefore, the second reviser should be another Manchu banner-man who was stationed in the Hangzhou garrison.

The *Kimeng* was reprinted many times in the Qing dynasty. An early version was printed in a year no earlier than 1730, which can be known according to the end of preface that says *hvwaliyasun tob i jakvqi aniya niyengniyeri sain inenggi,* meaning "a good day of the Spring in the eighth year of Yongzheng", while its corresponding Han-Chinese text tells that it was one of the first days of the early Spring[49] in the lunar calender of *geng xu.*[50]The print was preserved by the Hall for Advancement of Literature[51] in Suzhou[52] and the Manchu counterpart says *yung kui jai cang ban ban,* which must be the Version of Preserved Print in Permanent Chief of Study.[53] The Permanent Chief of Study in the Capital City[54] is a famous publisher in Beijing during the Qing dynasty. Evidence is that a famous medical book, named as the Same Principle for Treating Small Pox and Herpes,[55] was also published by Jingdu Yongkuizhai in the fifty-sixth year of Kangxi (1717),[56] which is a close date to the publication of *Kimeng.* All this information indicates that both Manchu and Chinese literati sponsored the printing of the book.

The *Kimeng* was originally composed in Manchu and translated into the Han Chinese language. This bilingual document is known as *Manchu Chinese Simultaneous Combination,*[57] which proves that the Manchus also adopted bilingual and multilingual language policies, like the other unifying regimes in Asian history.[58]

---

[48] Peihe 佩和
[49] mengchun zhi shuori 孟春之朔日
[50] Geng 庚 is the seventh position in the system of celestial stem; xu 戌 is the eleventh position in the system of terrestrial branch.
[51] hongwen ge 宏文閣
[52] Suzhou 蘇州
[53] yongkuizhai canban ban 永魁齋藏板版
[54] Jingdu Yongkuizhai 京都永魁齋
[55] Douzhen yiguan 痘疹一貫
[56] Sun Feiran (?-?), *Douzhen yiguan*, Jingdu yongkuizhai keben, Beijing, 1717.
[57] manhanhebi 滿漢合璧
[58] Rawski, Presidential Address, p. 838.

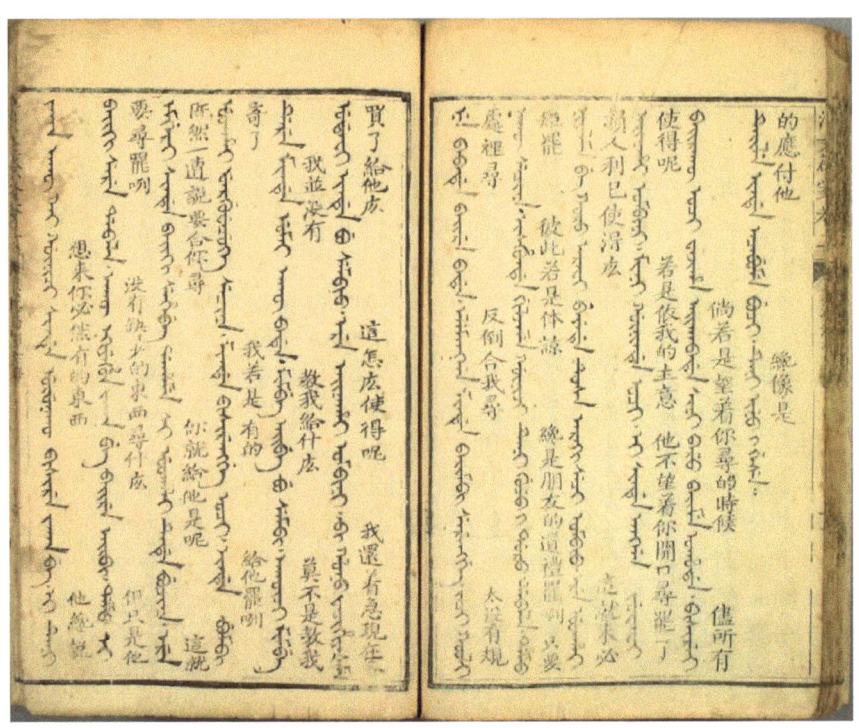

Picture 1: One Sample Page from Kimeng

In the nineteenth century, Alexander Wylie (1815-1887), a British missionary and historian, did comprehensive studies upon this *Kimeng*. In his groundbreaking work, Wylie composed a review of Manchu history dating from Confucius' time to the Qing dynasty, introduced tens of official documents about Manchu literature, prepared a table of Manchu alphabet, romanized the Manchu texts of *Kimeng* and translated them into English, analyzed Manchu grammar in light of English and listed key vocabulary for facilitating comprehension.[59] By assessing Wylie's publication, the print of *Kimeng* used by him must have been in a good shape and prevailing in the late Qing period, demonstrating that the Manchu language was still functioning as the official language across the empire.

---

[59] Wylie, Translation of the Ts'ing wan k'e mung, a Chinese Grammar of the Manchu Tartar Language with Introductory Notes on Manchu Literature.

Different editions and translations of *Kimeng* were well kept by Christian missionaries since the late eighteenth century. In 1790, M. Langlès mentioned that M. Raux wrote a publication about methods of learning Manchu language, which was extracted from *Kimeng* and its third edition went to the British Museum in London.[60] Furthermore, according to Wylie, a similar work based on the original was preserved in the Royal Library, and there were other Manchu grammar books that were produced from *Kimeng* stored in Europe and Russia.[61] In mainland China, libraries of the Forbidden City, Minzu University of China, and Dalian, also hold different editions of *Kimeng*, so does the East Asian Economic Research Institute of Yamaguchi University.

Oyonggo One and Two

The second primer is named as manju gisun i oyonggo jorin i bithe (qingwen zhiyao 清文指要), which means Book of Essential Elements of Manchu language. The third primer is sirame banjihuha nikan hergen i kamqibuha manju gisun oyonggo jorin bithe (xubian jianhan qingwen zhiyao 續編兼漢清文指要), which means the Continuously Compiled Essential Elements of Manchu-Language Book with Chinese Words Combined, being abbreviated as Oyonggo Two in the following text.

---

[60] Wylie, Translation of the Ts'ing wan k'e mung, a Chinese Grammar of the Manchu Tartar Language with Introductory Notes on Manchu Literature, p. lvi.
[61] Wylie, Translation of the Ts'ing wan k'e mung, a Chinese Grammar of the Manchu Tartar Language with Introductory Notes on Manchu Literature, pp. lvii-lviii.

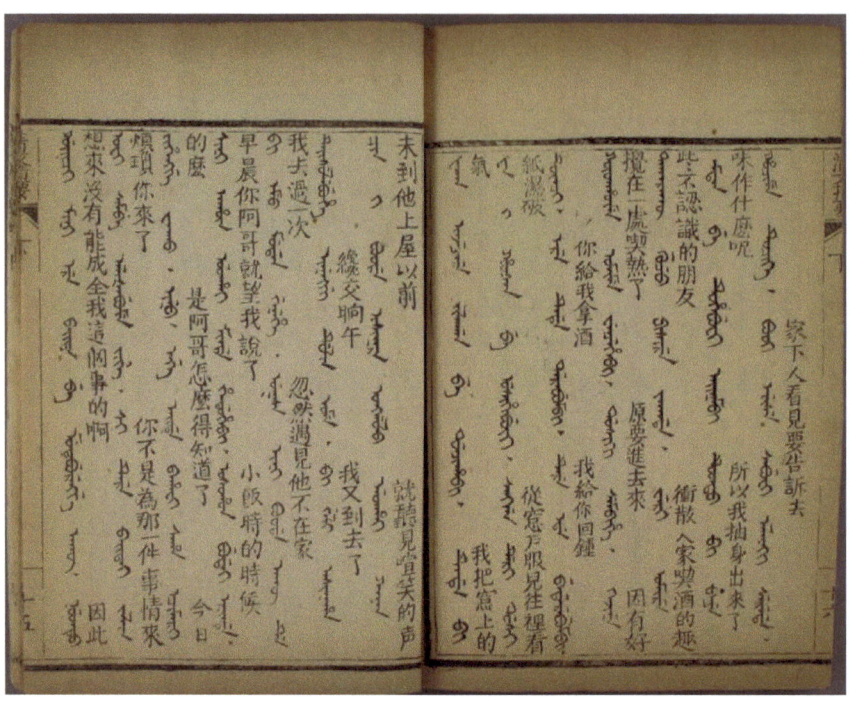

Picture 2: One Sample Page from Oyonggo One

According to research of Meilan Zhang, an earlier version was identified as a reprint of Sanhuai Tang[62] in the fourteenth year of the Jiaqing reign (1809) and another reprint took place in the twenty-third year of Jiaqing (1818) by the Bureau of Xi'an General;[63] Furthermore, a Qing scholar Zhi Xin[64] collected another version in his *Sanhe yulu*,[65] which contains one hundred and two chapters, being block-printed by Wuyuntang[66] in the tenth year of Daoguang (1830). Besides, there are other versions collected and published by British, Japanese and Korean scholars in the successive years, such as Sir Thomas Francis Wade in 1867, Hirose Sei[67] in

---

[62] Sanhuaitang 三槐堂
[63] Xi'an jiangjun shu 西安将軍署
[64] Zhixin 智信
[65] Sanhe yulu 三合語錄
[66] Wuyuntang 五雲堂
[67] Hirose 廣布精

1879, Fukushima Kyusei[68] in 1880 and Song Heon-Seok[69] in 1921.[70] The *Oyonggo One* has three volumes and the *Oyonggo Two* has two volumes, in forms of woodblock printing and traditional thread binding. Regarding its physical appearance, both primers were written in Manchu and Chinese languages, with white blanks[71] preserved in top, bottom and inner margins. In the binding process, the mark for folding book pages is a single-straight line, which is called the Single-Fish Tail[72] as the same style of the *Kimeng*. The periphery was framed with a bold line, being paralleledby a thin line from inside. This printing style is named as the Four-Periphery-Double Sides.[73] Each page is 16.5 centimeters long and fourteen centimeters wide.

Our version of the second and third primers was printed by the Hall of Three Chinese-scholar Tree,[74] being re-engraved in the fourteenth year of Jiaqing (1809). In ancient Chinese history, the term of Three Chinese-scholar Tree means Three Dukes[75] because in the Zhou dynasty (1046-256 BCE), when meeting the king, the government officials often stood in front of the Chinese-scholar trees.In the Northern Song dynasty (960-1127), *Sanhuaitang* became a synonym of a large Chinese family, Wang, due to an ambitious official Wang Hu[76] who consistently desired that one of his children would become a duke. Finally this dream came true because his son Wang Dan[77] took the office of Grand Councilor.[78] Later *Sanhuaitang* became more famous because of Su Shi's masterpiece entitled as the Inscription upon the Hall of Three Chinese-scholar Tree,[79] praising Wang's fine tradition in fostering good scholars and government officials. In the following dynasties, *Sanhuaitang* became a symbol of a

---

[68] Funari Fukushima 福島九成
[69] Song Xianshi 宋憲奭
[70] Zhang Meilan (2016), "Cong qingwenzhiyao manhan wenben yongci de bianhua kan manwen tezheng de xiaoshi", *Zhongguo yuwen*, 2016.5: 566-575.
[71] baikou 白口
[72] danyuwei 單魚尾
[73] sizhou shuangbian 四周雙邊
[74] sanhuaitang canban 三槐堂藏版
[75] sangong 三公
[76] Wanghu 王祜
[77] Wangdan 王旦
[78] zaixiang 宰相
[79] Su Shi 蘇軾 (1037-1101), *sanhuaitang ming* 三槐堂銘

prosperous family that lives out the principle of benevolence. In the Qing dynasty, the unification elites, including the banner-men stationed both in the capital [80] and throughout the empire, [81] closely associated with *Sanhuaitang* for carrying out good governance, especially in the aspect of publishing the Manchu primers.

The authorship of these two successive primers remains questionable.In *"Guidance of the Essential Elements of Manchu Language"*, [82] Zhang Huake suggested that these two primers share substantive similarities in contents with *"One Hundred Chapters of Manchu Language"*, [83] whose authorship is uncertain.According to Takekoshi's research, *tanggv meyen* was printed in the fifteenth year of the Qianlong reign (1750), [84] which is earlier than the reprinted version of *Oyonggo One* in the fourteenth year of Jiaqing (1809). Nonetheless, conventionally scholars believe that both primers were composed by Joot Fujun, [85] who was a Mongol under the Plain Yellow Banner. [86]

Several reasons might explain why some scholars assume Fujun as the author of the second and third primers. The *Draft of Qing History* says that Fujun was a Metropolitan Graduate in Translation, [87] from which scholars can ascertain that he must be proficient in Manchu, Mongol and Chinese languages for composing the primers in a bilingual form. However, as Zhang Huake indicates these two primers only appeared in the original Manchu version, with a few Chinese characters as annotations. Catering to the market need, the publisher *Sanhuaitang* found some experts and translated the Manchu texts into Chinese. [88] Zhang's description particularly meets the format of the *One Hundred Chapters of Manchu Language*, upon which the *Oyonggo One* and *Two* developed. The Chi-

---

[80] jingqi 京旗
[81] zhufang baqi 駐防八旗
[82] Qingwenzhiyao jiedu 清文指要解讀
[83] man. *tanggv meyen*; chin. *Qingwen baitiao* 清文百條, See Zhang Huake, *Qingwen-zhiyao jiedu*, Wenshizhe chubanshe, Taipei, 2005, p. 14.
[84] Takashi Takegoshi 竹越孝, 『一百條』・『清文指要』対照テキスト古代文字資料館発行, published by Ancient Character Museum, 149: 18.
[85] Zhuote fujun 卓特·富俊 (1749-1834)
[86] man. gulu suwayan gvsa; chin. zhenghuangqi 正黃旗
[87] *fanyi jinshi* 翻譯進士, See *Qingshigao*, Zhao Erxun deng zhuan, Di sanshiqi ce, Juan 342, Liezhuan 129, edition Beijing: Zhonghua shuju, 1977, p. 11119.
[88] Zhang Huake, *Qingwenzhiyao jiedu*, p. 24.

nese translation could be carried out by some officials who held degrees in the Translation examination, [89] specializing in translating Manchu-Chinese documents. In the second and third primers, the author elaborated methods of translating, passing the examination and serving in the government. He stressed that one should learn to speak Manchu first before undertaking translation work. This could be the reason why some scholars to believe that the author of the second and third primers is Fujun who was mentioned in *Draft of Qing History* as he specialized in translation.

There are more reasons for some scholars to assume Fujun was the author for the second and third primers. One of Fujun's memorials, which was filed in the fifth year of Daoguang (1825), shows that he was asking the Emperor for distributing Manchu-language textbooks and relevant regulations:

In the second month of the fifth year, [Fujun] memorialized: "Jilin is the place where our Court prospered, with honest customs and simple manners. All of the Eight Banner officials and bond-servants should prioritize our national language, riding and shooting. Besides riding and shooting, [the Court] should teach them Manchu and Chinese literature and skills, to let them know cardinal principles of righteousness. [Therefore, I] petition to [the Court] for bestowing and distributing regular books, Manchu-language textbooks and regulations to enlarge people's knowledge. " [The Court] agreed. [90]

Due to Fujun's official status, he was able to access the government resource for actualizing this program. It is reasonable to speculate that, under the sponsorship of him or someone like him, this *Oyonggo One* was widely circulated in the empire and gained scholars' attention. Another speculation is that Fujun could be honored as the author of the primers due to his successful career as a government official and military

---

[89] Zhang Huake, *Qingwenzhiyao jiedu*, p. 14.

[90] wunian eryue, zou: Jilin wei wochao faxiang zhidi, suhou fengchun, baqi chenpu jie dang yi guoyuqishe weizhong. qishe erwai, dang jiao yi qing han wenyi, shi zhi yifang. qing shang fa shuji, qingwen tiaoli, yikuo jianwen. congzhi. 五年二月，奏：
"吉林爲我朝發祥之地，俗厚風淳，八旗臣僕皆當以國語騎射爲重。騎射而外，當教以清、漢文藝，使知義方。請賞發書籍、清文條例，以擴見聞。"從之。 See Qingshi liezhuan, juan 34, p. 2619.

commander. Firstly, he was appointed as a Secretary in Ministry of Rites,[91] and later he worked as a Director in Ministry of Rites.[92] Gradually he was promoted to a Mongol Reader-in-waiting of Grand Secretariat,[93] Academician of Grand Secretariat[94] and simultaneously as Mongol Vice Commander-in-chief of Bordered Blue Banner.[95] In the first year of Jiaqing (1796), he was promoted to be the Vice Minister in Ministry of War,[96] reassigned to be a Manchu Vice Commander-in-chief of Bordered White Banner,[97] while assuming the position of Grand Minister Consultant in Kebuduo.[98] In the rest of his life, Fujun held critical posts such as General of Jilin,[99] Minister of the Court of Colonial Affairs,[100] Assistant Grand Secretary,[101] Chinese-Martial Commander-in-chief of Bordered Yellow Banner,[102] Grand Secretary of the Eastern Hall,[103] Inner Grand Minister,[104] and was granted with Grand Mentor of Heir Apparent after his death.[105] As a Mongol banner-man, he served in different positions, including Banner Commanders in three different ethnic groups,[106] which indicate his capabilities in three imperial languages.This rich experience in officialdom may have encouraged scholars of his time to accredit Fujun as the author of the primers.

The author of the *Oyonggo One* and *Two* repeatedly exhorted readers not to gamble and so did Fujun in his office. For example, in Section 49,

---

[91] libu zhushi 禮部主事
[92] libulangzhong 禮部郎中
[93] neige menggu shidu xueshi 內閣蒙古侍讀學士
[94] neige xueshi 內閣學士
[95] man. *kubuhe lamun gvsai monggo meiren i janggin;* chin. *xianglanqi menggu fudutong* 鑲藍旗蒙古副都統, See *Qingshiliezhuan*, Wang Zhonghan dianjiao, Zhonghua shuju, Beijing, 1987, p. 2614.
[96] bingbu shilang 兵部侍郎
[97] man. kubuhe xanggiyan gvsai manju meiren i janggin; chin. xiangbaiqi manzhou fudutong 鑲白旗滿洲副都統
[98] Kebuduo canzan dachen 科布多參贊大臣
[99] jilin jiangjun 吉林將軍
[100] lifanyuan shangshu 理藩院尚書
[101] xieban daxueshi 協辦大學士
[102] man. kubuhe suwayan gvsai ujen qoohai ejen; chin. xianghuangqi hanjun dutong 鑲黃旗漢軍都統
[103] dongge daxueshi 東閣大學士
[104] neidachen 內大臣
[105] *taizi taifu* 太子太傅, See *Qingshigao*, pp. 11119-11122.
[106] dutong 都統

one government official complained that in these days some Manchu friends jointly set up a gambling house and wanted him to take a partnership in running the business.[107] This government official excused himself for not having any free time due to being occupied by duties from now and then.[108] Besides, the law strictly prohibits people from gambling and finally he did not go.[109]

Another example is that in Section 53, the primer author designed a conversation of persuading people to quit gambling. One person said to his friend, "Nowadays you are addicted to gambling and owed a lot of debts."[110] This is a very serious matter so he exhorted that there was no end to gambling and nothing would be left if his friend continued being involved deeply.[111]

When Fujun was in office, he sternly forbade people from gambling.

It was reported that in the sixth month of the sixteenth year of Jiaqing (1811), Han Dingjin, an Investigating Censor,[112] memorialized that gambling was a strong local convention in Three Eastern Provinces beyond Shanhai Pass.[113] The emperor summoned Rong Lin, an Academician of Grand Secretariat,[114] who reported thatwhen Fujun took the office of General, he searched and arrested [gamblers] with a serious attitude, and the gambling phenomenon was slightly reduced. The Imperial Edict says, "Fujun ... strictly prohibited gambling, especially with a serious attitude."[115]

---

[107] ere uquri, musei tere emu feniyen agese dahvme aqafi, jiha efire falan neihebi, mimbe inu urunakv gene sembi,

[108] mini beye xolo akv be, teike teike alban isinjire be,

[109] jai fafun xajin umesi qira, bi jiduji genehekv,

[110] si te jiha efire de dosifi, utala bekedun araha sembi,

[111] jiha efire de, ai bube, lifa dosika sehede, ai bihe seme taksimbi,

[112] *yushi* 御史

[113] guandong sansheng 關東三省

[114] neige xueshi 內閣學士

[115] shiliunina liuyue, yushi Han Dingjin zou Guandongsansheng dufeng shenchi. shang zhaojian neige xueshi Ronglin, zoucheng Fujun qian zai jiangjun rennei, cha'na renzhen, shaojue lianji. yuyue: Fujun ... yanjin dubo, youshu renzhen."十六年六月, 御史韓鼎晉奏關東三省賭風甚熾。上召見內閣學士榮麟, 奏稱富俊前在將軍任內, 查拏認真, 稍覺斂跡。論曰: "富俊……嚴禁賭博, 尤屬認真。" See Qingshi liezhuan, juan 34, p. 2616.

This exhortation is in accordance with Fujun's policy that was described in *Biographies of Qing History*.[116] The above passages strongly signaled that both the author of *Oyonggo One* and Fujun opposed gambling and therefore scholars may consider them as the same person. Besides, one can see that the contents of Manchu primers act well in cooperation with government policies.

The publication of the primers must have been funded by the central or local government of the Qing empire. Zhang Huake suggests that the publication of the *Oyonggo One* and *Two* was sponsored by the Bureau of Xi'an General.[117] If this is true, according to the *Draft of Qing History*, in the fourteenth year of Jiaqing (1809), Saiqungga was transferred to take the post of Xi'an General.[118] Though Saiqungga was soon posted as Jilin General, the publication of *Oyonggo jorin i bihe* happened during his term of office.Nonetheless, according to Meilan Zhang's research, the sponsorship of the *Oyonggo One* in 1809 is unclear and the version published in 1818 was sponsored by the Xi'an General.[119] Thus, the sponsorship of the 1809 version still requires further research.

Given that Fujun was born in 1749 and passed away in 1834, the *Oyonggo One* was reprinted when he was sixty years old. Thus we have reasons to believe that the publication of the second and third primers could be sponsored by Fujun or someone like him, who held a high ranking official post and accordingly scholars honored him as the author of the primers. The contents of the *Oyonggo One* and *Two* were largely overlapped with the *One Hundred Chapters of Manchu Language*, which was published in 1750.Therefore, we can at least conclude that Fujun was not the original creator of these primers, but still, the preface of the second primer could be written by him if he sponsored the printing. Due to his high official rank and the sponsorship for some Manchu textbooks, it is reasonable to assume that scholars honored him as the editor of the second and third primers.

---

[116] qingshiliezhuan 清史列傳
[117] xi'an jiangjunshu 西安將軍署, See Zhang Huake, Qingwenzhiyao jiedu, p 13.
[118] 賽沖阿···十四年，調西安，尋調吉林。 See *Qingshigao*, juan 348, p. 11212.
[119] Zhang Meilan (2016), "Cong qingwenzhiyao manhan wenben yongci de bianhua kan manwen tezheng de xiaoshi", *Zhongguo yuwen*, 2016.5: 566-575.

Due to their popularity, the Oyonggo One and Two had little problems of surviving in the course of history. Libraries in Asia, Europe and North America hold various editions that are available for research. The earliest block-printed edition published by Double-peak Hall in 1789 is preserved in National Library of China.[120] The edition that was printed in 1809, known as the Inscription upon the Hall of Three Chinese-scholar Tree, is kept in the library of Beijing University, and so is the edition printed by the Bureau of Xi'an General in 1818. The One Hundred Chapters of Manchu Language, which contains the same content with the Oyonggo One and Two but in a different order of contents, was compiled by Thomas Francis Wade (1818-1895) into A Progressive Course Designed to Assist the Student of Colloquial Chinese as Spoken in the Capital and the Metropolitan Department, which was published in 1867 in London. This version can be found in the Harvard-Yenching Library, and the library of Beijing University also has an edition that was produced by the Five-cloud Hall in 1830. [121] Furthermore, other versions of the Oyonggo One and Two can be found in Japan and Korea, where they were published in the late nineteenth and early twentieth centuries. In 1879, by the Koishigawa Seizandosha Press, a Japanese scholar Hirobe Sei brought out his Compilation of Asian Language, which consists of Oyonggo One and Two under the name of Conversation Chapters. In 1880, through Ida Heisaku press, another Japanese scholar Hukushima Kyusei published his interpretation of Oyonggo One and Two, which is based on a version kept by the book-house Kugatsu Chikaramizu. In 1921 by a press called Moral-prosperity-book forest, a Korean scholar Song Heon-Seok published his compilation of Chinese languages, which included Oyonggo One and Two in the Book of Conversations in Old Movable-type Printing.[122] Basically, there were seven versions that are available for academic studies, which were summarized by Meilan Zhang and Jin Qi.[123]

---

[120] shuangfeng ge 雙峰閣, guojia tushuguan 國家圖書館
[121] wuyun tang 五雲堂
[122] jiu huoziben hanyu huihua shu 舊活字本漢語會話書
[123] Meilan Zhang and Jin Qi (2017), "The Decline of Manchu in Its Contact with Late Qing Chinese-A Case Study of Several Editions of *Qingwen Zhiyao*," in Dan Xu and

These three primers are important textbooks for Manchu people to learn their mother tongue in the Qing dynasty. Being similar to the first primer of *Kimeng*, the *Oyonggo One* is also divided into fifty-one sections, covering various topics, such as language learning, eating, drinking, religious beliefs, friendship, personalities, and even weather. One of the reasons for writing this book, as the author stated in the preface, is to help the *tuktan taqire urse*, which is the people who just start to learn the Manchu language. Another reason is that the author considered the Manchu language as the Manchu identity, and if one cannot speak Manchu, he has lost his identity.[124] As the author illustrated himself, one time he saw some people speaking Manchu, he found that they could not speak fluently as they were supposed to.[125] They felt really embarrassed for pausing from time to time.[126] In the author's opinion, it is because they did not usually practice their speaking.[127] Furthermore, the author observed that it is ridiculous for some people to start with learning translation without any capability of speaking the Manchu language.[128] In the author's opinion, even though their Chinese language capability is advanced when they write in Manchu, they fall short of vocabulary, common phrases and grammatical cohesion.[129] The author believed that these people turn into mediocre scholars even if they spend a lifetime on learning.[130] Thus, the author suggested that learners should focus on learning to speak Manchu as the first point, and then they can engage in translation.[131] Here, the author did not undermine the learning of Chinese but only prioritized learning Manchu. As Elliott stated in his *The Manchu Way,* certain

---

Hui Li (eds.), *Languages and Genes in Northwestern China and Adjacent Regions*, Springer, Singapore.

[124] aika manjurame bahanarakv,beyei ubu sibiya inu waliyabumbi kai,

[125] kemuni tuwaqi ememu urse manjurambihede, iletu bahanara gisun bime lak seme baharakv,

[126] deng seme ilinjafi gvniname bahatala, dere aifini dukseme fularakangge labdu,

[127] ere umai gvwa haran akv, gemu an i uquri kiqeme taqihakv urebume gisurehekv ofi kai,

[128] geli injequkengge, manju gisun oron unde de, afanggala ubaliyambure be taqirengge bi,

[129] fi nikebuhe manggi manju gisun eden dadun, tamin aqarakv, yohi banjinarakv be ainara,

[130] udu sakdatala taqiha sehe seme, eden baksi sere gebu qi guweme muterakv kai,

[131] ubaliyambure be taqire onggolo, nememe manju gisun taqire be oyonggo obure be saqi aqambi,

amounts of Manchu, Mongol and Han Chinese people were able to use at least two languages for communication.[132] As a banner-man, the creators of these Manchu primers just demonstrated that they were capable of using at least two languages, with Manchu as their first language.

However, as the author of the preface emphasized there are too many Manchu books, and it is impossible for beginners to to read them all.[133] Therefore, taking the opportunity of serving in the government, the author collected many oral traditions from the older generations. Combining what he has learned, one sentence by another, he accumulated one hundred sections.[134] He named the book as the "Essential Elements of Manchu Language" and used it to teach the children of his lineage.[135]

Regarding the application of primers, the author also claimed that if learners can consistently concentrate their minds on learning and repeatedly practice, they would be able to use Manchu language spontaneously, speaking in any way they want and making sentences accordingly without further worries.[136] Because his book contains many words, the author was afraid that readers would spend too much time on transcribing the sentences, so therefore he commissioned it to craftsmen for engraving.[137] "For friends who favor Manchu language as we do," in the author's conviction, "we would share this common interest."[138] Finally, the author said that even though this book brings little benefit to those knowledgeable sages, it still helps the beginners undoubtedly.[139]

These three primers are composed in similar written styles. They were all paralleled in bilingual forms, with the left column in Manchu and

---

[132] Elliott, *the Manchu Way*, p. 291.
[133] damu manju bithe umesi labdu geren, teni taqire urse waqihiayame hvlaqi, atanggi dube da,
[134] bi dolo yabure xolo de, sakdasai ulandume gisurede, mini taqifi ejehengge be, emu gisun emu gisun i aqamjahai, uheri tanggv meyen iktambufi,
[135] manju i oyonggo jorin, mini mukvn i deote juse be taqibuha,
[136] taqire urse unenggi ede gvnin girkvfi hing seme fuhaxame urebuqi, goidaha manggi ini qisui gvniha iqi forgoxome gamame mutembi, absi gisureqibe gisun banjinarakvngge akv be dahame, bahanarakv jalin de geli ai joboro,
[137] damu ere bithei hergen jaqi labdu, geli hvlara urse sarkiyame arara de hvsun baiburakv seme,
tuttu faksi de afabufi folobufi,
[138] musei adali manju gisun de amuran guquse de, uheleki sembi,
[139] udu hafuka saisa de nonggibure ba akv biqibe, tuktan taqire urse de majige niyeqequn akv semeo,

47

the right Chinese. Because the Manchus hold great esteem for the left side and the Chinese on the contrary, this array is acceptable for both of the ethnic peoples. Besides, taking the second and third primers for an example, the author illustrated an interesting phenomenon of bilingual education due to the decline of Manchu language education. In the preface he admitted that some Manchu people had already lost their identity due to being unfamiliar with their mother tongue. Elliott also mentioned a Manchu official memorialized to the emperor Yongzheng (r. 1723-1735) for establishing a Manchu school because of "a disturbing decline of Manchu ability".[140] Compared with the *Kimeng* that was compiled in an earlier time, Xeoping did not indicate there was a decline of Manchu language competence in the Hangzhou garrison. In Xeoping's *Kimeng*, the Chinese sentences were paralleled to the Manchu texts merely to facilitate learners' comprehension, which does not suggest a loss of Manchu language capability. Therefore, one can see that these three primers were created to maintain a Manchu identity while addressing different issues.

In conclusion, the primer of *Kimeng* was published in 1730, the *Oyonggo One* and probably with its sequel, was engraved again in 1809. The composition of these three Manchu textbooks covered about one hundred years of history regarding the cultural transformation within the Manchu communities. There are social norms, traditions, family life, personal hobbies, bad habits, laughter, tears, problems and hopes. In conversational texts, the authors and revisers exemplified people of different ethnic origins, which are Manchu, Chinese and Mongol, interacting with one another for individual purposes.The publication of these three primers involved publishers in both southern and northern China, with collaboration of local literati and unification elites with different ethnic identities, which depict a vivid picture of Manchu society in the eighteenth and early nineteenth centuries.

---

[140] Elliott, *The Manchu Way*, p. 296.

Banner as an Identity

People often assume that the Qing regime is nothing but another Chinese dynasty. The Chinese history books illustrate a picture that the Qing military troops entered the Shanhai Pass in 1644, annihilated the Ming's remaining forces and founded a new court in Beijing. But gradually the Manchus were assimilated into the advanced Han Chinese culture. Unlike the previous Mongol rulers, these new rulers were totally sinicized.[141] Nonetheless, researchers raised reasonable doubts about what actually happened in the past, as one way to pay respect to Leopold von Ranke's maxim, 'wie es eigentlich gewesen', as it actually was.[142] In *The Manchu Way*, Elliott also pointed out a common misconception as a pure "sinicizationist" thinking, which is used to cover a shameful fact that China was dominated by Manchu rulers.[143] Actually, the existing Manchu documents tell that the Qing regime is the achievement of Manchu unification, being supported by the unification elites of Mongols and Han Chinese, and this whole process was well documented since 1607, eight years after the creation of Manchu script, to the end of the regime (1912).

This Manchu enterprise was maintained by three traditions, which require the banner-men to practice all the time: Manchu language, shooting from stance and shooting from horseback,[144] often being paraphrased as "national language, riding and shooting".[145] In Elliott's research, these traditions were honored as the "Old Way" (*fe doro*), being stressed by the Khan Hong Taiji in 1636.[146] The original message is that Hong Taiji reminded all his subordinates, including the Chieftains, officials and royal kinsman, not to forget the Forefathers' Old Way: repeatedly they must

---

[141] hanhua 漢化
[142] Leopold von Ranke (1855), *Geschichiten der romanischen und germanischen Voelker von 1494-1514,* Saemtliche Werke vol.33, Leipzig, viii.
[143] Elliott, *The Manchu Way*, pp. 27-29.
[144] manju gisun, gabtambi, niyamniyambi
[145] guoyuqishe 國語騎射
[146] Elliott, *The Manchu Way*, p. 9.

wear Jurchen clothes, learn Jurchen language, and practice shooting from stance and horseback from time to time.[147]

In Section 41 of the *Kimeng*, the author Xeoping designed a conversation for a work interview, which started with questions about family background. The first question is to figure out what banner the interviewee belongs to and the answer is Plain Yellow Banner,[148] which is one of the Three Superior Banners[149] being directly led by the Emperor himself. This question indicates that the interviewee had a high reference point, which is unequal to the regular candidates. The second question is to know whether he belongs to a Superintendent Commander,[150] which commands a basic unit of the Imperial Household Department[151]that stays closer to the emperor. The third question is asking about the interviewee's Company,[152] which is a basic fighting community of the Eight Banners. The following conversations are discussing about official titles of his family members, who all served the Emperor directly as the Imperial Guard[153] and the Vice Director in the Ministry of War[154] in the Six Ministries.[155] Surprisingly, the interviewee's older brother had already become a sixth rank official who wore a blue feather in his hat.[156] As Kiyohiko Sugiyama suggested, being different than the Escort Guards who served the banner leaders, the Imperial Guards were selected to attend upon and protect the sovereignty, and they were granted with privileges ofholding important posts in the government.[157] This dialogue reveals remarkable

---

[147] ... dahvn dahvn i mafari de doro be ume onggoro, nioi ji etuku be etu, nioi ji gisun be taqi, gabtara niyamniyara be erindari urebu, See Fe dangse, pp. 8282-8283.

[148] man. gulu suwayan gvsa; chin. zhenghuangqi 正黃旗

[149] shangsanqi 上三旗

[150] man. hontoho; chin. guanling 管領

[151] neiwufu 內務府

[152] man. *niru*; chin. *niulu* 牛錄

[153] man. *hiya*; chin. *shiwei* 侍衛

[154] man. qoohai jurgan i aisilakv hafan; chin. bingbu yuanwailang 兵部員外郎

[155] *liubu* 六部

[156] man. lamun funggala; chin. lanling 藍翎

[157] Kiyohiko Sugiyama (2010), The Qing Empire in the Central Eurasian Context: Its Structure of Rule as Seen from the Eight Banner System, Collected in Comparative Imperiology (2010) , edited by Matsuzato Kimitaka, Slavic Research Center, Hokkaido University, Sapporo.

information regarding this young man's unique identity: as a Manchu, he is one of the unification elites.

In the same section of the *Kimeng,* the following conversation tells that this banner-man attended the examination the previous year, but had failed because of insufficiency in reading and writing.[158] After this long conversation, it turned out that all the dialogues were a test to evaluate the man's abilities.[159] The examiner was pleased with his performance and the next day he would report to his superior ministers and definitely provide the candidate's name to the leaders.[160] The candidate might need to take the examination again or he will be employed directly as an alternative.[161] In the following days, this young man was required to practice shooting from stance and horseback as usual and he should also learn reading and writing as before.[162] A messenger could quickly deliver the result of the examination and he should stay home so he will not miss the news.[163] This section evidently tells that a banner-man has to fulfill duties of maintaining language capability and martial skills, and thus enjoys certain privilege of attending examination or a direct employment. This banner-man's privilege was ethnic in nature, which sets a boundary between Manchus and Chinese commoners, and this distinction was consistently maintained through the Eight Banner system during the Qing dynasty.[164]

The Civil Examination System was very competitive in China's history.[165] Tens of thousands of candidates had to go through three major grades of examinations in order to earn an opportunity of working in the government. The lowest level is Prefecture Examination, which was supervised by a touring Provincial Education Intendant.[166] Successful can-

---

[158] simnehe bihe, gebu gaihakv, hvlarangge ararangge gemu eden ojoro jakade,

[159] bi jakan sinde utala gisun fonjihangge, gemu sini bengsen be qenderengge,

[160] tuwaqi sini taqihangge kemuni ombi, bi qimari ambasa de alafi, urunakv sini gebu be isibuki,

[161] eiqi dasame simnebure, eiqi uthai baitalara be gemu boljoqi ojorakv,

[162] ere udu inenggi dolo, sini gabtara niyamniyara babe, kemuni an i urebu, hvlara arara babe inu an i taqi,

[163] selgiyere be tuwame deyere gese feksihei jio, boode bisu, ume tookabure,

[164] Mark C. Elliott, *The Manchu Way*, p. 13.

[165] *keju* 科舉

[166] *Yuanshi* 院試 is supervised by officials of *tidu xueyuan* 提督學院

didates were called Cultivated Talents.[167] The middle level is Provincial Examination and men who successful passed were granted the title of Provincial Graduate.[168] The highest level is divided into two examinations: Metropolitan Examination and those who succeeded can attend the incoming Palace Examination,[169] which was nominally presided over by the emperor.[170] All the successful candidates were ranked into three degrees and designated as Metropolitan Graduates.[171] Usually only the Metropolitan Graduates would be assigned into different government branches for work.

The banner-men in the Qing court enjoyed certain privilege, which is a separate examination called Translation. Regularly, the Chinese candidates must be qualified as Cultivated Talents before they can attend the provincial examination, in which those who have succeeded can attend the metropolitan level. It is strictly regulated that Cultivated Talents are not allowed to attend the metropolitan examinations. However, the banner-men are not confined to this rule. In the fourth section of *Oyonggo One*, one banner-man worried that as a Cultivated Talent, he may not be permitted to attend a higher level of examination.[172] But his friend confirmed that any person like him, who was in the system of Eight Banners, was allowed to take the exam.[173] Furthermore, for the banner-men, even the poor students who go to public-funding schools, are qualified for the examination.[174] Because of the low entrance standard of the examination, the other speaker, who is also a banner-man, is taking every moment to read Manchu books for preparation.[175] Here, the author obviously is high-

---

[167] xiucai 秀才
[168] Those who passed *xiangshi* 鄉試 would become *juren* 舉人
[169] Those who passed *huishi* 會試 would attend *dianshi* 殿試, being recruited by the emperor in person, so that officials would become Disciples of the Emperor (*tianzi mensheng* 天子門生) and support the emperor's administration over the imperial issues.
[170] Charles O, Hucker (1988), *A Dictionary of Official Titles in Imperial China,* Taiwan Edition, Southern Materials Center, INC, Taipei, p. 93.
[171] jinshi 進士
[172] damu bithei xusai ainahai ombini,
[173] sini gesengge jakvn gvsa gemu simneqi ombime,
[174] tere anggala jurgangga taqikvi juse gemu ojoro bade,
[175] simneqi ome ofi, ... ere sidende teni haqihiyame manju bithe hvlambihai,

52

lighting the privilege of being a banner-man and the importance of mastering Manchu language.

As Elliott argued, this banner system was the crucial foundation to sustain the Old Ways of Manchu people and their ethnic identity, which was being exemplified by language ability, martial skills and a frugal life style.[176] The Eight Banner system designates a Manchu enterprise and dominance over the other peoples in history of East Asia and Central Eurasia.

---

[176] Elliott, *The Manchu Way,* xviii, Preface.

Manchu Language as an Identity

Manchu language is a Manchu identity. These three Manchu primers also emphasize this identity from different perspectives. In the beginning of the Kimeng, Xeoping made clear that people are supposed to learn every word thoroughly when reading Manchu books, and even a little carelessness is not allowed.[177] Here the author sets a high standard for Manchu language learning, which is different than the Han Chinese annotations that he put in parallel: coarse and vulgar. Xeoping's comment marks a lofty expectation as to how the author wanted to pass his mother tongue to the younger generations in a strict manner, which clearly proves that Manchu language should be carried on, not given up. Therefore, the phenomenon of "sinicization" was not tolerated by the Manchus of the time. Otherwise, the author should advocate readers to commit to Chinese language learning.

In Section 42 of the *Kimeng*, a Manchu man told his friend that his Company Commander[178] asked him to serve as a clerk every time when they met.[179] The man confessed that he only knows a few words when reading Manchu books, but he does not understand words in chunks.[180] Before going to his office for employment, this man had to study for a few months by reading books.[181] So he asked his friend to lending him a few Manchu books and he really wanted to transcribe and read them.[182] This passage also confirms that language capability is a duty for bannermen to fulfill.

In the preface of *Oyonggo One*, the writer the author explicitly claimed that Manchu language is the foundation of the Manchu communities and every Manchu person must know how to use the language and

---

[177] manju bithe hvlara niyalma oqi, urunakv hergen tome gemu getukeleme saqi aqambi, majige heoledeqi ojorakv,
[178] man. nirui janggin; chin. zuoling 佐領
[179] uthai baita de yabu yabu seme hendumbi, meni nirui janggin mimbe aqahadari,
[180] bi gvniqi manju bithe be udu hergen takara gojime, gisun seqi oron sarkv,
[181] baita de dosiqi, jai udu biyai bithe hvlafi,
[182] age sinde manju bithe biqi, udu debtelin juwen bureo, bi doolafi hvlaki,

incompetence is not tolerated.[183] The parallel Chinese translation of "Manchu language" is Qingyu 清語, which is the language that represents the Qing empire. Nevertheless, the concept of *manju halangga niyalma* means all people who bear the Manchu surnames, which highlights that Manchu language is the cohesion force that unites the Manchu people together as a community, quite distinct from the other ethnic groups. Also, the empire's future is dependent on these unification elites, whose identity is connected with the individual's practice of learning Manchu language.[184] Therefore, the maintenance of Manchu identity lies in the practice of using Manchu language to prevent acculturation.

Furthermore, as a banner-man, the author also considered himself as a fortunate member of the Manchu community, which is great and noble,[185] being distinguished from the unified people. In the author's conviction, Manchu language is an identity, and if one cannot speak it, the identity is being lost.[186] If one speaks Manchu language, he or she is part of the community. This banner-Mongol man is a Manchu by his identity.

Furthermore, the author considered learning Manchu books as the most important thing for banner-men.[187] In the conversation, the other person confessed that he had spent more than ten years on learning Chinese books, but gained little achievement.[188] If he does not read Manchu books, and does not learn how to translate, he would end up losing progress in both languages.[189] Therefore, he asked if the interlocutor would compile a few chapters of Manchu-language texts and teach him to read, as the way of gaining success.[190] In the context, we know that the final success means a government job. So Manchu language indicates more than an identity, but also a successful career.

In the second section of *Oyonggo One*, one person engaged conversation by complimenting the other man'sManchu pronunciation as good

---

[183] manju gisun serengge, manju halangga niyalmai fulehe da, yaya we bahanarakvqi ojorakvngge kai,
[184] Elliott, *The Manchu Way*, p. 11.
[185] muse jabxan de wesihun jalan i ayan suwayan manju ofi,
[186] aika manjurame bahanarakv, beyei ubu sibiya inu waliyabumbi,
[187] manju bithe taqimbi, musei ujui uju oyonggo baita,
[188] bi juwan aniya funqeme nikan bithe taqiha, tetele umai dube da tuqirakv,
[189] jai aikabade manju bithe hvlarakv, ubaliyambure be taqirakv oqi, juwede gemu sartabure de isinambi,
[190] udu meyen manju gisun banjibufi minde hvlabureo, bahafi hvwaxaqi,

and clear.[191] The other replied that his Manchu-language capability is not worth mentioning, but one of his friends speaks decent Manchu in a clear and fast way, without any Chinese accent.[192] Here we should note that in the parallel Chinese text, the expression of "without any Chinese accent" is originally "without even a little barbarian accent".[193] In the eyes of banner-men, the Chinese are considered as barbarians, as in the same way the Chinese looked at them, which exemplifies the distinction between the rulers and the people.

The examination of translation required candidates to be skilled in both Manchu and Chinese languages. In Section 3 of the *Oyonggo One,* one man (possibly referring to the author himself since he was a Metropolitan Graduate in Translation) suggested that it would be very easy for his friend to learn translating because he was good at reading Chinese books.[194] If his friend could concentrate on learning Manchu continuously, and learn step by step, he would make achievements naturally within two or three years.[195] Then the friend was persuaded, asking the man for help to correct his translation work.[196] The man praised his friend for making significant progress with smooth sentences and clear writing.[197] He would pass if he took the the examination.[198]

Learning Manchu language is always difficult, even for the banner-men whose first language is Manchu. In Section 5 of the *Oyonggo One,* one man compliments the other and said "your Manchu oral language sounds pretty good".[199] The other replied that he could understand what people said but he still cannot speak well.[200] Furthermore, he cannot speak like those who speak in chunks and he could not keep up when

---

[191] mudan gairengge sain bime tomorhon,

[192] mini manju gisun be ai dabufi gisurere babi, mini emu guqu i manju gisun sain, getuken bime daqun, majige nikan mudan akv,

[193] yidian'er manyin ye meiyou 一點兒蠻音也沒有

[194] ubaliyambure be taqiqi, umesi dabala, si nikan bithe bahanara niyalma kai,

[195] gvnin girkvfi giyalan lakqan akv, emu anan i taqime ohode, ini qisui dube da tuqimbi, juwe ilan aniya i sidende,

[196] age mini ubaliyambuhangge be tuwafi, majige dasatarao,

[197] sini taqihangge labdu nonggiubha, gisun arame tomorhon, hergen arame tomorhon,

[198] simneqi seferehei bahaqi ombi,

[199] sini manjurarangge majige muru tuqikebi,

[200] bi niyalmai gisurere be ulhire gojime, mini beye gisureme ohode, oron unde,

people speak four or five sentences in a row.[201] Moreover, he is afraid of making mistakes and thus he speaks indecisively and hesitatingly.[202] He believed that this was all he had achieved and he could no longer make progress.[203] The man consoled his friend and said that was because he did not practice enough. One method of improvement was, to engage conversations with anyone who spoke Manchu well, and then read books with good teachers.[204] "Speak with friends who are good at Manchu language and read everyday", the man said, " and you will remember those sentences.[205] Speak all the time and your tongue will be skillful.[206] If you learn this way, it only takes one or two years and you would speak as freely as you wish."[207]

In Section 7 of the *Oyonggo One,* one man asked what books his friend was reading.[208] His friend responded, "Not much, but some insignificant sentences.[209] Other than that, we read the Essential Elements of Manchu Language."[210] Here, the author advertised his book through this friend's word. Furthermore, these two men also talked about learning to write Manchu script in print style and to translate.[211] They also mentioned there were no Manchu schools in neighborhood.[212] One man said one of his lineage cousins was teaching the children of his family and he would introduce this banner-man to join.[213] This conversation indicates that Manchu language teaching, learning and other forms of education were-

---

[201] gvwai adali fiyelen fiyelen i gisureme muterakv, sere anggala, emu siran i duin sunja gisun, gemu sirabume muterakv,

[202] baibi taxaraburahv qalaburahv seme, tathvnjame gelhun akv kengse lasha gisurerakv,

[203] inu ere hvman dabala, nonggibure aibi,

[204] ere gemu sini urehekv haran, damu uqaraha uqaraha be tuwame amqatame gisure, jai bithede xungke sefu be baifi bithe hvla,

[205] manju gisun de mangga guquse de adanafi gisure, inenggidari hvlaqi, gisun ejembi,

[206] erindari gisureqi, ilenggv urembi,

[207] uttu taqime ohode, manggai emu juwe aniya i sidende, ini qisui gvnin i qihai anggai iqi tang sembikai,

[208] ne aiqi jergi bithe hvlambi,

[209] gvwa bithe akv, damu yasai juleri buyarame gisun,

[210] jai manju gisun i oyonggo jorin i bithei teile,

[211] ginggulere hergen, ubaliyambu,

[212] musei ubai xurdeme, fuhali manju taqikv akv,

[213] mini emu mukvn i ahvn, taqibure ele urse, gemu meni emu uksun i juse deote, sini funde majige gisureqi,

mainly conducted through communities like family and lineage, which are exclusive to the banner-men.

In Section 21 the author exemplified a harsh discipline for people who are slow in learning Manchu books. In a traditional approach, the teacher required students to recite the texts in the early morning but found out that the students performed worse and worse.[214] The teacher asked them to stop and gave them a lecture:[215] "Since you are reading Manchu books, you should learn with a single mind.[216] If you just make up a number and pursue a fame, what is the point of learning?"[217] The teacher worked in the government and committed his free time to teaching these students because they were lineage members.[218] This passage confirms that Manchu education was conducted through the community of lineage, which is not shared by the commoners.

The Manchus even admonished one another to maintain their identity by education, such as by reading. In Section 22, one banner-man was well fed everyday but indulged himself in playing music instruments.[219] The other banner-man criticized him that what he did was not a government business.[220] "We have good fortune because of our Manchu identity," the other man continued, "we eat official rice and use official silver.[221] In our whole family, from head to feet, everything comes from our Master's grace."[222] Here the author clearly points out the economic privileges enjoyed by the banner-men. In other words, the Manchus were the Emperor's servants and they should devote themselves to garrison, civil and military affairs, as Elliott described.[223] "But you are not improving your abilities, and you don't work hard in the government but only concentrate on learning these musical instruments.[224] You have disdained our Man-

---

[214] eqimari qeni bithe xejilebuqi, emke, emke qi eshun,

[215] tede bi takasu, mini gisun be donji,

[216] suwe manju bithe be hvlaqi tetendere, uthai emu julehen i taqiqina,

[217] ere gese ton arame, untuhun gebu gaiqi, atanggi dube da,

[218] te biqibe, mini beye alban kame, ineku giranggi yali ofi,

[219] inenggidari ebitele jefu manggi, fifan tenggeri be tebliyehei fitherengge,

[220] aika alban semeo,

[221] muse jabxan de manju ofi, jeterengge alban i bele, baitalarangge qaliyan i menggun,

[222] booi gubqi ujui hukxehe bethei fehuhengge, gemu ejen i kesi de bahangge,

[223] Elliott, *The Manchu Way,* pp. 133-134.

[224] erdemu be taqirakv, alban de faxxame yaburakv oso nakv, baibi ede gvnin girkvfi taqiqi,

chu reputation!"[225] The other man kept on, "You should read books because those who learn to sing can only stand behind the doors and those who learn to become scholars will sit with one another in opposites.[226] Learning musical instruments will only make you into something for people to be amused with and earn you a name of lowliness.[227] Would you consider playing instrument as an aptitude that is valued in decent and official occasions?[228] Among the high officials and ministers, if there is anyone who has an origin in playing the musical instrument, you can tell it out loud now! "[229]

In short, the emphasis of Manchu language competence is to maintain a line of separation between the unifying and unified populations, as suggested by Elliott in *The Manchu Way*.[230] In the *Oyonggo One*, the first ten lessons, out of fifty-one in total, were composed to emphasize the learning of Manchu language, involving taking examination for career purpose, going to school for education and reading Manchu books as private education, etc..Reading Manchu books as the advanced level of education is highlighted throughout the whole book, testifying the importance of learning Manchu language as the prioritized method of maintaining the Manchu identity. Furthermore, these three Manchu-language primers indicate that essentially language is a cultural norm, which contains messages about the identity of its speakers, who are the ruling elites in the context of Manchu unification.

---

[225] manju be gvtubuha ai dabala,
[226] bithe taqire de isirakv, uqun be taqihangge, uqe i amala ilimbi, baksi be taqihangge, bakqin de tembi,
[227] niyalma de efiku injeku arara dabala, nantuhvn fusihvn sere gebu qi guweme muterakv kai,
[228] jingkini siden i bade isinaha manggi, fithere haqin be bengsen obuqi ombio,
[229] ambasa hafasai dorgide, ya emke fithere qi beye tuqikengge be, si te tuqibu,
[230] Elliott, *The Manchu Way*, p. 5.

Martial Arts as an Identity

Essentially, banner-man is a military identity, which means all banner people are hereditary officers and soldiers whose profession is to fight wars. Nonetheless, as Elliott pointed out that relatively scholars payed little attention to the military aspect of banner life.[231] One of the intentions of this book is to endorse the study of Manchu martial acts.

Shooting from stance and horseback were basic skills in which Jurchens were proficient since the Khitan dominance of Northern China. With a military superiority, the Jurchens vanquished the Khitan Liao (916-1125) and the Chinese Northern Song dynasty (960-1127). After the fall of the Mongol Yuan empire (1271-1368), most of the Jurchen ethnic groups maintained the skills of riding horses and shooting arrows, as they hunted animals as means of living in Northeast Asia. Nurgaqi gradually constructed the Eight Banners on the basis of these warriors, upon which the state of Later Jin was constituted, also as Sugiyama' research indicated.[232] When Hong Taiji was in power, he repeatedly emphasized the practice of martial arts, along with Jurchen language and dress code, as the Jurchen identity that distinguishes themselves from the Han Chinese.[233] After the Manchu acquisition of China, the succeeding emperors continuously stressed this Manchu tradition of martial arts. Up to the Qianlong reign (r. 1735-1796), a vast empire came into being, stretching from the Fast East to Central Asia and down to South Asia, asshown in a map portrayed from Huang Qianren's work of 1767 (see Map 2).[234] This exponential land acquisition was built upon the durative emphasis of martial arts, comprising shooting from stance and horseback, supported by the firearms in certain conditions.

---

[231] Elliott, *The Manchu Way,* pp. 175-176.
[232] Sugiyama, The Qing Empire in the Central Eurasian Context: Its Structure of Rule as Seen from the Eight Banner System, p. 89-90.
[233] *Fe dangse*, pp. 8280-8283.
[234] Daqing wannian yitong tianxia quantu 大清萬年一統天下全圖

*Map 2: The Great Qing's Complete Map of All under Heaven,
148 x 235 cm, stored in Library of Congress, USA.*

These Manchu primers were composed in the process of drastic territory expansion, and though their texts convey messages in peaceful terms. In Section 41 of the *Kimeng*, the interviewer asked the young banner-man if he could shoot from both stance and horseback and the interviewee replied that he could only shoot from stance, not horseback.[235] When being asked "why didn't you learn shooting from horseback", he answered that he does not have a horse and therefore he has not yet learned.[236] The reason is surely not because of poverty since he comes from an eminent family and the interviewer did not pry further but only asked him to draw a bow.[237] Unfortunately the young man could not pull the string off the pads due to the stiff body of the bow.[238] Next, the interviewer asked the

---

[235] si gabtame niyamniyame gemu bahanambio, gabtame bahanambi, niyamniyame bahanarakv,
[236] si ainu niyamniyara be taqirakv, morin akv ofi taqihakv,
[237] si beri tatame tuwa,
[238] ere beri tebke be bi inu neime muterakv, absi mangga na,

man to read some chronicles and it turns out that, surprisingly, the young man has been learning for three years under the guidance of Jooli i Ama,[239] who was an academician of the Imperial Academy.[240] His teacher was proficient in translating, teaching, writing and shooting from stance and horseback,[241] which means he was capable of serving both in court and war. Therefore, as a student, this young banner-man must be qualified for working in the government.

In Section 8 of the *Oyonggo One* , the author gave an example of a good government official who has been honest, kindhearted, and good at learning knowledge besides shooting from stance and horseback since he was young.[242] In Section 14 of *Oyonggo One*, the author listed shooting from stance as an important thing for the Manchu people to do.[243] He admitted that shooting the arrows seems easy but it is very difficult to grasp the points.[244] Some people practice day and night but few excelled.[245] As a banner-man, the author is an expert of shooting and he pointed out that the secret is to straighten the body up, keep shoulders horizontally while being at ease.[246] Archers should select the strong bows, so that arrows will shoot powerfully and hit the target one by one.[247]

Next, through a conversation, one banner-man asked the other person to help with improvement in shooting from stance.[248] The banner-man said there was not much he could say about the other person but sooner or later by his "thumb", he would earn an official rank, which was a peacock tail feather in his headgear.[249] "Your gesture looks good and very skillful with a clean release", the banner-man commented, "If all people can be-

---

[239] dangse be hvlame tuwaki, ilan aniya hvlaha,

[240] man. bithei yamun; chin. hanlinyuan 翰林院

[241] bithe ubaliyambure giyangnara, hergen arara gabtara niyamniyara be bahana-rakvngge akv,

[242] nomhon bime sain, taqin fonjin de amuran, gabtara niyamniyamra,

[243] gabtambi serengge, musei manjusai oyonggo baita,

[244] tuwara de ja gojime, fakjin bahara de mangga,

[245] te biqi inenggi dobori akv tataxame, qolgoroko sain de isinafi, gebu tuqikengge giyanakv udu,

[246] beye tob, meiren neqin, umsei elhe sulfa,

[247] ere dade beri mangga, agvra tuqiburengge, geli da tolome goibure oqi,

[248] majige jorixame tuwanqihiya,

[249] sini gabtarangge ai hendumbi, yamji qimari ferhe de akdafi, funggala hadambi-kai,

come like you, what else would I expect?"[250] Furthermore, this expert at archery pointed out that his friend's bow was a little soft so the string was a little loose and it couldn't stabilize well.[251] If these improvements can be made, he will become outstanding in shooting.[252]

Shooting was an important skill, which promotes a banner-man's military career. One banner-man congratulated the other for being appointed and dispatched as a Company Commander.[253] The appointment of post is competitive between two alternatives: the First Candidate[254] and the Second Candidate.[255] This banner-man was selected as the first candidate yesterday, and the second candidate was a vanguard of ten soldiers who had no soldiers but only some men for hunting. Therefore, his friend thought the first candidate would surely take the office and wear a peacock tail, which is usually for officers beyond the fifth rank.[256] This first candidate was too old for such a position because all his friends had become high-rank ministers and even the younger ones had already succeeded him.[257] Besides, the first candidate fought a war and got wounded and at the moment he was serving as one of the Top Fifteen Shooters.[258] In his banner, there would be no one who has a better qualification.[259] Thus, we can tell that the promotion was closely related to a banner-man's shooting performance.

The capability of shooting from stance and horseback is emphasized as a requirement of being a Manchu, upon which the state functions. Manchu officers supervise all military units, including the Green Standards that mostly consist of Chinese soldiers.[260] Every Manchu has a duty to practice shooting for maintaining their identity as military officers and soldiers.

---

[250] durun sain, umesi urehebi, uksalarangge geli bolgo, niyalma gemu sini adali ome muteqi, ai baire,

[251] damu beri kemuni ajige uhuken, gunirembi, asuru toktobume muterakv,

[252] halaha sehede, toktofi geren qi tuqire dabala,

[253] man. janggin; chin. niulu zhangjing 牛錄章京

[254] man. *qohoho*; chin. *nizheng* 擬正

[255] man. *adabuhangge*; chin. *nipei* 擬陪

[256] sikse ilgame sonjoro de, mimbe qohoho, emu gabsihiyan i juwan i da, tojin funggala hadambi seme belhe,

[257] aniya goidaha, sini emgi yabuha guquse gemu amban oho, jai sini amala gaiha asihata, yooni sinqi enggelehebi,

[258] man. tofohon mangga; chin. shiwu shanshe 十五善射

[259] si hendu gvsade sinqi dulenderengge gemu weqi,

[260] lüying 綠營

Manchu Shamanistic Belief as an Identity

Religious or supernatural topics are not tolerated in the Confucian orthodox because Confucius refused to talk about extraordinary things, feats of violence, disorder and spiritual beings.[261] Being different from the Chinese tradition, the Manchu did not prohibit themselves from these unusual conversations. In Section 58 of the *Oyonggo Two*, the author depicted a house that was haunted.

One person asked the other about the house at the opposite of his door because his cousin was interested to buy it.[262] The other said the house was ominous and not suitable for living.[263] In the beginning the house was purchased by a lineage brother of the other person, and it was in a good condition. From the seven gate rooms to the five rooms behind the principal ones, everywhere was comfortable and clean.[264] When the property was passed onto his son, the wing rooms on the two sides were decayed and pulled down for reconstruction and then it was haunted.[265] In the beginning it was just causing a little disturbance and thus tolerable, but after a long time the ghost even made noises and appeared physically in daylight.[266] From time to time, women of the house got scared by encountering the ghost and so their life was disturbed.[267] The owner of the house invited Shamans to perform Shamanistic rituals and to cast out demons, but it did not work.[268] Consequently, there was nothing to do but to sell the house at a cheap price.[269] The reason for being haunted, from an individual perception, is bad fortune but not much about the house per

---

[261] zi bu yu guai, li, luan, shen 子不語怪力亂神

[262] suweni bakqin de bisire tere emu falga boo antaka, mini emu tara ahvn udaki sembi,

[263] tere boo teqi ojorakv, umesi doksin,

[264] da jokson de mini emu mukvn i ahvn udahangge, girin i boo nadan giyalan, fere de isitala sunja jergi, umesi iqangga sain bolgo bihe,

[265] mini ahvn i jui de isinaha manggi, juwe ergi hetu boo be sangsaraka seme efulefi, dasame weilehe turgunde, holkonde hutu ai dabkame deribuhe,

[266] suqungga daixahangge, hono yebe, bihe bihei, inenggi xun de asuki tuqibume arbun sabubuha,

[267] booi hehesi aika ohode, uthai buqeli be tunggalaha seme golofi ergen joqibuhangge gemu bi,

[268] samdaqi mekele, fudexeqi baitakv,

[269] ojoro jakade, arga akv, teni ja hvda de unqaha,

se.[270] If fortune is good, even demons and ghosts truly exist, one can dodge their harm and no one would get hurt.[271] At last, the inquirer said his brother was a very timid person and he would just honestly tell his brother what he has heard and it is his decision to buy or not.[272] This passage confirms that the Manchus, unlike the Chinese Confucian scholars, did believe in a mysterious force that affects human life. Though one man held a reasonable doubt about the existence of demons and ghosts, the owner of the house did invite Shamans for religious performance of exorcism. This is solid proof that Manchu people lived their life in a different conviction than the Confucian orthodoxy.

In Section 59 of the *Oyonggo Two*, one man told another that there was a fortune-teller who came to the suburb and he was extraordinarily good at his work.[273] According to what people said, this fortune-teller was like a supernatural being, who knew people's past in a way like people have already told him.[274] Because the fortune-teller could really calculate and find out about the past and future, many of our people came to him in a queue that filled up his workplace.[275] Since the fortune-teller was such a powerful man, this banner-man suggested that they also should pay a visit.[276] The other banner-man responded that he already knew such a thing because his friends had been there in groups.[277] Besides, the other banner-man went to the fortune-teller and showed him with the Eight Characters.[278] Surprisingly, the fortune-teller told everything correctly about how old his parents were, how many brothers he had, his wife's

---

[270] ere gemu forgon ehe i haran,yaya boode umai gai akv,

[271] forgon sain oqi, udu buxuku yemji bihe seme, inu jailatame burulara dabala, niyalma be nungneme mutembio,

[272] tuttu seme, mini ere ahvn umesi fahvn ajige, bi daqilaha yargiyan babe, inde alaqi wajiha, udaqibe udarakv oqibe, ini qihai gamakini,

[273] age si donjihakvn, jakan hoton i tule emu jakvn hergen tuwara niyalma ji-hebi,umesi ferguweguke mangga sembi,

[274] niyalma i alara be donjiqi,tere niyalma fuhali enduri adali banjihabi,musei dule-kele baita be, aimaka we inde alaha adali,

[275] jafaha sindaha gese bodome bahanambi, musei niyalma genehengge umesi labdu, siran siran i lakqarakv jalu fihekebi,

[276] ere gese xengge niyalma bikai, atanggi biqibe muse ahvn deo inu inde tuwabu-naki,

[277] bi aifini saha, mini guquse, ere udu uquri feniyen feniyelefi genere jakade,

[278] qananggi bi inu tubade isinaha,mini jakvn hergen be inde tuwabuhade,

surname, and the time when he acquired his official rank.[279] Every detail was right.[280] However, though the past was reckoned correctly, the future may not happen according to what the fortune-teller said.[281] The other banner-man replied that even so, the expense of fortune-telling is not much, and one should just consider it as amusement, which walks off one's bad mood.[282] Such a thing does not matter.[283] This passage tells that the Manchus had a different mindset regarding the past and future, which can be approached through an unusual way. Confucian scholars believed in achievements through hard work and would restrain themselves from activities such as fortune-telling. In the above conversation, these two Manchu men obviously demonstrated their curiosity of knowing the future through a fortune-teller, whose work is not tolerated by the Confucian scholars.

Other passages also refer to ghosts and supernatural beings for expressing strong feelings. For example, in the Section 32 of the *Oyonggo One*, a man who did not look after his parents well and the others criticized him, saying that such a person would not be pardoned by the Heaven and Earth and he would be hated by the ghosts and supernatural beings.[284] Therefore, an unfilial son would not end up well.[285] Another example is where the Section 45 of the *Oyonggo One* describes a stubborn person who refused to listen to good suggestions and behaved like being possessed by demons.[286] Such passages point out that the Manchus were different in ethnicity and practiced their unique religious beliefs, such as Shamanism. One may find similar phenomena in the Han Chinese communities, in which Shamanism is also practiced by individuals, but such conversations will not appear in language textbooks that teach people to maintain a tradition.

---

[279] ama eme ai aniya, ahvn deo udu, sargan hala ai, atanggi hafan bahangge,haqin haqin i baita, gemu tob seme aqanaha,
[280] heni majige taxarabuhakv,
[281] dulekengge udu aqanaha biqibe, damu jidere unde baita, ainahai ini henduhe songkoi ombini,
[282] tuttu seme, muse yamaka bade dere udu jiha fayarakv, eiqibe, si geli baita akv, boode bai tere anggala, sargaxara gese geneqi, alixara be tookabure ton okini.
[283] ai ojorakv sere babi,
[284] enteke niyalma, abka na baktamburakv, hutu enduri uhei seyere be dahame,
[285] adarame bahafi sain i dubembi,
[286] sain gisun be umai donjirakv, aimaka qargiqi tokoxoro adali,

Manchu Conventions as an Identity

Manchu education focused on history with little literature. In Section 36, the author emphasized that students should read books like Comprehensive History in Aid of Governance, [287] which helps them increase knowledge, remember things of the past, follow the good examples and learn lessons from the bad events.[288] Reading history can benefit one's mind and body greatly.[289] On the contrary, Manchus believe that novels are all groundless words made up by people, full of imagined fighting such as one person chopping with a sword and the other blocking with a spear; or fighting by inviting supernatural beings who are capable of sorcery, coming through clouds and going through fog.[290] The so-called magic is to turn grass into horses or throw away beans that will become into people, all of which are lies.[291] But the ignorant people would consider these magical capabilities true, get confused and listen with great interest.[292] When the knowledgeable and capable people saw this, not only would they laugh but also become really sick of it.[293] This passage shows a strong attitude against literature that is based on imagination, but in favor of history based upon narrative. On the other hand, these passages prove the existence of Manchu literature that is for recreational purposes. As Crossley has pointed out, all this Manchu literature work, along with education and examination system, was driven by political purposes for sustaining the empire in Manchu hands.[294]

---

[287] man. hafu buleku; chin. zizhitongjian 資治通鑑

[288] taqin fonjin nonggibumbi, julgei baita be ejeme gaifi, sain ningge be alhvdame yabure, ehengge be targaqun obure oqi,

[289] beye gvnin de ambula tusangga,

[290] julen bithe serengge, gemu niyalmai banjibuha oron akv gisun, tere loho i saqiqi, ere gida i sujaha, fa bahanara enduri se, gemu tugi qi jidere, talman deri genere,

[291] orho hasalafi morin ubaliyambi, turi sofi niyalma kvbulimbi, iletu holo gisun bime,

[292] hvlhi urse yargiyan baita obufi, menekesaka amtanggai donjimbi,

[293] sara bahanara niyalma sabuha de,basure teile akv, yargiyan i eimeme tuwambi kai,

[294] Pamela Kyle Crossley (1999), *A translucent mirror: history and identity in Qing imperial ideology*, University of California Press, Berkeley and Los Angeles, California, p. 192.

Hunting was a custom shared by all Manchu communities. As a traditional way of life, hunting was mixed with other modes of production, such as fishing and farming, pasturing and tributary trade to the neighboring Chinese dynasty.[295] Before the Manchu expansion into China proper, the Khan Nurgaqi made specific and strict regulations for hunting as a teamwork, which also functioned like a military maneuver that proceeds without making noises[296]. [297]

The author made hunting as the first lesson in the Oyonggo Two.

[295] Elliott, *The Manchu Way*, p. 49.
[296] sure kundulen han, daqi dain dailara de, aba abalara de fafun qira, jamaraburakv, jilgan tuqiburakv,
[297] *Fe dangse*, p. 145.

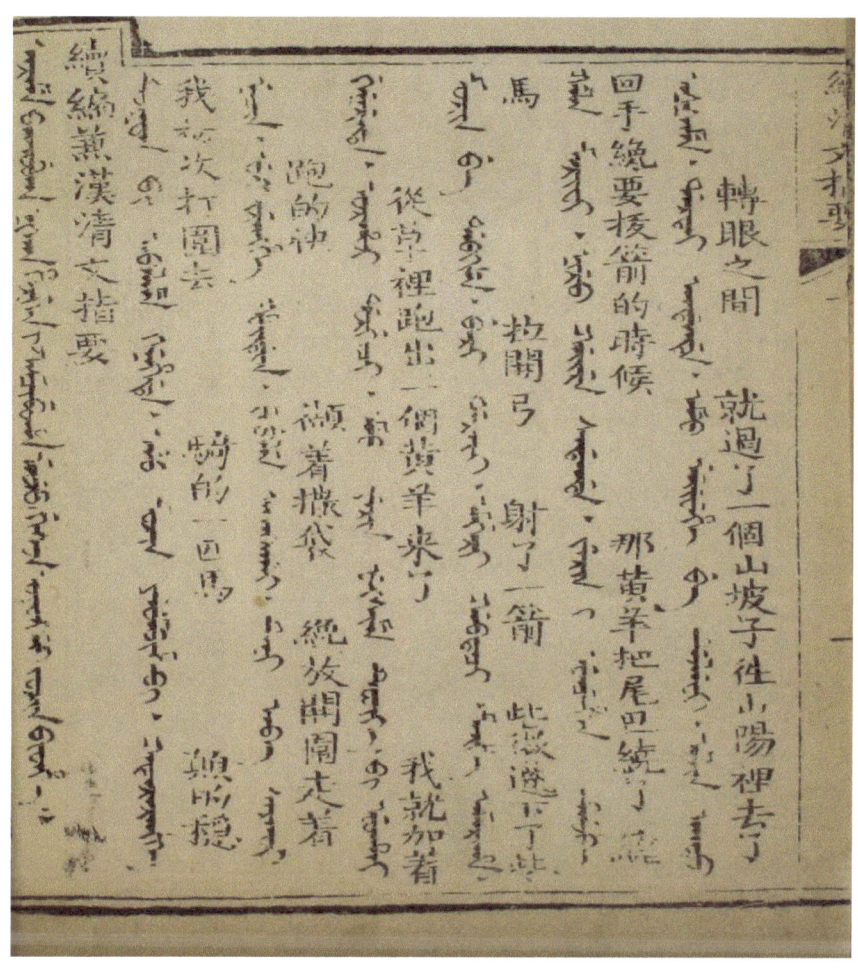

Picture 3:: One Sample Page from Oyonggo Two

A banner-man has given a detailed description of his first group hunting: his horse galloped steadily and fast and after the encirclement was relieved. He carried a quiver and moved forward.[298] Suddenly a gazelle came out of grass and he urged the horse, stretched the bow and made a shot.[299] He missed the target, and when he tried to pull out another arrow,

---

[298] tuktan bi abalame genehede, emu morin yalumbihebi, katararangge neqin, feksirengge hvdun, jebele ashahai, teni aba sarafi genehede,

[299] orhoi dorgiqi emu jeren feksime tuqike, bi uthai morin be dabkime, beri darafi emgeri gabtaqi,

the gazelle waggled its tail, ran over a hill and went up a hillside.[300] He followed up and shot again, but the arrow flew over the gazelle's head.[301] Unexpectedly, a deer came over from the other side[302] and was shot by the arrow he just released.[303] The hunter considered it as a good luck because the real prey escaped and he caught something he did not expect.[304] Here, the author used a word "murakvngge" that means the unexpected preys. According to the Manchu custom, hunters would blow a deer whistle to mimic the sound of stags in order that the females would be allured for mating. Hunters would take the moment and hunt. This is a particular tradition was maintained by the Manchus as one of their unique identities.

Another Manchu convention is frugality, which was listed as one essential character along with riding, shooting, and Manchu-language competence by Elliott.[305] In Section 65 of *sirame banjibuha Oyonggo One*, a banner-man sighed that their old way is all gone.[306] Back to the old days, even the teenagers could make clothes by spreading cotton and lining them with cloth.[307] It was a teamwork, in which this person sews the front and that person makes a shape, etc..[308] It took no more than one or two days before clothes were finished.[309] Besides, even hats were made at home.[310] People would laugh at you if you bought clothes or paid someone to make them.[311] However, the other banner-man responded by asking how current days could be compared with the old times.[312] Besides, people were making clothes for a wedding day, which was imminent and

---

[300] majige amariha, gala marifi niru gaire sidende, jeren i unqehen dube axxame, emu meifehe be dulefi, alin antu ergi be baime wesihun iqi genehe,

[301] tede bi morin be haqihiyahai hanqi amqanafi emgeri gabtaqi, geli uju be dabame duleke,

[302] gvnihakv qargiqi emu buhv fekesime ebsi jihe,

[303] tob seme mini gabtaha niru de goibufi,

[304] mayan sain, amqabuhangge turibuhe, murakvngge elemangga nambuha,

[305] Elliott, *The Manchu Way*, p. 276.

[306] muse fe kooli gemu wajiha,

[307] sakdasai forgon de juwan udu se i juse, gemu etuku xanggabume mutembihe, kubun sektefi, tuku doko aqabufi,

[308] si adasun be ufiqi, bi uthai jurgan gocimbi,

[309] manggaqi emu juwe inenggi sidende, uthai waqihiyabumbi,

[310] tere anggala, mahala qi aname, gemu boode weilembihe,

[311] basa bume tufifi weilebure, jiha menggun i udafi eture oqi, niyalma gemu oforo deri suk seme injembikai,

[312] tere forgon ere forgon de emu adali obufi gisureqi ombio,

so had to catch up day and night.[313] By rigidly adhering to the old rules, people just caused the wedding to be delayed with eyes being wide open.[314] Here the author seems to suggest that some specific situations require a different method to solve issues, rather than sticking to the old way. Frugality, such as making clothes by oneself, is a beautiful moral but some important occasions, such as a wedding, are not necessarily confined to this rule.

In Section 66, one banner-man claimed that if people should not eat good food or wear good clothes when they are young, for what reason should they do this other than to save money?[315] The other man replied that one should be happy if there is some money in hand.[316] But could people become happy if they are unlike the rich people who have ways of making profit?[317] As Elliott pointed out that banner people are not allowed to generate their own income through commerce and gradually they became poorer and poorer.[318] The man continued, "Shall I borrow money to buy clothes or shall I sell the house to eat well?[319] If I live a luxury life according to your suggestion, and spent all the money,[320] it would be better off that I just fell over to the ground and then died.[321] But if I didn't die, what could I do then?[322] You would not even help me when I stretch out my hands and beg from you!"[323]

Here, the author advocates a life of frugality. One reason is that the banner population grows fast, and, as Elliott pointed out, the Manchu people were multiplying daily[324] and the population of banner people grew exponentially after the unification. [325] In Section 62 of the *Oyonggo Two*, through another conversation between two banner-men, we know

---

[313] jai gaire inenggi umesi hanqi oho, dobori dulime haqihiyame weileqi,

[314] aika memereme fe kooli sehei, yasa gehun tookabure de isibuqi,

[315] te sakdara unde be amqame eturakv jeterakv oqi, jiha menggun fita jafarafi ainambi,

[316] minde ele mila biqi, sebjelerengge inu giyan,

[317] umai gvwa i gese funqen daban i bahara ba akv bade,

[318] Elliott, *The Manchu Way*, p. 313.

[319] eiqi bekdun arafi efu sembio, eiqi boo unqafi jefu sembio,

[320] sini gisun sonkoi ohode, fayaha ulin wajiha,

[321] uthai giyok seme buqeqi inu okini,

[322] talude buqerakv, tere erinde ainaqi ojoro,

[323] falanggv be alibume sinde baiqi, si ainahai anabumbini,

[324] sheng chi ri fan 生齒日繁

[325] Elliott, *The Manchu Way,* p. 314.

that one family raised nine children and they all survived.[326] In one of his memorials, Fujun reported to the Jiaqing Emperor:

In the third month of the eighteenth year, [Fujun's] analysis said, the subordinate Guangning county of Jinzhou prefecture in Fengtian province has been an Important Agency of communication center, with busyness, weariness and difficulty . In recent years, people are multiplying daily and the commercial shops in market are dense ... In the twelfth month, [Fujun] asked [the Court] for a regulation that all inner and outer officials must rotate every three years, plus that the pursuit of an extravagant life style should be prohibited and military preparations must be strengthened.[327]

The Emperor did not agree to rotate the posts of the officials every three years, but permitted the prohibition upon extravagant life.

The Imperial Edict said, "... As for gentries and commoners who hold a wedding, funeral, or banquet and reward with food and drink, they should conduct them according to their family circumstances and make ceremonies that suit the local situation, rather than to accommodate customs that make for flamboyancy. Nowadays men of extravagance admire one another, and, yet on the contrary, they consider men of frugality wrong, so that the contrast between the poor and the rich is remarkable. [People] obtain what they are not supposed to have and commit every bad deeds. The corrupt practices affect one another, and where is the end? Whereupon the Grand Ministers of Eight Banners and each province should well teach well and guide, so that every person knows and prioritizes courtliness, and senses the difference between honor and shame. All the flamboyant clothes, luxury food, unnecessary and over-elaborate formalities are not worth being cherished. Hopefully [people] would uphold

---

[326] uyun banjifi uyun taksiha

1. [327] shibanian sanyue, shu cheng: Fengtian Jinzhou shu Guangningxian xiangwei chongfanpinan yaoque, jinnian shengci rifan, shichan choumi, … shi'eryue, qing ding neiwai chengong gengdiao, bing jinzhi shemi, jiangqiu wubei 十八年三月，疏稱：奉天錦州屬廣寧縣向爲衝繁疲難要缺，近年生齒日繁，市廛稠密，……十二月，請定內外臣工三年更調，並禁止奢靡，講求武備"。 See Qingshi liezhuan, Juan 34, p. 2616.

74

practicality and reject flamboyancy so that local conventions and the people's mindset would reach simplicity."[328]

The intention of Fujun's memorial was to restrain people from pursuing a lavish lifestyle in the county of Guangning, but the Imperial Edict made it into a policy, demanding all Grand Ministers of Eight Banners and each province to educate their people for living in frugality.It is obvious that leaders of Eight Banners were required to exhort their bannermen to live according to the Court's decree.

In Section 83, a banner-man criticized his friend for wasting food. He suggested that the right way of living is to cherish and save the good stuff,[329] because the other banner-man did not give the leftovers to his bond-servants to eat but arbitrarily poured it down the drain.[330] According to the criticism, the other banner-man only knows eating well but ignores the difficulty of acquiring food such as rice.[331] This man then elaborated the hardship of toiling and transporting, thus even one grain was not easy to obtain.[332] Furthermore, it is difficult to manage one's desire of eating, thinking and spending lavishly.[333] The man believed that one should control impulses such as eating. As an old saying goes, if one eats frugally, food will be enough; if one wears frugally, clothes will be plenty.[334]The man concluded his criticism by saying that wasting food would under-

---

[328] yuyue: zhi shimin hunsangyanlao, ziying chen jia youwu, suiyi chengli, wuru renqingjingshang fuhua. xian shemizhe qunxiang xinxian, zhuanyi zhijianzhe weifei, suizhi pinfu xiangyao, qu fei qi you, misuo buwei. bixi xiangyan, yiyu hudi? zhuo baiqi ji zhisheng dayuan, shanwei huadao, shi renren zhi lirang weixian, lianchi weizhong. yiqie xianyimeishi, rujiefanwen, juwuzugui. shuji chongshi chuhua, fengsu renxin, keji rizhen chunpu. 諭曰: "至士民婚喪宴勞, 自應稱家有無, 隨宜成禮, 無如人情競尚浮華。現奢靡者羣相欽羨, 轉以質儉者爲非, 遂至貧富相耀, 取非其有, 靡所不爲。敝習相沿, 伊于胡底? 著八旗及直省大員, 善爲化導, 使人人知禮讓爲先, 廉恥爲重。一切鮮衣美食, 縟節繁文, 俱無足貴。庶幾崇實黜華, 風俗人心, 可冀日臻淳樸。" See Qingshi liezhuan, Juan 34, p. 2616-2617.
[329] sain jaka be hairame malhvxaqi teni banjire were niyalmai doro,
[330] jeme wajirakv funqehe buda be booi urse de ulebuqi, gvnin qihai waqihiyame ko sangga de doolahangge ainu,
[331] bele jeku i mangga babe sahakvbi,
[332] tarire niyalma juwere urse, ai gese jobome suilafi, emu belge seme ja de bahangge semeo,
[333] erebe jeme, terebe kidume, gvniha gvnihai uthai udafi, waliyan gemin i mamgiyambi,
[334] angga de ai kemun, jetere de ai dube, sakdasa i gisun, hairame jeqi jeku i da, hairame etuqi etuku i da sehebi,

75

mine one's blessings and there would be no time to regret when people suffer in famine times.[335] Therefore, the real intention of frugality is to avoid starvation in bad years.

One reason for Fujun to emphasize frugality and cherish food was because he knew the hardship of making a living for both banner people and commoners. The *Draft of Qing History* says that,

4. In the eighth year of Jiaqing (1803), [Fujun] was dispatched as General of Jilin and transferred to Shengjing.[Fujun] investigated and managed the problem of "commoners renting banner lands". Fujun analyzed that, "Within one year, some one thousand and six hundred cases were put on record, with about ten thousand people who were supposed to be held accountable. For years [the lands] were frequently rented, involving people in great numbers. Most banner people and commoners were poor and miserable, for committing crime and being prosecuted. The circumstance is indeed requires sympathy and thus ask for pardon for them all."[336]

With rapid population growth, substance for supporting a banner family was restricted.[337]The commoners faced the same problem. But the extent of cultivatable lands did not increase as fast as human population. For this reason, Fujun believed that both of the banner-men and commoners were excusable in the issue of land transaction and people should live in a style of frugality.

Another unique custom is eating Big Meat (pork), such as meat offered to ancestors,[338] or Lights-out Meat,[339] which is depicted in Section 30 of the *Oyonggo One*. This is a very unique Manchu custom. Accord-

---

[335] sini hvturi giyanakv udu, ere durun i sotaqi, omihon de amqabuha erinde, aliyaha seme amqaburakv kai,

2. [336] banian, chu wei Jilin jiangjun, diao Shengjing. Qing zhi min dian qidi... Fujun shuyan: yinian zhinei, yiqian liubai yu an, ying zhuijiaozhe buxia wanren, nianjiu zhuandian, zhulian fanduo. qi min duo qiongku, ji huozui, you po zhuihu, qing shi kemin, qing xi kuanmian.八年，出爲吉林將軍，調盛京。請治民典旗地……富俊疏言："一年之內，一千六百餘案，應追繳者不下萬人，年久轉典，株連繁多。旗、民多窮苦，既獲罪，又迫追呼，情實可憫，請悉寬免。"See Qingshigao, Di sanshiqi ce, Juan 342, Liezhuan 129, p. 11119.

[337] Elliott, *The Manchu Way,* p. 314.

[338] man. weqehe yali; chin. jishenderou 祭神的肉

[339] man. tuibuhe yali; chin. beidengderou 背燈的肉

ing to Zhang Huake, before the unification of China, the Manchus performed this ceremony in the native Manchu way. In order to honor their ancestors, such as Nurgaqi or deities, for abundant blessings upon their children, each household should not express their hospitality in the ritual of worship. Since the meat is essentially considered as a blessing of the ancestors, hosts do not invite or receive guests, but just provide meat for the visitors to eat. All visitors come to eat without invitation and they do not say thanks afterwards but just leave quietly.[340] The conversations in this section were carefully written to demonstrate this distinctive Manchu custom. One person said that he was supposed to invite his friend for eating the meat,[341] however, this friend knew this condition in relation to what he had or did not have at home.[342] The bond-servants killed pigs and cleaned the internal organs,[343] and all hands were occupied.[344] Therefore, no servants were sent to invite friends for eating the meat.[345] However, his friend knew this situation very well.[346] He would not wait for invitation.[347] Initially, he met a few friends and they all came to eat.[348] He was afraid that they had missed the opportunity,[349] but unexpectedly they made it in an easy way.[350] So far their behavior was appropriate, but, what happened next was a violation of rules. His friend suggested that all visitors should not bother the host,[351] and they should just sit in rows according to their ages and start to eat.[352] Furthermore, this friend asked the others to see if they wanted to boil the meat in broth.[353] Another man corrected his suggestion immediately and exclaimed, "Hey, what are you talking about?[354] This is wrong.[355] Did we have such a custom in the be-

---

[340] Zhang Huake, *Qingwenzhiyao jiedu*, p. 22.
[341] teike hono age be solinaki sembihe,
[342] age si sarangge, bisire akv,
[343] damu ere udu ahasi ulgiyan be tekdebure, duha do be dasatara de,
[344] ya gemu gala baiburakv,
[345] tuttu ojoro jakade niyalma takvrahakv,
[346] sinde niyalma akv be bi iletu sambikai,
[347] geli solire be aliyambio,
[348] bi guquse be guilefi, amba yali be jekenjihe,
[349] hono sitabuha ayoo sembihe,
[350] gvnihakv hib seme amqabuha,
[351] je, agese boigoji be ume gvnin jobobure,
[352] muse ahvn bodome ikiri teqefi jeki,
[353] agese jali jefu, sile e den barafi jeqina,
[354] ara, sini ere ai gisun,

ginning?[356] Meat is a blessing from the ancestors.[357] One should not be persuaded to eat,[358] and no one is supposed to receive guests and see them out.[359] Aren't you violating something by arranging seats in this way?"[360] As we discussed in the beginning of this passage, according to the old Manchu custom, all visitors should just come in, eat and leave quietly, without the etiquette of seating in a particular place.

A basic concept behind all these customs is the Manchu ethnicity, which is highlighted by modern historians as a characteristic distinctive from the Chinese and other ethnic groups. After the unification of China proper, the Manchus slowly modified their traditions, consciously or subconsciously, due to the influence of the Chinese culture. The above conversations intentionally remind the Manchus not to give up their tradition but to maintain their unique identity. This ethnicity theme deserves more attention in academic research. As Rawski has suggested, scholars should approach the Qing history from the perspectives of ethnicity and Manchu-language sources, in order to better interpret the recent past of China.[361]

Other habits, such as drinking liquor and rice wine, also appeared in these primers. Alcohol consumption has a long history in the Manchu communities. The Manchu word of distilled spirit is *arki,* which could have derived from the Mongolian word *arkhi.* In traditional Mongol societies, *arkhi* is an alcoholic beverage with circa ten percent alcohol due to simple equipment for distillation. In the Ming dynasty, the Chinese also had this loan word *alaji,*[362] which was used to indicate Fiery Wine in Li Shizhen's "Compendium of Materia Medica",[363] but its alcohol concentration can go up to 50% with good equipment of distillation. Initially, all these alien words took their origin in the Arabic invention of distilled

---

[355] taxafahabi,
[356] musei da jokson de ere gese kooli bihe,
[357] ere yali serengge, weqeku i kesi kai,
[358] haqihiyaqi ombio,
[359] antahasa jiqi geneqi, okdoro fudere ba hono akv bade,
[360] ere durun anahvnjaqi, soroki akv semeo,
[361] Rawski, *Presidential Address*, pp. 829-850.
[362] Alaji 阿剌吉
[363] Huojiu 火酒, See Bencao gangmu 本草綱目

78

liquor *arak,* which was introduced by the Arab merchants to East Asia during the Mongol Yuan time (1206-1368).

Another Manchu word for alcoholic drink is *nure,* which roughly corresponds with Chinese Rice Wine.[364] The excessive consumption of rice wine, in which alcoholic content ranges from 18-25%, can cause severe health issue. In our Manchu primers, there is a kind of Weak Rice Wine that was used to treat friends.[365] One should note that the expression of weak wine could be a conventional verbal exchange for etiquette, which in reality is a strong alcohol. In another case, a guest said that the rice wine is so strong and horrific that he got drunk from drinking only one cup.[366] The Manchu custom is to urge or encourage guests to drink a lot, on the grounds that wine is not poison and the guest can stay over night if he got drunk.

Nonetheless, alcohol consumption had turned into a problem for some Manchus who were capable of drinking.[367] In an exaggerated way, one person said that he could drink all day and would not get sick.[368] When his friend persuaded him to quit, he answered that he had got used to drinking on a daily basis and couldn't stop immediately.[369] The consequence is that, as his friend analyzed, he suffered from dry fever in the next morning, and he cannot bear the sight of looking at himself.[370] Another bad example, given by the author of the third primer, is a man who was dying due to addictions of wine and sex.[371] Furthermore, the author also mentioned an extreme case of alcohol consumption, in which a person drinks liquor and rice wine constantly to the extent of being paralyzed.[372] Such a problem was repeatedly pointed out by the author as a

---

[364] Mijiu 米酒

[365] man. *nitan nure*; chin. *bojiu* 薄酒

[366] ere nure umesi hatan nimequke, bi damu emu hvntahan omire jakade uthai soktoho kai.

[367] nure omire mangga niyalma.

[368] uthai mimbe emu inenggi xun tuhetele omibuha seme bi inu eimeterakv.

[369] damu bi seibeni omime taqiha, emu erindetargame muterakv.

[370] si nure omiha jai enenggi erde iliha manggi fuyakiyambio akvn. Fiyakiyahangge tuwara ba akv.

[371] nure boqo de dosifi.

[372] simbe tuwaqi, arki nure de haji, dartai andande seme aljabuqi ojorakv, omihadari urui lalanji heperefi,...

common phenomenon that haunts the Manchu society during the Qianlong era.

Drinking, along with gambling, has endangered the Manchu society by directing people's attention away from their old traditions, such as speaking their language, riding and shooting. One example is that to seek a marriage alliance, a Manchu father did not list his son's achievements, but emphasized that his son does not interact with people who drink, gamble and make trouble around.[373] Staying away from alcohol was considered a high moral standard among the Manchu people.

In light of Manchu-language primers, consuming liquor as "substance abuse" among the banner-men was well examined by Yves Trachsel, who surveyed many cases of excessive drinking in the mid-Qing time.[374] Prohibition against excessive alcoholic drinks, with both liquor and rice wine included, can be dated back to Nurgaqi's time, due to the relevant crimes of affray, injury (caused by riding horses after drinking), family issue, health problems, etc..[375] Due to the cold weather in Northeast Asia, implementing a total prohibition on drinking alcohol is hardly feasible. The khans, officials, officers and soldiers all favored drinking on different occasions and therefore, the drinking problem has accompanied the enterprise of Manchu empire from the beginning to the end.

---

[373] mini ere jui, udu qolgoroko erdemu ferguwequke bengsen akv biqibe, damu nure omire jiha efire ehe faquhvn urse de dayanfi, balai sargaxara jergi baita, inde heni majige akv.

[374] Yves Trachsel (2018), "Substance Abuse Among Bannermen and Banner Self-perception: An Analysis of Qing Language Primers", *Saksaha,* vol. 15.

[375] *Fe dangse,* pp. 3021-3024.

Conclusion

By the law of the Qing government, the Manchus were military people, which is the profession they were born into. The Manchus established their regime in Northeast Asia and then entered the Ming's capital Beijing to rule China proper. The Manchu identity, which stresses mounted archery and fluency in Manchu language, was formed mainly in the eighteen century,[376] during which time Tibet and part of Central Asia were also integrated into the Qing state. The Manchu language was used for communicating military information in territorial expansion, led by the Manchus.

These Manchu-language primers indicate an ethnic discourse of Manchu dominance and unification. Scholars must recognize that, as a non-Han Chinese regime, the Qing empire was a magnificent Manchu enterprise, which was documented in their own language. Thus, it is a necessary for scholars to reinterpret the Qing history by reading Manchu-language chronicles.

Besides, one can see that all these phenomena, including banner life, language competence, shooting from stance and horseback and various Manchu conventions, constitute a Manchu identity. From a further perspective, this Manchu identity was reinforced by maintaining these unique customs and practice, which represent a distinguished status of unification elites. After the Manchu unification of China proper in 1644, the Qing court successively unified Tibet, the Oirats Mongol and Muslim regimes in Central Asia, Jinchuan Tibetans, Burma and Gurkha, by which the military campaigns continued up to the year of 1792. These wars lasted over one and a half centuries, during which the Manchus adjusted their political principles for ruling different peoples of multiple cultures, while maintaining their own distinctive identity through speaking and writing Manchu language. Essentially, our three Manchu primers were written in this long period of warfare, which manifests itself as a unification of political culture, dominated by the non-Chinese unification elites.

---

[376] Rawski, Presidential Address, p. 838.

PART I
THE PRIMERS
THEIR MANCHU AND CHINESE TRANSCRIPTIONS

Chapter 1
qingwen kimeng

xutuqin 序

Preface: A Book for Beginners

1. qing wen ki meng bithe serengge,
清文啓蒙,

2. mini guqu xeoping siyan xeng ni fisembume arafi,
乃吾友壽平先生著述,

3. booi taqikv de taqibuhangge.
以課家塾者也。

4. ede sume sindaha nikan gisun,
其所註漢語,

5. udu umesi muwa qinggiya biqibe,
雖甚淺近,

6. teni taqire urse be neileme ulhiyen i ibebure de,
然開蒙循序,

7. miqihiyan qi xumin de dosinara,
由淺入深,

8. goro yabure de hanqi qi deribure gvnin tebukebi,
行遠自邇之寓意焉。

9. tere anggala tuktan yarhvdame taqibure de,
況廸之初,

10. enteke getuken iletu bithe waka oqi,
非此曉暢之文,

11. inu sara ulhire de mangga ombi,
亦難領會。

12. ere yargian i ajigan taqire ursei suqungga doobure ada,
誠幼學之初筏,

13. duka dosimbure doko jugvn kai.
入門之**捷徑**也。

14. bi kemuni siyan xeng ni erebe jafafi ajigan urse be taqibuha be tuwaqi,
余嘗目睹先生以此課蒙,

15. majige sureken ulhiqungga urse oqi,

稍能頴悟者，

16. taqime biyalame baiburakv,

學不匝月，

17. uthai hvlame arame mutembi,

而即能書誦，

18. sere anggala, jilgan mudan getuken bolgo[377], hergen i jijun tob tondo ojorakvngge akv[378],

且音韻筆畫，莫不明切端楷。

19. yala emgeri taqifi qalabure jequhunjere de isinarakv ombi,

一讀不致錯誤，

20. fulehe be tob se[l]giyen be bolgo obure gvnin ambula bisire dade,

大有正本清源之義，

21. geli gung tusa be hvdun ojoro ferguwequke babi,

更見功效提速之妙。

22. bi aifini jise be gaifi folobufi,

久欲請稿刊刻，

23. teniken taqire urse de durun tuwakv obuki seme baihade,

以爲初學津梁，

24. siyan xeng ohakv henduhengge,

而先生不許，曰，

25. ere bithe serengge,

此本，

26. mini booi juse be taqihiyame,

庭訓小子，

27. faksikan i gamame arahangge,

設法而作。

28. suhengge,

所註，

29. yooni buya qalgari gisun muwa albatu fiyan akvngge,

皆係俚言鄙語，麤俗不文。

30. folobuqi basuqun akv semeo sehe bihe,

付之梨棗，不無詒誚乎？

31. bi dahvn dahvn i hvsutuleme baire jakade,

---

[377] 'Getuken bolgo' means clear, corresponding with 明切 (ming qie).

[378] *'Ojorakvngge akv'* means something not impossible, which can be paraphrased as 'one has to admit', corresponding with 莫不 *(mobu)*.

予力請再三，

32. teni bahafi aqabume folobuha,
始獲校梓，

33. ede ajigan taqire urse de,
其於初學之士，

34. ainqi ambula niyeqequn tusa ojoro ba bidere,
大有裨益云。

35. hvwaliyasun tob i jakvqi aniya niyengniyeri sain inenggi,
雍正庚戌孟春之朔日

36. zo jung tang ni booi ejen qeng ming yuwan araha.
作忠堂主人程明遠題

Introduction: Reading Thoroughly

1. manju bithe hvlara niyalma oqi,
凡如读讀滿洲書的人

2. urunakv hergen tome gemu getukeleme saqi aqambi,
必定字字都该當明白知道

3. majige heoledeqi ojorakv,
些须怠慢使不得

4. aikabade ere bithede ejehengge getuken akv oqi,
倘或這個書上若記的不明白

5. gvwai bithede teisulebuhede,
別的書上碰见了

6. uthai tengkime same muterakv ombi,
可就不能的確知道

7. uttu sere anggala,
豈但這樣說

8. yaya niyalma de belge i gese erdemu biqi,
凡人有粟粒之技

9. beyede tusangga sehe bade,
尚且說于己有益

10. aikabade gvnin de teburakvqi geli ombio,
倘若不存心也使得麼

11. kiqerakvqi geli ombio.
若不用心也使得麼

Section 1: Knowing a Friend

1. age i amba algin be donjifi goidaha,
久矣听见了兄長的大名譽

2. damu wesihun cira be bahafi aqahakv,
就只没得會见尊面

3. enenggi jabxan de ,
今日万幸

4. emgeri takaha be dahame,
既然一遭認識了

5. age si waliyame gvnirakv oqi,
兄長你若是不棄想念

6. mini boode majige feliyereo,
求祈往我家行走一行走

7. sini gisurerenge umesi inu,
你說的狠是

8. esi yabumbi,
自然行走

9. bi hono age i jakade genefi taqibure be dongjiki seme gvnire bade,
我还想着要往兄長跟前领教去

10. sini boode feliyerakv mujanggao,
不往你家里行走的麼

11. damu yabuhai age de eimebure inenggi bikai,
只是走长了教阿哥厭煩的日子有啊

12. ai geli,
豈有此理

13. bi damu age si jiderakv ayoo sere dabala,
我只恐怕兄長你不肯来罷咧

14. jiqi tetendere,
既是肯来

15. urgunjehe seme wajirakv bade,
喜之不盡

16. eimere kooli bio.
厭煩的規矩有麼

Section 2: Asking for a Favor

1. age si atanggi genembi ,
阿哥你幾時去

2. geneki seqi uthai genembi seme hendu,

說要去就說去

3. generakv oqi uthai generakv seme hendu,
若不去就說不去

4. bi damu sini anggai qanggi genembi sehebe donjire dabala,
我只听见寡你的嘴说去罷咧

5. si emgeri yargiyan i genere be oron sabuhakv,
总没见你一遭儿真去

6. doigonde toktobume gisureqi,
预先說定了

7. gvwa niyalma inu uthai kenehunjerakv ombi seqina,
别人可就也不疑惑了

8. ere gese kooli akv baita geli bini,
這樣無理的事也有呢

9. bi geneki seqi,
我若是要去

10. inu mini qiha,
也由着我

11. generakv oqi,
若是不去

12. inu mini qiha dabala,
也由着我罷咧

13. urunakv sinde alafi ainambi,
必定告诉你作什麼

14. tere anggala bi qananggi tubade isinafi,
况且我前日到了那裡

15. ere emu baita jai baire turgun be suwaliyame,
把这一件事情并連懇求的缘故

16. gemu tede xanggabume gisurefi jihengge kai,
都合他说完畢了来的啊

17. si aibide bihe,
你在那裡来着

18. ere erinde teni jifi,
这时候纔来

19. gejing seme sinde waqihiyame ala seqi geli ombio.
絮絮叨叨的盡情都叫告訴你也使得麼

Section 3: Making an Inquiry

1. ere baita sinqi tulgiyen,
這個事情除了你之外

2. gvwa niyalma ainaha seme inu sarkv,
別人斷然也不知道

3. si unenggi sarangge getuken oqi,
你果然知道的明白

4. uthai minde ulhibume alarao,
求祈就告诉我知曉

5. bi yargiyan i sarkv kai,
我實實的不知道啊

6. saqi uthai sinde alambi dere,
若是知道就告诉你罷咱的

7. umai sarkv bade,
並不知道

8. mimbe aibe ala sembi,
叫我告诉什麼

9. akv oqi mimbe balai banjibufi ala sembio,
莫不是叫我胡编派了告诉麼

10. eiqibe suwe inu bahafi donjirengge kai,
總是你们也得听的见的啊

11. aiseme ekxembi,
何必忙

12. jooqina,
罷咧

13. bi tuwaqi gvwa niyalma sinde emu baita fonjiqi,
我看別人若問你一件事情

14. si uthai daqi dubede isitala,
你就从頭至尾

15. giyan giyan i alambi,
一件一件的告訴

16. bi aika sinde emu baita fonjime ohode,
我若是問你一件事情的时候

17. si uthai sarkv sere,
你就說不知道

18. donjihakv sere,
說没听见

19. baibi erken terken seme mini baru siltambi,

平白的支吾望着我推托
20. simbe geli niyalma seqi ombio.
你也算说是個人麼

Section 4: True Friendship

1. age si atanggi wesikengge,
阿哥你是幾時高陞了的
2. amba urgun kai,
大喜呀
3. bi oron inu bahafi donjihakv,
我連影兒也没得听见
4. donjimbihe biqi,
若是听见
5. urgun i doroi aqaname geneqi aqambihe,
該當賀喜去来着
6. sarkv ojoro jakade,
因爲不知道
7. tuttu urgun arame genehekv,
故此没有去賀喜
8. age ume ehe gvnire,
阿哥別要不好思量
9. bireme yooni waliyame gamarao,
諸凡求祈容谅
10. age ainu uttu gisurembi,
阿哥怎麼这樣说
11. muse gemu sain guqu kai,
咱们都是好朋友
12. dere aqaqi uthai wajiha,
见面就完了
13. urunakv untuhun doro be wesihulefi ainambi,
必定尚虚套礼作什麼
14. guqusei doro guqulerede,
朋友們裡頭相交之间
15. damu ishunde mujilen de tebume biqi,
只要彼此心裡想着
16. teni guqu i doro dabala,
繞是朋友的道理罷咧
17. tere durun i fiyanararangge gemu holo kai,

91

那樣做作的都是假呀

18. ememu urse untuhun doro de,
或有一等人们在虚套礼上

19. udu dembei habqihiyan biqibe,
雖然甚是响快

20. aikabade ini baru emu gvnin mujilen i baita be hebdeneqi,
倘若望着他去商量一件心腹的事儿

21. damu oilori deleri seme jabumbi,
只是浮面皮儿的答應

22. tere gesengge oqi,
若像那样的

23. ai amtangga.
有什麼趣兒

Section 5: Being Occupied by Work

1. sikese si aibide genehe bihe,
昨日你往那里去來着

2. bi niyalma takvrafi simbe solime ganabuqi,
我使了人去請你

3. sini booi niyalma simbe boode akv gvwabsi genehe sehe,
你的家人说你没在家往別處去了

4. bi simbe bodoqi,
我筹计着你

5. ainqi meni boode jimbi dere seme,
想是往我们家里来了罷

6. emu inenggi xun tuhetele aliyaqi,
等了一天直到日頭落

7. si umai jihekv,
你竟没有来

8. baibi emu inenggi aliyaha,
白等了一日

9. gvwa emu baita de geneki seqi,
別的一宗事上要去

10. geli simbe jiderahv sembi,
又恐怕你来

11. absi gvnin baibuha ni,
狠糟了心了呢

12. age sini ere uthai waka ohobi,

阿哥你这就不是了

13. we ya de emu hexu haxu i baita akv ni,
誰没有一个冗雜的事兒

14. damu weri boode feliyembio,
只是往人家行走麼

15. tere anggala mini beye xuntuhule alban de geme jabdurakv bime,
況且我的身子整日間應帶差事不得閒兒

16. weri qisui baita de daname gene seqi,
再叫管別人家的私事去

17. giyanakv xolo bio.
能有工夫麼

Section 6: Setting Your Heart at Rest

1. bi sinde yanduha baita be,
我烦你的事

2. si tede henduhebio,
你合他说了么

3. terei gvnin be tuwaqi ombio ojorakvn,
看他的意思使得不使得

4. bi tede henduhebi,
我合他说了

5. ini hendurengge,
他説的話

6. emu niyalma baita oqi,
若是一個人的事

7. kenuni ja bihe,
還容易来着

8. geren i baita ojoro jakade,
因是衆人的事

9. umesi mangga,
甚难

10. elheken i oso,
説叫缓缓的

11. ume hahilara sehe,
別急了

12. bi geli ere baita be jiduji atanggi teni yargiyan mejige bahara seme inde fonjiqi,
我又問他这個事情到底幾時纔得實信

13. ini gisun mejige bahaqi,
他的話説是一得信

14. sinde benebuqi uthai wajiha,
给你送去就完了

15. aiseme emdubei fonjimbi sehe,
不必侭着问

16. bi ini arbun be tuwaqi,
我看他的光景

17. inu baita be sartabure niyalma waka,
也不是誤事的人

18. si damu mujilen be sulakan i sinda,
你只管把心放宽着

19. sini baita be mutebuqi uthai wajiha,
把你的事成就了就完了

20. ede ai kenehunjere babi.
还有什麼疑惑的去處

Section 7: A Solid Word

1. si naranggi mimbe aibade gene sembi,
你到底是叫我往那里去

2. gaitai uttu oki sembime,
忽然要这們着

3. holkonde geli tuttu oki sembi,
忽然又要那們着

4. absi toktohon akv bai,
好沒個定凖罷

5. emu akdun gisun biqi,
若有一句結實話

6. gvwa niyalma inu dahame yaburede ja seqina,
別人也容易隨着行

7. ere gese angga ubaxakv niyalma geli bini,
這樣口嘴反覆的人也有呢

8. sini beye geneki sehe dabala,
是你自己說要去罷咧

9. we simbe gene sehe,
誰叫你去來

10. te biqibe,
譬如今

11. generakv niyalma be,
把不去的人
12. ergeletei gene seqi ombio,
壓派着叫去使得麼
13. niyalmai hendure balame,
可是人說的
14. niyalma be sahangge getuken,
傍觀者清
15. beyebe sahangge hvlhi sehe kai,
當局者迷啊
16. yaya baita de damu beyei qihakv babe,
凡事只把己所不欲的去處
17. inu niyalma de ume isibure oqi,
也別施之於人
18. ainqi ojorakv sere ba akv dere.
想必沒有使不得的去處了

Section 8: Trying to Make an Accomplishment

1. mini emu baita,
我的一件事情
2. baibi yabuqi ojorakv gese,
只像行不得
3. age si gosiqi,
阿哥你若是疼愛
4. mini funde genefi gisurefi mutebuhe manggi,
替我去說成了
5. bi age i ferguwequke gvnin be ainaha seme urgederakv,
我斷然不負了阿哥的盛情
6. urunakv ujui baili isibuki,
必定報答深恩
7. ere gumu an i jergi baita kai,
這都是平常的事啊
8. si uthai beye genefi gisurembi dere,
你就自己去說罷咧
9. ede niyalma de ai baire babi,
這有什麼求人的去處
10. tuttu seme,
雖然那樣說

11. te doigonde gisurerakv oqi ojorakv,
如今不可不預先說下

12. aikabade te mutembi seme hendufi,
倘或如今說了能得來

13. amaga inenggi muterakv ohode ainara,
日後不能的時候怎麼着

14. te muteburakv seme hendufi,
如今若說成不來

15. amaga inenggi mutebuhede geli ainara,
日後成了的時候可又怎麼

16. giyan be bodome ohode,
若論起理來

17. bi esi muterei teile faxxambi,
我自然儘着力兒巴結

18. talu de sini baita be mutebuqi,
萬一若能成你的事

19. si inu ume urgunjere,
你也別喜歡

20. sini baita be mureburakv oqi,
若不能成你的事

21. si inu ume ushara,
你也別惱

22. uttu ohode,
要是這們着

23. bi teni sini funde genefi faxxaqi ombi.
我纔可以替你去巴結

Section 9: Being a Good Friend

1. bi age be tafulahangge,
我勸阿哥的

2. simbe sain okini,
是叫你好

3. ehe taqirahv sere gvnin,
恐怕學壞了的意思

4. giyan de aqanara gese oqi,
若像合乎理

5. si uthai dahame yabu,
你就依着行

6. giyan de aqanarakv oqi,

若是不合理

7. uthai naka,

就罷

8. simbe ofi,

因爲是你

9. bi teni uttu gisurere dabala,

我纔這樣說罷咧

I would just say so.

10. gvwa de bihe biqi,

若是別人

11. bi inu uttu gisurerakv bihe,

我也不這樣說

12. eqi ai,

可不是麽

13. age si serengge gvnin saha guqu ofi,

皆因阿哥你是知心的朋友

14. teni uttu tafulara dabala,

纔這樣勸罷咧

15. aikabade arsari guqu ofi,

倘若是平常些的朋友

16. niyalmai endebuku be saha manggi,

見了人的過失

17. tafularakv sere anggala,

不但說不勸

18. hono basumbikai,

還要笑話呢

19. donjiqi tondoi gisun xan de iqakv biqibe,

常聽見說忠言逆耳

20. yabun de tusa,

有益於行

21. sain okto angga de gosihon biqibe,

良藥苦口

22. nimeku de tusa sehebi,

有益於病

23. gemu age i adali guquse de sain ningge,

都像阿哥合朋友好的

24. giyanakv udu bi.

能有幾個

Section 10: Which One is Good?

1. erebe sain seqi ojorakv,
這個說不得好

2. ereqi sain ningge ai yadara,
比這個好的有什麼缺少

3. erebe sain serakv oqi,
若把這個說不好

4. geli ai gesengge be sain sembi,
再把什麼樣的說好

5. si umesi sain ningge be sabuhakv ofi,
因爲你沒有看見着實好的

6. teni erebe sain sere dabala,
纔說這個好罷咧

7. ereqi sain ningge be sabuha sehede,
倘若看見比這個好的

8. geli terebe sain sembime,
又要說那個好

9. erebe sain serakv kai,
不肯說這個好了啊

10. sain jaka serengge,
若是好東西

11. yaya qi encu,
比別者另樣

12. musei teile sain serengge waka,
不止咱們說好

13. niyalma tome sabufi buyerakvngge akv,
人人看見沒有不愛的

14. terebe teni sain jaka seqi ojoro dabala,
那纔可以說得起是好東西罷咧

15. sain ehe ningge be ilgaburakv oqi,
若不分別一個好歹

16. bireme gemu sain seqi geli ombio.
一概都說好也使得麼

Section 11: Seeking Something

1. bi ini gisun i mudan be donjiqi,
我聽他的話音兒

2. sinde aika jaka baiki sere gese,

98

像要合你尋什麼東西

3. i minde ai jaka baiki sere,
他要合我尋什麼東西

4. minde umai baiqi aqara jaka akv kai,
我並沒有可尋的東西呀

5. gvniqi sinde urunakv bisire jaka be,
想來你必然有的東西

6. i teni baiki sere dabala,
他纔說要尋罷咧

7. akv ekiyekun jaka be baire aibi,
沒有缺少的東西尋什麼

8. damu i emgeri sinde baiki sehebe dahame,
但只是他既然一遭說要合你尋

9. si uthai tede buqina,
你就給他

10. ere uthai ferguwequke seqina,
這就奇了

11. minde bisirengge oqi,
我若是有的

12. inde bure dabala,
給他罷咧

13. minde umai akv bade,
我並沒有

14. mimbe aibe bu sembi,
叫我給什麼

15. akvqi mimbe udafi inde bu sembio,
莫不是叫我買了給他麼

16. ere ainahai ombini,
這未必使得呢

17. bi hono faqihiyaxame ne babade baire bade,
我還着急現在各處裏尋

18. elemangga minde baimbi serengge,
反到說合我尋

19. jaqi kooli akv seqina,
太無規矩罷

20. ishunde giljame gvniqi,
彼此體諒

21. teni guqui doro dabala,

纔是朋友的道理罷咧

22. damu niyalma be koro arafi beyede tusa araki seqi ombio,
只要損人利己使得麼

23. ere uthai ainahai ombini,
這就未必使得呢

24. mini gvninde oqi,
若是依我的主意

25. i sinde angga juwafi bairakv oqi wajiha,
他不望着你開口尋罷了

26. aikabade sini baru baime ohode,
倘若是合你尋的時候

27. bisirei teile inde aqabume buqi,
侭所有的應付他

28. teni inu gese.
纔像是

Section 12: Contending for Something

1. giyan i siningge oqi,
若該當是你的

2. si urunakv bahambi,
你必然得

3. temxefi ainambi,
爭作什麼

4. temxeqi uthai bahara,
若是爭就得

5. temxerakv oqi uthai baharakvn,
不爭就不得麼

6. sini bahara giyan oqi,
你若該當得

7. uthai temxerakv seme inu bahambi,
就不爭也得

8. sini bahara giyan waka oqi,
你若不該當得

9. udu temxehe seme inu baharakv,
縱然爭了也不得

10. niyalmai hendure balame,
可是人說的

11. anabuha niyalma alin be tuwakiyambi,

讓人不是癡

12. boxobuha niyalma boo be tuwakiyambi sehebi,
過後得便宜

13. mini gvnin de oqi,
依我的主意

14. oyomburakv bime baibi niyalmai baru temxere anggala,
於其沒要緊白向人爭

15. hono emu dere arara de isirakv,
還不如作一個情面

16. ai oqibe,
憑他怎樣

17. ini qisui emu doro giyan bi,
自然有一個道理

18. inu niyalmai haqihiyaqi ojorongge waka kai.
可也不是人勉強來得的

Section 13: Want It or Not?

1. si gaiki seqi,
你若是要

2. uthai gaisu,
就拿起來

3. te gaijarakv oqi,
如今若是不要

4. guwa gaiha de,
別人要了的時候

5. sini dolo ume ehe gvnire,
你心裏別不好思量

6. tere erinde oho manggi,
到了那時候

7. si aliyame gvniha seme inu amqarakv oho,
你後悔也來不及了

8. udu gaiki sehe seme inu baharakv kai,
縱然說要也不得

9. hvwanggiyarakv,
不妨事

10. ere emgeri miningge oho kai,
這個已經是我的了

11. we ai gelhun akv jifi mini ejelehe jaka be gaimbi,

誰敢來要我佔下的東西

12. si hon hairara gese oqi,
你若是狠捨不得的樣兒

13. uthai joo bai,
就罷呀

14. qihanggai bure oqi,
若是情願給

15. gaiqi inu amtangga dere,
要着也有趣兒

16. umai qihakv bade,
並不情願

17. gaiha seme ai amtangga.
縱然要了有什麼味兒

Section 14: A Trustworthy Man

1. si tede hendu,
你合他說

2. jiduji bumbio burakvn,
到底給不給

3. bure gese oqi,
若是說給

4. niyalma inu bahara seme ereme gvnimbi,
人也指望着想得

5. qananggi bumbi seme buhekv,
前日說給沒有給

6. sikse bumbi seme geli buhekv,
昨日說給又沒有給

7. si burekv oqi inu okini,
你若是不給也罷

8. damu emu yargiyan mejige isibuqi,
只給個實在信

9. kemuni majige yebe,
也還好些

10. baibi enenggi qimari seme anatarangge,
平白的今日明日推

11. qohome niyalma be eitererengge seqina,
竟是哄人

12. bure burakv de aibi,

給不給何妨

13. emu kengse lasha i gisun biqi,
若有一句簡決話

14. niyalma inu gasara ba akv,
人也沒有報怨的去處

15. damu anggai iqi gisurehe gojime,
只顧信着嘴說出來

16. amaga inenggi aqanara aqanarakv babe inu majige bodorakv oqi,
也不計算一計算日後應不應

17. erebe geli akdun bisire niyalma seqi ombio.
這也算是有信實的人麼

Section 15: An Official Business

1. ere gemu siden i baita,
這都是公事

2. qisui baita de duibuleqi ojorakv,
比不得私事

3. qisui baita oqi,
若是私事

4. kemuni ainame ainame oqi ombi,
還可以胡里瑪里使得

5. siden i baita de aika majige gvnin de teburakv heoledeqi,
在公事上若是些須不留心懈怠了

6. baita tuqike manggi ja akv kai,
事情出來了不輕啊

7. we alime gaimbi,
誰肯應承

8. si alime gaimbio,
你應承啊

9. bi alime gaimbio,
我應承啊

10. eiqi sinde alahakv sembio,
或是說沒有告訴你啊

11. eiqi simbe donjihakv sembio,
或是說你沒聽見啊

12. eiqi simbe donjirakv sembio,
或是說你不肯聽啊

13. dekdeni henduhengge sain,

常言道的好

14. angga jalu axu,
滿口含

15. ume angga jalu gisurere sehebi,
莫要滿口言

16. oihorilaqi ombio.
輕慢地麼

Section 16: To Go or Not to Go?

1. suwe tede aqanafi,
你們若是去見他

2. mimbe guilefi sasa yoki,
会着我一齊兒去

3. bi boode suwembe aliyara,
我在家裡等着你們

4. saikan eje,
好生記着

5. mini ere jergi gisun be ume onggoro,
別忘了我這些話

6. be simbe guilenjiqi ojorakv kai,
我們來會不得你啊

7. sini boo tehengge umesi goro,
你家住的很遠

8. geili sini boode isinjitele ai erin ombi,
再到你家裡可是什麼時候

9. nememe meni genere be tookabure de isinarakvn,
不反到誤了我們去麼

10. jai de oqi,
二則

11. meni gvnin de inu mudalime yabure be sengguwenderengge waka,
我們的心裡也不是怕繞着走

12. damu si geneki sembime geli generakv,
就只是你說要去又不去

13. generakv bime geli geneki sembi,
不去又說要去

14. emdubei amasi julesi niyalma be akabumbi,
促着來回勒揩人

15. umai toktoho gisun akv,

並沒個一定的話
16. ere gese uxan faxan de we hamire.
像這樣拉拉扯扯的誰受得

Section 17: Growing into a Good Person

1. i banitai uttu kai,
他生性是這樣啊

2. adarame halame mutembi,
怎麼能改

3. ai geli,
豈有此理

4. banitai uttu oqi,
生性是這樣

5. uthai halaqi ojorakv nio,
就改不得麼

6. enduringge niyalma seme hono endebuku be dasaki sere bade,
聖人尚且還要修過

7. jergi niyalma be ai hendure,
何況平常的人

8. ini gvnin i qihai yabure jakade,
所以任着意兒走

9. teni usun taqifi,
纔學厭了

10. emu geterakv niyalma oho kai,
成了一個不長進的人了啊

11. damu beyei saha teile oqi,
只以着自己的見識

12. aide isinambi,
到得那裏

13. kenuni mangga urse de adanafi,
還是就了高人去

14. terei taqin fonjin be taqire,
學他的學問

15. terei yabun be alhvdame yabume ohode,
仿他的品行

16. teni hvwaxafi emu sain niyalma oqi ojoro dabala,
纔可以長成一個好人罷咧

17. uttu hvluri malari yabuqi,

105

若是這樣哈里哈賑的行
18. oyombure aibi.
有何着要

Section 18: Being Straightforward

1. lalanji sini yabuha baita sembime,
拉累的說是你行的事
2. si alime gairakvngge,
你不肯應承
3. elemangga daljakv niyalma de anatambi,
反推不相干的人
4. yargiyan oqibe,
或真
5. taxan oqibe,
或假
6. dubentele daldaqi ojorakv,
終久瞞不得
7. ini qisui tuqinjimbi,
自然要出來
8. niyalma de anataha de,
推給了人
9. uthai ukqaqi ombio,
就脫得麼
10. guweqi ombio,
免得麼
11. te biqibe,
譬如今
12. si alime gajirakv oso nakv,
你不肯應承
13. hetu niyalma jifi sini yabuha baita mujangga sehede,
傍人來說是你行的事
14. tere erinde dosiqi inu waka,
那時候進也不是
15. bedereqi inu waka,
退也不是
16. Damu yasa gehun ojoro dabala,
只是大瞪着眼罷咧
17. jai faksidaki seqi,

再要巧辯

18. jabume mutembio,
答應得來麼

19. inemene emu yargiyan babe tuqibufi gisureqi,
索性說出一個實在去處

20. niyalma geli emu giljame gvnire babi,
人家另有一個體念處

21. erken terken i serengge,
支支吾吾的說

22. inu baitakv kai.
也不中用啊

Section 19: A Talented Man

1. suwe terebe bai tuwara de albatu dabala,
你們白看着他村粗罷咧

2. dolo umesi getuken kai,
心裡狠明白呀

3. waka oqi ai,
可不是什麼

4. bi imbe tuwaqi inu eme giltukan yebken niyalma,
我看他是一個秀氣敏捷的人

5. iqihiyahangge baita tome daqun,
所辦的事事兒急快

6. gisurehengge gisun tome mangga,
所說的句句話兒高強

7. eiten haqin de muterakv sere ba akv,
百樣兒無所不能

8. erebe tuwame ohode,
看起這個來

9. niyalma be qira i tuwaqi ojorakv,
人不可貌相

10. mederi muke be hiyase i miyaliqi ojorakv sehe gisun,
海水不可斗量的話

11. umai taxan akv kai,
竟不虛啊

12. ede inu damu niyalmai faxxara faxxarakv be hedure dabala,
這也只說人肯巴結不肯巴結罷咧

13. faxxaqi tetendere,

既肯巴結

14. ai haqi i mangga baita seme muteburakv ni.
什麼樣兒的難事不成呢

Section 20: Individual Matters

1. si tubaqi bahafi ukqaha sere be donjire jakade,
聽見說你得脫離了那個去處

2. bi umesi selaha,
我着實快活了

3. neneme donjiha gisun,
先聽見的話

4. hono buru bara bihe,
還恍恍惚惚的來着

5. amala dur seme gisurere jakade,
後頭亂烘烘說的時候

6. bi teni akdaha,
我纔信了

7. yala sini ere gese hvturingga niyalma,
果然你這樣有福之人

8. ainaha seme fengxen akv bade tuhenerakv seqina,
斷然不落那無福之地

9. damu sini onggolo gvnin bahabuha babe,
但是你預先得了主意

10. niyalma adarame bahafi sara,
人怎麼地知道

11. hetu niyalma sini jalin oihori faqihiyaxambihe,
傍人爲你好不着急來着

12. ere gemu age si an i uquri guquse de habqihiyan ofi,
着皆因是阿哥你平素間合朋友們和抄

13. teni gemu uttu hing seme gvnin de tebure dabala,
纔都這樣誠心塾着罷咧

14. sain ba akv bihe biqi,
若是沒有好處

15. we jifi hersembini,
誰肯來理呢

16. tere anggala bahaqi urgun seqi ojorakv,
況且得之不謂喜

17. ufaraqi koro seqi ojorakv,

108

失之不言虧

18. gemu meni meni teisu i dorgi baita,
都是各自分內的事

19. ini qisui emu toktoho giyan bi,
自然有一定的理

20. ede ai ferguwere babi.
還有什麼稱奇處

Section 21: Being Thankful

1. age i ferguwequke gvnin be bi waqihiyame saha,
阿哥的盛情我盡都知道了

2. ere durun i mujilen akvmbuha be,
這樣的盡心

3. bi hukxeme gvnirakv sere doro bio,
我不感念的理有麼

4. ne udu karulame muterakv biqibe,
現在雖然不能答報

5. amaga inenggi urunakv kiqeme faxxame karulambi,
日後自然效力圖報

6. damu ne bi aisere mujilen de hadahai ejefi,
但是現在我說什麼緊記在心裡

7. ainaha seme onggorakv obuki,
斷然也不肯忘

8. age ainu uttu gisurembi,
阿哥怎麼這樣說

9. ya gemu guqu waka,
那個都不是朋友

10. inenggi seqi mooi abdaha qi hono fulu kai,
論日子比樹葉兒還多呀

11. niyalma seme banjifi ya bade uqaraburakv ni,
人生何處不相逢呢

12. urunakv ser sere baqi aname,
必定按着些須的去處

13. yooni karulara be ereme gvniqi ombio,
都指望報答使得麼

14. age si jaqi gvnin fulu,
阿哥你太心多

15. jaqi kimqikv bai.
特仔細了罷

Section 22: Being Content

1. si ai uttu elequn be sarkv,
你怎麼這樣不知足

2. gemu sini adali oqi inu joo kai,
都像你也罷了啊

3. labdukan i baharangge komsokon i baharade isirakv,
多得不如少得

4. komsokon i baharangge ne baharade isirakv,
少得不如現得

5. labdu memerefi lalanji niyanggome muterakv oqi,
貪多嚼不爛

6. inu baitakv,
也是無用

7. damu dergi de duibuleqi isirakv biqibe,
但是比上雖不足

8. fejergi de duibuleqi funqetele bi seqi uthai wajiha,
比下有餘就罷了

9. urui julesi genere gojime,
只望前去

10. amasi forofi tuwarakv oqi ombio.
不望後看使得麼

Section 23: Great Concern

1. si tere baita be majige faxxaqina,
你把那個事巴結一巴結

2. ai uttu heolen,
怎這樣懈怠

3. tere baita holbobuhangge ujen amba,
那個事關係的重大

4. ambula narhvxaqi aqambi,
着實該當細致

5. balai niyalma de firgembuqi ojorakv kai,
胡洩露于人使不得啊

6. baita serengge ai boljon,
事情有何定準

7. doigomxorakvngge uthai waka seqina,
不預備提防的就不是話了

8. aikabade si olgoxoro dade geli olgoxoro,

若是你小心上又小心

9. ginggulere dade geli ginggulere,
謹慎上又謹慎

10. jai durun kemun qi jurqerakv,
再不錯規矩制度

11. tob sere gvnin be jafafi yabume ohode,
拿着正主意行的時候

12. ainqi eiten baita de gemu dosobumbi dere,
想是諸事上都奈得住罷咧

13. ere bai mini saha i teile sinde jombuhangge,
這白是俺我所知提你

14. adarame iqihiyame gamaqi aqara babe,
該怎樣辦理的去處

15. sini lashalara de bi,
在乎你決斷

Section 24: A Burdensome Matter

1. yaya baita be emgeri waqihiyabuqi sain dabala,
凡事一遭兒完畢了好罷咧

2. juwedere de isinaqi,
若到二次

3. ai sain ba banjinara,
生出什麼好處來

4. baita xanggafi jabqara anggala,
于其埋怨于事畢

5. deribure onggolo olhoxoro de isirakv,
不如小心于起初

6. ere baita kemuni ijishvn seqi ombi,
這事還算順當

7. asuru murtashvn sere ba akv,
沒有什麼捻扭別的去處

8. la li seme waqihiyaqi ombi,
可以爽爽利利完地

9. ede ai dahvn dahvn i fonjire babi,
這有什麼再三再四的去處

10. si sarkv,
你不知道

11. ere baita be urunakv juwedere de isinambi,

這事必到二次

12. adarame seqi,

怎麼說呢

13. amba muru be tuwaqi,

看起大概

14. uthai umesi xadaquka baita,

就是個很勞神的事

15. aikabade da sekiyen be getukeleburakv oqi,

倘若看不清楚了根源

16. amaga inenggi urunakv debkebure de isinambi.

日後必至翻騰起來

Section 25: To Know It Exactly

1. ememu urse uttu gisurembi,

或者這們樣說

2. ememu urse geli tuttu gisurembi,

或者又那們樣說

3. gvniqi gemu taxan,

想來都是虛

4. ainahai yargiyan ni,

未必是真呢

5. te ya be akdaqi ojoro,

如今可信那一個

6. ya be donjiqi ojoro,

可聽那一個

7. elemangga mujilen farfabure jakade,

反倒亂了心

8. ere baitai aisi jobolon mutebure efujere babe,

把這小事的利害成破

9. inu gemu toktobume muterakv ohobi,

也都定不來了

10. te absi ohode sain jiye,

如今可怎麼樣的好啊

11. sarkv seme araki seqi,

若要裝作不知道

12. yargiyan be taxan obuqi ojorakv sere anggala,

別說以真作假使不得

13. taxan be yargiyan obuqi inu ojorakv,

以假作真也使不得

14. uru be waka seqi ojorakv sere anggala,
以是說非使不得

15. waka be uru seqi inu ojorakv,
以非說是也使不得

16. Eitereqibe,
總而言之

17. urunakv uru waka yargiyan taxan i babe,
必定把是非真假之處

18. tengkime saha manggi,
知道切實了

19. teni ojoro dabala,
纔可得罷咧

20. nambuhai nambuhai uthai hvlhidame gisureqi ombio.
撈把住就糊里糊塗的說使得麼

Section 26: An Obvious Thing

1. si uthai aqara be tuwame yabu,
你就酌量着行

2. jai ume daqilara,
再別討示下

3. ere umesi iletu baita be dahame,
这个即是很顯然的事

4. ainaha seme sirkedeme goidabure de isinarakv,
斷不至于悠恋遲誤

5. aika giyalu jaka i ba biqi,
若有什么破綻空子之處

6. niyalmai fiktu baire de gelera dabala,
怕人尋因由兒罷咧

7. ere gese haqin demun umai akv bade,
並沒有這等異樣條款

8. hoo hio seme yabuqi,
慷慷慨慨的行

9. uthai wajiha,
就完了

10. ede geli ai tathvnjara babi,
這有什麼遊疑的去處

11. damu baita de teisulehe manggi,

只是碰着了事情

12. foihori tuwarakv,
不輕看

13. neneme emu jergi narhvxame gvninjafi,
先細想一番

14. jai yabume ohode,
再行的時候

15. urui jabxaji bisire dabala,
定有便宜的事儿罷咧

16. ainahai ufaraki ba bini.
未必有吃虧的去處呢

Section 27: Keep Your Words

1. ere jergi gisun gemu sini gvnin qi tuqinjihenggeo,
這些話都是從你心裡發出來的啊

2. aiqi bai buhiyeme gisurehenggeo,
或是白猜防着說的啊

3. sini ere gese xan be gidafi honggon be hvlhara baita be,
似你這樣掩耳盜鈴的事

4. yaya bade isinafi inu yabume banjinarakv,
不拘到那裏也行不去

5. si simbe alime muterakv seqi,
你說你當不起

6. i sinqi geli alime muterakv kai,
他比你更當不起呀

7. qananggi lalanji si alime gaisu sefi,
前日屢屢的說叫你應承

8. enenggi jio nakv uthai angga ubaliyakangge,
今日一道來就改變了嘴

9. erebe niyalmai waka semeo,
這是人家的不是啊

10. beyei waka semeo,
是自己的不是啊

11. ai oqibe,
憑他什麼

12. beye alifi yaburengge wesihun,
自己應承了行的高

13. ere durun i niyalma de ten gairengge,

這樣合人家討憑據的
14. hihanakv bai.
不稀罕罷

Section 28: A Predetermined Principle

1. asihata majige fede,
小夥子們上緊些

2. ere gese sain nashvn be ufarabuha manggi,
失去了這樣的好機會

3. jai ere uqaran be gvniqi geli bahambio,
再想着際遇還得麼

4. erin forgon oyonggo seqi,
時候兒說要緊

5. faxxarangge inu oyonggo,
巴結也要緊

6. bi simbe tuwaqi,
我看你

7. ememu fonde hon hahi,
有一時太急

8. ememu fonde elehun dabahabi,
有一時過於皮鬆

9. sini henduhe ere jergi gisun inu biqibe,
你說的這些話雖是

10. si damu emken be saha gojime, juwe be sara unde,
你但知其一不知其二

11. yaya baita ini qisui emu bajinara doro bi,
凡事自然有一個造定的理

12. bahara giyan oqi,
若是該得

13. gvnin akv bade kemuni uqarabumbi,
無心處常硼着

14. bahara giyan waka oqi,
若是不該得

15. udu hvsun mohotolo faxxaha seme inu baitakv kai.
縱然盡力巴結了也不中用啊

Section 29: A Fixed Conclusion

1. age be baibi takara adali,
倒像認得阿哥

2. yaka bade aqaha gese absi qira be takambi,
在那裏會過樣的好面善

3. enenggi jabxan de geli age be aqaha,
今日萬幸又會見了阿哥

4. adarame bahafi sini emgi emu bade bifi, daruhai age i taqibure be don-jiqi,
怎麼得同你在一處常常領阿哥的教

5. tere yala mini kesi oho seqina,
那真是我的造化了

6. turgun adarame seqi.
情由怎麼說呢

7. sain urse de adanaqi,
就好人

8. ulhiyen ulhiyen i sain de ibenembi,
漸漸進於好

9. ehe urse de dayanaqi,
歸壞人

10. bihe bihei ehe de uxabumbi serengge,
久而連累壞

11. toktoho leolen kai,
乃是定論

12. niyalmai sain ehe be urunakv inenggi goidaha manggi, teni takambi semeo,
人的好歹必定到日久纔認得麼

13. dartai andande inu takabumbikai.
傾刻之間也認得出來的啊

Section 30: A Bitter Memory

1. emgeri duleke baita be geli jonofi ainambi,
一遭兒過去了的事又提起來作什麼

2. jongko dari bi yertexembime korsombi,
回回兒提起來愧而且恨

3. haha niyalma baita biqi,
漢子家有事

4. teng tang seme yabure,
響響亮亮的行

5. hoo hio seme arbuxara oqi,
慷慷慨慨的動作

6. teni inu dabala,
纔是罷咧

7. niyalmai afabuha be alime gaiha manggi,
受了人的託付

8. geli niyalmai baita be duhemburakv bime,
又不終人之事

9. elemangga juwe sidenderi sain niyalma arame,
反從兩下里作好人

10. damu beyei waka be niyalma de guribuki sembi,
只要把自己的不是挪給人

11. tuttu bime enggiqi bade balai bardanggilame,
然而在背地裏胡誇口

12. geren i juleri baita be geli lashalame muterakv,
衆人面前又不能決斷事

13. erebe geli bengsen bisire niyalma seqi ombio.
這也稱得起是有本事的人麼

Section 31: To Pay Respect

1. qohome age i elhe be fonjime,
特候兄長的安

2. deo bi gingguleme jasiha,
弟謹寄信

3. age i wesihun beye saiyun,
兄長的貴體好麼

4. booi gubqi gemu saiyun,
家裏都好麼

5. age qi fakqahaqi ebsi,
自別兄長以來

6. elhe be fonjime jasiki seqi,
欲要寄信候安

[I] wanted to send regards by mails.
7. ildun i niyalma be baharakv ofi,
因不得順便之人

8. tuttu bahafi jasihakv bihe,
所以沒得寄信

9. deo bi jing kidume gvnime bisirede.
弟正在想念之間

10. holkonde age i jasigan isinjiha,

117

忽然兄長的書信到來

11. bi yala alimbaharakv urgunjembime yertexembi,
我真乃不勝歡喜又是慚愧

12. tuttu seme muse ahvn deo i beye udu juwe bade giyalabuha biqibe,
雖其那樣說咱兄弟身雖相隔兩處

13. gvnin mujilen be umai giyalabuha ba akv,
心情並無相隔

14. uttu be dahame,
即是如此

15. ereqi amasi yaya ildun de,
今後凡係順便

16. age beyei elhe babe kemuni jasireo,
望乞常將兄長身體平安之處寄來

17. deo bi selame donjiki,
弟欲樂問

18. jai meni beyese agei kesi de yooni sain,
至于我等身體托賴兄長全好

19. erei jalin gingguleme jasiha.
爲此謹寄

Section 32: School Education

1. ere uquri suweni sefu kemuni jimbio akvn,
這一向你們師傅還來不來

2. jimbi,
來

3. emu inenggi de urunakv emu mudan jimbi,
一日必定來一次

4. tuttu oqi,
若是那們樣

5. inenggidari jifi gemu suwede ai jergi gisun taqibumbi,
每日來了都教給你們些什麼話

6. meni ere sefu i taqibuhangge,
我們這個師傅教的

7. gemu yasai juleri gisurere an i gisun,
都是眼面前說的尋常話

8. jai fonjire jabure muwa gisun,
再問答的粗話

9. umai enqu haqin i mangga gisun akv,

118

並沒有另樣的難話

10. age suweni ere taqihangge umesi doro waka oho,
阿哥你們這學的狠不是道理了

11. ainu terebe syxu i bithe be giyangnaburakv,
為什麼不叫他講四書

12. ubaliyambure be taqirakv,
不學翻譯

13. aniya hvsime ere jergi muwa gisun be taqifi ainambi,
成年甲學這些粗話作什麼？

14. agei henduhengge umesi inu,
阿哥說的狠是

15. taqibuhangge umesi giyangga,
教導的狠有理

16. tuttu sehe seme,
雖其那樣說

17. age si damu sini beyebe sara dabala,
阿哥你只知道你自己罷咧

18. meni beyebe sarkv kai,
不知道我們的身子啊

19. be aikabade gemu age i adali ere gese sure sektu bihe biqi,
我們若是都像阿哥這樣聰明伶俐

20. syxu i bithe be taqiki sere anggala,
別說學四書

21. uthai sunja nomun geren dz i bithe seme,
就便是五經諸子

22. inu gemu hvlaqi aqambi,
也都該當讀

23. meni beyebe jafafi age de duibuleqi geli ombio,
拿着我們的身子比阿哥也使得麼

24. meni taqihangge inenggi qinggiya bime,
我們所學的日子淺

25. bahanahangge geli eden,
會的又少

26. tuttu bime angga modo,
然嘴又遲鈍

27. emu siran i sunja ninggun gisun biqi,
一連若有五六句話

28. uthai gisureme muterakv,

就說不來

29. aikabade gisureme ohode urui tanjambi,
若是我一定打登兒

30. hendure balame,
可是說的

31. hono miqume bahanahakv bade,
還沒有會爬

32. uthai feliyere be taqiqi ombio.
就學得走麼

Section 33: Being III

1. qananggi dobori majige xahvrara jakade,
前日夜裡略受了些涼

2. ere juwe inenggi beye umesi qihakv,
這兩日身子狠不受用

3. jeke jaka singgerakv bime,
吃的東西不消化

4. teqibe iliqibe elhe akv,
坐立也不安

5. beyei gubqi hvsun akv,
渾身無力

6. damu gvwaidame deduki sembi,
只要歪蒯倒着

7. sikese yamji furgisu i muke be fuifufi,
昨日晚上熬了些生薑湯

8. nei gaime majige omire jakade,
喝了些出了汗

9. enenggi beye teni majige sulakan oho,
今日身子纔略鬆散了些

10. eqi kai,
可不是麼

11. ere uquri yooni uttu kai,
這一向都是這樣啊

12. uthai mini beye ere udu inenggi i dolo,
就是我的身子這幾日裏頭

13. inu asuru la li akv,
也甚是不爽快

14. dolo qehun bime kuxun,

120

心裡膨悶又嘈雜

15. jeqi omiqi amtan baharakv,
飲食不得味

16. beye pio seme bethei fejile kubun i farsi be fehuhe adali,
身子虛飄飄腳底下踹着棉花瓜子是的

17. elekei maktabuhakv bihe,
險些兒沒有撩倒來着

18. arga akv katunjahai arkan seme duleke,
沒法兒強扎掙着剛剛兒的好了

19. gvniqi gemu ere aniya erin forgon i geri sukdun i haran dere
想來都是今年的時氣的過失罷.

Section 34: A Difficult Time

1. bi te umesi banjire de mangga ohobi,
我如今狠難過了

2. booi anggala geren bime,
家口衆

3. geli niyalma de edelehe bekdun bi,
又該下人的債

4. tuqibure ba labdu,
出去的多

5. dosinjire ba komso,
進來的少

6. geli hvda maiman akv,
又沒有買賣生意

7. niyalma de alaha seme,
縱告訴了人

8. inu gemu akdarakv,
也都不信

9. qe elemangga mimbe jortai tuttu arahangge sembi,
他們倒說是我故意裝作那們樣的

10. age si simbe banjire de mangga seqi,
阿哥你說你難過

11. mini ere beyere omiholoro gosihon i babe,
我這挨冷受餓的苦處

12. wede alanara,
告訴誰去

13. tei forgon juwan booi dorgi uyun boode gemu hesihedeme inenggi be hetumbure dabala,
如今的時候十家內九家都是打着幌兒度日罷咧

14. ya emu boode tuttu elgiyen tumin banjimbini,
那一家是那樣豐富殷實過地呢

15. niyalmai hendure balame,
可是人說的

16. boo tome guwan xi yen seqi,
家家觀世音

17. babade o mi to fo sembikai.
處處念彌陀

Section 35: Grass Has Ears

1. age si kemuni faksidafi ainambi,
阿哥你還巧辯作什麼

2. urunakv angga aqabuki sembio,
必定要對口麼

3. eiqibe sinde majige muru bifi,
縱是你有些影兒

4. niyalma teni tuttu gisurere dabala,
人纔那樣說罷咧

5. tese ainu mini beyebe laidarakv ni,
他們怎麼不賴我呢

6. yaya yabuha baita,
大凡行的事

7. damu niyalma be daldaqi ojoro dabala,
只可瞞得人罷咧

8. dergi abka be gidaqi ojorakv kai,
瞞不得上天啊

9. dekdeni henduhengge,
俗語說的

10. jugvn de gisureqi,
路上說話

11. orho i dolo donjire niyalma bi sehebi,
草裡有人聽

12. edun darakv oqi,
風若不刮

13. mooi abdaha geli axxambio.
樹葉兒也動麼

122

Section 36: Don't be So Polite

1. age geli webe anahvnjara,
阿哥再還讓誰

2. uthai tafafi dulimbade teki,
就請上去在當中坐

3. qembe inu mende majige ba anabu,
叫他們也讓給我們一點地方

4. be inu tembi dere,
我們也坐下罷

5. ere agei gisun inu,
這阿哥的話是

6. age si uthai qin i te,
阿哥你就正坐

7. ere age be adame tekini,
叫這阿哥挨着坐罷

8. age si inu ume marara,
阿哥你也別推辭

9. uthai ere agei sirame teki,
就接着這阿哥坐

10. bi uthai uttu bakqilame teki,
我就這們對着坐

11. yaya demun i teqendufi jeki bai,
不拘怎麼樣的大家坐下吃罷

12. ere doro be ainambi,
用這禮行作什麼

13. geli yengsi sarin waka,
又不是喜慶筵席

14. aibe dele wala sembi.
什麼叫作上頭下頭

Section 37: What is True?

1. age si hetu niyalma gisun be ume donjire,
阿哥你別聽傍人的話

2. i mimbe gisurehe seqi,
他說是我說了

3. uthai gisurehe okini,
就算是我說了罷

4. eiqi wei juleri gisurehe bihe,

或是當着誰的面前說來着

5. inu emu siden bakqin bidere,
也有一個對證罷咧

6. tere aika mimbe niyalma be waha seqi,
他若說我殺了人

7. uthai mimbe niyalma be waha sembio,
就說我殺了人了麼

8. age hon ume niyalma be sui akv adunggiyara,
阿哥別太無故的挫磨人

9. ujui ninggude genggiyen abka bikai,
頭上有青天啊

10. sakdasai gisun hendure balame,
可是老人家說的話

11. yasai sabuhangge be yargiyan sembi,
眼見的是實

12. xan i donjihengge be taxan sembikai.
耳聽的是虛啊

Section 38: Time Flies

1. erin forgon absi hvdun,
時候兒好快

2. herqun akv de geli emu aniya ofi,
不覺的又是一年

3. aniya biyade isinjiha,
到了正月裡了

4. abka kesi de geli emu se nonggiha,
托賴老天爺又添了一歲

5. yala xun biya homso maktara adali niyalma be sakdabume xorgimbi seqina,
果然是日月如梭催人老

6. bi se asigan i fonde,
我年少的時候

7. inu aniya haqin i uquri be buyeme erembihe,
也愛盼望年節來着

8. te se de ofi,
如今因上了年紀

9. ere gese erehunjere mujilen yooni akv sere anggala,
不但說這樣盼望的心全都沒了

10. damu haqin inenggi sere be donjiha de,
只一聽見了人說節令的話
11. uju gemu fintambikai.
頭都疼啊

Section 39: Cannot Promise

1. minde emu baita bifi,
我有一件事
2. qohome age de yandume baime jihe,
特煩求阿哥來了
3. musei fe guqulehe be gvniqi,
若想咱們的舊相遇
4. mini ere baita be,
把我這個事情
5. urunakv tere looye de ulame gisurereo,
望祈必定轉那位老爺說
6. je,
哦
7. bi genefi muterei teile gisureme tuwaki,
我去儘量兒說着瞧
8. i dahaqi si inu ume urgunjere,
他若是依你也別喜歡
9. i daharakv oqi,
他若是不依
10. age inu ume gasara,
阿哥也別報怨
11. bi terei baru bai an i guqulembi,
我合他白平常相遇
12. asuru gvlika ba akv,
沒甚相厚處
13. ere baita be mutebure muteburakv be,
這個事成得來成不來
14. bi inu akdulame muterakv kai.
我也保不住啊

Section 40: Expecting for a Reply

1. mentuhun ahvn i gingguleme unggihe bithe,
愚兄謹發字帖

2. ere uquri simbe umai bahafi sabuhakv,
那些時竟沒得看見你

3. erin hvdun geri fari ofi,
因是光陰迅速恍惚間

4. ethai ududu aniya oho adali,
就像幾年

5. beye sini wesihun boode tuwanaki seqi,
欲要親身到你尊府看望

6. geli bahafi aqarakv ayoo seme gvnimbi,
想着又恐不得會見

7. mergen deo sain niyalma be dahame,
賢弟乃是善人

8. urunakv sain ojoro be,
必然吉利

9. ai gisurebure babi,
有何說處

10. qananggi si gosime,
前者蒙你疼愛

11. sini baru gaire jaka be,
向你所要之物

12. minde bure sehe,
已說給我

13. ertele umai benjibuhekv,
至今並沒送來

14. aiqi wesihun booi niyalma jabdurakv aise,
想是貴家不得閒空

15. simbe geli jobobume benjibure anggala,
于其又勞你送來

16. bi qohome meni ajige haha jui be ganabuha,
我特令我們小廝去取

17. mergen deo hahilame bufi unggire be,
賢弟速速給發

18. ne bi dukai beren de nikefi ereme aliyahabi,
我現倚門待望

19. bure burakv be urunakv emu bithe arafi amasi unggireo.
給于不給望祈必寫一字發回

Section 41: Interview for Work

1. age si ya gvsangge,
阿哥你是那旗的

2. bi gulu suwayan ningge,
我是正黃旗的

3. hontohonggeo,
是渾托和的啊

4. nirunggeo,
是牛錄上的

5. nirungge,
牛錄上的

6. wei niru debi,
在誰牛錄上

7. qangxeo niru debi,
在常壽牛錄上

8. hala ai,
姓什麼

9. hala jeo,
姓周

10. gebu ai,
名子叫什麼

11. gebu fengxengge,
名子叫豐盛額

12. wei jui,
誰的兒子

13. uju jergi hiya gingguji i jui,
頭等侍衛京屋吉的兒子

14. udu se oho,
幾歲了

15. juwan uyun se oho,
十九歲了

16. ai aniya,
屬什麼的

17. muduri aniya,
屬龍的

18. mukvn bio,
有戶中

19. akv,
沒有

20. mukvn bi,
有戶中

21. wei mukvn,

誰的戶中

22. jalan i janggin bayantu i mukvn,
參領巴煙兔的戶中

23. ahvn deote gemu bio,
弟兄們都有麼

24. gemu bi,
都有

25. sini ahvn ai alban debi,
你哥哥在什麼差事上

26. mini age ne lamun funggala,
我哥哥現在是藍翎子

27. sini deo se adarame,
你兄弟什麼年紀

28. teni ninggun se ohobi,
纔六歲了

29. kemuni ajigen,
還小呢
Still young.

30. banjiha inenggi atanggi,
生日是幾時

31. aniya biyai orin sunja de inu,
是正月二十五日

32. sini boo aibide tehebi,
你家在那裏住

33. gu leo i juleri xun dekdere ergi de tehe bi,
在鼓樓前頭東邊住

34. qoohai jurgan i aisilakv hafan hvri i ama sinde ai ombi,
兵部員外郎呼哩阿媽是你什麼

35. minde ahvn ombi,
是我哥哥

36. ini ama sinde ai ombi,
他父親是你什麼

37. minde eshen ombi,
是我叔叔

38. banjiha eshen,
親叔叔麼

39. inu,
是

40. banjiha eshen,

親叔叔

41. si gabtame niyamniyame gemu bahanambio,
你馬步箭都會射麼

42. gabtame bahanambi,
會射步箭

43. niyamniyame bahanarakv,
不會射馬箭

44. si ainu niyamniyara be taqirakv,
你爲什麼不學馬箭

45. morin akv ofi taqihakv,
因爲沒有馬不曾學

46. si beri tatame tuwa,
你拉拉弓瞧

47. je,
哦

48. ara,
哎呀

49. ere beri i tebke be bi inu neime muterakv,
這個弓的墊子我也開不開

50. absi mangga na,
好硬啊

51. tuttu oqi,
那們都

52. beri be sinda,
把弓放下

53. dangse be hvlame tuwaki,
念念檔子看

54. je,
哦

55. si udu aniaya bithe hvlaha,
你讀了幾年書了

56. ilan aniya hvlaha,
讀了三年了

57. bithe giyagnahoo,
講過了書

58. akvn,
沒有

59. giyangnaha,

講過了

60. yaya bithe be si gemu giyangname mutembio,
不拘什麼書你都能講得來麼

61. mutere ba inu bi,
能的去處也有

62. muterakv ba inu bi,
不能的去處也有

63. aikabade narhvn somishvn ba oqi,
倘若是細微之處

64. bi uthai muterakv,
我就不能

65. si ya sefu i taqikv de bithe hvlambi,
你在那個師傅學裡讀書

66. jao sefu i taqikv de hvlambi,
在趙師傅的學裡念

67. ere jao sefu aibide tehebi,
這個趙師傅在那裡住

68. mini tehe booi dukai bakqin de bisire,
在我住的房子對門

69. tere amba boo uthai ini boo kai,
那個大房子就是他的家呀

70. jao sefu i qolo be ai ama sembi,
趙師傅的號叫什麼字兒

71. jooli i ama sembi,
叫作拙哩阿媽

72. ne aide bi,
現在什麼上頭？

73. daqi bithei yamun i asgan i bithei da de bihe,
原是翰林院的學士來着

74. beye jadahalaha turgunde,
因爲身子殘疾了

75. asgan i bithei da qi nakaha,
辭了學士了

76. bithe de antaka,
書上如何

77. sain,
好

78. bakqin akv i mangga,

無對手的高強

79. bithe ubaliyambure giyangnara,
翻譯講書

80. hergen arara gabtara niyamniyara be bahanarakvngge akv,
寫字馬步箭沒有不會的

81. xabisa be kadalarangge inu qirao,
管徒弟們也緊嗎

82. age ere babe ume jondoro,
阿哥別提這個

83. ajige juse damu ini jilgan be donjiha de,
小孩子們只一聽見他的聲兒

84. fayangga gemu tuhembi,
魂都掉

85. si inu tede gelembio,
你也怕他麼

86. ara ere ai gisun,
哎呀這是什麼話

87. sefu serengge uthai ama i adali kai,
師傅就是父親一樣啊

88. sefu de gelerakv oqi,
不怕師傅

89. geli we de gelembini,
還怕誰呢

90. terei booi banjirengge antaka,
他家過的如何

91. inu damu fe bihe hethe be tuwakiyame banjire dabala,
也只是守着舊有的產業過罷咧

92. ereqi tulgiyen i enqu geli bahara ba bisire be bi sarkv,
除此之外他另有所得去處我不知道

93. ne ini jakade bithe hvlara xabise udu bi,
現在他跟前念書的徒弟有多少

94. ne bisirengge ainqi tanggv isime bi,
現在有的想是夠着一百

95. si duleke aniya de inu simnembiheo akvn,
你去年也考來着沒有

96. simnehe bihe,
考來着

97. hvlarangge ararangge gemu eden ojoro jakade,

因爲念的寫的都差池

98. gebu gaihakv,
沒取名子

99. dule turgun uttu biheni,
原來情由是這樣來着呢

100. bi jakan sinde utala gisun fonjihangge,
我方纔問你的這許多話

101. gemu sini bengsen be qenderengge,
那是試探你的本事的

102. tuwaqi sini taqihangge kemuni ombi,
看你所學的還去得

103. bi qimari ambasa de alafi,
我明日告訴了大人們

104. urunakv sini gebu be isibuki,
必定送你的名子

105. eiqi dasame simnebure,
或是叫從考

106. eiqi uthai baitalara be gemu boljoqi ojorakv,
或是即用都定不得

107. ere udu inenggi dolo,
這幾日裡頭

108. sini gabtara niyamniyara babe,
把你的馬步箭

109. kemuni an i urebu,
還是照舊演習

110. hvlara arara babe inu an i taqi,
念的寫的去處也照舊學

111. boode bisu,
在家裡

112. gvwa bade ume genere,
別往別處去

113. selgiyere be tuwame deyere gese feksihei jio,
瞧着傳去如飛的跑了來

114. ume tookabure,
別誤了

115. je saha.
哦知道了

Section 42: Borrow Books

1. age si absi genembi,
阿哥你那里去

2. gvwa bade majige baita bifi genembi,
別處有點兒事情去

3. age yabu,
阿哥走

4. taka meni boode dari,
且順便到我家裡

5. joo bai,
罷咧

6. bi enenggi emu ekxere baita bifi xolo baharakv,
我今日有一宗緊事情不得工夫

7. enqu inenggi jai dariki bai,
另日再到去罷

8. age si neneheqi mujilen ambula gvwaliyakabi,
阿哥你比先心大變了

9. muse daqi ishunde targaqun akv gisureme,
咱們原是彼此說話沒有忌教

10. ton akv yabumbihengge kai,
行走沒有遍數兒來着的呀

11. si utala inenggi mini duka de umai enggelenjirakv bime,
你許多日子竟不登我的門

12. aqafi geli uttu anduhvri duyen ohongge,
見了又這樣冷淡

13. we simbe ainaha nio,
誰把你怎麼樣了麼

14. si sarkv,
你不知道

15. bi jiderakvngge waka,
非是我不來

16. damu booi joboshvn turgunde,
只爲家艱難的緣故

17. inenggidari ekxeme,
每日忙

18. umai xolo baharakv bade,
竟不得工夫

19. mimbe seme ainara,

叫我怎麼樣

20. age si booi joboshvn i jalin waka,
阿哥你不是爲家艱難

21. anqi aisi be ujeleme sain guqu be aldangga obume,
想是重利疏遠好朋友

22. mimbe tulgiyen gvnimbi dere,
外想着我罷

23. age sini ere ai gisun serengge,
阿哥你說的這是什麼話

24. musei guqulehengge,
咱們的相于

25. gvwa de duibuleqi ombio,
比得別人麼

26. si ainu ere gese gisun tuqimbi,
你爲何發出這樣話來

27. je je wajiha,
遮遮完了

28. enenggi mini baita be uthai tookabuqi,
今日我的事就便誤

29. tookabukini,
誤去罷

30. bi genere be nakafi,
我止住去

31. bgei boode darinaki,
到阿哥家里

32. bi eiqi generakv ohode,
我若是不去了

33. si kemuni mimbe wakaxambio,
你還怪我麼

34. age uttu oqi,
阿哥若這樣

35. teni guqu i doro,
纔是朋友的道理

36. daxose aba,
大小子在那里

37. morin gaisu,
接馬

38. je,

134

哦

39. ere morin be amargi hvwa de gamafi hvwaita,
把這個馬拿到後院子裡栓着

40. dukai jakade ume hvwaitara,
別拴在門口兒

41. ehe urse de guwelke,
仔細壞人

42. julahv be burgiyen de lakiya,
扯手掛在鞍喬子上

43. tohoma be inu hete,
墊子也撩起來

44. je,
哦

45. age yabu,
阿哥走

46. dosiki,
進去

47. age nagan de tafa,
阿哥上炕去

48. bi tafaki,
我上去

49. age ergi de sain,
阿哥這邊好

50. ubade inu sain,
這裡也好

51. jai majige wesi,
再上陞些兒

52. uthai uttu ohode umesi iqangga,
就是這樣很舒服

53. daxose aba,
大小子在那裡

54. si tule ainambi,
你在外頭作什麼呢

55. bi ubade morin hvwaitame bi,
我在這裡栓馬呢

56. ere waburu morin be hvwaitafi jiqi wajiha,
這個砍頭的栓上馬來罷了

57. emdubei hvwaitambio,

侭着栓麼

58. buqehe aha geli bini,
死奴才也有呢

59. hvdun dambagu tebufi benju,
快裝煙送來

60. si jai dosifi hendu,
你再進去說

61. qai be halukan i wenjefi benju se,
叫把茶熱的溫溫的送來

62. sun be labdukan i sinda,
把奶子多着些

63. tumikan oso,
稠稠的

64. hon ume genggiyen ojoro,
別太清了

65. je,
哦

66. taitai i beye saiyvn,
太太身體好麼

67. sain,
好

68. axa saiyvn,
嫂子好麼

69. sain,
好

70. juse gemu saiyvn,
孩子們都好麼

71. sain,
好

72. ara,
哎呀

73. daxose aba,
大小子在那里

74. qaibe ainu benjirakv,
把茶怎不送來

75. gajiha,
拿來了

76. age uthai gaisu,

阿哥就拿罷

77. age si inu gaisu,
阿哥你也拿

78. ai geli,
豈有此理

79. age si nene,
阿哥你先來

80. bi uthai neneme gaiki,
我就先拿咧

81. age bi hengkilerakv kai,
阿哥我不磕頭了啊

82. ai geli,
豈有此理

83. emu moro untuhun qai de geli hengkilembi serengge ai gisun,
一碗空茶也說磕頭是什麼話

84. age bi geli donjiqi,
阿哥我又聽見

85. si taqikv de dosifi bithe hvlambi sere yargiyvn,
說你進學讀書是真麼

86. inu,
是

87. meni nirui janggin mimbe aqahadari,
我們牛錄章京遭遭兒見了我

88. uthai baita de yabu yabu seme hendumbi,
就說當差事罷當差事罷

89. bi gvniqi manju bithe be udu hergen takara gojime,
我想滿洲書雖認得幾個字兒

90. gisun seqi oron sarkv,
若說是話總不知道

91. jai udu biyai bithe hvlafi,
再念幾個月的書

92. baita de dosiqi,
上差事去

93. inu goidabumbi sere ba akv,
也不算遲

94. tuttu ofi duleke biyai juwan ilan de,
所以上月十三日

95. geli taqikv de dosika,

又上了學了

96. si adarame bahafi donjiha,
你怎麼得聽見了

97. qananggi jooli i ama age mini boode jifi,
是前日卓哩阿媽阿哥來我家裡

98. bi tede simbe fonjiha bithe,
我望他問你來着

99. i minde alara jakade,
他告訴我的時候

100. bi teni saha,
我纔知道了

101. age sinde manju bithe biqi,
阿哥你有滿洲書麼

102. udu debtelin juwen bureo,
借于幾本

103. bi doolafi hvlaki,
我抄了念

104. wajiha manggi uthai sinde amasi benjire,
完了就于你送回來

105. minde bithe akv,
我沒有書

106. bi guquse de baime tuwaki,
我合朋友們尋着瞧

107. baha manggi niyalma be takvrafi sinde benebure,
得了使人送于你去

108. ere uthai age minbe gosiha kai,
這就是阿哥疼我了啊

109. ai gisun serengge,
說的是什麼話

110. age si uttu sithvme bithe hvlaki sembime,
阿哥你這樣上緊要讀書

111. bi udu debtelin bithe be baifi sinde doolaburakv sere doro bio,
我連幾本書不尋給你抄的理有麼

112. je je wajiha,
遮遮完了

113. bi inu gvwa de bairakv kai,
我也不合別人尋了啊

114. age gvwa de ume baire,

138

阿哥別合別人尋

115. bi baifi sinde benebure sehe kai,
我已是說了尋了給你送去

116. inu,
是

117. age bi geneki,
阿哥我去咧

118. buda jefi gene,
吃了再去

119. si ai uttu ekxembi,
你怎麼這們忙

120. buda dagilabume uthai bahambikai,
飯收拾着就得啊

121. joo bai,
罷呀

122. minde yargiyan i ekxere baita bi,
我當真地有忙事情

123. emu guqu minbe baita hebdembi seme,
一個朋友叫我商量事

124. i boode aliyahabi,
他在家裡等着你

125. bi generakv ohode,
我若是不去

126. tere mimbe jabqarakvn,
他不埋怨我麼

127. yargiyvn,
真麼

128. ai geli,
豈有此理

129. ede geli ai holtoro babi,
這有什麼撒謊的去處

130. unenggi oqi,
若是真

131. bi simbe biburakv,
我不留着你

132. damu age jifi untuhun tehe kai,
但是阿哥來了空坐了啊

133. jai jio,

再來呀

134. age si inu dosiki bai,
阿哥你也進吧

135. emu juwe inenggi oho manggi,
過一兩日

136. bi geli age be tuwanjiki.
我還來瞧阿哥

Section 43: Visiting a Friend

1. age saiyvn,
阿哥好麼

2. sain,
好

3. age sini beye inu saiyvn,
阿哥你的身體也好麼

4. sain,
好

5. ere uquri si aibide bihe,
這一向你在那里來着

6. umai simbe sabuhakv,
竟沒見你

7. bi jing age be tuwanjiki sembihe,
我正要來瞧阿哥來着

8. gaitai emu ajige baita de uxabure jakade,
忽然被一件小事拉扯住

9. tuttu bahafi jihekv,
故此沒得來

10. qananggi arkan seme baita teni wajiha,
前日將將兒事情纔完了

11. sikse xolo bahafi jiki sehe biqi,
昨日得了工夫將說要來

12. geli agame deribuhe,
又下起雨來了

13. age si sarangge,
阿哥你知道的

14. minde nemerku jangqi gemu akv,
我雨衣氊褂子都沒有

15. morin inu akv,

馬也沒有

16. jugvn geli lifagan,
路上又爛泥

17. tuttu ofi,
因是那們

18. geli bahafi jihekv,
又沒得來

19. enenggi galga ojoro jakade,
今日晴了

20. bi yafahalame,
我步行

21. qohome age be tuwanjime jihe,
特來瞧阿哥來了

22. ara uttu goro de,
哎呀這們遠的

23. mini jalin agei beyebe suilabuhangge,
爲我勞動阿哥的駕

24. bi adarame alime mutembi,
我如何當得起

25. yala bi hukxeke seme wajirakv,
真真的我感之不盡

26. ai geli,
豈敢

27. age bi boode emhun tehede jing umesi alixambihe,
阿哥我在家裡獨坐正狠悶的慌來着

28. sini beye jihengge tob seme mini gvninde aqaha,
你來的正合了我的主意

29. tuttu bime age be kiduha gvnin be,
然而想念阿哥的心

30. inu bahafi selabuha,
也得快活了

31. muse ahvn deo enenggi dere aqaha be dahame,
咱們弟兄今日既是會見面了

32. untuhusaka simbe unggire kooli akv,
沒有空空叫你去的規矩

33. emu hvntahan nitan nure be dagilafi,
收拾一杯薄酒

34. muse juwe nofi bakqilame omiqame,

咱們二人對飲

35. majige leoleme teqeki,
坐着敍談一敍談

36. age si mimbe uttu gosiki sere be dahame,
阿哥你既然這樣要疼愛我

37. bi marara ba akv,
我不推辭

38. urunakv agei gvnin de aqabuki,
必定合阿哥的意思

39. damu turgun akv de jobobuhangge,
只是無故騷擾

40. giyan de aqarakv,
不合理

41. ai geli,
豈敢

42. kesitu aba,
克十兔在那裡

43. mure anju dagilabufi benju se,
說叫收拾酒菜送來

44. je,
哦

45. kesitu si ere falan be ainu erirakv,
克十兔這個地你怎麼不掃

46. dere be inu dasihiyarakv,
桌子也不揮

47. si baibi boode bifi ainambihe,
你白白的在家裡什麼來着

48. bi aifini erihe bihe,
我早已掃了來着

49. edun dahai umai nakarakv,
風佁着刮竟不住

50. jai uqe de geli hide lakihakv ofi,
再房門上又沒掛簾子

51. uttu nantuhun oho,
是這們臟了

52. ere doro sarkv waburu aha geli bini,
這個不知禮的砍頭奴才也有呢

53. kemuni tabsidaki sembio,

142

還有強嘴麼

54. hasa nure be tuwana,
快看酒去罷

55. je,
哦

56. age muse ere xolo de,
阿哥咱們稱着這個工夫

57. neneme dere be hvwa de guribufi teki bai,
先把桌子挪在院子裡坐着罷

58. ere booi dolo umesi halhvn kai,
這屋裡狠熱呀

59. umesi inu,
狠是

60. muse tule guribuqi,
咱們若望外挪

61. tere singgeri xan i mooi fejile sain,
那槐樹底下好

62. tubade sebderileme teqi iqangga,
那裡稱陰涼兒坐着舒服

63. tuba ehe,
那裡不好

64. moo de bisire umiyaha labdu emdubei tuhembi,
樹上的蟲子多不住的掉

65. amargi hvwai sihin i fejile sain de isirakv,
不如後院子房檐底下好

66. tuttu oqi uthai amargi hvwa de okini,
若是那們着就是後院裡罷

67. eitereqibe,
總而言之

68. hvwa i dolo booi torgiqi serguwen,
院子裡比屋裡涼快

69. esi,
自然

70. tere anggala boo hafirahvn,
況且屋窄

71. niyalma geli geren oqi,
人又多

72. tehei uju liyeliyexeme mujilen farfabumbi seqina,

坐久了頭眩心亂

73. bi banitai inu halhvn de hamirakv,
我生來的也受不得熱

74. age te niyengniyeri dubei forgon de,
阿哥今當春末的時候

75. tumen jaka gemu fulhurefi,
萬物都發生了

76. jing alin de sargaxare muke be tuwara sain erin,
正是遊山看水的好時節

77. mini ere ajige bithei booi hvwa,
我這個小書房院子

78. udu gebungge yafan ferguwequke ba waka biqibe,
雖然不是名院勝景

79. inu alin weji qi enqu akv,
也不亞如山林

80. tob seme musei jergi ursei somime tere ba kai,
正是吾輩隱居之處啊

81. eqi ai,
可不是麼

82. ara,
哎呀

83. emdubei sula gisun be leolerede,
俱着敘談閒話

84. nure darabure be gemu onggolo,
把讓酒都忘記了

85. daxose nure tebu,
大小子斟上酒

86. age si emu hvntahan omi,
阿哥你喝一鐘

87. bi omiha,
我喝過了

88. ere nure umesi hatan nimequke,
這個酒狠釅利害

89. bi damu emu hvntahan omire jakade uthai soktoho kai,
我只喝了一鐘就醉咧

90. absi serengge,
說的是那里話

91. teni hvntahan be tukiyeme,

纔舉鍾子

92. hono angga de gamara unde de,
還未沾脣

93. uthai soktoho sere doro bio,
就說醉了的理有麼

94. si jaqi holtorongge mangga,
你特會撒謊

95. mini holtorongge waka,
非我撒謊

96. bi daqi omime bahanarakv bihe,
我原本不會飲酒

97. age ere durun i mimbe gosime ofi,
只爲阿哥這樣疼愛我

98. teni emu hvntahan omiha dabala,
纔喝了一鍾

99. gvwa bade oqi,
若是別處

100. ainaha seme omirakv,
斷然不喝

101. age aika akdarakv oqi,
阿哥若是不信

102. booi urse de fonjiqi enderakv kai,
問家人們便知

103. sini gisun be bi gemu akdarakv,
你的話我都不信

104. omime bahanara bahanarakv be bi inu darakv,
會喝不會喝我也不管

105. si damu mini ilan hvntahan nure be omire wajiha manggi,
你只飲完了我的三盃酒

106. bi simbe guwebure,
我饒了你

107. nure seqi geli horon i okto waka,
酒又不是毒藥

108. oktolome wara de kelembio,
怕藥殺了麼

109. je je wajiha,
遮遮完了

110. ede aibi,

145

這有何妨

111. ere ilan hvntahan nure de,

這三盃酒

112. uthai soktome buqeqi inu okini,

就便醉死也罷

113. bi omiki,

我喝

114. age si tuwa,

阿哥你瞧

115. gemu omime waqihiyaha,

都喝乾了

116. tule inu yamjiha,

外頭也晚了

117. bi geneki bai,

我去罷

118. age ubade emu dobori dedufi,

阿哥在這裡睡一夜

119. qimari jai geneki,

明日再去

120. joo bai,

罷呀

121. qimari boode baita bi,

明日家裡有事

122. generakv oqi ojorakv,

不去使不得

123. uttu waka bihe biqi,

若不是這樣

124. uthai sini boode emu dobori indembihe,

就在你家過一夜

125. age sinde aika xolo bahaqi,

阿哥你若是得來工夫

126. inu meni boode emu mari geneqina,

也往我們家裡去一遭兒

127. urunakv genembi,

必定去

128. je baniha kai,

遮 生受了啊

129. ai geli,

146

豈敢

130. ai jekeni,
吃了什麼

131. geli baniha sembi,
又道生受

132. je age si untuhun genehe kai.
遮阿哥你空去了啊

Section 44: A Banquet

1. tule emu niyalma bifi duka hvlambi,
外頭有一個人叫門

2. weqi,
是誰

3. bi takarakv,
我不認得

4. eljitu si teqifi tuwana,
二吉兔你出去瞧

5. je,
哦

6. tule emu niyalma morin de yalufi age be baime ai gisun alanjiha sembi,
外頭一個人騎在馬上說找阿哥告訴什麼話來了

7. ai alara be si fonjihakvn,
告訴什麼你沒問麼

8. bi fonjiha bihe,
我問來着

9. i age be aqaha manggi, teni alambi sehe,
他說見了阿哥纔告訴

10. tuttu oqi bi genefi tuwanaki,
若是那們着我去看

11. ara age si jiheo,
哎呀阿哥你來了麼

12. aibiqi jihengge,
從那里來的

13. beye gubqi gemu buraki qanggi,
渾身都是灰土

14. age boode dosiki,
阿哥請進家裡去

15. joo bai,

罷呀

16. bi dosirakv,
我不進去

17. sinde gisun alafi uthai yombi,
告訴了你話就走

18. ainu uttu ekxembi,
怎麼這們忙

19. gvwa bade emu guqu bifi mimbe aliyahabi,
別處有一個朋友等着我呢

20. xolo jabdurakv,
不得工夫

21. ai geli,
豈有此理

22. uthai gvwa bade guqu bikini,
就是別處有朋友罷

23. taka mini boode dartai dosifi emu hvntahan genggiyen qai omifi jai geneki,
暫且進我家裡去喝一盃清茶再去

24. sini dolo adarame,
你心下如何

25. bi dosiki seqi,
我若是要進去

26. aifini uthai dosika kai,
早已就進去了呀

27. geli sini anahvnjara be aliyambio,
又等你讓麼

28. tere anggala, age ere durun i mimbe kunduleqi,
況且阿哥這樣的敬我

29. bi emu doro giyan be inu sarkv mujanggao,
我連一個道理也不知道麼

30. jabdurakvngge yargiyan,
不得工夫是真

31. age si enenggi aikabade mini boode dosirakv oqi,
阿哥你今日倘若不進我家裡去

32. bi yargiyan i simbe ushambi,
我實實的惱你

33. bi taka sinde fonji,
我且問你

34. si urunakv mimbe dosimbufi minde ai jaka ulebuki sembi,

148

你必定叫我進去要給我什麼東西吃

35. yadara boo kai,
窮人家呀

36. ai sain jaka bi,
有什麼好東西

37. emu moro untuhun buda dagilafi sinde ulebure dabala,
收拾一碗空飯給你吃罷咧

38. ereqi tulgiyen gvwa jaka akv kai,
除此之外沒有別的東西啊

39. sini boode aika migan yali niongniyaha yali biqi,
你家裡若有小豬子肉鵝肉

40. bi dosifi jeki,
我進去吃

41. akv oqi bi dosirakv,
若是沒有我不進去

42. bi ajigan qi untuhun buda be jeme taqihakv,
我自幼兒沒有吃慣空飯

43. age si damu dosiqina,
阿哥你只管進去

44. untuhun budai teile sinde ulebure kooli geli bio,
寡空飯給你吃的規矩也有麼

45. uthai migan yali niongniyaha yali jeki seqi,
就便要吃小豬子肉鵝肉

46. inu umesi ja,
也狠容易

47. asuru mangga ba akv kai,
沒甚難處啊

48. boode beleni bisirengge,
家裡現成有的

49. tuttu oqi si neneme dosi,
若是那們着你先進去

50. ai geli,
豈敢

51. mini boo kai,
是我家呀

52. bi nendeqi ombio,
我先走使得麼

53. eljitu aba,

二吉兔在那里呢

54. nagan de sektefun sekte,
炕上鋪坐褥

55. fileku de yaha nonggi,
火盆裡添上炭

56. sun qai aqabu,
對奶子茶

57. dambagu tebufi benju,
裝煙送來

58. je,
哦

59. sakda mafa boode bio,
老太爺在家裡麼

60. boode akv,
沒在家

61. absi genehe,
那去了

62. emu guqu i boode enenggi metembi seme yali jeme genehe,
一個朋友家今日還願吃肉去了

63. uttu oqi mafa amasi jihe manggi,
如此太爺回來了

64. si mini funde sain seme fonji,
你替我問好

65. inu,
是

66. age muse taka sula gisun be bargiya,
阿哥咱們且把閒話收起來

67. si arki omimbio,
你喝燒酒啊

Do you drink liquor,

68. nure omimbio,
喝黄酒啊

69. yaya okini gemu sain kai,
不拘什麼都好呀

70. buda booha be inu hahilame dagilabu,
把飯菜也叫快着收拾

71. bi kemuni aliyahai jeki sembikai,
我還等着要吃

72. nure anju be neneme banju,

150

先送酒菜來

73. hahila se,
說叫快着

74. age si wesihun te,
阿哥你上坐

75. tubai nagan niome xahvrun de teqi ojorakv,
那里的炕冰骨涼坐不得

76. qasi majige guri,
往那們挪一挪

77. qeni qihai teqekini,
由着他們坐着去罷

78. ume dara,
別要管

79. age si dosifi booha be majige haqihiyaqina,
阿哥你進去催一催菜去

80. eiqi bujuhengge qolahangge be,
或是煮的炒的

81. ya beleni oqi,
那個若是現成

82. hvdun gajifi mende ulebumbi dere,
快拿來給我們吃罷咧

83. asarafi suweni boode elheken i beye jeki semeo,
收着你們家裡慢慢的自己吃麼

84. age ekisaka te. Ume balai gisurere,
阿哥悄默聲的坐着別胡說

85. uttu oilohon balama ohode,
若這樣輕狂

86. weri de basuburahv,
不怕人笑話麼

87. eljitu nure tebu,
二吉兔斟酒

88. ere emu hvntahan nure,
這一盃酒

89. bi simbe kundulerengge,
是我敬你的

90. si urunakv waqihiyame omi,
你必定喝干

91. ai geli,

豈有此理

92. si damu mimbe takambio,
你只認得我麼

93. inu gvwa agese de kunduleqina,
也敬敬別的阿哥們

94. mimbe ume haqihiyara,
別催我

95. bi serengge omihai soktoro de isinarakv oqi inu nakarakv sere niyalma kai,
我是不喝到醉也不歇手的人啊

96. geren agese suwe inu udu hvntahan omiqina,
衆位阿哥你們也喝幾鍾是呢

97. ainu gemu uttu antahaxara mangga ni,
怎麼都會這樣作客

98. si serengge boigoji niyalma kai,
你是主人家呀

99. si jeterakv oqi,
你若不吃

100. antaha inu omirakv seqina,
客也不飲

101. bi ainu jeterakv,
我爲什麼不吃

102. esi jembi,
自然吃

103. suwe emgeri jihe be dahame,
你們既是來了

104. giyan i jetere bade oqi,
該當吃的去處

105. uthai ebitele jefu,
就往飽裡吃

106. omiqi aqara bade oqi,
該當喝到去處

107. uthai soktotolo omi,
就往醉裡喝

108. uttu oqi teni inu dabala,
如此纔是罷咧

109. ere gese goqishvdame bai tefi,
這樣謙謙遜遜的白坐着

110. darabuha seme umai omirakv,

讓這竟不喝

111. inu sabkalarakvngge,
也不動筷兒

112. ainqi mini nure hatan akvn,
想是我的酒不醶

113. sogi booha amtangga akvn aise,
菜沒有味麼

114. be age sini darabure be baiburakv,
我們不用阿哥你讓

115. gemu ubade jembi omimbi kai,
都在這裡吃呢喝呢啊

116. eljitu aba,
二吉兔在那里

117. morin dahalara urse de nure omibu, buda ulebu,
給跟馬的人們酒喝飯吃

118. ayaya meni booi niyalma de ume nure omibure,
哎呀呀別給我們的家下人酒喝

119. qe gemu omime bahanarakv,
他們都不會喝

120. tumen de emgeri soktoho sehede,
萬一醉了

121. adarame membe dahalabumbi,
怎麼跟我們

122. suwe mujilen sinda,
你們放心

123. hvwanggiyarakv,
無妨

124. bi damu qembe labdu omiburakv oqi uthai wajiha,
我只不叫他們多喝就完了

125. age si daqi nure omire mangga niyalma bihe kai,
阿哥你原是善飲的人來着啊

126. enenggi ainaha ni,
今日怎麼了

127. umai omirakv,
竟不喝

128. si sarkv,
你不知道

129. bi neneme majige omihabi,

我先喝了些

130. akv bihe biqi,
若不然

131. uthai mimbe emu inenggi xun tuhetele omibuha seme,
就便叫我喝一日到晚

132. bi inu eimeterakv,
我也不嫌厭煩

133. buda jembi seqi,
若論吃飯

134. bi yargiyan i sinde isirakv,
我實在不及你

135. nure omiki seqi,
若要喝酒

136. si minqi qingkai eberi,
你比我不及遠了

137. tuttu sehe seme,
雖其那樣說

138. si tere durn i omiqi,
你若是那樣喝

139. buda jetere be tookambi sere anggala,
不但說耽誤飯食

140. amaga inenggi se de oho manggi,
日後上了年紀

141. urunakv tede kokirabumbi,
必然受他的傷損

142. bi simbe tafulahangge gemu sain gisun,
我勸你的都是好話

143. akdara akdarakv gemu sini qiha okini,
信不信都任憑你

144. ere gemu age mimbe gosime ofi,
這都是阿哥疼愛我

145. teni uttu jombure dabala,
纔這樣提罷咧

146. gosirakv biqi,
若不疼愛

147. ainaha seme ere gese gosihvn gisun i tafularakv,
斷然不這樣苦言相勸

148. damu bi seibeni omime taqiha,

但只是我素日喝慣了

149. emu erinde targame muterakv,
一時忌不住

150. tuttu waka,
不是那們着

151. si dabame omirakv oqi uthai sain,
你若不過餘喝就好

152. hon taragaha de nememe ehe ombi,
太戒了反倒不好

153. bi geli sinde fonjire,
我再問你

154. si nure omiha jai enenggi erde iliha manggi fuyakiyambio akvn,
你喝了酒的第二日清早起來乾嘔不乾嘔

155. fuyakiyahangge tuwara ba akv,
乾嘔噁心的看不得

156. tuttu oqi,
若是那們着

157. ere uthai nure i haran dere,
這就是酒之故耳

Section 45: An Ungrateful Person

1. age si ere baili qashvlaha niyalma be jonorakv oqi,
阿哥你若不提起這背恩的人來

2. bi inu fanqarakv bihe,
我也不氣
I will not get angry.

3. si emgeri jonohode,
你一遭提起來

4. mini ki uthai wesihun jolhofi bilga sibohabi,
我的氣就往上涌堵住嗓子

5. tere udu aniya de,
那幾年

6. i meni booi dukai bokson be gemu feshelebume manabuha bihe,
他把我們家裡的門坎子都踢破了來着

7. eturengge akv oqi,
若是沒了穿的

8. mini beye qi sufi inde etubumbi,
從我身上脫給他穿

155

9. baitalarangge akv oqi,,
若是沒了用的
10. mini menggun jiha be gamafi baitalambi,
拿我的銀錢去使
11. jeterengge akv oqi,
若是沒了吃的
12. amba fulhv de tebufi meiherefi gamambi,
大口袋裝上米背了去
13. aika emu mohoho baita tuqikede,
倘若出來一件困乏的事情
14. uthai mini jakade jifi giohoxome baimbi,
就往我跟前來哀求
15. age si mimbe umesi sarangge kai,
阿哥你是最知道我的啊
16. ini tere bairede,
他那求的上頭
17. mini mujilen geli nitarafi,
我的心又回了
18. udu akv biqibe,
雖然沒有
19. inu guquse de juwen gaifi inde aqabume bumbi,
也合朋友們借來應付他
20. yala mini ai jaka be i jekekv,
真乃我的什麼東西他沒吃過
21. ai jaka be i gamahakv,
什麼東西他沒拿去
22. damu mini doko yali be faitafi inde ulebuhekv bihe sere dabala.
就只是我腿班裡的肉沒有割給他吃罷咧

Section 46: Qingming Festival

1. ere uquri absi kumungge,
這一向好熱鬧
2. hangsi inenggi ojoro jakade,
因爲是清明
3. waliyara niyalma hoton qi tuqikengge ton akv,
上墳的人從城裡出來的沒數兒
4. tuwaqi sejen kiyoo morin lorin umai lakqarakv yabumbi,
只見車轎驟馬竟不斷的走

156

5. buda doboro nure hisalarangge inu bi,
也有供飯奠酒的

6. boihon nonggire hooxan jiha deijirengge inu bi,
也有添土燒紙的

7. eifu i oyo be tebeliyefi songgorongge songgoqombi,
抱着墳頭哭的一齊哭

8. mooi fejile borhome teqefi omirengge omiqambi,
樹下團坐飲的大家飲

9. yala gasara niyalma be sabuqi mujilen efujembi,
真乃是見了哭的人傷心

10. sebjelere niyalma be sabuqi injeku banjimbi seqina,
見了樂的人長笑

11. erebe tuwame ohode,
看起這個來

12. jalan i urse juse omosi be ujihangge,
世上的人養子孫

13. gemu tanggv aniya i amaga baitai jalin kai.
都爲是百年之後的事啊

Section 47: Lie to Me

1. age si absi toktohon akv,
阿哥你好沒定準

2. qananggi jimbi seme ainu jihekv,
前日說來爲什麼沒來

3. qananggi jabduhakv okini,
前日沒得工夫罷了

4. sikse geli ainaha,
昨日又怎麼了

5. giyan i jiqi aqambi kai,
理該來呀

6. ainu geli jiderakv ni,
怎麼又不來呢

7. enenggi oqi qimari sembi,
今日說明日

8. qimari ohode qoro be anatambi,
明日推後日

9. enenggi qimari sehei,
侭着說今日明日

10. inenggidari niyalma be eiterembio,
每日哄人麼

11. age si uttu oqi ojorakv kai,
阿哥你若是如此使不得呀

12. ereqi amasi jai ume uttu ojoro,
從今後再別這樣

13. holtoqi inu damu emgeri juwenggeri oqi ojoro dabala,
若是撒謊也只可一次兩次罷咧

14. daruhai holtoqi,
若常常的撒謊

15. jai geli sini gisun be akdara niyalma bio.
再還信你的話的人有麼

Section 48: An Honest Man

1. suwe tere niyalma be ambaki seqi,
你們若說那個人大道

2. yargiyen i terebe muribuhabi,
真真的冤屈了他了

3. umesi emu ujui uju jergi nomhon niyalma,
狠是一個頭等頭的老實人

4. uthai niyalmai juleri seme inu weihuken i gisurerakv,
就是人前也不肯輕言

5. emu gisun biqi teni emu gisun be gisurembi,
有一句纔說一句

6. ini banin uthai tuttu,
他的性情就是那樣

7. imbe sarkv urse oqi,
若是不知道他的人

8. terebe durun arambi sembi,
說他是捏款

9. suwe terei emgi emu bade bihekv ofi,
因爲你們沒有合他在一處

10. terei yabun axxan be sarkv dabala,
不知道他爲人動作罷咧

11. bi ini baru feliyeme yabuha bihe be dahame,
我是于他行走過的

12. ini banin be sambi sere anggala,
不但知道他的秉性

158

13. banjire were babe suwaliyame yooni gemu tenggime sambikai.
連過活的去處全都知道的真確啊

Section 49: A High Expectation

1. age si inu largin bai,
阿哥你特也煩絮罷

2. erebe buqi si inu gairakv,
給這個你也不要

3. terebe buqi si inu ehe sembi,
給那個你也說不好

4. ambakan ningge be beneqi,
送大些兒的去

5. si geli amba oho sembi,
你又說大了

6. ajigesi ningge be benjiqi,
送小些兒的來

7. si geli jaqi ajige oho sembi,
你又說太小了

8. uttu de inu waka,
這們着也不是

9. tuttu de inu waka,
那們着也不是

10. maka ai gesengge be,
不知什麼樣的

11. teni age i gvninde aqabumbi,
纔合阿哥的主意

12. si urunakv tere emu adalingge be gaiki seqi,
你必定要像那一樣的

13. niyalma be aibide baihanabure.
叫人往那里尋去

Section 50: A Foolish Man

1. age si absi mentuhun jiye,
阿哥你好愚啊

2. sinde jiha biqi,
你若有錢

3. jiha jafafi niyalma be dangnambi,
拿錢擋人

4. jiha akv oqi,
若是無錢

5. sain gisun i neqihiyeme baime gisurembi,
用好言撫濟求着說

6. uttu oqi,
若是如此

7. teni inu dabala,
纔是罷咧

8. niyalmai der sere xeyen menggun be juwen gajifi,
借了人的白花花的銀子

9. beye madagan be yooni toodame burakv bime,
本利全不還給

10. elemangga weri xorgime gaire be wakaxaqi,
反倒怪人家催討

11. ere geli ombio,
這也使得麼

12. ere uthai gvnin tebuhei juwen gamafi toodame hurakv oki sere niyalma kai,
這就是存心借了去不還給的人啊

13. aikabade gemu uttu etuhuxere guwangguxara oqi,
倘若都是這些以強賭光棍

14. jai we geli gelhun akv bekdun sindara,
再誰還敢放債

15. suwe emu ergi de oqi menggun be baitalaki sere jalin,
你們一邊是爲要使銀子

16. emu ergi de oqi madagan be bahaki sere turgun,
一邊是圖得利錢

17. sui akv meni akdulara niyalma be uxabufi ainambi,
無辜的拉扯我們保人們作什麼

18. ere emken inu mimbe hvlambi,
這一個也叫我

19. tere emken inu mimbe baimbi,
那一個也尋我

20. daqi suwembe akdulahangge,
原保了你們

21. sain mujilen bihe dabala,
是好心來着罷咧

22. we aika suweni jetere omire be alime gaiha babio.
誰接了你們的什麼吃喝麼

160

Section 51: A Wordy Man

1. age si ai uttu gisun fulu,
阿哥你怎麼這樣話多

2. jihedari anggai dolori biyadar seme balai iqi gisurembi,
遭遭兒來了嘴裡瓜答答答亂說

3. si inu majige eimederakvn, angga inu xadarakvn,
你一點兒也不嫌厭煩麼 嘴也不累麼

4. gisurehengge kemuni tere udu fe gisun i teile bime,
說的還是那幾句舊話

5. emdubei alame wede donjibumbi,
侭着告訴給誰聽

6. sakda ahvn si mini gisun be sijirhvn seme ume wakaxara,
老長兄你別怪我的話直

7. sini beye sereburakv dabala,
你自己不覺得罷咧

8. hetu niyalma donjirede,
傍人聽着

9. gisun majige yeye gese,
話似絮叨些

10. si ere sede uthai uttu oiboko oqi,
你這個年紀尚就這樣老悖回了

11. se i baru oho manggi,
上了年紀之後

12. adarame boo boigon be jafame baita be iqihiyaqi ombi.
可怎麼樣掌家業料理事

abkai wehiye i xahvn meihe aniya niyengniyeri ujui biyade
乾隆辛巳年春正月

Chapter 2
manju gisun i oyonggo jorin i bithe

Introduction: The Root of Manchu People

1. manju gisun serengge,
清語者

2. manju halangga niyalmai fulehe da,
乃滿洲人之根本

3. yaya we bahanarakvqi ojorakvngge kai,
任憑是誰不會使不得

4. adarame seqi,
怎麼說呢

5. muse jabxan de wesihun jalan i ayan suwayan manju ofi,
我等幸而生在盛世 因是滿洲

6. aika manjurame bahanarakv,
若不會說清語

7. niyalma be aqaha dari fonjiha de,
每遇人問及

8. angga gahvxara yasa xarinjara oqi,
就張口翻眼

9. ereqi giqukengge bio,
比這可羞的有麼

10. ereqi fanqaqukangge geli bio,
比這可氣的有麼

11. ede niyalmai yekerxeme basure be hono aisembi.
這上頭別說人家譏笑打趣

12. beyei ubu sibiya inu waliyabumbi kai,
連自己的身份也丟了

13. hairakan akv semeo,
豈不可惜

14. kemuni tuwaqi ememu urse manjurambihede,
嘗見有一等人說起滿洲話來

15. iletu bahanara gisun bime lak seme baharakv,
分明是會的話 恰乎不得

16. deng seme ilinjafi gvniname bahatala,
猛然止住 及至想起來

17. dere aifini dukseme fularakangge labdu,

早已臉上臊紅了的很多

18. ere umai gvwa haran akv,
這沒有別的緣故

19. gemu an i uquri kiqeme taqihakv urebume gisurehekv ofi kai,
皆是平時未學 未習練着說之故也

20. geli injequkengge,
又有可笑者

21. manju gisun oron unde de,
滿洲話還沒有影兒

22. afanggala ubaliyambure be taqirengge bi,
就先學翻譯的

23. enteke niyalma yala yuwei gurun de genembime sejen be amasi fo-
roro,
這等人何異北轅赴粵

24. yonggan be bujumbime buda okini sere qi ai enqu,
煮沙要飯者乎

25. nikan bithe de ai haqin i mangga okini,
任憑漢文怎麼精奧

26. fi nikebuhe manggi
下筆時

27. manju gisun eden dadun,
奈何清語短少

28. tamin aqarakv[379],
不合卯榫

29. yohi banjinarakv be ainara,
不成套數

30. udu sakdatala taqiha sehe seme,
雖學至老

31. eden baksi sere gebu qi guweme muterakv kai,
難免庸愚名色

32. muwaxame duibuleqi uthai boo arara adali,
粗比即如蓋房

33. taibu tura wase feise i jergi haqingga jaka akv oqi,

---

[379] The Manchu expression of 'tamin aqarakv' means 'the edges of fur do not match well'. The Chinese translation of 榫卯 (sunmao) means 'carpenters assemble furniture accurately without using rivets'. 不合榫卯 (buhe sunmao) means 'the connecting parts of furniture cannot match each other well'.

若無杜柱磚瓦等項

34. faksisa be teile gajiha seme,
獨把匠人們叫來

35. aini weilebumbi,
拿什麼做呢

36. gala joolafi tuwara dabala,
惟有束手觀望而已

37. boo xanggara kooli akv kai,
無有成房之理呀

38. erebe tawahade
以此看來

39. ubaliyambure be taqire onggolo,
未學翻譯以前

40. nememe manju gisun taqire be oyonggo obure be saqi aqambi,
當知先學清語為要

41. damu manju bithe umesi labdu geren,
但清語甚煩

42. teni taqire urse
初學之人

43. waqihiyame hvlaqi
全行誦讀

44. atanggi dube da,
幾時是了

45. uttu ofi
因此

46. bi dolo yabure xolo de
我在裡頭走的空兒

47. sakdasai ulandume gisurehe,
將老輩傳說

48. mini taqifi ejehengge be,
並我學記的

49. emu gisun emu gisun i aqamjahai,
一句一句的集湊着

50. uheri tanggv meyen iktambufi,
共集百句

51. mini mukvn i deote juse be taqibuha
教我族中子弟

52. bithei gebu be manju i oyonggo jorin sehe,

以書名曰 清文指要

53. erei dorgide

此內

54. wasinara iqi tuhenere kemun,

貫串落腳

55. haqingga manjurara fakjin

各種說清語的方法

56. udu akvmbume yongkiyahakv biqibe,

雖不周旋

57. amba muru yasai juleri baitalaqi aqara oyonggo oyonggongge gemu belhehebi,

大概眼前應用最緊要者俱備

57. taqire urse unenggi ede gvnin girkvfi hing seme

學者果能專心致志

58. fuhaxame urebuqi,

反覆熟習

58. goidaha manggi ini qisui gvniha iqi forgoxome gamame mutembi,

久之自能隨意運用

59. absi gisureqibe

任憑怎樣說去

60. gisun banjinarakvngge akv be dahame,

無有不成話的

60. bahanarakv jalin de geli ai joboro,

又何愁不會呢

61. damu ere bithei hergen jaqi labdu,

但此書字句甚多

62. geli hvlara urse sarkiyame arara de hvsun baiburakv seme,

又恐讀者抄寫費力 [380]

63. tuttu faksi de afabufi folobufi,

故此付匠役刊刻

64. musei adali manju gisun de amuran guquse de

凡我等好清語的朋友

65. uheleki sembi,

公於同好

65. udu hafuka saisa de nonggibure ba akv biqibe
雖無益於通家

66. tuktan taqire urse de
在初學

67. majige niyeqequn akv semeo
未必無小補云

Some Basic Rules of Pronunciations

1. te tuktan taqime manjurara asihata de ulhibuqi aqara
今敘明初學清文少年

2. udu gisun be getukeleme arafi,
應知數語

3. giyangnara urebure de ja obuhabi,
以便講習

4. manjurara de, i sere hergen, ni sere hergen be ilgame hvlara,
讀說清語分別伊 尼伊

5. gisurerengge umesi oyonggo,
最爲緊要

6. erebe saqi aqambi,
應知之

7. juwan juwe ujui dolo,
十二字頭內

8. damu duiqi ujui hergen i fejergi de,
惟第四頭字下

9. i seme araqi aqarangge be,
當寫伊者

10. gemu i seme araqibe,
雖寫伊者

11. ni seme hvlambi, gisurembi,
卻讀尼伊 說尼伊

12. duibuleqi, ejen i kesi, gurun i hvturi seme hvlara gisurere adali,
譬如或讀 或說 皇上的恩 國家的福

13. erei badarambume gamame,
推而廣之

14. duiqi ujui hergen i fejergi de,
第四頭字下

15. yaya i seme araqi aqarangge be,

凡當寫伊者

16. gemu i seme araqibe,
皆寫伊

17. ni seme hvlara, gisurerengge,
讀尼伊 說尼伊

18. yooni ere songko.
悉本此

19. sunjaqi ujui hergen i fejergi de,
第五頭字下

20. i seme araqi aqarangge be,
當寫伊者

21. gemu ni seme arambi,
皆寫尼伊

22. inu ni seme hvlambi, gisurembi,
亦讀尼伊 說尼伊

23. duibuleqi, wang ni dukai hiya, gung ni harangga hafan seme hvlara, gisurere adali,
譬如或讀 或說 王子門上護衛 公屬下官員

24. erei badarambume gamame,
推而廣之

25. sunjaqi ujui hergen i fejergi de,
第五頭字下

26. yaya i seme araqi aqarangge be,
凡當寫伊者

27. gemu ni seme arara,
皆寫尼伊

28. ni seme hvlara, gisurerengge,
讀尼伊 說尼伊

29. yooni ere songko,
悉準此

30. duiqi, sunjaqi ere juwe uju qi tulgiyen
除第四第五此二頭外

31. funqehe juwan ujui hergen i fejergi de,
其餘十頭字下

32. i seme araqi aqarangge oqi,
應寫伊者

33. gemu i seme arambi,
皆寫伊

34. i seme hvlambi,

168

讀伊

35. gisurembi,
說伊

36. aniya, inenggi, dobori, niyengniyeri, juwari, bolori, tuweri i jergi
hergen i fejergi de,
年 日 夜 春 夏 秋 冬等字下

37. eiqi isinaha,
或有至

38. eiqi teisulehe sere jergi gisun bisirengge ohode,
遇等句

39. de, sere hegen baitalaraqi tulgiyen
用德額外

40. funqehe isinaha, teisulehe sere jergi gisun akvngge oqi,
其餘無至 遇等句者

41. gemu de sere hergen baitalarakv,
皆不用德額

42. duibuleqi,
譬如或寫或說

43. eiqi tere aniya, tere inenggi, tere dobori de isinaha manggi,
俟至某年某日某夜

44. jai kimqime iqihiyaki,
再行酌辦

45. tere niyengniyeri, tere juwari, tere bolori, tere tuweri de teisulehe
erinde,
俟遇某春某夏某秋某冬

46. jai toktobume gisureki seme arara,
再行定議

47. gisurere adali ere uthai aniya, inenggi, dobori, niyengniyeri, juwari,
bolori, tuweri sere hergen
i fejergide,
此即年 日 夜 春 夏 秋 冬字下

48. de sere hergen baitalarangge,
用德額者

49. aika isinaha, teisulehe sere jergi gisun akv,
如無至遇等句

50. xuwe fejergi gisun be sirabume arara, gisurere de oqi,
直接下文寫說者

51. gemu de sere hergen baitalarakv,
皆不用德額

52. duibuleqi, eiqi niowanggiyan morin aniya dosika tukiyesi,
譬如或寫或說甲午年中的舉人

53. niohon honin aniya dosika dosikasi,
乙未年中的進士

54. tere aniya tere biyai iqe de,
某年某月初一日

55. wesimbuhede,
奏

56. ineku inenggi hese,
本日奉旨

57. saha
知道了

58. sehe,
欽此

59. erei jalin gingguleme wesimbuhe,
爲此謹奏

60. erei jalin gingguleme alibuha seme arara gisurere adali,
爲此上呈

61. ere gemu aniya, inenggi, jai jalin sere hergen i fejergide,
此皆年日及爲字下

62. de sere hergen baitalarakv,
不用德額

63. ne yabubure kooli durun,
現行式樣

64. han i araha ubaliyambuha dasan i nomen de henduhengge,
御製翻譯書經有曰

65. aniya biyai dergi,
正月上日

66. wen zu han i juktehen de duben be alime gaiha sehebi,
受終於文祖廟

67. ere gisun xun han i kooli i fiyelen de bi.
語在舜典

68. han i araha ubliyambuha irgebun i nomun de henduhengge,
御製翻譯詩經有曰

69. inenggi elben ganambi,
晝爾于茅

70. dobori futa murimbi sehebi,
宵爾索綯

71. ere gisun bin gurun i taqinun i fiyelen de bi,

語在豳風

72. Enduringge taqihiyan be neileme badarambuha bithede henduhengge,
聖諭廣訓有曰

73. damu joboxorongge,
所慮

74. jeku ambula bargiyara aniya,
年穀豐登

75. embiqi isabume asarara be gvnirakv,
或忽於儲蓄

76. suje boso elgiyen baha uquri,
布帛充贍

77. embiqi mamgiyame fayame baitalara oqi,
或侈於費用

78. malhvxarakv ufaraqun, kiqehekv qi enqu akv sehebi,
不儉之弊與不勤等

79. ere gisun usin nimalan be ujeleqi,
語在重農桑

80. eture jetere be tesubure haqin de bi.
以足衣食

81. geli henduhengge,
又曰

82. suweni geren qooha irgen xumin dobori kimqime seolefi,
爾兵民清夜自思

83. mini gvnin de aqabuqi aqambi sehebi,
其咸體朕意

84. ere gisun jeku qaliyan be waqihiyafi hafirame boxobure ba akv obure
haqin de bi,
語在完錢糧以省催科

85. han i araha julgei xu fiyelen i xumin bulekv bithede henduhengge,
御製古文淵鑒有曰

86. niyengniyeri sonjome abalame,
春蒐

87. juwari usin i jalin abalame,
夏苗

88. bolori wame abalame,
秋獮

89. tuweri kame abalame,
冬狩

90. gemu usin i xolo de baita be deribumbi gisun,

皆於農隙以講事也

91. ere gisun lu gurun i zang hi be nimaha butara be tuwanara jalin tafulara fiyelen de bi.

語在臧僖伯諫觀魚

92. ereqi wesihun udu meyen,

以上數段

93. gemu aniaya, inenggi, dobori, niyengniyeri, juwari, bolori, tuweri, jai
jalin sere hergen i

fejergide,

皆年 日 夜 春 夏 秋 冬及爲字下

94. de sere hergen baitalarakv yargiyan temgetu.

不用德額字確據

95. manju gisun i dorgide, be, me, qi, fi i jergei untuhun hergen umesi
labdu,

清語內伯額 墨額 妻伊 飛伊等虛字甚多

96. umai jorihakv bime

在所不論

97. damu i, ni, de sere udu hergen be tuqibume araha,

惟舉伊 尼伊 德額數字

98. ne yabubure kooli durun be alhvdakini sehe dade,

既以現行格式爲法

99. geli nomun, taqihiyan be yarufi dahin dabtan i getukeleme
tuqibuhengge

而又引經據訓 往復發明

100. ai gvnin seqi,

其意何居

101. qohome gehun iletu bolgo getuken,

蓋因彰明皎着

102. niyalma tome gemu sarangge ofi,

人所共知者

103. dahime dalhidara be baiburakv,

毋庸重贅

104. dubifi kimqirakv,

忽焉不察

105. ja i farfaburengge be emke emken i jorime tuqibufi,

易於混淆者一一指出

106. sonjofi baitalara de belhehe,

以備採擇

107. eitereqibe mentuhun gvnin be majige akvmbufi,

無非稍盡鄙懷

108. taxaraha jurqenjehe babe tuwanqihiyaki sere turgun.

正其錯謬

109. inu urhuhe babe niyeqetere

亦補偏

110. eyehe taqin be maribure jalin emu erinde deribuhebi dere,

救弊之一端耳

111. tere anggala i sere hergen, ni sere hergen fudarame forgoxobure babe halame

況伊 尼伊顛倒

112. dasara be gvnirakvngge,

不思改正

113. ele manju gisun i qilqin,

尤爲清語之疵

114. uthai berten bisire saikan gu be,

即如美玉有瑕

115. yongkiyaha gu seqi ojorakv adali,

不得謂之完璧

116. manju gisun de qilqin biqi,

清語帶疵

117. inu narhvn sain ojoro be erehunjeme banjinarakv,

亦難望其精通

118. manjurame muteqi tetendere,

既能清語

119. gulhun muyahvn ojoro be kiqerakv oqi,

不務完全

120. ambula hairaqun.

深爲可惜

121. unenggi terei holbobuhangge oyonggo be safi,

誠能知其所關緊要

122. ere bithe be dahin dabtan i fuhaxame tuwafi,

將此編反覆翻閱

123. tengkime ejefi,

切實記憶

124. erindari gvnin tebufi kimqime,

時加檢點

125. taxarara jurqenjehe babe tuwanqihiyaqi,

正其錯誤

126. kiqeme genehei inenggi goidaha manggi,

用功日久

127. ulhiyen i elehun de isinafi,

漸進自然

128. gisun ede narhvn akv sere basuqun qi guweqi ojoro teile akv,

不特可免殘缺不精之譏

129. umesi urehe bime qilqin akv sere maktaqun bahaqi ombi,

並可成熟練無疵之美

130. yala sain akv semeo,

豈不休哉

131. ningguqi ujui nadanju juwe hergen i unqehen i teisu hashv ergide,

第六頭七十二字尾左

132. gemu juwe tongki bi,

皆有雙點

133. geli ere juwe tongki akv dehi hergen i dorgi,

又有無此雙點四十字內

134. manju gisun de holbobufi,

關係清語

135. kemuni arara orin hergen be,

不時書寫者二十字

136. ejere de umesi mangga,

殊難記憶

137. ofi tuttu nadata hergen ninggun gisun i uqun banjibuha,

是以編作七言六句之歌

138. erebe ureme ejehe de,

將此記熟

139. uthai ilgame muteqi taxaraburakv ombi,

則能辨別無差矣

140. nadata hergen ninggun gisun i uqun

七言六句歌

141. e 字爲始 fu 其終

if a sentence begins with 'e' and ends with 'fu',

142. ne, se, de, le, me, qe 同

then 'ne', 'se', 'de', 'le', 'me' and 'qe' are the same;

143. be, pe, je, ye 與 hv 類

the combinations of 'be', 'pe', 'je' and 'ye' are similar to 'hv ';

144. ke, ku 二句一樣通

sentences that end with 'ke' and 'ku' will all make sense.

145. 再加 fe 來二十整

plus 'fe', there will be twenty words

146. *毋庸雙點尾皆弓*

whose appearances all look like a bow, without two dots attached.

Section 1: The Most Important Thing

1. donjiqi si te manju bithe taqimbi sembi.
聽見你說如今學滿洲書呢

2. umesi sain.
狠好

3. manju gisun serengge
清話呀

4. musei ujui uju oyonggo baita
是喒們頭等頭要緊的事

5. uthai nikansai meni meni ba i gisun i adali.
就像漢人各處的鄉談一樣

6. bahanarakvqi ombio
不會使得嗎

7. inu waka oqi ai
可不是什麼

8. bi juwan aniya funqeme nikan bithe taqiha
我學漢書十年多了

9. tetele umai dube da tuqirakv
至今並無頭緒

10. jai aikabade manju bithe hvlarakv
再要是不念滿洲書

11. ubaliyambure be taqirakv oqi
不學翻譯

12. juwede gemu sartabure de isinambi
兩下里都至於耽誤了

13. uttu ofi
因此上

14. bi emde oqi
我一則

15. age be tuwanjiha
來瞧阿哥

16. jai de oqi
再還有

17. geli sakda ahvn de baire babi

懇求老長兄的去處

18. damu baibi angga juwara de mangga

但只難於開口

19. ede aibi

這有什麼

20. gisun biqi

有話

21. uthai gisure

就說

22. mini mutere baita oqi

要是我能的事

23. sinde bi geli marambio

你跟前我還推辭嗎

24. mini bairengge

我求的是

25. age gosiqi

阿哥疼愛我

26. xadambi seme ainara

就是乏些也罷

27. xolo xolo de

得空兒

28. udu meyen manju gisun banjibufi

求編幾條清話

29. minde hvlabureo

教我念念

30. deo bi bahafi hvwaxaqi

兄弟若能出息

31. gemu age i kesi kai

都是阿哥恩惠啊

32. ainaha seme baili be onggorakv

斷不肯忘

33. urunakv ujeleme karulaki

必然重報

34. ainu uttu gisurembi

什麼這們說呢

35. si aika gurun gvwao

你還是別人嗎

36. damu sini taqirakv be hendumbi dere

只說你不學罷咧
37. taqiki seqi tetendere
既然要學
38. bi nekulefi simbe niyalma okini sembikai
我巴不得的叫你成人啊
39. karulaki serengge
報答
40. ai gisun
是什麼話
41. musei dolo gisureqi ombio
嗒們裏頭也說得嗎
42. tuttu seme
雖是那們說
43. bi hukxeme gvniha seme wajirakv
我可感念不盡
44. damu hengkixeme baniha bure dabala
就只是拜謝罷咧
45. aisere
說什麼呢

Section 2: Concentrate on Learning

1. age sini manju gisun,
阿哥你的清話
2. ai xolo de taqiha,
什麼空兒學了
3. mudan gairengge sain bime tomorhon,
話音好又清楚
Your pronunciation is made good and clear.
4. mini manju gisun be ai dabufi gisurere babi,
我的清話那裡提得起來
5. age gosime uttu dabali maktambi,
阿哥疼愛這們過獎
6. mini emu guqu i manju gisun sain,
我的一個朋友清話好
7. getuken bime daqun,
明白又快
8. majige nikan mudan akv,
一點兒蠻音沒有

9. umesi urehebi,
狠熟了
10. tuttu bime xan geli fe,
而且聽見的老話又多
11. tere teni mangga seqi ombi,
那才算得精
12. tere sinqi antaka,
他比你如何
13. bi adarame inde duibuleqi ombi,
我如何比得他
14. fuhali terei bakqin waka,
總不是他的對兒
15. abka na i gese giyalabuhabi,
天地懸隔
16. turgun ai seqi,
什麼緣故呢
17. ini taqihangge xumin,
他學的深
18. bahanahangge labdu,
會的多
19. bithede amuran,
好讀書
20. tetele hono angga qi hokoburakv hvlambi,
至今還不住口的念
21. gala qi aljaburakv tuwambi,
不離手的看
22. imbe amqaki seqi,
要趕他
23. yargiyan i mangga,
實在難
24. age sini ere gisun, majige taxarabuhakv semeo,
阿哥你這話不錯了些兒嗎
25. hing sere oqi, hada hafumbi sehebi,
有心專山可通的話呀
26. tere inu taqifi bahanahangge dabala,
他也是學會的罷了
27. umai banjitai bahanarangge waka kai,
並非生來就會的
28. muse tede isirakvngge ya ba,

嗒們那一塊兒不如他

29. i ai haqin i urehe bahanahangge okini,
憑他是怎麼樣的精熟

30. muse damu mujilen be teng seme jafafi,
嗒們只是拿定主意

31. gvnin girkvfi taqiqi,
專心學去

32. udu tere ten de isiname muterakv biqibe,
雖然不能到他那個地步

33. inu urunakv haminambidere.
也必定差不遠罷咧

Section 3: Your are Making Progress!

1. si nikan bithe bahanara niyalma kai,
你是會漢書的人啊

2. ubaliyambure be taqiqi, umesi ja dabala,
學翻譯狠容易罷咧

3. gvnin girkvfi giyalan lakqan akv,
專心不間斷

4. emu anan i taqime ohode,
挨着次兒學了去

5. juwe ilan aniya i sidende,
二三年間

6. ini qisui dube da tuqimbi,
自有頭緒

7. aika emu inenggi fiyakiyara, juwan inenggi xahvrara adali taqiqi,
要像一暴十寒的學

8. uthai orin aniya bithe hvlaha seme,
就念二十年的書

9. inu mangga kai,
也難啊

10. age mini ubaliyambuhangge be tuwafi,
求阿哥看了我的翻譯

11. majige dasatarao,
改一改

12. sini taqihangge labdu nonggibuha.
你學得大長了

13. gisun tome ijishvn,

句句順當

14. hergen arame tomorhon,
字字清楚

15. majige qilqin fuhali akv,
沒有一點乞星

16. simneqi seferehei bahaqi ombi.
要考操券可得

Section 4: To Attend an Exam

1. ere mudan ubaliyambure be simnere de,
這一次考翻譯

2. gebu alibuhao, akvn,
遞了名字了沒有

3. simneqi oqi,
要考得

4. esi sain oqi,
自然好麼

5. damu bithei xusai ainahai ombini,
但是文秀才未必使得

6. wei kooli,
那格的例呢

7. sini gesengge jakvn gvsa gemu simneqi ombime,
像你這樣的八旗的都許考

8. sini beye teile simneburakv doro bio,
有獨不准你考的理嗎

9. tere anggala jurgangga taqikvi juse gemu ojoro bade,
況且義學生都還使得

10. xusai be ai hendure,
秀才何用說呢

11. simneqi ome ofi,
因爲考得

12. sini deo ere sidende teni haqihiyamc manju bithe hvlambikai,
你兄弟這個空兒才上緊念清書呢

13. hvdun gebu yabubu,
快行名字

14. nashvn be ume ufarabure.
別錯過了機會啊

180

Section 5: Practice Makes Perfect

1. sini manjurarangge majige muru tuqikebi,
你的清話說的有了些規模了

2. aibide,
那裡

3. bi niyalmai gisurere be ulhire gojime,
人說的我雖然懂得

4. mini beye gisureme ohode, oron unde,
我說起來總還早呢

5. gvwai adali fiyelen fiyelen i gisureme muterakv, sere anggala,
不但不能像別人說的成片段

6. emu siran i duin sunja gisun, gemu sirabume muterakv,
一連四五句話都接不上

7. tere anggala,
況且

8. hono emu aldungga babi,
還有一個怪處

9. gisurere onggolo,
從未說話

10. baibi taxaraburahv qalaburahv seme,
只恐怕差錯了

11. tathvnjame gelhun akv kengse lasha gisurerakv,
說的遲疑不敢簡斷

12. uttu kai, mimbe adarame gisure sembi,
這樣光景教我仔麼說呢?

13. bi inu usaka,
我也灰了心了

14. gvniqi ai haqin i taqiha seme,
想來就是怎麼樣的學去

15. inu ere hvman dabala,
不過這個本事兒罷了

16. nonggibure aibi,
那裡能長進

17. ere gemu sini urehekv haran,
這都是你沒有熟的緣故

18. bi sinde taqibure,
我教給你

19. yaya webe seme ume bodoro,

別論他是誰

20. damu uqaraha uqaraha be tuwame amqatame gisure,
只是大凡遇見的就趕着他說

21. jai bithede xungke sefu be baifi bithe hvla,
再找書理通達的師傅念書

22. manju gisun de mangga guquse de adanafi gisure,
就了清話精熟的朋友去說話

23. inenggidari hvlaqi,
每日家念

24. gisun ejembi,
話就記得了

25. erindari gisureqi,
時刻的說

26. ilenggv urembi,
舌頭就熟了

27. uttu taqime ohode,
要這樣學了去

28. manggai emu juwe aniya i sidende,
至狠一二年間

29. ini qisui gvnin i qihai anggai iqi tang sembikai,
自然任意順口不打蹬兒的說上來了

30. muterakv jalin geli aiseme jobombi ni.
又何愁不能呢

Section 6: Receiving a Guest

1. absi yooha bihe,
往那裡去來着

2. bi ergi emu niyamangga niyalmai boode genehe bihe,
我往這裡一個親戚家去來着

3. ere ildun de mini boode darifi majige teki,
順便到我家裡坐坐

4. age si ubade tehebio,
阿哥你在這裡住着麼

5. inu,
是

6. jakan gurinjihe,
新近搬了來了

7. uttu oqi,

要是這樣

8. musei tehengge giyanakv udu goro,
嗒們住的能有多遠

9. saha biqi aifini simbe tuwajjirakv biheo,
要知道早不看你來了嗎

10. age yabu,
阿哥走

11. ai geili,
豈有此理

12. mini boode kai,
是我家裡

13. age wesifi teki,
阿哥上去坐

14. ubade iqangga,
這裡舒服

15. si tuttu tehede,
你那們坐下

16. bi absi tembi,
我怎麼坐呢

17. sain,
好啊

18. teme jabduha,
已經坐下了

19. ubade emu nikere babi,
這裡有個靠頭兒

20. booi urse aba,
家裡人呢

21. yaha gaju,
拿火來

22. age bi dambagu omirakv,
阿哥我不吃煙

23. angga furunahabi,
長了口瘡了

24. tuttu oqi,
要是那樣

25. qai gana,
取茶去

26. age qai gaisu,

阿哥請茶

27. ko,
咢

28. absi halhvn,
好熱呀

29. halhvn oqi,
要熱

30. majige tukiyeqebu,
叫揚一揚

31. hvwanggiyarakv,
無妨

32. mukiyebukini,
晾一晾罷

33. je,
咢

34. buda be tuwana,
看飯去

35. beleni bisirengge be hasa benju se,
說把現成的快送來

36. akv,
不啊

37. age ume,
阿哥別

38. bi kemuni gvwa bade geneki sembi,
我還要往別處去呢

39. ainahabi,
怎麼了

40. beleni bisirengge sini jalin dagilahangge geli waka,
現成的又不是為你預備的

41. majige jefi geneqina,
吃點去是呢

42. joo bai,
罷呀

43. emgeri sini boo be takaha kai,
一遭認得你家了

44. enqu inenggi jai qohome jifi,
另日特來

45. gulhun emu inenggi gisureme teqeki.
坐着說一天的話兒罷

Section 7: Going to School

1. age si inenggidari ederi yaburengge,
阿哥你終日從這們走

2. gemu aibide genembi.
都是往那裡去

3. bithe hvlaname genembi,
念書去

4. manju bithe hvlambi, wakao,
不是念清書嗎

5. inu,
是

6. ne aiqi jergi bithe hvlambi,
如今念些甚麼書啊

7. gvwa bithe akv,
沒有別的書

8. damu yasai juleri buyarame gisun,
眼前零星話

9. jai manju gisun i oyonggo jorin i bithei teile,
再秖有清語指要

10. suwende ginggulere hergen taqibumbio akvn,
還教你們清字楷書啊不呢

11. te inenggi xun foholon,
如今天短

12. hergen arara xolo akv,
沒有寫字的空兒

13. ereqi inenggi xun sidaraka manggi,
從此天長了

14. hergen arabumbi sere anggala,
不但叫寫字

15. hono ubaliyambu sembikai,
還叫翻譯呢

16. age bi bithe hvlara jalin,
阿哥我為念書

17. yala uju silgime
實在鑽頭覓縫兒的

18. aibide baihanahakv,
那裡沒有找到呢

19. musei ubai xurdeme,

我們方近左右

20. fuhali manju taqikv akv,
竟沒有清書學房

21. gvniqi sini taqire ba,
想來你學的地方

22. ai hendure,
有什麼說處

23. atanggi biqibe, bi inu bithe hvlanaki,
多咨我也去念書罷

24. mini funde majige gisureqi ojoroo,
可以替我說說嗎

25. age si mende taqibure niyalma be we sembi,
阿哥你當教我們的是誰啊

26. sefu sembio
是師傅嗎

27. waka kai,
不是啊

28. mini emu mukvn i ahvn,
是我一個族兄

29. taqibure ele urse,
所有教的

30. gemu meni emu uksun i juse deote,
都是我們一家兒的子弟

31. jai niyaman hvnqihin,
再是親戚

32. umai gvwa niyalma akv,
並無別人

33. adarame seqi,
仔麼說呢

34. mini ahvn inenggidari yamulambi,
我阿哥終日上衙門

35. jabdurakv,
不得閒

36. ineku be erde yamji nandame genere jakade,
也是我們早晚找着去的上頭

37. arga akv,
不得已

38. xolo jalgiyanjafi membe taqibumbi,

匀着空兒教我們

39. waka oqi,
要不是

40. age bithe hvlame geneki sehengge,
阿哥要念書去

41. sain baita dabala,
好事罷咧

42. sini funde majige gisureqi,
替你說一說

43. minde geli ai wajiha ni.
又費了我什麼了呢

Section 8: A Successful Man

1. tere age serengge,
那個阿哥

2. musei fe adaki kai,
是嗒們舊街坊啊

xame tuwame mutuha juse,
看着長大的孩子

3. giyalafi giyanakv udu goidaha,
隔了能有幾年

4. te donjiqi mujakv hvwaxafi, hafan oho sere,
如今聽見說着實出息作了官了

5. suqunnga bi hono akdara dulin kenehunjre dulin bihe,
起初我還半信半疑的來着

6. amala guquse de fonjiqi,
後來問朋友們

7. mujangga, erebe tuwaqi
果然看起這個來

8. mujin bisirengge, baita jiduji mutebumbi,
有志者事竟成

9. se mulan de akv sehe gisun,
不在年紀的話

10. taxan akv ni,
不假呀

11. age i gisun inu,
阿哥的話是

12. tuttu seqibe,

187

雖是那們說

13. inu terei sakdasa de wajirakv sain ba bifi,
也是他的老家兒有餘蔭

14. teni ere gese dekejingge juse banjiha,
才生出這個樣的成人的孩子來了

15. nomhon bime sain,
樸實又良善

16. taqin fonjin de amuran,
好學問

17. gabtara niyamiyara,
馬步箭

18. eiten hahai erdemu,
大凡漢子的本事

19. se de teisu akv, ambula taqihabi,
他那博學的身分 不對他的年紀

20. an i uquri, boode biqi,
素常在家裡

21. bithe tuwara dabala,
看書罷咧

22. balai bade emu okson seme inu feliyerakv.
混賬路一步兒也不肯走

23. tere anggala, siden i baita de oqi,
況且公事上

24. ginggun olhoba
小心謹慎

25. bahara sara bade oqi,
所得的去處

26. fimenere ba akv.
總不沾染

27. ere tob seme sain be iktambuha boode
這個正與積善之家

28. urunakv fonqetele hvturi bi sehe gisun de aqanaha seqina.
必有餘慶的話 相合了

Section 9: Bumping into a Friend

1. age yalu,
阿哥騎着

2. bi sinde jailaha kai,

我躲了你了

3. xadame geli aiseme ebumbi,
乏乏的又下來作什麼

4. ai gisun serengge,
甚麼話呢

5. sabuhakv
若沒有看見

6. oqi ainara,
怎麼樣呢

7. bi kejine aldangga qi uthai simbe sabuha bade,
我老遠的就看見了你了

8. morilahai dulere kooli bio,
有騎過去的理嗎

9. age boode dosifi terakvn,
阿哥不進家裡坐坐嗎

10. inu kai,
是啊

11. muse aqahakvngge kejine goidaha,
嗒們許久不見了

12. bi dosifi majige teki,
我進去略坐坐吧

13. ara,
哎吆

14. utala haqingga moo ilha tebuhebio,
栽了這些各種的花木

15. geli utala boqonggo nisiha ujihebi
又養着許多金魚

16. wehe ai jibsime iktambuhangge inu sain,
山子石堆疊的也好

17. gvnin isinaha ba umesi faksi,
想頭甚巧
The creative mind is very ingenious.

18. jergi jergi de gemu doro yangse bi,
層層都有款致

19. ere bithei boo, yala bolgo,
這個書房甚乾淨

20. absi tuwaqi,
怎麼看

21. absi iqangga,
怎麼順

22. tob seme musei bithe hvlaqi aqara ba,
正是喈們該讀書的地方

23. damu korsorongge
但所恨的

24. minde asuru guqu gargan akv,
我沒有什麼朋友

25. emhun bithe taqiqi,
獨自念書

26. dembei simeli,
甚冷落

27. ede ai mangga,
這有何難

28. si aika eimerakv oqi,
你要不厭煩

29. bi sinde guqu arame jiqi antaka,
我來給你作伴 如何

30. tuttu oqi,
若是那樣

31. minde tusa oho,
與我有益了

32. solinaqi hono jiderakv jalin joboxombikai,
還愁請不到呢

33. yala jiqi,
果然要來

34. mini jabxan dabala,
我有幸罷咧

35. simbe sere doro geli bio.
豈有厭煩的理呢

Section 10: Reading is the Key

1. niyalma seme jalan de banjifi,
人生在世

2. ujui uju de taqirengge oyonggo,
頭等頭 是為學要緊

3. bithe hvlarengge,
讀書啊

4. qohome jurgan giyan be getukelere jalin,
特爲明義理

5. taqifi jurgan giyan be getukelehe sehede,
學的義理明白了

6. boode biqi niyaman de hiyooxunlara,
在家孝親

7. hafan teqi gurun boode hvsun bure,
作官給國家出力

8. ai ai baita be ini qisui mutebumbi,
諸事自然成就

9. te biqibe,
即如

10. unenggi taqiha erdemu biqi,
果然學的有本事

11. yaya bade isinaha manggi,
不拘到那裡

12. niyalma kundelere teile akv,
不但人尊敬

13. beye yabure de inu hoo hio sembi,
自己走着也豪爽

14. ememu urse,
有一宗人

15. bithe hvlarakv,
不念書

16. yabun be dasarakv,
不修品

17. baibi gvldurame enqehexeme, urui sihexeme yabure be bengsen oburengge,
只是以鑽幹逢迎爲本事

18. terei gvnin de absi ojoro be sarkv,
不知他心裡要怎麼

19. bi yargiyan i ini funde girume korsombi,
我真替他愧恨

20. entekengge,
這們樣子的

21. beye fusihvxabure yabun efujere be hono aisembi,
豈但辱身壞品

22. weri ini ama aja be suwaliyame gemu toombikai,
人家連他的父母 都是要罵的呀

23. age si bai gvnime tuwa,
阿哥你白想着瞧

24. ama eme i baili, jui oho niyalma tumen de emgeri karulame mutem-bio,
父母的恩 爲人子的 豈能答報萬一

25. fiyan nonggime eldemburakv oqi, joo dere,
不能榮耀增光咧

26. fudarame firume toobure de isibuqi,
反到叫受人的咒罵

27. gusherakvngge ai dabala,
就是一個沒有出息的東西罷了

28. erebe kimqime gvniha de niyalma ofi,
細想起這個來 爲人

29. bithe hvlarakvqi ombio,
豈可不讀書

30. yabun be dasarakvqi ombio.
不修品呢

Section 11: Where Did You Go?

1. sikse wei boode genehe,
Yesterday whose house did you go to?

2. tuttu goidafi teni jihe,
來的那樣遲

3. mini emu guqu be tuwanaha bihe,
看我一個朋友去來着

4. qeni tehengge goro,
他們住的遠

5. wargi heqen i genqehen de bi,
在西城根底下

6. ere dade, geli yamji buda ulebure,
又搭着給晚飯吃

7. jakade majige sitabuha,
所以遲了些

8. bi sinde emu gisun hebdeki seme,
我要和你商量一句話

9. ududu mudan niyalma takvrafi solinaqi,
打發人去請了好幾次

10. sini booi urse,

你家裡人們說

11. simbe sejen tefi tuqike,

你坐了車出去了

12. aibide genembi seme,

往那裡去

13. gisun werihekv sembi,

沒有留下話

14. bodoqi,

估量着

15. sini feliyere ba umesi tongga kai,

你走的地方甚少

16. manggai oqi musei ere udu guqu i boode dabala,

不過嗒們這幾個朋友家罷了

17. toktofi mini ubade darimbi seme aliyaqi,

一定到我這裡

18. aba, xun dabsitala

竟等到日平西

19. umai jihekv,

總沒有來

20. mekele emu inenggi aliyaha seqina,

算是徒然等了一天

21. inu,

是

22. age i boode niyalma isinara onggolo

阿哥家裡人還沒有到去

23. bi aifini duka tuqike,

我早出了門了

24. amasi jifi

回來

25. booi urse i alahangge,

家裡人告訴

26. age niyalma unggifi

阿哥打發了人

27. emu siran i juwe ilan mudan jio sehe,

一連叫了我兩三次

28. nergin de uthai jiki sembihe,

彼時就要來着

29. abka yamjiha,

天晚了

30. geli hiyatari yaksirahv sembi,
又恐怕關柵欄

31. tuttu bi enenggi jihe.
所以我今日來了

Section 12: Just Work Harder

1. alban kame yabure niyalma
當差行走的人

2. damu meni meni nashvn uqaran be tuwambi,
只看各自的際遇

3. forgon juken oqi,
時運要平常

4. baibi ishunde ijishvn akv,
只是彼此相左

5. yaya baita tuwaha tuwahai mutebure hanqikan ome,
凡事眼看着將成了

6. urui niyalma de sihelebufi,
偏被人阻撓

7. fasilan tuqimbi,
生出枝杈來了

8. ememu mayan sain
有一宗彩頭好

9. wesihun bethe gaiha urse,
走好運氣的人

10. yala ini gvniha iqi bodoho songkoi,
實在照所想所算的

11. lak seme gvnin de aqanarakvngge akv,
無有不爽爽利利隨心的

12. yasa tuwahai dabali dabali wesimbi,
眼看着超等優陞

13. age si uttu gisurembi wakao,
阿哥你不是這們說嗎

14. mini gvnin de tuttu akv,
我心裡卻不然

15. damu faxxara faxxarakv be hendure dabala,
只論有作爲沒作爲罷咧

16. aika vren i gese baibi qaliyan fulun jeme,

194

要是尸位素餐

17. aniya hvsime yaburakv oqi,
整年家不行走

18. hono nakabuqi aqara dabala,
還是當退的罷咧

19. wesire be ereqi ombio,
如何指望得陞呢

20. damu alban de kiqebe oyonggo,
只是差事上要勤謹

21. guqu sede hvwaliyasun dele,
朋友們裡頭以和爲主

22. ume iqi kani akv ojoro,
不可不隨合

23. baita biqi, niyalma be guqihiyererakv,
有事不攀人

24. teisulebuhe be tuwame,
凡所遇見的

25. beye sisafi iqihiyara,
撲倒身子辦

26. julesi funtume yabure ohode,
勇往向前的行走了去

27. toktofi sain jergi de ilimbikai,
定有好處

28. wesirakv doro bio.
豈有不陞的理嗎

Section 13: Eating Meat

1. age si ainu teni jihe,
阿哥你怎麼纔來

2. bi suwembe aliyahai
我只管等你們

3. elei elei amu xaburaha,
幾乎沒有打睡

4. bi sinde alara,
我告訴你

5. be teni axxafi,
我們纔要動身

6. sini boode jiderengge,

195

往你們家來

7. uksa emu eimebure niyaha yali be uqaraha,
忽然遇見一塊討人嫌的爛肉

8. gisun dalhvn bime oyomburakv,
話粘又不要緊

9. uttu sere tuttu sere,
怎長怎短的

10. ja ja de bahaqi wajirakv,
容易不得完

11. baita akv de,
沒事情的時候

12. lolo sere de aibi,
嘮叨些何妨

13. qihai alakini dere,
只管隨他告訴是呢

14. geli simbe aliyarahv seme,
又恐怕你等着

15. tede arga akv
因此沒有法兒

16. mende baita bi,
說我們有事

17. qimari jai gisurekv seme,
明日再說吧

18. ini gisun be meitefi jihe seqina,
竟是把他的話截斷來的

19. akvqi aifini qi jifi teme xadambihe,
不然早來坐乏了

20. weke aba,
誰在那裡呢

21. hvdun dere be sinda,
快放桌子

22. gvniqi agese gemu yadahvxaha,
想是老爺們都餓了

23. buda ai be lak se,
飯啊什麼都教簡決些

24. age si ere absi,
阿哥你這是怎麼說

25. faitaha yali biqi, wajiha kai,

有割的肉就完了

26. geli utala booha saikv be ainambi,
又要這些餚饌作什麼

27. membe antaha i doroi tuwambio,
把我們當客待嗎

28. bai emu gvnin okini,
不過是一點心

29. giyanakv ai sain jaka bi,
能有什麼好東西

30. age se boohalame majige jefu,
阿哥們就着吃些

31. si uttu ambarame dagilahabi kai,
你這樣盛設了麼

32. be esi jeqi
我們自然吃

33. ebirakv oqi, inu sabka sindara ba akv,
不飽也不放筷子

34. tuttu oqi, ai hendure,
要那樣 有什麼說的

35. deo be gosiha kai.
疼了兄弟了

Section 14: Shooting An Arrow

1. gabtambi serengge,
射步箭啊

2. musei manjusai oyonggo baita,
是嗒們滿洲要緊的事

3. tuwara de ja gojime,
看着容易

4. fakjin bahara de mangga,
難得主宰

5. te biqi inenggi dobori akv tataxame,
即如晝夜的常拉

6. beri be tebeliyehei amgarangge gemu bikai,
抱着睡覺的都有

7. qolgoroko sain de isinafi,
到了超羣的

8. gebu tuqikengge giyanakv udu,

好出名的 能有幾個

9. mangga ba aide seqi,
難處在那裡

10. beye tob,
身子要正

11. haqin demun akv,
沒有毛病

12. meiren neqin,
膀子要平

13. umesi elhe sulfa,
狠自然

14. ere dade beri mangga,
又搭弓硬

15. agvra tuqiburengge hvsungge,
箭出的有勁

16. geli da tolome goibure oqi,
再根根着

17. teni mangga seqi ombi,
才算得好啊

18. age si mini gabtara be tuwa,
阿哥你看我射步箭

19. neneheqi hvwaxahao, akvn,
比先出息了沒有

20. aika iqakv ba biqi,
要有不舒服的去處

21. majige jorixame tuwanqihiya,
撥正撥正

22. sini gabtarangge ai hendumbi,
你射步箭有什麼說的

23. yamji qimari ferhe de akdafi
早晚仗着大拇指

24. funggala hadambikai,
頭戴翎子的麼

25. durun sain,
樣子好

26. umesi urehebi,
狠熟

27. uksalarangge geli bolgo,

撒放的又乾淨

28. niyalma gemu sini adali ome muteqi,
人都能像你

29. ai baire,
還少什麼

30. damu beri kemuni ajige uhuken,
但只弓還軟些

31. gunirembi,
吐信子

32. asuru toktobume muterakv,
有些定不住

33. ere udu babe ejefi,
把這幾處記着

34. halaha sehede,
要說是改了

35. yaya bade isinafi gabtaqi,
不拘到那裡去射箭

36. toktofi geren qi tuqire dabala,
一定是出衆的

37. gidabure aibi.
如何壓的下去呢

Section 15: A Frank Person

1. si serengge emu wajirakv sain niyalma,
你竟是一個說不盡的好人

2. dolo majige hede da akv,
心裡沒有一點渣滓

3. damu angga jaqi sijirhvn,
但只嘴太直

4. niyalma i uru waka be saha de,
知道人的是非了

5. majige ba burakv,
一點分兒也不留

6. uthai kang seme gisurembi,
就直言奉上

7. guquse de endebuku be tuwanqihiyara doro biqibe,
雖說朋友裡頭有規過的道理

8. banjire sain juken be bodome tafulambi dere,

也論相與的好不好勸罷咧

9. damu gequ sere de emu adali seqi,
只說朋友都是一樣

10. tere ainahai ojoro,
那未必使得

11. teike ere emu fiyelen i gisun be,
方纔這一段話

12. si sain gvnin sembi wakao,
你說不是好心嗎

13. ini gvnin de labdu iqakv,
他心裡很不舒服

14. buling bulinjame,
目瞪着眼疑惑着說

15. ara,
哎呀

16. guweleke,
仔細啊

17. ere mimbe tuhebuhe be boljon akv seme kenehunjembikai,
恐怕是陷害我吧

18. age i gisun,
阿哥的話

19. fuhali mimbe dasara sain okto,
竟是治我的良藥

20. bi hungkereme gvnin dahambi,
我心裡狠服

21. ere eiqi mini emu jadaha ba,
這竟是我的一宗病了

22. bi sarkv ainaha,
我豈不知道

23. damu ere gese baita de teisulebuhe manggi,
但只是遇到這樣的事情

24. esi seqi ojorakv angga yojohoxombi,
不由的嘴癢癢

25. gisureqi ojorakvngge de gisureqi, gisun be ufaraha sehebi,
有不可與言 而與之言 失言的話

26. enenggi qi bi umesileme halaki,
從今日起我痛改吧

27. jai uttu oqi,

再要這樣

28. fulu aisembi,
多說什麼

29. age uthai dere be baime qifele,
阿哥就望着我臉上吐唾沫

30. bi qihanggai janquhvn i alime gaimbi.
我情願甘心領受

Section 16: A Difficult Friendship

1. suwe umesi banjire sain kai,
你們狠相好啊

2. te ainaha,
如今怎麼了

3. fuhali sini duka i bokason de fehunjirakv ohoni,
總不登你的門檻子了

4. sarkv je,
不知道啊

5. we ya aika inde waka sabubuha ba biqi,
要有誰得罪過他的去處

6. geli emu gisurere babe,
還有一說

7. umai akv bade,
總沒有

8. hoqikosaka yabumbihengge,
好端端的來往的人

9. gaitai, ya emu gisun de ni gidafi,
忽然那一句上記了過失

10. fuqe nakv lasha feliyerakv ohobi,
惱的決然不走了

11. yaburakv oqi inu okini,
不走也罷咧

12. enggiqi bade baibi mimbe uttu ehe sere,
背地裡只是說我這樣不好

13. tuttu nimequke sere,
那樣厲害

14. mini takara ele guquse be aqaha dari,
所有遇見我認得的朋友

15. gisun i fesin obume jubexehengge gojime,

201

就作話柄兒 毀謗是怎麼說

16. jakan mini jui de urun isibure de,
新近給我孩子娶媳婦

17. bi hono dere de ainara seme,
我還臉上過不去

18. imbe solinaha bihe,
請他去來着

19. indahvn inu emke takvraha ba akv,
狗也沒打發一個來

20. mini uqaraha uqarahangge,
我所遇見的

21. gemu ere gese guqu kai,
都是這樣的朋友

22. mimbe jai adarame guquleme sembi,
叫我再怎麼相與呢

23. tere niyalmai gisun yabun holo kukduri,
我沒說過那個人語言品行

24. akdaqi ojorakv seme bi aika henduhekvn,
虛假誇張不可信麼

25. tere fonde si geli hersembio,
彼時你還理來着嗎

26. hono mujakv mimbe iqakvxameliyan i bihe,
還着實有些不受用我來着

27. niyalmai qira be takara gojime,
識人的面貌罷咧

28. gvnin be adarame xuwe hafu sambini,
心裡如何知道的透徹呢

29. sain ehe be ilgarakv,
不分好歹

30. bireme gemu umesi haji guqu seqi ombio.
一概都說得是很好的朋友嗎

Section 17: A Stingy Friend

1. ere uquri
這一向

2. si geli aibide xodonoho bihe,
你又往那裡奔忙去了

3. mudan talude mini jakade inu majige feliyeqina,

間或到我這裡走走是呢

4. ainu sini dere yasa be oron saburakv,
怎麼總不見你的面目

5. bi aifini age be tuwajiki sembihe,
我早要看阿哥來着

6. gvnihakv emu daljakv heturi baita de siderebu nakv,
不想被一件旁不相干的事絆住

7. fuhali lahin taha
竟受了累了

8. inenggidari fusu fasa jaka xolo aika bio,
終日匆忙還有空兒嗎

9. akvqi enenggi bahafi ukqame muterakv bihe,
要不是今日還脫不開來着

10. minde hahi oyonggo baita bi seme kanagan arame gisurehei
只管推託着說我有急事

11. arkan teni mimbe sindaha,
將將的纔放了我了

12. jihengge umesi sain,
來的甚好

13. jing alixahabi,
正悶在這裡

14. gvniqi sinde inu asuru oyonggo baita akv,
想來你也沒有什麼要緊的事

15. muse emu inenggi gisureme teki,
喒們坐着說一日的話兒罷

16. beleni buda jefi gene,
現成的飯吃了去

17. bi inu enqu booha dagilarakv,
我也不另收拾菜

18. damu jihe dari,
但只來勤

19. baibi age simbe gaxihiyaburengge,
只管騷擾阿哥

20. mini gvnin de elhe akv,
我心裡不安

21. tuttu ofi, gelhun akv ta seme jiderakv,
因此不敢常來

22. si ainu tulgiyen obufi gvnimbi,

你怎麼外道

23. muse atanggi si bi seme ilgambihe,
嗒們從幾時分彼此來着

24. jai udu inenggi giyalafi jiderakv oqi,
若要再隔幾日不來

25. bi hono majige jaka belhefi,
我還要預備些東西

26. qohome simbe helneki sere bade,
特請你去

27. emu erin i beleni untuhun buda be,
一頓現成的空飯

28. geli aiseme dabufi gisurembi,
又何足論呢

29. tere anggala, siningge be,
況且你的東西

30. bi ai jekekv,
我什麼沒吃過

31. erebe tuwaqi
看起這個來

32. iletu mimbe sini boode, jai jai ume genere serengge kai.
竟是明明的叫我再別往你們家去了啊

Section 18: Encountering a Stubborn Man

1. bi daqi sini ere baita be,
我原說你這一件事

2. tede gisureqi,
向他說着

3. umesi ja sembihe,
狠容易來

4. eimede tuttu jayan qira fangnai ojorakv be, we gvniha,
誰想竟遇見了一個厭物 那樣牙關緊 決不肯依

5. ede mujakv gvnin baibuha seqina,
因此竟狠費了心了

6. musei hebdehe babe, inde alaha de,
把嗒們商量的去處告訴了他

7. dere efulefi[381],
放下臉來

8. mini gisun be fudasihvn i fiyo sembi,
以我的話爲乖謬之談

9. tede bi hvr sehe,
所以我的火上來

10. jili monggon i da deri oho,
性子到了脖梗子上了

11. ainaqi ainakini dabala seme,
要作什麼就作罷咧

12. imbe neqiki sere gvnin jalu jafaha bihe,
滿心裡要惹他一惹

13. amala gvnifi,
後來想了一想

14. beyebe beye fonjime,
自己問着自己

15. si taxarabuhabi,
你錯了

16. ere jihengge, beyei baita waka
這來意不是自己的事

17. guqu i jalin kai,
爲的是朋友啊

18. imbe majige baktambure de
就畧容着他些

19. geli ai wajimbi
又費了什麼

20. seme ini elere ebsihei akxulame beqere be kirime,
所以忍着他的儘量痛責

21. emu jilgan tuqikekv,
一聲也不哼

22. ijishvn i alime gaiha,
順順的領受了

23. geli kejine goidame tefi,
又坐了好一會

24. terei arbun be tuwafi,

---

[381] 'Dere efulefi' literally means 'face is ruined'.

看他的光景

25. iqi aqabume elheken i baire jakade,
順着他慢慢的央求

26. arkan teni uju gehexehe,
剛剛的纔點了頭了

27. si gvnime tuwa,
你想着瞧

28. mini jili majige hani oqi,
我的性子要畧急些

29. sini baita faijume bihe wakao.
你的事情不有些不妥當了嗎

Section 19: A Good Rain

1. sikse erde iliha manggi,
昨天清早起來

2. booi dolo dembei farhvn,
屋裡狠黑

3. bi ainqi kemuni gehun gerere unde aise seme,
我說想是天還沒狠亮

4. hvwa de tuqifi tuwaqi,
出院子裡看

5. dele luk seme tulhuxehe ni,
原來陰得漆黑

6. dere obofi teni yamulaki sere de,
洗了臉纔要上衙門

7. sebe saba aga i sabdan tuhenjihe,
一點兩點的下雨了

8. baji aliyara sidende,
畧等了一會

9. xor seme asuki tuqikebi,
下響了

10. geli majige te manggi,
又坐了一坐兒

11. emu hvntahan qai omiha biqi,
吃了一鍾茶的空兒

12. gaitai kiyatar seme, emgeri akjan akjame,
忽然一聲打起焦雷

13. hungker seme agame deribuhe,

下起傾盆大雨來了

14. bi ere bai emu burgin i huksidere dabala,
我只說這不過一陣暴雨罷咧
I thought it was a rainstorm for a period of time,

15. duleke manggi jai yoki seqi,
過去了再走罷

16. aibide yamjitala hungkerehe bime,
那裡直傾到晚

17. dobonio geretele umai nakahakv,
又徹夜至天明 纔沒有住

18. enenggi budai erin otolo,
到今日飯時

19. teni buru bara xun i elden be sabuha,
纔恍恍惚惚看見日光了

20. yala erinde aqabure sain aga,
真是應時的好雨啊

21. gvniqi ba ba i usin bafukakvngge akv kai,
想來各處的地畝 沒有不透的

22. bolori jeku elgiyen tumin i bargiyarakv ainaha.
秋天的莊稼 豈有不豐收的呢

Section 20: A Role Model

1. sini daqilarangge, tere age wakao,
你打聽的不是那個阿哥麼

2. tere serengge,
他呀

3. fulhv i dorgi suifun kai,
是囊中之錐子啊

4. atanggi biqibe, urunakv qolgorome tuqimbi,
幾時必要出頭

5. turgun ai seqi,
甚麼緣故呢

6. banitai ujen jingji ambula taqihabi,
生來的沉靜博學

7. yabuqi durun axxaqi kemun,
行動是榜樣準則

8. alban de oqi,
差事上

9. emu julehen i yabumbi,
一拿步兒的走
10. boode oqi
居家呢
11. emu suihen i banjimbi,
一樸心兒的過
12. yargiyan i ajige haqin demun akv,
實在的沒有一點毛病
13. ama eme de hiyooxungga,
父母跟前孝順
14. ahvn deo de haji,
兄弟之間親熱
15. ere dade guqu gargan de,
況且朋友裡頭
16. umesi karaba,
狠護衆
17. yaya we inde emu baita yandure de,
不拘誰托他一件事
18. alime gaijarakv oqi wajiha,
不應就罷了
19. uju gehexehe sehede,
要說是點了頭
20. urunakv beye sisafi sini funde faqihiyaxambi,
必然撲倒身子替你設措
21. muteburakv oqi nakara kooli akv,
不成不肯歇手
22. uttu ofi,
因此
23. we imbe kundulerakv,
誰不敬他
24. we hanqi oki serakv,
誰不要親近他
25. sain niyalma abka aisilambi sehebi,
有吉人天相之說
26. enteke niyalma
這樣的人
27. mekele banjifi untuhuri wajire aibi,
豈有虛生空完的呢

28. abka urunakv hvturi isibure dabala.
天必降福罷了

Section 21: A Harsh Discipline

1. eqimari qeni bithe xejilebuqi,
今日早起叫他们背書

2. emke, emke qi eshun,
一個比一個生

3. eke eke seme gahvxame,
哼啊哼的張着嘴

4. deng deng seme ilinjambi,
格蹬格蹬的打磕拌

5. tede bi takasu,
那上頭我說暫住

6. mini gisun be donji,
聽我的話

7. suwe manju bithe be hvlaqi tetendere,
你們既念清書

8. uthai emu julehen i taqiqina,
就一拿步兒學是呢

9. ere gese ton arame,
像這樣充着數兒

10. untuhun gebu gaiqi,
沽虛名

11. atanggi dube da,
幾時纔有頭緒

12. yala suwe inenggi biya be untuhuri manabuha sere anggala,
可是說的不但你們虛度光陰

13. bi inu mekele hvsun baibuha seqina,
我也是徒然費力啊

14. eiqi suweni beyebe suwe sartabuha sembio,
還算是你們自己誤了自己

15. eiqi bi suwembe tookabuha sembio,
或是算我誤了你們呢

16. qiksika amba haha oso nakv,
已成了壯年的大漢子

17. hendutele,
說着說着

18. geli uttu xan de donjire gojime
又這樣耳朵裡聽了

19. gvnin de teburakvngge,
心裡廢棄的光景

20. dere jaqi silemin bai,
太皮臉了啊

21. mini ere gosihon gisurere be,
把我這苦口的話

22. suwe ume gejenggi sere,
你們別說嘴碎

23. ume fiktu baimbi sere,
別說尋趁

24. te biqibe, mini beye alban kame
即如我當了差

25. funqehe xolo de,
剩的空兒

26. majige ergeqi oihori,
受用受用何等的好呢

27. baibi suwembe qanggi
只管合你們

28. ere tere serengge
這樣那樣的

29. ai hala,
爲什麼呢

30. ineku giranggi yali ofi,
也因爲是骨肉

31. suwembe hvwaxakini,
叫你們出息

32. niyalma okini sere gvnin kai,
叫你們成人的意思啊

33. ainara,
可怎麼樣呢

34. bi gvnin akvmbume taqibure de
我該盡心教的

35. giyan be dahame taqibuqi wajiha,
按着理教就完了

36. donjire donjirakvngge suweni qiha dabala,
聽不聽隨你們罷了

37. mimbe aina sembi.
叫我怎麼樣呢

Section 22: To Protect our Manchu Reputation

1. waka,
不是啊

2. sini ere absi serengge,
你這是怎麼說

3. inenggidari ebitele jefu manggi,
終日吃的飽飽的

4. fifan tenggeri be tebeliyehei fitherengge,
抱着琵琶弦子彈的光景

5. aika alban semeo,
還算是差事啊

6. gebu gaiki sembio,
還要成名嗎

7. eiqi ede akdafi banjiki sembio,
或是要仗着這個過日子啊

8. muse jabxan de manju ofi,
喈們幸而是滿洲

9. jeterengge alban i bele,
吃的是官米

10. baitalarangge qaliyan i menggun,
使的是帑銀

11. booi gubqi ujui hukxehe bethei fehuhengge,
闔家頭頂腳跴的

12. gemu ejen i kesi de bahangge,
都是拖着主子的恩典得的

13. erdemu be taqirakv,
不學本事

14. alban de faxxame yaburakv oso nakv,
不當差效力

15. baibi ede gvnin girkvfi taqiqi,
只管在這上頭專心去學

16. manju be gvtubuha ai dabala,
玷污滿洲哩呀

17. baitangga gvnin be baitakv bade fayabure anggala,
與其將有用的心思費於無用之地

211

18. bithe taqire de isirakv,
不如讀書啊

19. uqun be taqihangge,
學唱的

20. uqe i amala ilimbi,
立門僻

21. baksi be taqihangge
學儒的

22. bakqin de tembi
坐對膝

23. sehebi,
有此一說

24. ai haqin i ferguwequke mangga de isinaha seme,
就學到怎樣精良地步

25. niyalma de efiku injeku arara dabala,
不過供人的玩笑罷了

26. nantuhvn fusihvn sere gebu qi guweme muterakv kai,
不能免下賤的名色啊

27. jingkini siden i bade isinaha manggi,
到了正經公所

28. fithere haqin be bengsen obuqi ombio,
會彈也算得本事嗎

29. mini gisun be temgetu akv,
要說我的話沒憑據

30. akdaqi ojorakv seqi,
不可信

31. ambasa hafasai dorgide,
大人們裡頭

32. ya emke fithere qi beye tuqikengge be,
那一個是從會彈出身的

33. si te tuqibu.
你如今說出來

Section 23: Being Promoted!

1. age urgun kai,
阿哥喜啊

2. janggin sindara de tomilaha sembi,
說是派出放章京來了

3. inu,
是啊

4. sikse ilgame sonjoro de,
昨日揀選

5. mimbe qohoho,
把我擬了正了

6. adabuhangge we,
擬陪的是誰

7. bi takarakv,
我不認得

8. emu gabsihiyan i juwan i da,
是一個前鋒什長

9. inde qooha mudan bio akvn,
他有兵沒有呢

10. akv,
沒有

11. aba i teile,
單有圍

12. bi sini funde ureme bodoho,
我替你打算熟了

13. tojin funggala hadambi seme belhe,
預備帶孔雀翎子

14. bi ai ferguwequke,
我算什麼奇特

15. minqi sain ningge ai yadara,
比我好的要多少

16. urunakv bahambi seme ereqi ombio,
如何指望必得呢

17. ama mafari kesi de,
托着祖父

18. jabxan de herebure be boljoqi ojorakv,
僥倖撈着了也定不得

19. ai gisun serengge,
甚麼話呢

20. si ai erin i niyalma,
你是什麼時候的人啊

21. aniya goidaha,
年久了

22. fe be bodoqi,

論陳

23. sini emgi yabuha guquse gemu amban oho,
合你走的朋友都作大人了

24. jai sini amala gaiha asihata,
再在你後頭挑的少年們

25. yooni sinqi enggelehebi,
都比你強了先了.

26. yabuha feliyehe be bodoqi,
論行走

27. qooha de faxxaha feye baha,
出過兵得過傷

28. tuttu bime,
而且

29. ne tofohon mangga,
現是十五善射

30. si hendu gvsade sinqi dulenderengge gemu weqi,
你說旗下過於你的是誰

31. bi saha,
我知道了

32. eiqi sini urgun nure be omime jiderahv seme,
想是恐怕來吃你的喜酒

33. jortanggi uttu gisurembi dere,
故意的這們說罷咧

34. ai geli,
豈有此理

35. yala bahaqi,
要果然得了

36. nure be aisembi,
別說酒

37. sini gvnin de aqabume soliki,
合着你的主意請罷

38. bai yobo maktambi,
白說着頑

39. bi urgun arame jiqi giyan ningge,
我該來賀喜

40. fudarame siningge be jeqi,
倒吃你的東西

41. geli ombio.
也使得嗎

Section 24: Some Strange Visitors

1. enenggi yaka jihebio,
今日誰來了嗎

2. age duka tuqime,
阿哥一出門

3. dahanduhai juwe niyalma tuwanjiha bihe,
跟着有兩個人瞧來着

4. age be wesike seme,
說阿哥陞了

5. qohome urgun de aqanjiha sehe,
特來道喜

6. we tuqifi jabuha,
誰出去答應了

7. mini beye dukai jakade iliha bihe,
我在門口站着來着

8. bi mini ahvn boode akv,
我說我哥哥不在家

9. looyesa dosifi teki seme,
讓老爺們進去坐坐

10. anahvnjaqi fangnai dosirakv,
斷不進來

11. amasi genehe,
回去了

12. ai gese niyalma,
什麼樣的人啊

13. adarame banjihabi,
怎麼個長像兒

14. emke yalihangga,
一個胖子

15. age qi majige dekdehun,
比阿哥略猛些

16. beye teksin,
勻溜身子

17. xufangga salu,
連鬢鬍子

18. yasa bultahvn,
豹子眼

19. fahala qira,

紫棠色

20. tere emke yala yobo,
那一個真可笑

21. nantuhvn manggi fuhali tuwaqi ojorakv,
穢的竟瞧不得

22. yasa gakda
一隻眼

23. bime hiyari,
又邪着

24. kerkenehe kerkeri,
醬稠的麻子

25. hoshori salu,
倒捲着的鬍子

26. terei demun i mini baru
那個樣子望着我

27. emgeri gisurere jakade,
一說話

28. bi elekei busa seme injehe,
我幾乎沒有笑出來

29. tere yalihangga,
那個胖子

30. bi saha,
我知道了

31. ere emke geli we bihe,
這一個又是誰呢

32. bi qeni hala be fonjiha bihe,
我問他們的姓來着

33. minde emte justan gebu jergi araha bithe werihebi,
每人給我留了一個職名

34. bi gajifi, age de tuwabure,
我拿來給阿哥看

35. ara,
哎呀

36. ere suisirengge aibiqi jihe,
這個孽障起那裡來了

37. si tere be ume
你別說

38. yokqin akv seme

216

他不成材料

39. ja tuwara,
輕看了

40. beye giru udu waiku daikv biqibe,
他身量雖然歪邪

41. fi de sain,
筆下好

42. dotori bi,
有內囊

43. imbe jonoho de
提起他來

44. we sarkv,
誰不知道

45. aifini gebu gaiha,
早有了名了

46. seibeni oihori koikaxambihe kai.
夙昔何等的攪渾過的來着啊

Section 25: Looking for a Friend

1. meni juwe nofi,
我們兩個人

2. daqi banjire sain bime,
原相好

3. te geli ududu ursu niyaman daribuhabi,
如今又有好幾層親

4. utala aniya bahafi sabuhakv seme,
因多少年沒得見

5. bi qoohai baqi amasi isinjiha de
我從出兵的地方回來

6. uthai imbe baihanafi,
就要找了他去

7. kiduha jongko be gisureki sembihe,
敘敘想念的情況來着

8. gvnihakv baita de siderebu nakv,
不略被往事絆住

9. fuhali xolo baharakv,
總沒得工夫

10. sikse ildun de ini boode darifi fonjiqi,

昨天順便到他家問起來

11. gurifi kejine goidaha,
搬去許久了

12. ne siyoo giyai dolo wargi ergi genqehen i murihan de tehebi sembi,
說現在小街裡頭西邊轉彎處住着呢

13. alaha songkoi baime genefi tuwaqi,
照着告訴的話找去了瞧

14. umesi koqo wai,
狠背的小地方

15. duka yaksifi bi,
關着門呢

16. duka neiqi seme hvlaqi
叫開門呢

17. umai jabure niyalma akv,
總沒人答應

18. geli duka toksime kejine hvlaha manggi
又敲着門 叫了好一會

19. emu sakda mama tame afame tuqike,
一個老婆子磕磕絆絆的出來了

20. mini ejen boode akv,
說我的主兒不在家

21. gvwa bade yoha sembi,
往別處去了

22. bi sini looye amasi jihe manggi ala,
我說你老爺回來告訴

23. mimbe tuwanjiha se sere de,
說我看來了

24. xan umesi jigeyen,
耳朵很沉

25. fuhali donjihakv,
總沒聽見

26. tuttu ofi, bi arga akv,
所以我沒法兒

27. qeni adaki ajige puseli de fi yuwan baifi,
合他們間壁小鋪兒裡尋了個筆硯

28. mini genehe babe bithelefi werihe.
把我去了的話寫了個字兒留下了

Section 26: Happy New Year!

1. age iqe aniya, amba urgun kai,
阿哥新年大喜啊

2. je,
是

3. ishunde urgun okini,
同喜啊

4. age teki,
阿哥請坐

5. ainambi,
作什麼

6. age de aniyai doroi hengkileki,
給阿哥拜年

7. ai gisun serengge,
什麼話呢

8. sakda ahvn kai,
老兄長啊

9. hengkilengge giyan waka semeo,
不該當磕頭的嗎

10. je,
咢

11. hafan hali wesikini,
陞官

12. juse dasu fusekini,
多養兒子

13. bayan wesihun banjikini,
過富貴日子

14. age ili wesifi te,
阿哥起來上去坐

15. beleni bujuha hoho efen udu fali jefu,
現成的煮餃子吃幾個

16. bi booqi jefi tuqike,
我從家裡吃了出來的

17. jekengge tuttu ebihebio,
吃的那樣飽嗎

18. asihata teike jeke seme
年青的人就是纔吃了

19. uthai yadahvxambikai,

219

也就餓啊

20. si ainqi manggaxambi dere,
你想是爲難罷咧

21. yargiyan,
實在

22. age i boode, bi geli antaharambio,
阿哥的家裡我還粧假嗎

23. gelhun akv holtorakv,
不敢撒謊

24. je,
嚛

25. wajiha,
罷了

26. qai aqabufi benju,
對茶送來

27. age bi omirakv,
阿哥我不喝

28. ainu,
怎麼

29. bi kemuni gvwa bade dariki sembi,
我還要到別處去

30. geneqi aqara boo labdu,
應去的人家多

31. onggofi xadafi,
忘了乏了

32. jai geneme ohode,
再去的時候

33. niyalma gemu gvninjara de isinambi,
人都犯思量了

34. age uthai jefu,
阿哥就吃

35. mimbe ume fudere,
別送我

36. amtan gamarahv,
看帶了滋味去

37. ai geli,
豈有此理

38. uqe be tuqirakv kooli bio,

那裡有不出房門的禮

39. je,

咢

40. xadaha kai,

乏了

41. jifi untuhusaka,

來了空空的

42. qai inu omirakv,

茶也不喝

43. boode isinaha manggi sain be fonjiha se.

到家裡說我問好了

Section 27: Don't Fall into Buddhism!

1. sain baita be yabumbi sehengge,

作好事啊

2. musei akvmbuqi aqara hiyooxun deoqin tondo akdun jergi haqin be henduhebi,

說的是嗒們當盡的孝弟忠信之類

3. umai gemu fuqihi enduri be doboro, hvwaxan doose de ulebure de bisirengge waka,

並非全在供神佛 齋僧道

4. duibuleqi ehe be yabure urse,

比方說作惡的人

5. ai haqin i xayolame jugvn jukiha doohan qaha seme,

任憑怎樣的吃素補路修橋

6. ini weile be suqi ombio,

豈能解他的罪呢

7. udu fuqihi enduri seme hvturi isibume banjinarakv kai,

就是神佛 也不便降福啊

8. xayolara urse abkai tanggin de tafambi,

吃素的遊天堂

9. ergengge warangge na i gindana de tuxambi sere,

殺牲的下地獄的

10. hala haqin i gisun

各樣話

11. gemu hvwaxan doose i angga hetumbure kanagan,

都是僧道借着餬口的托詞

12. hiri akdaqi ombio,

221

豈可深信

13. qe aika uttu tuttu sere nimequke gisun i niyalma be jaldame hoxxo-rakv,
他們要不拏着怎長怎短的利害話 詆騙人

14. fuqihi xajin be dahame,
遵着佛教

15. juktehen i duka be yaksifi,
關着廟門

16. ekisaka maqihi jafara,
靜靜的持齋

17. nomun hvlara oqi
念經

18. jeqi jeterengge akv, etuqi eturengge akv, ombikai,
就要吃沒吃的 要穿沒穿的

19. we qembe ujimbi,
誰養贍他們呢

20. edun ukiyeme banji sembio.
喝風度日麼

Section 28: A Respectable Leader

1. sakda amban erdemu daqun kafur sembi,
老大人才情敏捷決斷

2. yaya baita isinjime jakan uthai giyan fiyan i iqihiyabumbi,
凡事一到 就教辦的有條有理

3. ere dade, dolo getuken,
而且心裏明白

4. niyalma be takambi,
認的人

5. sain ehe be ini yasa de fuhali enderakv,
好歹斷然瞞不過他的眼睛去

6. alban de kiqebe yebken asihata be watai gosimbi,
極憐愛差事勤 少年的英俊人

7. wesire forgoxoro bade isinaha manggi,
到了陞轉的去處

8. meihereme dahabumbi seqina,
只說是提拔保薦罷

9. aikabade alban de bulqakvxame,
要是差事上猾懶

222

10. dede dada sain sabubume,
抖抖搜搜的獻好

11. jabxan be baime yabure ohode,
希圖僥倖

12. tede faraka seme bodo,
可打算着在他的跟前發昏罷

13. nambuha sehede
要說撈把着了

14. ja sindara kooli akv,
斷無輕放的規矩

15. hendure gisun uttu,
說的話是這樣

16. deote inenggidari yasa tatafi xame
兄弟們終日眼巴巴的

17. tuwame minde akdafi niyalma hvwaxabumbi kai,
盼望要仗着我成人

18. tukiyeqi aqarangge be tukiyerakv,
要是應薦舉的不薦舉

19. jafataqi aqarangge be jafatarakv oqi,
應約束的不約束

20. sain niyalma aide huwekiyembi,
如何能勸善

21. ehe niyalma aide isembi sembi,
懲惡呢

22. banitai gvnin tondo angga sijirhvn,
生成的心直口快

23. gisun yabun tob hoxonggo,
說話行事因爲端方

24. niyalma gemu hungkereme gvnin dahafi,
所以人都傾心賓服

25. ishunde huwekiyendume,
彼此勸勉

26. julesi faqihiyaxame hvsun bumbi.
向前努力啊

Section 29: A Good Old Man

1. fe be amqabuha niyalma,
趕上舊時候的人

2. qingkai enqu,
總是不同

3. niyalma be aqaha de keb seme haji halhvn,
見了人極其親熱

4. emu bade teqefi
坐在一處

5. bithe qagan taqin fonjin be leolembihede,
論起書籍學問來

6. watai urgunjembi,
非常的喜歡

7. yar seme xun dositala gisurehe seme
連接不斷的說一日話兒

8. xadara ba inu akv,
也不乏

9. niyalma de jorixaqi aqara bade jorixambi,
該指撥人的去處 指撥

10. taqibuqi aqara bade taqibumbi,
該教導的去處 教導

11. julgei baita be yarume,
援引古來的事

12. te i niyalma de duibuleme,
比方如今的人

13. asihata be nesuken gisun i sain bade yarhvdambi,
把少年們用和藹的言語往好處引導啊

14. geli umesi gosingga,
又極仁德

15. dembei karaba,
狠護衆

16. niyalma i gosihon be sabuha de,
見了人的苦處

17. uthai beye tuxaha adali faqihiyaxame,
就像自己遭遇的一樣着急

18. urunakv muterei teile aitubume tuwaxatambi,
必定儘力兒搭救看顧

19. yala sujei gese, ler sere emu hvturi isibure sengge seqina,
實在竟是一位乾淨厚重積福的老人家啊

20. uttu ofi,
因此

21. udu inenggi giyalafi tuwanarakv oqi

要隔幾日不去看

22. gvnin de baibi ojorakv,
心裡只是不過意

23. dekdeni henduhengge,
俗話說的

24. emu niyalma de hvturi biqi
一人有福

25. booi gubqi kesi be alimbi sehebi,
托戴滿屋

26. erei boo boigon qiktarara,
這樣家業便當

27. juse omosi mukdenderengge,
子孫興旺

28. gemu sakda niyalmai yabuha sain karulan de kai.
都是老人家行爲的好報應啊

Section 30: The Right Way of Eating Meat

1. sikse weqehe yali jeke be dahame,
昨日吃過祭神的肉

2. uthai joo kai,
也就罷了

3. geli tuibuhe yali be benefi ainambi,
又送背燈的肉去作甚麼呢

4. teike hono age be solinaki sembihe,
方纔還要請阿哥去來着

5. age si sarangge,
阿哥你是知道的

6. bisire akv,
有的沒的

7. damu ere udu ahasi
這幾個奴才們

8. ulgiyan be tekdebure,
宰豬

9. duha do be dasatara de,
收拾雜碎

10. ya gemu gala baiburakv
那上頭都不費手

11. tuttu ojoro jakade niyalma takvrahakv,

225

因爲那樣沒使人去

12. sinde niyalma akv be bi iletu sambikai,
我明知道你沒有人

13. geli solire be aliyambio,
還等着請嗎

14. uttu ofi,
因此

15. bi guquse be guilefi
我會了朋友們

16. amba yali be jekenjihe,
來吃大肉來了

17. hono sitabuha ayoo sembihe,
還恐怕遲誤了來着

18. gvnihakv hib seme amqabuha,
不想儘自在從容的趕上了

19. je,
嗻

20. agese boigoji be ume gvnin jobobure,
阿哥們別叫主人家勞神

21. muse ahvn bodome ikiri teqefi jeki,
喒們序齒一溜兒坐着吃

22. agese yali jefu,
阿哥們請吃肉

23. sile be den barafi jeqina,
泖湯吃是呢

24. ara,
哎呀

25. sini ere ai gisun,
你這是什麼話

26. taxarahabi,
錯了

27. musei da jokson de ere gese kooli biheo,
喒們起初有這樣的規矩來着麼

28. ere yali serengge,
這個肉啊

29. weqeku i kesi kai,
是祖宗的恩惠呀

30. haqihiyaqi ombio,

226

強讓得麼
31. tere anggala antahasa jiqi geneqi,
況且賓客們來去
32. okdoro fudere ba hono akv bade,
還不接送
33. ere durun anahvnjaqi,
像這樣讓起來
34. soroki akv semeo.
不忌諱嗎

Section 31: Brotherhood

1. ahvn deo serengge,
弟兄啊
2. emu eme i banjihangge,
是一個母親生出來的
3. ajigan fonde
幼年間
4. jeqi uhe,
同吃
5. efiqi sasa,
同頑
6. umai beri beri akv,
並沒彼此
7. antaka senggime, antaka haji bihe,
何等的相親相愛來着
8. mutufi ulhiyen i fakqashvn ohongge,
長起來了漸漸的生分的緣故
9. amba muru gemu sargan guweleku i xusihiyere gisun de hvlimbufi,
大約都因惑於妻妾調唆的話
10. boo boigon temxere,
爭家私
11. hetu niyalmai jakanabure gisun de donjifi,
聽了傍人離間的話
12. teisu teisu gvnin tebureqi
各自留心上
13. banjinahangge umesi labdu,
起的狠多
14. adarame seqi,

227

怎麼說呢

15. inenggidari ere jergi ehequre gisun be donjifi,
終日聽了這些讒言

16. gvnin de tebuhei dolo jalupi,
心裡都裝滿了

17. emu erinde kirime muterakv,
一時不能忍的上頭

18. uthai beqen jamandekdere de isinafi,
就至於打架拌嘴

19. kimun bata i gese ohobi,
成了讎敵一樣了

20. gvnime tuwa,
想着瞧

21. hethe wajiqi,
產業完了

22. dasame ilibuqi ombi,
可以再立

23. sargan ufaraha de dasame gaiqi ombi,
女人失閃了可以再娶

24. ahvn deo i dorgide,
弟兄裡頭

25. emken kokiraha sehede,
要說是傷一個

26. uthai gala bethe emke bijaha adali,
就像手足折了一隻

27. dahvme bahaqi ombio,
豈可再得呢

28. talu de kesi akv,
偶然不幸

29. emu jobolon baita tuqinjihe de,
出一件禍患事

30. inu ahvn deo siren tatabumbi,
也還是弟兄脈絡相關

31. ergen xelefi faqihiyaxame aitubure dabala,
拼命的巴結着搭救罷咧

32. hetu niyalma uxaburahv seme
旁人恐怕掛帶

33. jailame jabdurakv bade

還躲不疊當

34. sini funde hvsutulere mujanggo,
肯替你用力麼

35. erebe tuwaqi,
看起這個來

36. ahvn deo de isirengge akv,
沒有如兄弟啊

37. niyalma ainu ubabe kimqime gvnirakv ni.
人爲什麼不細想這些呢

Section 32: Raising Children to Take Care of Parents

1. juse be ujirengge,
養兒

2. daqi sakdaka de belhere jaka,
原爲防備老

3. jui oho niyalma,
爲人子的

4. ama eme jobome suilame ujihe hvwaxabuha kesi be gvniqi,
要想着父母勤勞養育的恩

5. niyaman i sakdara onggolo be amqame,
該當趁着父母未老之前

6. sain etuku etubume,
將好衣服

7. iqangga jaka be alibume,
美食物事奉

8. injere qira, ijishvn gisun i urgunjebuqi aqambi,
和顏悅色的叫喜歡

9. aikabade eture jetere be darakv,
要是吃穿不管

10. beyere yuyure be fonjirakv,
飢寒不問

11. jugvn yabure niyalma adali tuwame,
視如路人

12. sakdasa be akara gingkara de isibuqi,
致令老人家傷心氣悶

13. akv oho manggi,
百年之後

14. ai haqin i gosiholome songgoho seme,

任憑怎麼樣的痛哭

15. ai baita,
中什麼用啊

16. unenggi gvnin qi tuqikengge seme,
就說是出於誠心

17. we akdara,
誰信呢

18. niyalmai basure de geleme,
不過是怕人恥笑

19. holtorongge dabala,
假粧罷咧

20. ai haqin i iqangga amtangga jaka doboho seme,
就供什麼樣的甘美東西

21. fayangga sukjihe be we sabuha,
誰見魂靈來受享了呢

22. ineku weihun urse sisiha dabala,
也還是活人攘塞了罷了

23. ufaraha niyalma ai baha ni,
沒的人得甚麼了呢

24. geli dabanahangge ama eme be se de goqimbuha,
甚至於說父母上年紀

25. sakdafi oiboko seme,
老悖晦了

26. daixahai ergeleme boo delhebuhengge gemu bi,
鬧着逼着叫分家的都有

27. gisun ede isinjifi,
說到這裡

28. niyalma esi seqi ojorakv,
人不由的

29. nasambime fanqaquka,
嗟嘆憤懑

30. enteke niyalma,
這樣的人

31. abka na baktamburakv,
天地不容

32. hutu enduri uhei seyere be dahame,
鬼神共恨

33. adarame bahafi sain i dubembi,

230

焉得善終呢

34. damu ekisaka tuwa,
只靜靜的看着

35. giyanakv udu goidambi,
如何能久

36. yasa habtaxara sidende,
展眼之間

37. ini juse omosi songko de songko ombikai.
他的子孫也就晒着蹤跡照樣的了

Section 33: A Greedy Man

1. ai baharakv ferguwequke jaka,
什麼不得異樣的東西

2. sabuha dari
每遭見了

3. baibi gejing seme,
只管絮煩

4. nandame gairengge,
向人尋

5. jaqi derakv kai,
太沒體面啊

6. weri dere de eterakv de,
人家臉上過不去

7. ineku sinde kejine buhe,
也給了你好些

8. gvnin de kemuni eleme sarkv,
心裡還不知足

9. ergeletei waqihiyame gaji serengge,
壓派着全都要的

10. ai doro,
是何道理

11. sinde buqi baili,
給你是人情

12. burakv oqi teisu kai,
不給是本分

13. fudarame jilidame, niyalma be lasihidarangge,
翻倒使性子捽搦人

14. mujakv fiyokoroho ai dabala,

大錯謬了罷咧

15. duibuleqi uthai sini jaka okini,
比方就是你的東西

16. niyalma buyeqi
人要愛

17. si buyerakvn,
你不愛麼

18. fuhali sinde saliburakv,
全不由你主張

19. fere heqeme kob seme gamaqi,
徹底都要拿了去

20. sini gvnin de adarame,
你心裡如何

21. sikse mini beye ofi,
昨日因爲是我

22. sini nantuhvn jili be kiriha dabala,
你那行次的性子 我忍了罷咧

23. minqi tulgiyen,
除了我

24. yaya we se he seme
不拘是誰

25. sinde anabure aibi,
豈肯讓你

26. mini gisun be eje,
記着我說的

27. halaha de sain,
改了好啊

28. si jakan aimaka fuhali enqehen akv oqi,
你方纔要是總沒能奈的

29. geli emu hendure babi,
又有一說

30. jeqi kemuni bahara etuqi kemuni mutere ergide bikai,
還在個得吃能穿的一邊

31. urui majige jabxaki be baime yaburengge
只管要佔小便宜

32. ai turgun,
是什麼緣故

33. enggiqi bade niyalma simbe yasa niowanggiyan serakvn.
背地裡 人不說你眼皮子淺嗎

Section 34: Why Did I Help?

1. We qihanggai ini baita de danaki sembihe,
誰情願去管他的事來着

2. bi serengge hoqikosaka boode tere niyalma kai,
我是好好家裡坐着的人

3. i aibideri ulan ulan i daqila nakv,
他從那裡灣轉打聽着

4. mimbe tere niyalma be takambi seme,
我認得那個人

5. nurhvme ududu mudan jihe,
一連來了好幾次

6. mini baru age mini ere baita fita sinde akdahabi,
向我說阿哥我這一件事作定仗着你了

7. xadambi seme ainara,
就說乏些可麼樣呢

8. gosiqi mini funde gisurereo seme,
要疼愛替我說說

9. fisai amala dahalahai aika mimbe sindambi sembio,
在背後跟着肯放嗎

10. mini dere daqi uhuken be,
我起根兒臉軟

11. si tengkime sarangge,
你狠知道

12. weri uttu hafirabufi niyakvn hengkin i baimbi ni,
人家這樣的着急跪拜央求

13. ai hendume yokto akv i amasi unggimbi,
怎麼好意思的叫他無趣兒回去呢

14. anatame banjinarakv ofi,
因爲推脫不開

15. tuttu bi alime gaifi,
我所以應承了

16. tere guqu de giyan giyan i hafukiyame alaha,
明明白白的通告訴那個朋友了

17. gvnihakv ini emhun i baita waka,
不成望不是他一個人的事

18. niyalma geren mayan tatabumbi seme alime gaihakv,
說人多掣肘沒肯應承

19. tede bi kemuni iqixame gisureki sembihe,

因此我還要看光景說來着

20. amala gvnifi,
後來想了一想

21. joo,
說罷呀

22. baita i arbun be tuwaqi,
看事情樣子

23. maribume muterakv kai,
不能挽回

24. yasa niqu nakv ergeleme alime gaisu sere kooli geli bio,
豈有盯着眼睛壓派着叫人應承的理呢

25. uttu ofi,
故此

26. bi amasi inde mejige alame genehe de
我回去告訴他個信

27. elemangga ini baita be efujehe seme,
反倒說我壞了他的事

28. mini baru dere waliyatambi,
望着我撩臉子

29. absi koro,
好虧心

30. saha biqi,
早知道

31. aiseme gisurembihe ai jojin biheni.
無緣無故爲什麼去說來着吭

Section 35: An Awkward Situation

1. age si teng seme uttu mararangge,
阿哥你這樣固辭的光景

2. bi yala sesulame wajirakv,
我不勝駭然

3. mimbe jihengge sitaha seme
說我來的遲了

4. uttu arbuxambio,
這們個舉動嗎

5. eiqi adarameo,
還是怎麼樣呢

6. ai i uquri hono ta seme feliyembime,

素常尚且不時的行走

7. sakda niyalma i sain inenggi,
老家兒的好日子

8. bi elemangga jiderakv oqi
我倒不來

9. guqu sere de aibi,
如何算是朋友呢

10. oron sarkvngge tumen yargiyan,
實在的總不知道

11. unenggi saqi,
果然知道

12. yala onggolo jiqi aqambihe,
當真的該預先來

13. mini beye biqi fulu akv,
雖說是有我不多

14. akv oqi, ekiyehun akv biqibe,
沒我不少

15. sini funde antahasa be tuwaxaqi inu sain kai,
替你待待客也好啊

16. te biqibe, wesihun niyaman hvnqihin i benjihe sain jaka,
即如貴親戚送來的好東西

17. ai yadara,
少什麼呢

18. gvniqi jeme wajirakv kai,
想來吃不了的

19. mini ser sere majige jaka be geli dabufi gisureqi ombio,
我這些微的一點東西 又何足掛齒

20. tuttu seme inu mini emu gvnin kai,
然而也是我一點心啊

21. ai gelhun akv urunakv sakda niyalma be jefu sere,
那裡敢說必定請老人家吃呢

22. damu majige angga isiqi
但只略嘗嘗

23. uthai mimbe gosiha,
就是疼了我了

24. mini jihe gvnin inu wajiha,
我來的意思也完了

25. si emdubei bargiyarakv oqi,

你只管不收

26. bi eiqi ubade tereo,
我還是在這裡坐着呀

27. amasi genereo,
還是回去呢

28. yargiyan i mimbe mangga de tabuhabi.
實在叫我爲難了啊

Section 36: Reading the Right Books!

1. bithe tuwaki seqi hafu buleku be tuwa,
要看書看通鑑

2. taqin fonjin nonggibumbi,
長學問

3. julgei baita be ejeme gaifi,
記得了古來的事情

4. sain ningge be alhvdame yabure,
以好的爲法

5. ehengge be targaqun obure oqi
以不好的爲戒

6. beye gvnin de ambula tusangga,
於身心大有益啊

7. julen bithe serengge,
小說

8. gemu niyalmai banjibuha oron akv gisun,
都是人編的沒影兒的話

9. udu minggan minggan debtelin tuwaha seme
就是成千本的看了

10. ai baita,
中什麼用

11. niyalma hono dere jilerxeme niyalma de donjibume hvlambi,
人還皮着臉念給人聽

12. tere gurun i forgon de
那一國的時候

13. wei emgi udu mudan afaha,
合誰上過幾次陣

14. tere loho i saqiqi,
那個用刀砍

15. ere gida i sujaha,

這個用鎗架

16.ere gida i tokoqi,

這個用鎗刺

17.tere loho i jailabuha,

那個用刀搪

18.burulaha sehede

要說是敗了

19.solime gajihangge,

請來的

20.gemu tugi qi jidere,

都是雲裡來

21.talman deri genere,

霧裡去

22.fa bahanara enduri se,

會法術的神仙

23.orho hasalafi morin ubaliyambi,

剪草變馬

24.turi sofi niyalma kvbulimbi sembi,

撒豆變人

25.iletu holo gisun bime,

明明是謊話

26.hvlhi urse yargiyan baita obufi

糊塗人們當作真事

27.menekesaka amtanggai donjimbi,

獸頭獸腦 有滋有味的聽

28.sara bahanara niyalma sabuha de,

有識見的人看見

29.basure teile akv,

不止笑話

30.yargiyan i eimeme tuwambi kai,

實在厭煩啊

31.ede gvnin fohodofi ainambi.

這上頭用心作什麼呢

Section 37: Living a Simple life

1. age si donjihao,

阿哥你聽見了嗎

2. gisun i ujan xala de

他那話頭話屑的口氣

3. gemu mimbe hoilashvn
都刻薄我

4. seme yekerxembi,
說穿的曹少

5. bi bardanggilarangge waka,
不是我誇口

6. tere serengge,
他呀

7. teniken juse kai,
是個奶黃未退的小孩子

8. giyanakv udu inenggi siteku,
能幾日的溺精

9. ere qeni sara baita waka mujangga,
這也果然不是他們知道的事啊

10. iqe etuku serengge,
新衣服

11. inu emu baita sita de etuqi aqarangge,
該當有事情的時候 穿的

12. mini ere bai an i eturengge kai,
我這不過是平常穿的啊

13. majige ferengge de aibi,
舊些何妨

14. uthai majige manaha de geli aibi,
就破些又何妨

15. haha i erdemu akv jalin
因爲沒有漢子的本事

16. giruqi aqambidere,
可恥罷咧

17. eture eturakv de,
穿不穿

18. ai holbobuha babi,
有什麼關係的去處

19. te biqibe,
即如

20. bi udu sain ningge eturakv biqibe,
我雖然不穿好的

21. gvnin dolo elehun,
心裡卻安然

22. adarame seqi
怎麼說呢

23. niyalma de giohoxome bairakv,
不求告人

24. bekdun edelerakv,
不欠債負

25. ere uthai giquke nasaquka sere ba akv,
這就沒有可恥可愁的去處

26. aika qeni gese asihata be oqi,
要像他們那樣少年

27. mini yasai hoxo de inu daburakv kai,
我眼脊角裡也不夾呀

28. damu ginqihiyan ningge etufi maimadame
只知道穿着華麗衣服

29. gohodoro be sara dabala,
搖搖擺擺的充體面罷咧

30. haha i erdemu taqire be sambio,
知道學漢子的本事麼

31. tentekengge udu gequheri junggin i hvsibuha seme,
那個樣子的就着蟒緞錦緞裏了

32. ai ferguwequke,
有什麼奇處

33. umesi buya fusihvn,
極下賤

34. yasa faha akv urse,
沒眼珠兒的人們

35. balai febgiyeme,
胡說夢話的樣

36. imbe derengge wesihun seme,
說他體面尊貴

37. onqohon maktafi tuwara dabala,
仰望着罷了

38. bi terebe lakiyara golbon sembikai.
我叫他是罣衣裳的架子啊

Section 38: An Irresponsible Servant

1. tere bithe be gajihao,
那個書拿來了嗎

2. kemuni gajire unde,
還沒取來呢

3. webe takvraha,
使喚誰去了

4. ertele hono jiderakv,
這早晚還不來

5. terebe unggifi ganabuha,
打發某人取去了

6. neneme, be imbe gene seqi,
先我們叫他去

7. i meni gisun be fonjimbio,
他肯問我們的話嗎

8. ebi habi akv,
沒精打采的

9. erin xun be tookaha,
耽擱時候

10. emdubei jibgexembi,
只管延遲

11. amala age i gisun bi sere jakade
後來說有阿哥的話

12. teni ebuhu sabuhv genehebi,
纔急忙去

13. emu yohi duin dobton wakao,
一部不是四套麼

14. ekexeme saksime genefi,
慌速去了

15. damu ilan dobton gajiha,
只拿了三套來

16. tede emu dobton melebuhe.
遺漏了一套

17. si jai hvdun gene,
說你再快着去

18. akvqi guwelke,
不然仔細

19. age jihe manggi,

阿哥來了

20. si nikqaha seme bodo,
你打算着要吃虧

21. sere de, elemangga meni alahangge, hvlhi, getuken akv,
他倒說我們告訴的糊塗不明白

22. ai wei seme gasahai genehe,
怎長怎短的抱怨着去了

23. tetele kemuni jidere unde,
至今還沒來

24. niyalma takvrafi imbe okdobuki seqi,
要差人迎他去呢

25. geli jugvn de jurqenjere ayoo sembi,
又恐怕走岔了路

26. ere gese bulqakv jaka geli bini,
這樣的滑東西也有呢

27. urunakv ya simengge bade efime genehe dabala,
必定往那個熱鬧地方頑去了罷咧

28. qiralame jafatarakv oqi ainaha seme banjinarakv,
要不嚴嚴的管或斷然不行

29. jihe manggi
來了的時候

30. huthufi nixa emu jergi ura tvqi
捆起来屁股上重重的打一頓

31. teni sain,
纔好 .

32. akvqi,
不然

33. taqiha manggi tuwara ba akv ombi.
慣了他就不堪了

Section 39: To Help a Friend

1. age de emu baita yanduqi,
託阿哥一件事

2. baibi angga juwara de manggaxambi,
只是難張口

3. turgun ainu seqi,
甚麼緣故呢

4. baiha mudan jaqi labdu ohobi,

求的遭數太多了

5. damu sinde bairakv oqi,
只是不求你

6. sinqi tulgiyen
除你之外

7. gvniqi mini ere baita be muteburengge akv,
想來沒有能成全我這個事的啊

8. uttu ofi simbe alixabume jihe,
因此煩瑣你來了

9. si tere baitai jalin jihengge wakao,
你不是爲那一件事情來的麼

10. inu,
是

11. age aide bahafi saha,
阿哥怎麼得知道了

12. eqimari sini ahvn uthai minde henduhebi,
今日早晨你阿哥就望我說了

13. osohon budai erinde,
小飯時的時候

14. bi emu mudan genehe,
我去過一次

15. uksa ini boode akv de teisulebuhe,
忽然遇見他不在家

16. inenggi dulin ome,
纔交晌午

17. bi geli isinaha,
我又到去了

18. qin i boode isinara onggolo
未到他上屋以前

19. uthai kaka faka injeqere jilgan be donjihabi,
就聽見喧笑的聲氣

20. tede bi fa i hooxan be usihibufi
我把窗上的紙溼破

21. sangga deri dosi tuwaqi,
從窗戶眼兒往裡看

22. ere tede darabumbi,
你給我拿酒

23. tere ede bederebumbi,

242

我給你回鍾
24. kvthvme omime wenjehebi,
攢在一處吃熱了
25. dosiki sembihe,
原要進去來
26. kejine takarakv guqu bisire jakade,
因有好些不認識的朋友
27. weri omire amtan be tuhebufi ainambi,
衝散人家吃酒的趣味作什麼呢
28. tuttu bi beye goqime tuqike,
所以我抽身出來了
29. booi urse sabufi alanaki serede,
家下人看見要告訴去
30. bi ekxeme gala lasihime ilibume,
我急忙擺手攔住了
31. si ume ekxere,
你別急
32. bi qimari farhvn suwaliyame genefi,
我明日黑早去
33. tede xanggatai gisureqi wajiha.
向他說妥當就完了

Section 40: Traveling Faraway

1. si kemuni jurara undeo,
你還沒起身麼
2. yamji qimari jurambi,
早晚起身
3. aqiha fulmiyen eiten gemu giyan fiyan i dasatame wajiha,
馱子行李諸凡都整理妥畢了
4. damu kunesun i menggun kemuni eden,
只是盤纏銀子還短
5. tasha be jafarangge ja,
擒虎易
6. niyalma de bairengge mangga sehe gisun be,
告人難的話
7. enenggi teile teni akdaha,
我今日才信了
8. dere felefi,

捨着臉

9. ba bade juwen gaiqi

各處借貸

10. baharakv,

不得

11. arga akv ofi,

因沒法兒

12. age i jakade jihe,

阿哥跟前來了

13. menggun oqibe,

或銀子

14. damtun oqibe

或當頭

15. minde majige aisilarao,

求幫我些

16. amasi jihe manggi

回來的時候

17. beye madagan be bodome toodame buki,

本利算着還罷

18. jabxan de sini jihengge erde,

幸而你來的早

19. majige sitabuqi

畧遲些

20. inu amqaburakv ombi,

也趕不上

21. jakan tokso qi udu yan menggun gajiha,

方纔屯裡拿了幾兩銀子來

22. kemuni baitalara unde,

還沒有用呢

23. si dulin gamafi takvra,

你拿一半去使

24. qai omiha manggi,

吃了茶

25. dengnefi sinde bukini,

秤了給你

26. si ere tuktan mudan bigarame yabumbi wakao,

你不是初次出外麼

27. inu,

是
28. sinde emu babe alaki,
我告訴你此話
29. goromime yabure doro,
遠行的道理
30. guquse de hvwaliyasun dele,
朋友們裡頭以和爲上
31. jai fejergi,
待下呢
32. alban urse be tuku doko seme faksalarakv,
官人們不必分內外
33. emu adali gosi,
一樣的愛惜
34. uthai menggun bahara jiha butara ba bihe seme,
就有得銀子掙錢財的去處
35. dere oyonggo,
臉面要緊
36. ume gala golmin ojoro,
別手長了
37. tuttu ohode,
要是那樣
38. labdu gebu algin de holbobuhabi,
於聲名大有關係
39. age i jombuhangge
阿哥提撥的
40. aisin gu i gese gisun kai,
金玉一樣的話呀
41. bi ufuhu de ulime fahvn de falime ejeki.
我牢託肘腸罷

Section 41: A Good Harvest

1. age atanggi tokso qi jihe,
阿哥幾時從屯裡來的
2. bi isinjifi kejine inenggi oho,
我到了好些日子了
3. age jihe be fuhali oron donjihakv,
阿哥來我總沒有聽見
4. donjiha biqi,

要聽見

5. inu tuwanjimbihe,
也來瞧來着

6. musei tehe falga enqu
嗻們住的方向不同

7. geli alban beye,
又是官身子

8. donjihakvngge giyan dabala,
聽不見是該當罷咧

9. suweni usin aibide bi,
你們地畝在那裡

10. birai qargi ba jeo i harangga bade bi,
住河那邊霸州所屬的地方

11. huenhe bira wakao,
不是渾河嗎

12. inu, huenhe bira,
是 渾河

13. ere aniya tubai jeku antaka,
今年那裡的莊稼如何

14. sain,
好

15. umesi elgiyen,
狠豐盛

16. ambula bargiyahabi,
大收了

17. neneme bisaka sere
先說潦了

18. geli hiyaribuha sere tere
又說旱了

19. gemu yoro gisun,
都是謠言

20. akdaqi ojorakv,
信不得

21. gvwa haqin be aisembi,
何必說別的

22. sahaliyan turi hvda mujakv ja seqina,
黑豆只說着實賤罷

23. juwan udu jiha de emu moro hiyase bahambi,

十幾個錢得一升

24. utala aniya inu ere gese akv bihe,
這幾年也沒像這們樣的

25. yargiyvn,
真嗎

26. mujangga,
果然

27. age jai aika booi niyalma takvraqi,
阿哥再要使喚家裡人去

28. mini funde udu hule sahaliyan turi udabureo,
叫替我買幾石黑豆

29. udu yan menggun salibure babe hengkileme
折多少銀子

30. bodofi minde alakini,
扣算了告訴我

31. bi da udaha ton i songkoi age de menggun benjibure,
我照原買的數目叫給阿哥送銀子來

32. inu,
是啊

33. sini boode ududu morin hvwaitahabi kai,
你家栓着好幾匹馬

34. ere giyan ningge,
這是該的

35. musei ubade mangga hvdai udara anggala,
與其喈們這裡拿貴價兒買

36. tubaqi udafi gajiqi ubui jabxan bahambikai.
從那裡買了拿了來加倍的便宜啊

Section 42: A Sight-seeing

1. qananggi meni udu nofi,
前幾日我們幾個人

2. ai sargaxambi,
什麼是遊頑

3. fuhali sui tuwaha kai,
竟受了罪了

4. hoton tuqifi,
出了城

5. jingkini jugvn be yaburakv oso nakv,

放着正經道路不走

6. feme mudalime aibide genere be sarkv,
不知混繞到那裡去了

7. jugvn i unduri aname fonjihai
沿路問着

8. arkan seme kakv de isinaha,
將將的到了閘口跟前

9. jahvdai de tefi,
就坐上船

10. ishunde gisurendume,
彼此說着話

11. omiqame,
吃着酒

12. dung gao sere ilhai yafan de isinafi,
趕到東皋花園

13. geli amasi kakv de isinjitele,
又回到閘口上

14. aifini xun dabsihabi,
早已日平西了

15. buda jeme wajime,
纔吃完了飯

16. bi uthai agese yoki,
我就說阿哥們走吧

17. muse gemu yafahan kutule
喒們都是步行家裡人

18. sandalabuhangge geli kejine goro seqi,
離的又狠遠

19. fahame te nakv,
實排排的坐着

20. axxara ba inu akv,
動也不動

21. amala xun dosire hamika be sabufi,
後來見日頭將入了

22. teni morilafi haqihiyame amasi jimbi,
纔騎上馬 急着回來

23. yaluhai guwali de isinaha biqi,
到了關廂裡

24. buruhun i biyai elden gemu sabuha,

248

恍惚看見月色了

25. hoton i dorgiqi tuqike niyalma
城裡頭出來的人

26. gemu hasa amqame,
都叫快趕

27. duka emu gargan dasihabi sere jakade,
掩了一扇門了

28. gvnin i dolo ele kexehe,
心裡更着了急

29. morin dabkime emu ergen i feksime
加着鞭子催着馬一氣兒跑着趕

30. amqahai dubeheqi amqabuha,
趕上了個末尾兒

31. meni beyese arkan dosinjihabe,
我們自己雖然將將的進來了

32. booi urse sibxa tutafi,
家裡人邋在老遠的

33. gemu tule yaksibuha,
都關在外頭了

34. yala amtangga i genehe,
實在竟是有滋有味的去

35. usatala amasi jihe seqina.
傷心失意的回來了

Section 43: A Condescending Man

1. teike bi yamulafi, amasi jidere de,
方纔我上了衙門回來

2. kejine aldangga qi kunggur seme emu feniyen i niyalma
從老遠的轟的一羣人

3. morilahai ebsi jihe,
騎着馬往這們來了

4. hanqi isinju nakv,
到了跟前

5. qinqilame emgeri takaqi,
細認了一認

6. musei fe adaki tere,
是喈們的舊街坊某人

7. etuhe yaluhangge absi saikan,

穿的騎的好壯觀

8. tarhvn morin, weihuken furdehe,
肥馬輕裘

9. qira xehun xahvn,
面貌軒昂

10. ambula tulejehe,
大胖了

11. mimbe sabure jakade,
看見我

12. fonjire ba inu akv,
問也不問

13. dere qasi forofi,
把臉往那們一紐

14. abka be xame tuwame duleke,
望着天過去了

15. nergin de bi uthai terebe hvlame ilibufi,
彼時我就要叫住

16. umesileme girubuki sembihe,
着實的羞辱他來着

17. amala gvniqi
後來想了一想

18. joo ainambi,
說罷作什麼

19. i mimbe hersere de,
他理我

20. bi uthai derengge sembio,
我就體面了嗎

21. i gvwa be holtombi dere,
他哄別人罷咧

22. age si aika sarkv,
阿哥你豈有不知道的

23. ilan aniyai onggolo,
三年以前

24. muse i ubade
喒們這裡

25. tere geli we bihe,
他又是誰來着呢

26. fungsan yadahvn kai,

250

窮的腥氣

27. erde jeke manggi
早起吃了

28. yamjingge be bodombi,
打算晚上的

29. inenggidari hergire fayangga adali,
終日遊魂一樣

30. omihon be kirime,
餓着肚子

31. ba bade faqihiyaxame,
各處張羅

32. emu dangxan orho tunggiyeme bahaqi,
拾着一根草

33. gemu hihan ningge,
都是希罕的

34. emu inenggi emu siran i juwe ilan mudan meni boode jifi,
一日至少也來我們家裡兩三遍

35. erebe bairakv oqi,
不是尋這個

36. terebe nandambi,
就是尋那個

37. miningge i ai jekekv,
我的東西他什麼沒吃過

38. sabka simibuhai gemu manaha,
筷子都咂明了

39. te niyalma de bairakv oho seme,
如今說求不着人了

40. emu qimari andande uthai gvwaliyafi fe be onggohobi,
一旦之間變的忘了舊了

41. beyebe beye tukiyeqengge waka,
不是自己擡舉自己

42. ini nantuhvn be we geli yasa de dabumbi.
他那行次 誰又把他放在眼裡呢

Section 44: A Beautiful Snow Scene

1. sikese dobori absi beikuwen,
昨日夜裡好冷

2. amu tolgin de geqehei getehe

睡夢裡凍醒了

3. abka gereme,
天一亮

4. bi ekxeme ilifi,
我急着起來

5. uqe neifi tuwaqi,
開了房門看

6. dule xahvn ambarame nimarambi nikai,
原來白花花的下了大雪了

7. buda jefi
吃了飯

8. inenggishvn oho manggi
傍晌午的時候

9. labsan labsan i kiyalmame ele amba oho,
大片飄飄雪越下大了

10. bi ere baita akv de
我想着這無事的上頭

11. adarame bahafi emu niyalma jifi
怎麼地一個人來

12. gisureme teqeki serede,
坐着說說話兒

13. booi niyalma dosifi niyalma jihe seme alara jakade,
家裡人進來告訴說 人來了

14. mini dolo se selaha,
我心裡狠爽快了

15. emu derei nure booha be dagilabuha,
一面叫收拾酒菜

16. emu derei qing sere emu fileku yaha dabuha,
一面點了一盆旺火

17. tereqi deote be helneme gajitala,
趕請了兄弟們來

18. nure booha en jen belheme jabduha,
酒餚早已齊備了

19. tukiyefi elhei omiqaha,
抬上來慢慢的吃着酒

20. hida be den hetefi tuwaqi,
高高的捲起簾子來看

21. nimanggi arbun

雪的光景

22. yaya qi bolgo saikan,
比諸樣的都清雅

23. sor sar sembi,
紛紛的印着

24. abka na tumen jaka
天地萬物

25. gemu der seme xeyen oho,
都煞白了

26. tuwahai ele yenden nerebufi,
看着益發高興了

27. sain de gurire endebuku be halara doro be gisurehei,
講論遷善改過的道理

28. yamji buda jefi,
直到吃了晚飯

29. dengjan dabuha manggi
點了燈

30. teni faqaha.
纔散了

Section 45: Don't Mess with Him

1. simbe tuwaqi
看起你來

2. bai angga qanggi,
只是寡嘴

3. giru getuken gese biqibe,
外面雖像明白
[Your] appearance looks clever,

4. dolo surhvn akv,
心裡不豁亮

5. tere sinde latunjirakv oqi,
他不尋趁你來

6. uthai sini jabxan kai,
就是你的便宜

7. si terebe neqifi ainambi,
你惹他作什麼呢

8. sain gisun be umai donjirakv,
總不聽好話

9. aimaka qargiqi tokoxoro adali
倒像神鬼指使一樣
10. murime genefi naranggi
牛強着去了
11. giruqun tuwabuhabi,
倒底受了辱磨了
12. tere xakxan be si we sembi,
那個刁頭你說他是誰
13. ja akv,
不非輕
14. gebungge nimequke niyalma kai,
有名的利害人啊
15. atanggi niyalma de ba bumbihe,
從幾時給人留分兒來着
16. tede daljakv baita oqi ombi,
與他無涉的則可
17. majige uxabure tatabure ba biqi,
有一點妨礙的去處
18. yaya we de seme ba burakv kai,
不拘誰不給留分兒啊
19. fakjilahai urunakv giyan be ejelefi,
疊着勁兒必要佔住理
20. jabxaha manggi teni nakambi,
得了便宜才休歇
21. je ere kai,
這不是麼
22. jiduji deduhe tasha be dekdebu nakv,
倒底把臥着的老虎哄起來
23. kangsiri foribufi,
碰了釘子
24. munahvn i amasi jihe,
敗興回來了
25. ere ai yokto,
這是什麼趣兒呢
26. teifungge tuherakv,
可是說的有柺棍不跌跤
27. gebungge ufararakv sehebi,
有名望不失着

28. sini emhun saha teile oqi,
光你一個人知道

29. aibide isinambi,
能到那裡呢

30. ai oqibe,
任憑怎樣

31. bi sinqi lakqafi udu se ahvn kai,
我比你長着好幾歲

32. unenggi yabure giyan oqi,
要果然該行的

33. sini gvnin de kimqime giyangnarakv oki seme,
就是你心裡不要講究

34. bi hono jombume haqihiyame gene sembikai,
我還提撥催着你去呢

35. fudarame ilibure kooli bio.
豈有倒攔阻你的規矩嗎

Section 46: Dealing with a Drunk

1. We ini baru ere tere sehe,
誰望着他講長講短了

2. ini gisun de boxobufi, mimbe gisurebumbikai,
被他的話逼着叫我說呀

3. gvwa be daldaqi ojoro dabala,
矇蔽得別人罷咧

4. sinde gidaqi ombio,
瞞藏得你嗎

5. aniya araha qi ebsi,
從過年以來

6. i aika alban de yabuha babio,
還走了什麼差事了嗎

7. enenggi aibideri omifi jio nakv,
今日起那裡吃了酒

8. dosinjime jaka,
剛一進來

9. ara,
唉呀

10. bi ainu teni simbe sabumbi sembi,
我怎麼纔見你啊

255

11. tuttu oqi,
要是那樣

12. bi tookan akv,
我不脫空

13. daruhai biyalame sini fonde alban de dangnahangge,
成月家裡常替你當差的

14. elemangga waka baha,
倒得了不是了

15. ere gisun de,
這個話上

16. mini jili uthai monggon i da deri oho,
我的性子就到了脖梗兒上了

17. enenggi aiseme gisurembi,
今日說甚麼

18. qimari jai bolgoki,
明日再決勝負罷

19. age si ainu ini gese sasa temxendumbi,
阿哥你怎麼望他一般一配的爭啊

20. tere tuttu yobodome taqiha be,
他那樣頑慣了的

21. si aika sarkv nio,
你有什麼不知道的呢

22. gvniqi,
想來

23. geli suisime omiha,
又是飲的撒酒瘋了

24. damu sabuhakv donjihakv ton okini,
只當是沒看見 沒聽見是呢

25. aiseme gisurembi,
說什麼

26. age si sarkv,
阿哥你不知道

27. ere gese ja de ja, mangga de mangga sere niyalma de,
像這樣丁是丁 卯是卯的人

28. ba buqi i huwekiyembi,
要給他留個分兒 他就高興了

29. si ine mene bi yobodombi herqun akv de gisun okjoslaha seqi,
你率性說我是頑不覺的話冒失了

30. niyalma embiqi waliyame gamambi dere,

256

人或者撩的開手罷咧

31. qira fuhun unenggilembi kai,
一連怒氣認真的說呀

32. we inde ombi,
誰合他過的去呢

33. age si ume fanqara,
阿哥你別生氣

34. bi ere suihutu be dalda bade gamafi,
我把這醉行次帶在僻靜處

35. yasa korime,
剜着眼睛

36. emu jergi girubume beqefi,
辱磨他一番

37. sinde ki fulhaki.
給你出氣罷

Section 47: A Cheater

1. tuktan imbe aqaha de,
起初見了他

2. niyalmai baru dembei habqihiyan kvwalar sembi,
望着人很親熱響快

3. terei banin eldengge fiyangga,
他的相貌軒昂

4. angga senqehe daqun sain,
口齒便利

5. mujakv buyeme tuwaha,
看着很羨慕了

6. adarame bahafi ini baru guquleme seme,
想着怎麽合他相與呢

7. angga qi tuheburakv maktambihe,
不住嘴的誇獎來着

8. amala feliyefi,
後走上了

9. emu bade fumerehei,
一處混混着

10. ini yabuha ele baita be kimqiqi,
細體察他所行的事情

11. dule emu tondokon niyalma waka biheni,

原來不是一個正經人

12. fiyanarara mangga holo qanggi,
駕虛弄空

13. terei yargiyan taxan be aibideri nambumbi,
他的真假 那裡撈得着呢

14. tuttu bime gvnin butemji,
而且心裡陰險

15. niyalma de sain jugvn bahaburakv,
不給人好道兒走

16. anggai ergide sini baru banjire sain sere gojime,
口裡雖說是向你好

17. enggiqi bade tuheburengge ja akv,
背地裡陷害的不輕

18. terei hvbin de dosika sehede sarbaitala ombi,
要入在他的圈套兒裡 就是一個仰面筋斗

19. te biqibe, ini gala de joqibuha niyalma, aika komso sembio,
即如在他手裡坑害的人還少嗎

20. simhun bukdafi toloqi wajirakv kai,
指不勝屈啊

21. ede guquse imbe jondombihede,
因此朋友們提起他來

22. gemu emekei seme,
都說是可怕呀

23. uju fintarakvngge akv,
無有不頭疼的

24. yarha i boqo oilo,
豹的顏色在浮皮

25. niyalmai boqo dolo sehengge,
人的成色在內裡的話

26. qohome ere gese niyalma be henduhebi,
特說的是這樣的人啊

27. yala mini jabxan,
實在是我的僥倖

28. gvnin werixefi aldangga oburakv seqi,
要不留心遠着他

29. ini geoden de tuhenerakv biheo.
有不落在他的局騙裡頭的嗎

258

Section 48: A Stupid Man

1. Tumen jaka qi umesi wesihun ningge be niyalma sembi,
比萬物最尊貴的叫作是人

2. niyalma ofi,
為人

3. sain ehe be ilgarakv,
要不辨好歹

4. doro giyan be faksalarakv oqi,
不分道理

5. ulha qi ai enqu,
与畜類何異

6. ne biqibe guqusei doro,
即如朋友們的道理

7. si bi ishunde kunduleqi,
你我彼此相敬

8. sain akvn,
豈不好麼

9. jaqi ohode aidahaxame latunju nakv,
動不動的尋了來發豪横

10. dere ura be tuwarakv,
不顧頭尾

11. anggai iqi balai lasihidame toorengge,
混捧掇信口兒罵

12. beyei bengsen arambio,
算了自己的本事了嗎

13. adarame,
是怎麼的啊

14. banjiha demun be tuwaqina,
看那長的怪樣兒是呢

15. hefeli wakjahvn
鼓着個大肚子

16. fuhali beliyen wajiha
竟是個獸人

17. bime xuqileme taqi nakv,
又學充懂文脈

18. absi niyalma be yali madabumbi,
好叫人肉麻呀

19. indahvn i gese ger sere be,

像狗齜着牙叫一樣

20. niyalma gemu ek sefi donjirakv oho kai,
人都厭煩不聽了

21. majige niyalmai gvnin biqi,
要略有人心的

22. inu sereqi aqambihe,
也該知覺來着

23. kemuni jilerxeme,
還恬不知恥

24. aimaka we imbe saixaha adali,
倒像誰誇他的一樣

25. ele huwekiyehengge,
益發興頭起來

26. ainu,
是怎麼說呢

27. erei ama inu emu jalan i haha seme yabumbihe kai,
他的老子也是一輩子行走的漢子來着

28. aide sui arafi,
那上頭作了孽

29. ere gese fusi banjiha,
養了這樣的賤貨

30. ai,
可嘆啊

31. waliyaha,
撩了的了

32. hvturi gemu ini amai fayangga gamaha
福分都叫他老子的魂靈兒帶了去了

33. ere uthai ini dube oho kai,
這也就是他的盡頭處了

34. geli wesiki mukdeki seqi ainahai mutere.
再要想陞騰未必能了

Section 49: Abiding the Law

1. musei dolo kai,
喒們裡頭

2. si aika gurun gvwao,
你還是外人麼

3. mimbe tuwaqi,

瞧我

4. uthai xuwe dosimbi dere,
就直進來

5. geli hafumbure de ai ganaha,
又何必通報呢

6. duka de isinju nakv,
既到門口

7. uthai amasi genehengge,
就回去的

8. booi niyalma mimbe boode akv sehe gisun de ushahao,
家裡人說我不在家的話上惱了嗎

9. ainahao,
是怎麼樣呢

10. turgun be tuqibume alarakv oqi,
若不告訴出緣故來

11. ainambahafi sara,
怎麼地知道呢

12. ere uquri,
這一向

13. musei tere emu feniyen agese
喈們那一羣阿哥們

14. dahvme aqafi,
合着夥兒

15. jiha efire falan neihebi,
開了耍錢場兒了

16. jakan jifi
方繞來

17. gashvme garime,
起誓發願的

18. mimbe inu urunakv gene sembi,
也必定叫我去

19. mini beye xolo akv be, si sarkv aibi,
你豈不知道我不得空兒

20. teike teike alban isinjire be
一會一會兒的有差事

21. ai boljon,
如何定得呢

22. jai fafun xajin umesi qira,

再王法很緊

23. talu de emu baita tuqinjiqi,
偶然出來一件事

24. dere be absi obumbi,
把臉放在那裡呢

25. uttu ofi ushaqi hvi ushakini dabala,
因此惱就憑他惱去罷

26. bi jiduji genehekv,
我到底沒去

27. booi urse de henduhengge,
說給家裡人們

28. yaya we mimbe baihanjiqi,
不拘誰來找我

29. boode akv seme jabu sehe,
答應不在家

30. gvnihakv sini beye jihede,
不想你來了

31. dulba ahasi
懵懂奴才們

32. inu songkoi jabufi
也照樣的答應

33. unggi nakv,
打發去了

34. teni dosifi minde alaha,
纔進來告訴了我

35. tede bi ekxeme niyalma takvrafi amqabuqi,
所以我急着差人去趕

36. amqabuhakv serede,
說沒趕上

37. mini dolo labsa,
我心裡着實失望

38. yala absi yabsi ojoro be sarkv ohobi.
不知道要怎麼樣了

Section 50: Visiting the Grave

1. si qananggi yafan de waliyame genehe biheo,
你前日往園裡上墳去來着嗎

2. inu,

是 .

3. ainu enenggi teni jihe,
怎麼今日纔來

4. sandalabuhangge umesi goro,
相隔的很遠

5. ineku inenggi mudari amasi jiqi muterakv ofi,
因為當日不能打來回

6. tubade juwe dobori indehebi,
在那裡歇了兩夜

7. suqungga inenggi hoton i duka neire ishun uthai juraka,
頭一日 頂着城開就起了身

8. yamjitala yabufi teni isinaha,
直到晚上纔到去了

9. sikse buda dobofi,
昨日供了飯

10. geli emu dobori indehe,
又歇了一夜

11. enenggi alin jakarame,
今日東方明兒

12. uthai jurafi amasi jihe,
就起身回來了

13. jugvn de udelereqi tulgiyen,
路上除了打尖

14. majige teyehe ba inu akv,
也總沒歇息

15. arkan seme hoton i duka be amqabuha,
剛剛的趕上城門了

16. age gorokon bade umbume sindahangge,
阿哥在遠些的地方埋葬

17. udu sain baita biqibe
雖是好事

18. juse omosi de enqehen akv oqi,
要是子孫沒力量

19. erin de aqabume waliyara de mangga,
難按着時候上墳啊

20. eiqi ainara,
可怎麼說呢

21. fe yafan de fuhali ba akv oho,

舊園子總沒地方了

22. fengsi tuwara urse,
看風水的人們

23. gemu tere babe sain sere jakade,
都說那個地方好的上頭

24. teni tubade eifu kvwaran ilibuha,
纔在那裡立了墳院

25. eitereqibe,
總說了罷

26. muse biqi,
喒們有呢

27. bisire doro,
是有的道理

28. akv oqi,
沒有呢

29. akv i doro,
是沒的道理

30. ai haqin i hafirahvn suilashvn sehe seme,
憑他怎麼樣窄累

31. yafan de genefi,
也往園裡去

32. inu emu hvntahan arki hisalambi dere,
奠一鍾酒啊

33. juse omosi de isinaha manggi,
到了子孫們跟前

34. damu terei dekjire dekjirakv be hendure dabala,
只論有出息沒出息罷咧

35. aika tere gese geterakv juse banjiha sehede,
要是養了那樣不長進的兒子

36. ini beye uthai yafan de tekini,
他的身子就住在園裡

37. hono ainahai emu afaha hooxan jiha deijimbini.
還未必燒一張紙錢呢啊

Section 51: Being Caught in a Rain

1. ara,
哎呀

2. ere gese amba aga de aibide genehe bihe,

這樣大雨 往那裡去來着

3. hvdun dosi,
快進去

4. mini emu guqu akv oho,
我的一個朋友不在了

5. giran benefi jihe,
送了殯來了

6. eqimari abka tulhvxemeliyan,
今日早晨天陰陰的

7. agara muru biqibe,
雖有下雨的光景

8. inenggi dulin de isinafi
到了晌午

9. gehun gahvn galakabi,
很晴明了

10. amasi marifi yabure de tuwaqi,
回來走着看

11. tugi geli bombonofi yur seme sektehe,
又一片一片的鋪開稠雲了

12. tede bi booi urse i baru,
那上頭我望着家裡人說

13. ere abka faijume,
這天氣不妥當

14. hasa yabu,
快走

15. akvqi
不然

16. muse toktofi aga de amqabumbi kai seme,
嗒們一定要着雨啊

17. hendutele,
正說着

18. uthai xor seme agame deribuhe,
就刷刷的下起雨來了

19. age si hendu,
阿哥你說

20. xehun bigan de kai,
在漫荒地裡

21. aibide jailanambi,

265

往那裡去躲

22. nereku jangqi etume jabduhakv de,
雨衣氈褂子沒穿疊當

23. beyei gubqi xeketele usihibuhe,
渾身溼透了

24. hvwanggiyarakv,
不妨

25. mini etuku bi,
有我的衣裳

26. tuqibufi si hala,
拿出來你換

27. abka inu yamjiha,
天也晚了

28. qimari jai hoton i dolo dosi,
明日再進城去

29. meni ere koqo wai yafan de
我們這個幽僻彎曲的園子裡

30. sain jaka akv biqibe,
雖然沒有好東西

31. boode ujihe mihan niongniyaha kemuni udu fali bi,
家裡養的小豬兒鵝還有幾個

32. emu juwe wafi sinde ulebure,
宰一兩個給你吃罷

33. jetere be ai sembi,
別說是吃

34. damu ere gese beyebe tomoro sain ba bahaqi,
但得這樣的好地方棲身子

35. uthai jabxan kai,
就是便宜了

36. akvqi,
不然

37. aga be funtume yaburakv,
不冒着雨走

38. aika fa bio.
還有法子嗎

Chapter 3
sirame banjibuha nikan hergen i kamqibuha manju gisun oyonggo jorin bithe

Section 52 : Go Hunting

1. tuktan bi abalame genehede,
我初次打圍去
2. emu morin yalumbihebi,
騎的一匹馬
3. katararangge neqin,
顛的穩
4. feksirengge hvdun,
跑的快
5. jebele ashahai,
襯着撒袋
6. teni aba sarafi genehede,
纔放開圍走着
7. orhoi dorgiqi emu jeren feksime tuqike,
從草裡跑出一個黃羊来了
8. bi uthai morin be dabkime,
我就加着馬
9. beri darafi
拉開弓
10. emgeri gabtaqi,
射了一箭
11. majige amariha,
些微遲下了些
12. gala marifi niru gaire sidende,
回手纔要拔箭的時候
13. jeren i unqehen dube axxame,
那黃羊把尾巴繞了一繞
14. dartai andande,
轉眼之間
15. emu meifehe be dulefi,
就過了一個山坡子
16. alin antu ergi be baime wesihun iqi genehe,
徃山陽裡去了

17. unqehen dahalahai amqanaha biqi,
我跟着尾巴趕去

18. geli alin be dabame, boso ergi be wasime genehebi,
過了山又徃山背裡去了

19. tede bi morin be haqihiyahai hanqi amqanafi emgeri gabtaqi,
所以我加馬趕到跟前 射了一箭

20. geli uju be dabame duleke,
又從頭上過去了

21. gvnihakv qargiqi emu buhv fekesime ebsi jihe,
不想一個鹿從那邊徃這邊跑了來了

22. teni alin be dabame ishun jiderengge
纏過了山迎着來

23. tob seme mini gabtaha niru de goibufi
正中在我射的箭上

24. kub seme tuheke,
撲的一聲就跌倒了

25. yala yala injeku,
實在是個笑話兒

26. mayan sain,
彩頭好的呀

27. amqabuhangge turibuhe,
趕上的放跑了

28. murakvngge elemangga nambuha,
沒哨的倒得了

29. sarkv urse de alaqi,
若要是告訴那不知道的人

30. aimaka yasa gehun holtoro adali.
倒像睜着眼睛撒謊一樣

Section 53: Gambling

1. ara, si ainahabi,
哎呀你怎麼了

2. muse giyanakv udu biya aqahakv,
喈們沒見面能有幾個月

3. ai hvdun de,
怎麼這們快

4. salu xarapi,
鬍子白了

5. sakda fiyan gaiha,
有了老模樣了
6. age si mimbe angga sijirhvn seme ume wakaxara,
阿哥你別怪我的嘴直
7. urahilame donjiqi,
風聞說
8. si te jiha efire de dosifi,
你如今頑起錢來
9. utala bekedun araha sembi,
作了好些賬
10. yala oqi,
要是真
11. efiku waka kai,
可不是頑的呀
12. majige bargiyaha de sain,
料收着些纔好呢
13. ere gemu oron akv gisun niyalmai banjibuhangge,
這全是人編造的沒影兒的話
14. si akdarakv oqi,
你要不信
15. narhvxame fujurulaqina,
可細細的打聽是呢
16. ai gisun serengge,
什麼話
17. beye i yabuhangge ba, beye endembio,
自己走的自己不知道嗎
18. guquse gemu simbe leolehe be tuwaqi,
看起朋友們全議論你的來
19. sinde majige bifi dere,
你料有些兒罷
20. jiha efire de, ai dube,
頑錢啊 那是了手
21. lifa dosika sehede,
要說是貪進去了
22. ai bihe seme taksimbi,
就說是有什麼能存得住呢
23. wajime dubede weile daksin ararakv oqi,
終久不遭罪戾
24. uthai majige hede funqeburakv, boo boigon fulahvn wajifi,

269

即將產業蕩盡毫無所存之時

25. teni nakambi,
纔歇手呢

26. ere gesengge musei xan de donjiha yasa de sabuhangge,
像這樣的 嗒們的耳躲裡聽見 眼睛裡看見的

27. labdu akv biqibe,
雖然不多

28. absi akv tanggv funqehebi,
只少也有一百還多

29. si bi muse saha tuwaha guqu kai,
嗒們是知己的朋友呀

30. aika same tafularakv
要是明知不勸

31. wei guwanta seqi,
說與誰什麼相干

32. banjire sain serengge aide,
豈說得是相好嗎

33. ainame akv oqi,
要是沒有的事

34. sain dabala,
好罷咧

35. bi fujurulafi ainambi.
我打聽作什麼呢

Section 54: A Terrible Weather

1. sikse umai edun su akv,
昨日並沒風

2. abka hoqikosaka bihengge,
是好好的天氣来着

3. gaitai eherefi sohon xun i elden gemu fundehun ohobi,
清清亮亮的日色忽然變的冷颼颼的了

4. tede bi faijuma,
那個上我說

5. ayan edun dara isika,
大風要來了呀

6. edun dekedere onggolo,
乘着風還未起

7. muse yoki sefi,

嗻們走罷

8. beri beri faqafi
所以各自各自散了

9. boode isinarangge,
將到家裡

10. hoo seme amba edun dame deribuhe,
就亂起大風來了

11. mooi subehe edun de febume lasihibure asuki,
把樹梢刮的亂摔的聲音

12. absi ersun,
好醜聽

13. hvjime dahai,
吹哨子樣的一直響

14. dobori dulin otolo
刮到半夜裡

15. teni majige toroko,
纔料料的定了些

16. eqimari ebsi jiderede,
今日早起徃這裡來

17. jugvn giyaide yabure urse,
走着見街道上的人

18. gemu ilime muterakv,
全站不住

19. ho ha seme sujumbi,
喝喝哈哈的跑啊

20. bi aika edun i qashvn bihe biqi,
我要順着風来

21. hono yebe bihe,
還好来着

22. geli edun i ishun ojoro jakade,
又是迎着風的上頭

23. dere ai ulme tokoro i adali, qak qak sembi,
把臉凍的像針扎的一樣疼

24. gala simhun beberefi, xusiha jafara de gemu fakjin akv ohobi,
手指頭凍拘了 拿鞭子的勁全沒了

25. juliyaha qifenggu na de isinanggala,
吐的吐沫 將到地下

26. uthai juhene,

271

就凍成冰

27. katak seme meyen meyen i lakqambi,
跌的幾節子了

28. adada,
好冷啊

29. banjiha qi
有生以來

30. ebsi rere gese beikuwen be, we dulembuhe ni.
這樣的冷啊 誰經過来着呢

Section 55: Kung Fu Fighting

1. si sarkv,
你不知道

2. ini ere gemu se asihan, senggi sukdun etuhun i haran,
這全是他年輕血氣強壯的過失

3. udu mudan koro baha manggi,
吃過幾遭虧

4. ini qisui amtan tuhembikai,
他那高興自然就去了

5. aide saha seqi,
從什麼上知道了呢

6. bi daqi uthai basilara de mujakv amuran,
我從前就狠好鬧硬浪

7. mini emu mukvn i ahvn i emgi
和我一個戶中的阿哥

8. inenggidari urebumbihe,
每日在一處演習来着

9. mini ahvn i gidalahangge umesi mangga,
我的阿哥的長鎗耍的狠精

10. juwan udu niyalma sehe seme,
就說是十幾個人

11. ini beyede hanqi fimeqi ojorakv,
不能到他的跟前

12. uttu bime,
這樣的

13. hono emu mangga bata be uqarahabi,
後來還遇見一個對手呢

14. nakqu i boode jihe emu toksoi niyalma,

272

徃舅舅家來的一個屯裡的人

15. bethe doholon,
瘸着腿子

16. loho maksime bahanambi sembi,
會耍腰刀

17. juwe niyalma emu bade uqarafi,
他們二人會在一處

18. erdemu be qendeki seme,
要試試本事

19. teisu teisu agvra be gaiha manggi,
各自各自拿了軍器

20. mini age yasa de geli imbe dabumbio,
我的阿哥眼裡還有他来着嗎

21. anahvnjara ba inu akv,
也不謙讓一下

22. uthai gida be dargiyafi,
就顫動長鎗

23. niyaman jaka be baime emgeri gidalaha,
徃心窩裡一扎

24. tere doholon majige ekexerakv,
那個瘸子也不慌也不忙

25. elhe nuhan i jeyen exeme,
慢慢的拿刀斜磕一下

26. emgeri jailabume saqime ofi,
（爲了避開刀砍）382

27. gida i dube uthai mokso emu meyen genehe,
把長鎗的頭兒就磕折了一節子去了

28. gida be goqime jabdunggala
將抽鎗時

29. loho aifini monggon de sindaha,
那腰刀早已放在脖子上了

30. teni jailaki serede,
纔要躲時

31. monggon be hahvra nakv,

---

382 Originally there was no Chinese translation for the corresponding Manchu sentence. I added a Chinese translation to facilitate comprehension of Manchu text.

被刀把脖子纏住

32. lasihime emgeri fahara jakade,
跟着就要砍的上

33. ududu okson i dubede maktafi,
倒退了好幾步

34. kub seme tuheke,
噗的一聲就跌倒了

35. tereqi niyanqan bijafi,
從那個上把高興打斷

36. jai jai taqirakv oho,
再也不學了

37. erebe tuwaqi,
以此看來

38. abkai fejergi amba kai,
天下最大啊

39. mangga urse ai yadara.
能人豈少嗎

Section 56: A Beautiful Scenery

1. qananggi, be wargi alin de oihori
我们前日往西山裡去

2. sebjelehe bihe,
何等的快樂来着

3. inenggi xun de sargaxara efire be hono ai sembi,
白日裡遊頑的 說他作什麼

4. dobori oho manggi,
到了晚上

5. ele se selaha,
越發爽快了

6. meni udu nofi yamji buda jefi,
我們幾個人吃了晚飯

7. jahvdai de tehe manggi
坐上了船

8. goidahakv,
不多的時候

9. biya mukdefi
月已升高

10. gehun elden fosokongge,

274

光輝射照的

11. uthai inenggi xun i adali,
就像白日裡一樣

12. elhei xurubume
慢慢的撐着船

13. edun i iqi wasihvn genehei,
順着風去

14. alin i oforo be murime dulefi tuwaqi,
轉過山嘴子去一看

15. abka birai boqo fuhali ilgaburakv hvwai sembi,
竟是天水一色 幽靜匪常

16. yala alin genggiyen muke bolgo seqi ombi,
真可謂山青水秀

17. selbihei ulhv noho i xumin bade isinaha biqi,
又撐着船將到了蘆葦深處

18. holkonde jungken i jilgan yang seme edun i iqi xan de bahabure jakade,
忽然從順風裡聽見喈喈的鐘聲到了那個時候

19. tumen haqin i gvnin seolen ede isinjifi,
竟把那萬宗的思慮

20. uthai muke de oboho adali,
付與流水

21. geterembuhekvngge akv,
無有不乾乾淨淨了

22. udu jalan qi qolgorome tuqike enduri sehe seme,
雖說是超凡出世的神仙

23. manggai tuttu sebjelere dabala,
也不是那樣的樂罷咧

24. tuttu ofi
因是那樣

25. ishunde amtanggai omiqahai
彼此暢飲

26. herqun akv adarame gereke be gemu sarkv ohobi,
不知怎樣的天就亮了

27. niyalma seme jalan de banjifi,
人生在世

28. enteke genggiyen biya sain arbun giyanakv udu,
能遇見幾遭那樣的美景明月呢

29. untuhuri dulembumbi, hairakan akv semeo.
（徒然放過） 不可惜嗎

Section 57: Caught a Cold

1. si ainahabi,
你怎麼了

2. qira biyabiyahvn kob seme,
氣色煞白的

3. wasifi ere durun ohobi,
消瘦的這樣了

4. age si sarkv,
阿哥你有所不知

5. ere udu iennggi ulan fetere de wa su umesi ehe,
這幾日刨溝的氣味 狠不好

6. tere dade, geli gaitai xahvrun, holkonde halhvn
又搭着忽冷忽熱的上

7. fuhali toktohon akv,
竟沒有定準

8. tuttu ofi,
所以

9. niyalma gemu beyebe ujire an kemun baharakv,
人不能照常的將養身子

10. qananggi budai erinde
而且前日飯時

11. xahvruxaka bihengge,
是涼涼快快的来着

12. gaitai halhvn ofi, niyalma hamiqi ojorakv fathaxambi,
忽然叫人受不得煩躁的狠

13. beyei gubqi hvmbur seme nei tuqire jakade,
出了通身的汗的上

14. sijigiyan be sufi majige serguwexeki seme,
把袍子脫了涼快着

15. emu moro xahvrun qai omiha biqi,
喝了一碗涼茶的上

16. ilihai andande uthai [uju] nimeme deribuhe,
立刻的頭就疼起來了

17. oforo inu wanggiyanaha
鼻子也嚷了

18. bilha inu sibuha,
嗓子也啞了
19. beye tugi de tehe adali hvi sembi,
渾身發冷狠覺着昏沉了
20. sini beye teile waka,
並不是你一個人那樣的
21. mini beye inu asuru qihakv,
我的身子也有些不舒服
22. axxara be bambi,
懶怠動轉
23. jabxan de sikse jekengge omihangge be waqihiyame oksiha,
幸而昨日吃了的喝了的東西全吐了
24. akvqi enenggi inu katunjambi ojorakv oho,
不然今日也不能勉強来着
25. bi sinde emu sain arga taqibure
我教給你一個好方法兒
26. damu hefeli be omiholobu
把肚子餓着
27. komsokon i jefu,
少吃東西
28. ume labdulara,
不要多貪了
29. tuttu ohode
要是那樣的時候
30. uthai majige xahvraka seme,
就是着點冷兒
31. inu ainaha seme hvwanggiyarakv.
也是再無妨的呀

Section 58: Being Haunted

1. suweni bakqin de bisire tere emu falga boo antaka,
你們對門的那一所房子怎麽樣
2. si terebe fonjifi ainambi,
你問那個做什麽
3. mini emu tara ahvn udaki sembi,
我的表兄說是要買
4. tere boo teqi ojorakv,
那個房子住不得

277

5. umesi doksin,
狠兇

6. da jokson de mini emu mukvn i ahvn udahangge,
起初是我一個族兄買的

7. girin i boo nadan giyalan,
從門房七間

8. fere de isitala sunja jergi,
到照房五層

9. umesi iqangga sain bolgo bihe,
狠舒服乾淨来着

10. mini ahvn i jui de isinaha manggi,
到了我阿哥的兒子的手裡

11. juwe ergi hetu boo be sangsaraka seme efulefi,
因爲那兩邊的廂房糙爛的上全拆了

12. dasame weilehe turgunde,
從新翻蓋的上

13. holkonde hutu ai dabkame deribuhe,
忽然間就鬧起鬼什麼來了

14. suqungga daixahangge, hono yebe,
起初鬧的還好

15. bihe bihei,
久而久之

16. inenggi xun de asuki tuqibume arbun sabubuha,
清天白日裡就出聲色 現了形了

17. booi hehesi aika ohode, uthai buqeli be tunggalaha seme
家裡的女人們動不動兒的就說是遇見了鬼了

18. golofi ergen joqibuhangge gemu bi,
竟有怕死了的

19. samdaqi mekele,
跳神呢是個白

20. fudexeqi baitakv
送幣呢是無用

21. ojoro jakade,
因那個上

22. arga akv,
沒有法兒

23. teni ja hvda de unqaha,
賤賤的賣了

24. age si sambio,

阿哥你知道嗎

25. ere gemu forgon ehe i haran,
這也是運氣不好的過失

26. yaya boode umai gai akv,
無論什麼房子裡並沒緣故

27. forgon sain oqi,
運氣要好

28. udu buxuku yemji bihe seme,
雖有邪魅外道

29. inu jailatame burulara dabala,
也就躲開了

30. niyalma be nungneme mutembio,
豈能侵害人嗎

31. tuttu seme
而且

32. mini ere ahvn umesi fahvn ajige,
我這個阿哥膽子狠小

33. bi daqilaha yargiyan babe, inde alaqi wajiha,
我把打聽的實在的緣故告訴他就完了

34. udaqibe udarakv oqibe,
或買與不買

35. ini qihai gamakini.
由他自己定奪去罷

Section 59: A Fortune Teller

1. age si donjihakvn,
阿哥你沒聽見嗎

2. jakan hoton i tule emu jakvn hergen tuwara niyalma jihebi,
新近城外頭來了一個算命的

3. umesi ferguwequke mangga sembi,
狠是出奇的好啊

4. niyalma i alara be donjiqi,
聽見人告訴

5. tere niyalma fuhali enduri adali banjihabi,
那個人竟是一個神仙了

6. musei dulekele baita be,
把喒們過去的事情

7. aimaka we inde alaha adali,

279

倒像誰告訴了他的一樣

8. jafaha sindaha gese bodome bahanambi,
會拿着算到

9. musei niyalma genehengge umesi labdu,
喒們人去的狠多

10. siran siran i lakqarakv jalu fihekebi,
接連不斷 填的滿滿的了

11. ere gese xengge niyalma bikai,
既有這樣的神人啊

12. atanggi biqibe muse ahvn deo inu inde tuwabunaki,
多喒喒們弟兄們也去叫他瞧瞧

13. bi aifini saha,
我早知道了

14. mini guquse, ere udu uquri feniyen feniyelefi genere jakade,
我的朋友們這幾日會成羣兒去的上頭

15. qananggi bi inu tubade isinaha,
前日我已經到了那裡去了

16. mini jakvn hergen be inde tuwabuhade,
把我的八個字兒給他看了

17. ama eme ai aniya,
他竟把父母的什麼年紀

18. ahvn deo udu,
弟兄幾個

19. sargan hala ai,
女人什麼姓氏

20. atanggi hafan bahangge,
多喒得的官

21. haqin haqin i baita, gemu tob seme aqanaha,
按件都算的對當

22. heni majige taxarabuhakv,
一點兒也不錯

23. dulekengge udu aqanaha biqibe,
已過去的雖然對了

24. damu jidere unde baita,
但只未来的事

25. ainahai ini henduhe songkoi ombini,
未必就照他那說的呢

26. tuttu seme,

可是那樣說

27. muse yamaka bade dere udu jiha fayarakv,
喈們那裡沒花過那幾個錢

28. eiqibe
揣說了罷

29. si geli baita akv,
你又無事

30. boode bai tere anggala,
與其在家裡白坐着

31. sargaxara gese geneqi,
莫若閒曠的一樣

32. alixara be tookabure ton okini.
消着愁悶兒去走走

33. ai ojorakv sere babi,
人有什麼使不得的去處呢

Section 60: A Silly Man

1. ini tere arbuxarangge
你看他那行景

2. absi yabsi,
不知要怎麼樣的

3. neneme sebkesaka imbe aqaha de,
原先纔見他的時候

4. nomhon ergide bi sembihe,
還在老實一邊来着

5. jaka tuwaqi fuhali niyalma de eleburakv,
近來一點叫人看不上

6. albatu ten de isinahabi,
粗村的至極了

7. niyalma juleri bubu baba
在人前頭磕磕絆絆的

8. absi fonjire absi jabure babe gemu sarkv,
連一問一答的話全不知道

9. qiqi goqi
縮頭縮腦的

10. adarame ibere, adarame bederere be gemu ulhirakv,
連怎麼進退也不懂得

11. geteqibe weri i amgara adali,

醒着倒像睡覺的一樣

12. bai niyalma i ton dabala,
白一個人數罷咧

13. hvlhi lampa i adarame banjihabi,
糊里糊塗的怎麼活着呢

14. suwe banjire sain bihe kai,
你們相與的好啊

15. tede majige jorixaqi jorixaqi aqambi dere,
該當指撥指撥他纔是呢

16. age suwe emu bade guquleme goidahakv ofi,
阿哥你們皆因並未久交

17. hono tenkime sara unde,
知道的尚不透徹

18. ereqi injequke baita geli bini,
比這個可笑的事還有呢

19. ishunde teqefi gisun gisurembihede,
彼此一處坐着講話的時候

20. erebe gisureme bihengge
正說着這個

21. holkonde terebe gvninafi leolembi,
忽然又題起那個來了

22. akvqi angga labdahvn
要不是把嘴唇子搭拉着

23. ergen sukdun akv,
沒氣兒一樣

24. yasai faha gurinjerakv
眼珠兒也不動

25. hadahai simbe tuwambi,
直直的望着你

26. gaitai gaitai emu uju unqehen akv beliyen gisun tuqikede,
忽然間又說出一句沒頭尾的傻話來

27. niyalma duha be lakqatala fanqame injebumbi,
把人的腸子都笑斷了

28. qananggi mimbe tuwaname genehe,
前日他瞧我去

29. amasi genere de xuwe yaburakv,
回來的時候並不是一直的走

30. fisa forofi amasi sosorome tuqimbi,

轉過脊背往外倒退着出去

31. tede bi age bokson de guwelke sere
那個上我說阿哥仔細門檻子啊

32. gisun wajinggala,
話還未了

33. i bethe tafi saksari onqohon tuhenere be,
他那脚就絆在上頭 仰面跌倒了

34. bi ekxeme julesi ibefi
我急忙上前

35. hvsun muterei ebsihei tatame jafara jakade,
盡力將將的攙扶起來了

36. arkan tamalibuha,
[剛剛收拾好了][383]

37. neneme bi hono ton akv tafulambihe,
我起初還沒數兒的勸過他来着

38. amala dasara halara muru akv be tuwaqi,
後来見他沒有改過的樣兒

39. hvwaxara tetun waka kai,
不是個成器的東西上

40. aiseme angga xadabume gisurembi.
爲什麼費着唇舌說呢

Section 61: An Alcoholic

1. age si tuwa,
阿哥你看

2. te geli isika,
如今又是分了

3. lalanji omifi ilime toktorakv ohobi,
喝的爛醉 連脚兒全站不住了

4. bi tere baita be si tede alahao akvn seme fonjiqi,
我問他你把那件事情告訴他了沒有

5. heihedeme
搖晃着身子

6. yasa durahvn i mini baru gala alibumbi,

[383] There was no Chinese counterpart in the first place. The translation is added according to the Manchu text.

眼睛直直的望着我遞手

7. dutu hele ai geli waka,
又不是聾子啞叭

8. jaburakvngge ainu,
爲什麼不答應

9. ere gese niyalma be fanqaburengge geli bini,
像這個叫人生氣的也有呢

10. enenggi mimbe fiyaratala tantaburakv oqi,
今日要不重重的打他的時候

11. bi uthai gashvkini,
我就要說誓了

12. age joo ume,
阿哥算了別

13. i ainqi onggofi genehekv,
他大畧忘了沒去罷

14. ini waka babe i endembio,
他的不是他豈不知道嗎

15. tuttu ofi olhome jabume gisun baharakv ohobi,
皆因是那樣怕的上沒有答應的話了

16. enenggi bi ubade bisire be dahame,
今日遇見我在這裡

17. mini dere be tuwame
看我的臉上

18. ere mari onqodome guwembureo,
饒過這一次罷

19. ereqi julesi,
徃後

20. nure omire be eteme lashalakini,
永遠斷了酒捴不許喝

21. hendure balama,
反過來說

22. kangnaqi eihen ja,
驢子容易騎

23. bungnaqi aha ja sehe,
奴才容易壓派

24. si jingkini sonqoho jafaha ejen kai,
你實在是摸着頭頂的主子啊

25. aibide ukqambi ,

他可徃那裡去

26. halaqi halaha,
要改就改了

27. aikabade halarakv
要是不改

28. kemuni uttu suihume omiqi,
還要是這樣喝的爛醉的時候

29. age qingkai isebu,
隨阿哥的意見兒責罰罷

30. bi udu jai uqaraha seme
我雖再遇見了

31. inu baire de mangga ombi,
也就難求情了

32. age si ainambahafi sara,
阿哥你如何知道呢

33. banitai emu gusherakv fayangga,
生來是一個不成器的魂灵兒

34. arki omimbi serede,
一說喝酒

35. uthai buqembi
就死也不肯放

36. ini amai senggi qi hono haji,
比他阿媽脖子上 [384]的血還（親 [385]）

37. ere mudan guwembuhede
這一次饒過了的時候

38. uthai halambi semeo,
就說是改了嗎

39. manggai oqi, emu juwe inenggi subuhvn dabala,
也不過減等着一兩日清醒不醉罷咧

40. duleke manggi
過去了

41. kemuni fe an i omimbi.
又是照舊的喝啊

---

[384] The phrase 脖子上 (*bozishang*, on the neck) was added by the original translator. There is no corresponding words in this Manchu sentence.

[385] The word 親 (*qin*) did not appear in the original translation. It is added according to the Manchu word 'haji' (intimate).

Section 62: Raising Children

1. age ere jui uduqingge,
阿哥的這個孩子是第幾個的

2. ere mini fiyanggv,
這是我的老搭兒

3. mama erxeheo,
出了花兒了嗎

4. unde,
還沒有呢

5. ese gemu ikiri ahvn deo,
他們全是連胎生的

6. uyun banjifi uyun taksiha,
弟兄九個 全存下了

7. age bi yobodorongge waka,
阿哥我不是頑

8. axa mergen kai,
嫂子好手段啊

9. juse banjire de silkabuhabi,
是第一個善養孩子的呀

10. omosi mama seqi ombi,
竟是個子孫娘娘了

11. si yala hvturi yongkiyaha niyalma kai,
你實在是個有福的人啊

12. ainaha hvturi,
未必是福

13. gajiha sui kai,
生來的孽啊

14. amba ningge hono yebe,
大些的還好些

15. ajigesi ningge inenggidari gar miyar sehei banjimbi,
小的們終日裡哭哭喊喊的

16. alimbaharakv yangxan,
不勝嘮叨

17. dolo gemu urehebi,
心裡全熟了

18. jalan i niyalma uthai uttu,
世上的人就是這樣的

19. juse bayan urse

孩子們多的人

20. gemu eimeme gasambi,
都厭煩埋怨

21. meni juse haji niyalma de emke biqina seqi, aba,
像我們這樣愛孩子的 要一個那裡有

22. abka inu mangga kai,
天就難測了啊

23. sini tere nionio waliyarakv bihe biqi,
你那一個兒子要是不死的時候

24. inu uyun juwan se ohobi,
也有九歲十歲了

25. yala emu sain jui,
實在是個好孩子

26. tetele jongko dari,
到如今（每次提起）從心裡

27. bi sini funde nasame gvnimbi,
我替你想念啊

28. tere banin wen,
他那模樣兒

29. gisun hese,
言語兒

30. gvwa juse qi qingkai enqu,
與別的孩子們迥乎不同

31. kur kar etufi,
穿上衣裳雄雄寔寔的

32. niyalma be sabumbihede,
一見了人

33. beyebe tob seme obufi,
端然正立

34. fixur seme elhei ibefi sain be fonjimbi,
慢慢的進前問個好

35. jilakan manggi, tere ajige angga
招人疼的那個小嘴

36. ai sigun bahanarakv,
什麼話兒不會說

37. tede emu baita fonjiha de,
要問他一件事情

38. aimaka we inde taqibuha adali,

像是誰教給他的一樣

39. daqi dubede isitala,
從頭至尾

40. haqingga demun i akvmbume mutembi,
各樣的情節都能罄盡情告訴

41. tentekengge emken biqi
那樣的要有一個

42. juwan de teherembikai,
就勝強十個啊

43. utala baitakvngge be ujifi ainambi.
養活着那些無用的作什麼呢

Section 63: A Fur Coat

1. ere sekei kurume puseli de udahanggeo,
這個貂鼠褂子 在鋪子裡買的嗎

2. puselingge waka,
不是鋪子裡的

3. juktehen de udahangge,
廟上買的

4. hvdai menggun udu,
價錢多少

5. si tubixeme tuwa,
你畧估畧估

6. ere absi akv
這個任憑怎麼樣的

7. ninju yan menggun salimbi dere
也值六十兩罷

8. gvsin yan menggun qi nonggihai,
從三十兩銀子上

9. dehi yan de isinafi,
添到四十兩

10. uthai unqaha,
就賣了

11. hvda ai uttu wasikabi,
價兒怎麼這樣的賤下來了

12. nenehe forgon de
先前的時候

13. ere gesengge juken jakvnju yan menggun unqaqi bahambi,

這樣一般的得賣八十兩銀子啊

14. boqo sahaliyan
顏色黑

15. funiyehe luku,
毛厚

16. weilehengge inu bokxokon,
做的精緻

17. fuserekengge inu teksin,
鋒毛兒也齊

18. tuttu bime tuku suje jiramin,
而且面子的緞子狠好

19. iqe ilhangga, erin i durun,
時樣的花兒

20. yargiyan i umesi salimbi,
實在狠值

21. mini ejehengge
我記得

22. sinde inu emken bihe,
你也有一件来着

23. mini tere ai ton,
我那個那裡算得數

24. bai emu gebu dabala,
白是個褂子名兒罷咧

25. funiyehe manaha,
毛也磨了

26. simen wajiha,
火力完了

27. tulesi etuqi ojorakv ohobi[386],
反穿不得了

28. fulun baha manggi,
關了俸銀的時候

29. giyan i emu sain ningge udambi dere,
就買一件好的呀

30. suweni gese asihata,
你們少年人

---

[386] Because the glaze/color is gone, it would be very ugly to wear the hair-side out.

31. jing wesihun iqi genere niyalma kai,
正是往高裡走的人啊

32. yamulara isara bade,
上衙門或是會齊

33. etuqi miyamiqi,
穿個樣子

34. giyan ningge,
是該當的

35. minde geli ai yangse,
我又要什麼樣兒

36. erin dulekebi,
過了時候了

37. damu halukan oqi joo kai,
煖和就罷了啊

38. sain ningge etuqi,
就是穿上好的

39. fiyan tuqirakv bime,
不但沒樣兒

40. elemangga kuxun
反倒不舒服

41. tere anggala,
況且

42. mini ere hithai alban de inu teisu akv,
我這分差使也不對當

43. inemene ferke manahangge
不論什麼舊的破的

44. elemangga minde fitheme aqanambi.
倒與我對裝了

Section 64: A Funeral Affair

1. qeni boode we akv oho,
他們家裡誰死了

2. qananggi bi tederi dulere de
前日我從那裡過

3. tuwaqi booi urse xahvn sinahi hvwaitahabi,
看見家裡的人們穿着煞白的孝

4. bi ekxeme idu gaime jidere jakade,
我因急着來接班的上

290

5. bahafi fonjihakv,
沒得問問

6. jakan ini eshen ufaraha,
新近他叔叔死了

7. banjiha eshen wakao,
不是親叔叔嗎

8. inu,
是

9. si jobolon de aqanahao akvn,
你道惱去來沒有

10. sikse nomun i dooqan arara de,
昨日念經作道場

11. bi gulhun emu inenggi tubade bihe,
我整一日在那裡来着

12. atanggi giran tuqibumbi,
幾時出殯

13. donjiqi biya i manashvn de sembi,
聽說是月盡頭

14. qeni yafan ya ergide bi,
他們的墳園在那裡

15. meni yafan de hanqi,
與我們的園裡相近

16. tuttu oqi
要是那樣

17. jugvn goro kai,
路遠啊

18. dehi ba isinambi dere,
四十来的里

19. ere sidende
這個空兒上

20. jai imbe aqaqi,
再要是遇見了他

21. gasabuha se,
說是道惱了

22. bi idu qi hokoho manggi,
等我下了班

23. simbe guilefi sasa aqaname genere,
會着你一同去走走罷

24. giran tuqibure onggolokon,

送殯的以前些

25. minde emu mejige bu,
給我一個信兒

26. bi ten de isiname muterakv okini,
我就是不能送到終點

27. hoton i tule isibume beneki,
也要送到城外頭

28. an i uquri be feliyerakv biqibe,
素日雖然不常往來

29. sabuha dari mini baru dembei sebsihiyan,
一見了我狠親熱

30. niyalma seme jalan de banjifi,
人生在世

31. ya gemu guqu waka,
那個不都是朋友

32. weri ere gese baita de
人家有了這樣的事情

33. muse beye isinaqi,
嗒們的身子要是到去了

34. gvniqi amqatambi seme leolere niyalma akv dere.
想來沒有說是攀援附勢的

Section 65: Making Clothes

1. ere hojihon de bure etuku wakao,
這個不是給女婿的衣裳嗎

2. inu,
是

3. ese ainarangge,
這些人都是作什麼的

4. turime gajiha faksisa,
僱了來的匠人們

5. ai,
可嘆

6. muse fe kooli gemu wajiha,
嗒們的舊規矩全完了

7. sakdasai forgon de
老時候

8. juwan udu se i juse,

十幾歲的孩子們

Even the teen-aged children

9. gemu etuku xanggabume mutembihe,

could make a complete clothes,

10. kubun sektefi,

續上了棉花

11. tuku doko aqabufi,

合上了裡面

12. ubaxaha manggi,

翻過來的時候

13. si adasun be ufiqi,

你縫大襟

14. bi uthai jurgan goqimbi,

我就行

15. ere ogo jafara

這個拿腰坎

16. tere monggon hayara hethe

那個上領子

17. huwexerengge hethe huwexeme,

烙袖子的烙袖子

18. tohon hadarangge tohon hadame,

釘鈕子的釘鈕子

19. manggaqi emu juwe inenggi sidende,

不過一兩天的工夫

20. uthai waqihiyabumbi,

就做完了

21. tere anggala,

不但那樣

22. mahala qi aname, gemu boode weilembihe,

連帽子全是家裡做來着

23. basa bume turifi weilebure,

給工錢僱人做

24. jiha menggun i udafi eture oqi,

或者拿銀錢買着穿的時候

25. niyalma gemu oforo deri suk seme injembikai,

人家全從鼻子眼裡笑的

26. age i gisun giyangga biqibe,

阿哥的話雖有理

27. si damu emken be saha gojime juwe be sahakvbi,

但你只知其一不知其二

28. tere forgon ere forgon de emu adali obufi gisureqi ombio,
那個時候與這個時候 作爲一樣說得麼

29. jai gaire inenggi umesi hanqi oho,
再者娶的日子狠近

30. simhun fatame bodoqi,
掐着指頭算來

31. arkan karkan juwan inenggi xolo bi,
恰好能有十日

32. ere sidende jaka
這個工夫

33. xolo tuqibureakv,
一點空兒不給

34. dobori dulime haqihiyame weileqi
不分晝夜的趕着做了去

35. amqara amqarakvngge,
趕的上趕不上

36. hono juwe sidenderi bikai,
還在兩可之間呢

37. aika memereme fe kooli sehei,
要是拘擬舊規矩

38. gio turibuhe balama,
旗杆底下悞了操

39. yasa gehun tookabure de isibuqi
睜着眼睛至於悞了時候

40. ai yokto.
什麼趣兒呢

Section 66: Being Frugal

1. niyalma ofi, tanggv se de banjirengge akv kai,
人沒有活一百歲的呀

2. ere taka banjire beye yala tolgin i gese,
這就是浮生若夢

3. sebjelere ba giyanakv udu,
爲歡幾何

4. xun biya homso maktara adali,
日月如梭的一樣

5. geri fari uju funiyehe xahvn xarapi,

一仰一合 頭髮就白了

6. eide de baitakv oho manggi,
各處全不中用了

7. elemangga juse omosi i senqehe be xame tuwame
反倒望着孩子們的下頦子

8. banjire dabala,
過日子罷咧

9. ai amtan,
什麼趣兒呢

10. jai sube giranggi mangga oho sehede,
再者筋骨說是硬了的時候

11. etuqi fiyan tuqirakv,
穿的沒樣兒

12. jeqi amtan baharakv,
吃的沒味兒

13. bihe seme ai baita
就是活着何用

14. te sakdara unde be amqame
今趁還未年老

15. eturakv jeterakv oqi,
若不吃不穿

16. jiha menggun fita jafarafi ainambi
把銀錢緊緊的攢着作什麼呢

17. si dababume mamgiyarakv dere,
你就不過費罷咧

18. bahara ufuhi be bodome
算着得的分兒

19. majige sebjeleqi heo seme ombi,
料樂些狠彀了啊

20. dabali seqi ojorakv,
要說是過於了使不得啊

21. sini ere gisun mimbe same gisurehenggeo,
你這個話是知道着說我的麼

22. eiqi sarkv de bai tubixeme gisurehenggeo,
或是不知道約模着說的麼

23. minde ele mila biqi,
我要手裡有些

24. sebjelerengge inu giyan,

樂也是應該的

25. umai gvwa i gese funqen daban i bahara ba akv bade,
並不像別人富富裕裕的有得的去處

26. mimbe adarame sebjele sembi,
叫我怎麼樂呢

27. eiqi bekdun arafi etu sembio,
作下賬弄穿的嗎

28. eiqi boo unqafi jefu sembio,
或是花了產業吃呢

29. sini gisun songkoi ohode,
要是照着你的話的時候

30. fayahai ulin wajiha,
把財帛花盡了

31. uthai giyok seme buqeqi inu okini,
一跤跌死了纔好

32. talude buqerakv,
倘若不死

33. kemuni ergen tafi banjiqi,
還戀着命兒活着

34. tere erinde ainaqi ojoro,
那個時候怎麼纔好啊

35. falanggv be alibume sinde baiqi,
伸着手向你要

36. si ainahai anabumbini.
你還未必給呢呀

Section 67: To be Reliable

1. yaya niyalma damu akdun biqi,
大凡人要有信實

2. niyalma teni gvnin bahambi,
人才心服

3. enenggi oqi qimari sere
今日推到明日

4. qimari oho manggi
到了明日

5. geli qoro sere,
又說後日

6. erken terken i inenggi anatahai,

這樣那樣的支悞日子

7. atanggi dube da,
幾時才是了手

8. alime gaisu manggi
應允了

9. geli angga aifure,
又要改嘴

10. eqimari uttu ojoro,
早晨這樣

11. yamji tuttu ojoro oqi
晚上那樣

12. niyalma jai adarame sini gisun be akdambi,
人再怎麼信你的話呢

13. ere durun i uxan faxan
像這樣拉拉扯扯的

14. kengse lasha akv ojoro anggala,
不但沒簡斷,

15. doigon qi emu yargian babe inde ulhibuqi,
就是預先把實在處給他知道了的時候

16. niyalma inu gvnin usafi,
人也心裡煩了

17. jai ereme gvnirakv ombi,
再不指望了

18. waka,
不是啊

19. bi yamaka i bade baita akdun ufaraha babio,
我或者在那裡有失信的去處嗎

20. si te jorime tuqibu,
你如今指出來

21. ai ai onggolo,
什麼什麼的裡頭

22. uttu algingga jubengge,
就這樣揚聲誹謗的

23. baita oron unde kai,
沒影兒的事情啊

24. mini funde faqihiyaxafi ainambi,
替我着什麼急

25. baita de teisulebufi,

遇見了各樣的事情了的時候

26. kimqiha dade kimqifi,
斟酌了又斟酌

27. fakjin baha manggi,
得了主意了

28. jai niyalma be wakaxaqi,
再說人的不是

29. Niyalma inu dahambi,
人也服啊

30. si getuken i sarkv bade
你知道的不真切

31. baiqi mimbe wakaxaqi ombio
白白的怪我使得嗎

32. tere anggala,
況且

33. yabuqi mini qiha,
走也在我

34. yaburakv oqi inu mini qiha
不走也在我

35. si xorgifi ainambi,
你催我作什麼

36. bi banitai uthai uttu qamangga,
我生來就是這樣寧折不屈的呀

37. baita be yargiyalahakv de
把事不見真酌的時候

38. bukdame jafafi mimbe uttu oso seqi,
就冤屈着叫我這樣的

39. bi ainaha seme yabure ba akv
我再也是不肯行的呀

40. adarame seqi
怎麼說呢？

41. tenteke basuqun werifi
留那樣笑話

42. gisun i anakv ojoro,
行那樣話柄兒的事情

43. baita be bi ajigan qi taqihakv,
自幼兒沒學過

44. i akdaqi aliya se,

他要信得就等着

45. akdarakv oqi,
要是不信

46. qihangga bade genefi enqu niyalma de yandukini dere,
任意別處求人去罷

47. we imbe ilibuhabio.
誰叫他停着等來呢

Section 68: A Ghost

1. ere udu inenggi
這幾日

2. gvngkame halhvn ojoro jakade,
因爲悶熱的上

3. fa be sujahai
把窗戶支着

4. dorgi giyalan boode amganha bihe,
在外間夜裡睡覺来着

5. sunjaqi ging ni erinde isinafi,
到了五更的時候

6. dosi forome jing amgame bisire de,
轉過去面徃裡正睡着

7. xan de asuki bahabumbi,
耳朵裡聽見響了一聲

8. amu suwaliyame yasa neifi tuwaqi,
帶困睜開眼睛一看

9. ujui ninggude emu aldungga jaka ilihabi,
頭前裡一個怪物站着呢

10. dere xanyan hooxan i adali,
臉像紙一樣的白

11. yasa qi senggi eyembi,
眼睛裡流血

12. beyei gubqi xahvn
渾身雪白的

13. ujui funiyehe lekdehun,
蓬着頭髮

14. na de fekuqeme bi,
在地下跳呢

15. sabure jakade,

我一見了

16. bi ambula gvwaqihiyalaha,
大吃了一驚

17. ara,
哎呀

18. ere uthai hutu serengge inu dere,
這個大署就是鬼罷

19. ini ainara be tuwaki seme,
想看他怎麼樣

20. yasa jiberefi tuwaqi
密縫着眼看時

21. fekuqehei goidahakv,
不想他跳了一會

22. horho be neifi
把箱子開了

23. etuku adu be kejine tuqibufi oho de,
拿出了好些衣裳

24. hafira nakv
夾在胳肢窩裡

25. fa deri tuqifi genehe,
要從窗戶裡出去了

26. tede bi gaihari ulhifi
因那個上我猛然明白了

27. dolori gvnime,
心裡想着

28. hutu oqi
要是鬼

29. etuku be gamara kooli bio,
也有拿衣裳的理嗎

30. seme ilifi,
站起來

31. loho be goqime tuqibufi,
拔出腰刀

32. jabdurakv de
給他個湊手不及

33. masilame emgeri genqehelere jakade,
結結實實的用刀背一砍

34. ara sefi,

唉的一聲

35. na de aro tuheke,
就撲通的跌在地下來了

36. booi urse be hvlame gajifi
叫了家裡的人們

37. dengjan dafufi tuwaqi,
點上燈看時

38. umesi yobo,
狠可笑

39. dule emu butu hvlha
卻原來是一個竊賊

40. jortai hutu arame niyalma be gelebumbiheni.
裝作鬼來嚇人來了的呀

Section 69: A Marriage Interview

1. feten bifi,
有緣分的上

2. be niyaman jafaki seme baime jihe,
我們來求作親來了

3. mini ere jui,
我的這個兒子

4. udu qolgoroko erdemu ferguwequke bengsen akv biqibe,
雖然沒有出類超羣的本事

5. damu nure omire jiha efire
但只喝酒耍錢

6. ehe faquhvn urse de dayanfi,
與那混賬人們

7. balai sargaxara jergi baita,
胡曠等項的事情

8. inde heni majige akv,
一點也沒有

9. looyesa hatame gvnirakv ofi,
老爺們要是不嫌

10. emu gosire gisun bureo,
給句疼愛的話罷

11. age si julesiken i jio,
阿哥你徔前些來

12. muse looyesa de hengkixeme baiki,

嗒們給老爺們磕着頭求啊

13. looyesa ume,
老爺們別

14. teqefi mini emu gisun donjire,
坐下聽我一句話

15. muse gemu fe niyaman,
嗒們呢全是舊親戚

16. gese gese giranggi yali,
而且一樣兒的骨頭肉兒

17. webe we sarkv,
誰不知道誰的

18. damu eigen sargan serengge,
但只夫妻啊

19. gemu nenehe jalan i toktobuha salgabun,
全是前世裡造定的啊

20. niyalmai qihai oqi ojorakv,
不是由着人的啊

21. juse be ujifi
養活着孩子們啊

22. beye xame tuwame emu sain juru aqabuqi,
親身眼看着成雙成對的了

23. ama eme oho niyalma i joboho suilaha gvnin inu wajimbi,
爲父母的那些勞苦心腸也就完了

24. tuttu sehe seme,
雖然那們說

25. emude oqi,
頭一件

26. minde ungga jalan i niyaman bi,
我有老家兒

27. ere age be sabure unde,
沒見這個阿哥

28. jaide oqi,
第二件

29. jihe taitai sa,
來的太太們

30. mini mentuhun sargan jui be inu majige tuwaki,
也瞧瞧我的醜女兒

31. inu,

302

是啊

32. looyesa i gisun umesi ferguwequke genggiyen kai,
老爺們的話狠聖明

33. ere gisun be uthai musei jihe taitai sade hafumbu,
把這話就通知嗒們來的太太們

34. gege be tuwaha manggi,
瞧了姑娘的時候

35. age be inu hvlame dosimbufi,
把阿哥也叫進去

36. ubai taitai sade tuwabuki,
給這裡的太太們瞧瞧

37. ishunde gemu gvnin [de] aqahame sehede
彼此全說是合式了

38. jai hengkileqi,
再磕頭

39. inu goidarakv kai.
也不遲啊

Section 70: Bad Marriage

1. qeni eigen sargan be baqihi sembio,
你說他們是結髮夫妻嗎

2. sirame gaihangge,
是繼娶的啊

3. ere emile ududu eigen anahabi,
這個女人妨了好幾個漢子了

4. banin giru sain,
身形兒好

5. gala weilen inu ombi,
針指兒也好

6. damu emu ba eden,
但只一件

7. juxun jetere mangga,
平常好吃醋

8. eigen susai se tulitele,
漢子直過了五十歲了

9. umai juse enen akv bime,
並沒有後

10. guweleku sindambi, sula hehe takvraki serede,

說要放妾使小
11. hetu dedufi ojorakv,
他就橫倘着不依
12. fasime buqeki sere,
說要吊死
13. beyebe beye araki sere,
又是要自盡
14. haqingga demun i gelebume daixambi,
各樣的嚇鬧
15. fisiku aihvma geli eberi ten,
自己耽誤的忘八
16. sargan de ergelebufi
被女人嚇的
17. fuhali horon gaibuha,
一點不能施威
18. imbe umainame muterakv bime,
竟把他不能怎麼樣的
19. beye niohon jili banjihai,
而且忍着氣兒
20. ergen susaka,
死人一樣的
21. erebe tuwaqi,
看起這個來
22. jalan i baita teksin akv mujangga,
世上的事情實在不齊啊
23. meni tubai emu age,
我們那裡一個阿哥
24. jakan sunja tanggv yan menggun de,
新近用五百兩銀子
25. emu hehe udafi beyede goqika,
買了個女人 收在跟前
26. fuhali ini oho i funiyehe i adali,
竟像寶貝一樣
27. aikan faikan i gese gosime,
要怎麼樣的就怎麼樣的疼的
28. ai seqi,
說怎麼樣的時候
29. jai gelhun akv majige jurqerakv,

再也不敢畧有錯

30. ere hayan i aha be
把這個奴才

31. uju de hukxehe bime,
拿頭頂着

32. jingkini sargan be elemangga aha nehv de isiburakv adunggiyambi,
反把正經女人倒不如奴才樣的折磨

33. inenggidari tantahai fasime buqere de isibuha,
每日裡打過來打過去 至於吊死了

34. danqan i urse habxaha,
被她那娘家的人告了

35. telele kemuni wajire unde,
到如今還沒完呢

36. ere felehun hehe,
這個惹禍的老婆

37. tere doksin haha de,
那個凶惡的男人

38. jing emu juru kai,
正是一對

39. abka ainu eigen sargan obume holboburakv ni.
老天怎麼就沒配成老婆漢子呢

Section 71: Getting into Trouble

1. musei tere oshon ningge,
喈們那個野東西

2. amba jobolon neqihebi,
惹了大禍了

3. ainahabi,
怎麼了

4. ainaha niyalma be tantame waha,
把一個什麼人打死了

5. turgun adarame,
怎麼一個緣故

6. fili fiktu akv kai,
無緣無故啊

7. qeni emu adaki be,
把他們一個街房

8. ini dukai dalbade sitehe seme,

說是在他們門傍邊撒了尿了

9. fonjin hese akv,
也不問一問

10. fahame tuhebu nakv, aktalame tefi,
就摔個仰面觔斗拉倒 [跨坐着]

11. dere yasa be baime tantame deribuhe,
照着臉龐眼睛打起來了

12. suqungga tantara de hono toome surembihe,
起初打還罵着叫喊

13. amala gudexehei,
後來只管搥打的上

14. nidure jilgan gemu akv oho,
連哼的聲兒也全沒了

15. borhome tuwara urse
打攢看的人們

16. arbun faijime be safi
知道光景不好了

17. tantara be ilibufi,
止住了打

18. tuwaqi aifini ergen yadahabi,
看時早已斷氣了

19. ede yafahan uksin sa imbe jafafi gamaha,
所以步兵們把他拿了去

20. buqehe niyalmai booi gubqi gemu jifi,
死人家裡的人們全來了

21. ini boo nahan be susubuha,
把他家鬧了個七零八落

22. agvra tetun be hvwalaha,
傢伙器皿打了個淨

23. wase qi aname yooni kolaha,
連瓦全揭了

24. kaiqara jilgan juwe ilan bai dubede isitala donjihabi,
喊叫的聲音 直聽到二三里路遠

25. sikse jurgan de isinaha,
昨日到部裡去了

26. enenggi erun nikebuhe sembi,
說今日上了刑了

27. age si donjihakvn,

306

阿哥你沒有聽見說嗎

28. ehe niyalma de ehe karulan bi sehebi,
惡人自有惡人報應啊

29. ere ini beye baihangge dabala,
這是他自己惹的罷咧

30. wede ai guwanta.
與誰什麼相干

Section 72: Real Friends

1. guquleki seqi,
要說是交結朋友啊

2. julgei guwan jung boo xu be alhvda,
可學那古時候的管仲鮑叔啊

3. ere juwe nofi,
這兩個人

4. emu iennggi xehun bigan yabure de
一日走到曠野地方

5. tuwaqi jugvn i dalbade,
看見道傍邊

6. emu aisin i xoge maktafi bi,
有一個金錁子放着

7. ishunde anahvnjahai,
彼此相讓

8. yaya we gaijarakv,
誰也不肯拿

9. waliyafi generede,
撂了去了

10. emu usin i haha be uqarafi
遇見一個莊稼漢子

11. jorime hendume,
指着說

12. tubade emu aisin i xoge bi,
那裡有一個金錁子

13. si genefi gaisu serede,
你去取來罷

14. tere usin i haha ekxeme genefi gaiqi
那個莊稼漢子急忙前去取時

15. aisin be saburakv,

不見金子

16. juwe ujungga meihe be sabuha,
是一個兩頭蛇

17. ambula golofi,
吃了一大驚

18. homin i meihe be juwe meyen obume lashalame saqiha,
拿鋤頭把蛇砍爲兩段

19. amqanafi jamarame hendume,
趕回來吵鬧着說

20. bi suwende aika kimun bio,
我與你們有仇嗎

21. juwe ujunggameihe be, ainu aisin xoge seme holtome alambi,
把兩頭蛇怎麼哄我說是金錁子

22. elekei mini ergen be joqibuha serede,
幾乎送了我的命啊

23. juwe nofi akdarakv,
二人不信

24. emgi sasa genefi tuwaqi,
一同前去看時

25. da an i aisin xoge,
照舊還是金錁子

26. saqibufi juwe dalame ofi, na de bisire be,
可砍爲兩段在地下

27. guwan jung, boo xu emte dulin gaiha,
管仲 鮑叔各取了一半來了

28. tere usin i haha
那個莊稼漢子

29. kemuni untuhun galai amasi genehe,
仍舊空手去了

30. julgei niyalma guqulere doro uttu,
古人交結朋友的道理是這樣

31. ere udu julen i gisun de hanqi biqibe,
這個雖與野史相近

32. yargiyan i te i forgon i aisi be temxere urse de,
實在可與如今爭利的人

33. durun tuwakv obuqi aqambi.
作個榜樣啊

Section 73: A Dirty Old Man

1. ere udu inenggi meni tubade absi simengge,
這幾日我們那裡好熱鬧

2. juktehen de hiyan dabume genehe hehesi umesi labdu,
去寺裡燒香的女人們真多

3. emken qi emke saikan,
一個比一個標致

4. uyun dabkvri qi ebunjihe, enduri gegei adali banjihangge gemu bi,
生的似九天仙女下凡塵的也有

5. hoqikon dere,
俊美的臉龐

6. der seme xeyen,
潔白

7. yaqin faitan yar seme,
黑青的眉 細細長長

8. nilgiyan irgaxara hojo yasa bolori mukei adali,
光潤的媚眼有如秋水

9. sunggeljere kanggili beye,
軟顫苗條的身子

10. niyengniyeri fodoho i gese,
春柳一般

11. emgeri oksoqi,
一旦移步

12. ashaha gu fiyahan kalang kiling seme guwembi,
佩玉瑪瑙鏗鏗鏘鏘的響

13. axxaha dari xungkeri ilha jarin i wa,
每一行動 蘭花麝香的香味

14. guksen guksen i jimbi,
一陣一陣飄來

15. suweni gese
你們的樣子

16. asihata sabuha sehede,
雖說是來看少年

17. maka absi arbuxara be sarkv ombikai,
要是不知如何舉動成嗎

18. waka,
不是啊

19. bi simbe gisurerakv oqi,

我要不說你

20. baibi dosorakv,
怪受不得的

21. hairakan niyalmai sukv,
可惜一張人皮

22. adarame sinde nerebuhe,
怎麼給你披上了

23. ninju se fargame genehe niyalma kai,
徃六十歲上去的人呀

24. kemuni ajigen semeo,
還小嗎

25. boihon monggon dere isinjifi,
土到了脖子上了

26. saliyan i ujui koika funqehebi,
寡剩了點頭皮兒了

27. yasa kaikara nakv,
斜着眼兒

28. urui hehesi feniyen de,
必定在婦人們的羣裡

29. guwele mele gohodorongge,
躲躲閃閃的晃着稀軟的身子擺浪子的

30. adarame,
怎麼說呢

31. duibuleqi niyalma enenggqi bade,
譬如人在背地裡

32. sini sargan be uttu tuttu seme leoleqi,
怎長怎短的講論你的女人的時候

33. sini gvnin de ai sembini,
你心裡怎麼樣呢

34. karu de karu,
所謂善有善報

35. furude de furu serengge,
惡有惡報

36. sain ehe i karulan helmen beyede dahara adali,
善惡的報應如影隨形的一樣

37. utala se unufi,
偌大的年紀了

38. majige butui erdemu be isaburakv,

一點陰德兒不積

39. baibi ere gese hamu dundara baita yabuqi,
寡要行這樣吃屎的事情

40. tei forgon i abka fangkala kai,
如今的天低啊

41. absi sini funde joboxombi.
叫怎麼替你愁呢

Section 74: Spring Outing

1. ere niyengniyeri dubesilehe erinde,
這是春末的時候

2. boode norohoi biqi,
靜坐在家裡

3. absi alixaquka,
何等的愁悶啊

4. sikse mini deo jioi,
昨日我兄弟來會我

5. hoton i tule sargaxaqi aqambi seme, mimbe guilefi,
說該徃城外頭曠去

6. ildun dukai tule genehe,
所以出了便門

7. xehun bigan de isinafi tuwaqi,
到了曠野地方一看

8. niyengniyeri arbun absi buyequke,
春景何等的可愛

9. birai xurdeme emu girin i bade,
沿河一帶

10. toro ilha fularjambi,
桃紅似火

11. fodoho gargan sunggeljembi,
綠柳被風擺動搖扭活軟

12. qeqike i jilgan jingjing jangjang,
雀鳥兒亂哨

13. mooi abdaha niowari nioweri,
樹葉兒青青

14. niyengniyeri edun falga falga dame,
春風兒陣陣

15. orhoi wa guksen guksen jimbi,

草味兒衝衝

16. bira de jahvdai bi,
河內有船

17. dalan de moo bi,
岸上有樹

18. jahvdai de fithere uqulerengge,
船內彈唱的

19. siran siran i lakqarakv,
接連不斷

20. mooi fejile ilgaxame yaburengge,
林內看花的

21. ilan sunja feniyelehebi,
三五成羣

22. tere dade,
那上頭

23. yen jugvn deri birgan be baime welmiyerengge,
又有從茅路上尋找小河兒去釣魚的

24. yala oihori,
實在好極里呀

25. xumin i bujan dolo,
在深林內

26. sebderi de serguwexeme,
乘着涼

27. nure omiqi,
飲着酒

28. umesi amtangga,
狠有趣

29. jai terei xurdeme emu girin i bade,
再着那一帶地方的

30. ilha yafan gemu sain,
花園兒也全好

31. amba juktehen inu bolgo,
大廟也潔淨

32. tuttu ofi,
所以

33. be eletele emu inenggi sargaxaha,
我們盡量曠了一天

34. giyan be bodoqi,

312

論理

35. simbe guileqi aqambihe,
該當會你来着

36. sinde mejige isibuhakvngge,
沒給你信的緣故

37. umai gvnin bifi simbe goboloki serengge waka,
並不是有心偏你

38. erei dorgide sinde aqarakv niyalma bifi kai.
這裡頭有你不對當的人啊

Section 75: A Prodigal Son

1. donjiqi,
聽說

2. muse tere gabula gaqilabufi,
嗒們那個饞阿哥窮透了

3. umesi oitobuha,
艱難的至極

4. hexenehe giohoto i adali,
衣裳狠糟濫跟討吃的一樣了

5. dardan seme ilban nahan de xoyohoi,
打着戰兒咕推在光土炕

6. emu farsi manaha jibehun nerehebi sembi,
披着一個破被窩呢

7. hojo sanggv waburu,
好啊呀 砍頭的

8. wasihvn bethe gaiha aise,
豈不是走到四達運氣裡了嗎

9. duleke aniya ai sui tuwahakv,
去年什麼罪沒受過

10. ai gosihon dulembuhekv,
什麼樣的苦沒經過呢

11. majige niyalma gvnin biqi,
料有一點人心的時候

12. inu aliyame gvnifi halahabi,
也悔改里呀

13. dekdeni gisun
俗話說的

14. bayan sebe amqambi sehei,

313

學着富的去了的時候

15. bethe niohuxun ombi sehebi,
必要窮的淨光的呀

16. akaburengge,
受着罪

17. ai gvnin bifi,
還有什麼心腸說

18. ubai nure tumin,
這裡的酒豔

19. tubai booha amtangga seme,
那裡的菜好

20. bayan urse i gese sasa babade sargaxambi,
像[富]有的人們一樣各處裡去曠的上

21. tede bi gequhun i erinde isinafi,
我到了那凍着的時候

22. jai tuwara dabala seqi,
再瞧罷咧

23. te yala keikehebi,
如今實在苦了

24. uttu henduqibe,
雖然這樣說

25. eiqi ainara
或者怎麼樣的

26. yargiyan i tuwame buqebumbio,
眼看着叫死嗎

27. mini gvnin de,
我心裡

28. muse uhei majige xufafi inde aisilaqi teni sain,
喒們公同攢湊攢湊纔好

29. menggun hono tusa akv,
銀子還無益

30. adarame seqi,
怎麼說呢

31. ini banin be si sarkv aibi,
他的毛病兒你豈不知道嗎

32. gvniqi gala de isina nakv
想來到了手裡

33. jeke yadahai wajifi,

314

吃完了的時候

34. da an i fulahvn ojoro dabala,
仍就是光光的罷咧

35. ai funqembi,
剩下什麼呢

36. ine mene emu jergi etuku udafi buqi,
將計就計的買一套衣裳給他

37. inde hono tusangga dere.
倒像有益的樣

Section 76: A Sparrow

1. bi sinde injeku alara,
我告訴你一個笑話兒

2. teike mini emhun ubade terede,
將纔我自己一個在這裡坐着

3. fa i duthe de emu qeqike dohabi,
窗欞上落着一個雀兒

4. xun i elden de helmexeme,
日頭影兒上照着

5. emgeri qongkifi, emgeri fekuqembi,
一啄一跳的

6. ede bi asuki tuqiburakv,
這個上我不出聲兒

7. elhei oksome hanqi isinafi,
慢慢的邁步走到跟前

8. leb seme emgeri jafara jakade,
忽然一拿的時候

9. fa i hooxan be fondo hvwajafi lakdari,
把窗戶紙抓破了

10. nambuha tuwaqi
拿住了看時

11. emu fiyasha qeqike,
是一個家雀兒

12. gala guribume,
換手的上

13. pur seme deyehe,
噗啦的一聲飛了

14. ekxeme uqe dasifi jafaqi

急着關上門拿時

15. namburilame,
將要拿住

16. geli turibuhe,
又放跑了

17. uba tuba jing amqame jafara sidende,
這裡那裡正趕着拿的上

18. buya juse qeqike baha sere be donjire jakade,
小人兒們聽見說得了雀兒了

19. kaiqaha gio i gese tuhere afarai sujume jifi,
叫喊着磕磕絆絆的跑了來了

20. bur seme amqarangge amqame,
撲着趕的趕

21. jafarangge jafame,
拿的拿

22. mahala gaifi ungke nakv baha,
拿帽子叩着得了

23. amala bi niyalma hono ergengge jaka udafi sindambikai,
後來我說人還要買雀兒放生呢

24. oron giyan akv,
無故的

25. muse erebe jafafi ainambi,
喒們拿他作什麼

26. sindaki serede,
放了吧

27. buqume susame ojorakv,
就死也不依

28. lakdahvn i wasifi gaji sembi,
一定瓜搭着臉要

29. jiduji buhe manggi
到底給了

30. teni urgunjefi fekuqehei genehe.
纔喜歡着跑了去了

Section 77: A Dilemma

1. sini tere baita absi oho,
你那件事怎麼樣了

2. bi ede jing gvnin baibumbikai,

我因爲這個正犯着思想呢

3. yabuki seqi
要行呢

4. majige holbobuha ba bisire gese,
又像有關係的樣子

5. de qi yaburakv aldasi nakaqi,
不行半途而廢罷

6. umesi hairakan,
又狠可惜

7. ne je angga de isinjiha jaka be
眼看着到了嘴裡的東西了

8. bahafi jeterekv,
不得吃

9. baibi niyalma de anabumbi,
白白的讓給人了

10. yabuqi waka,
行罷不是

11. nakaqi geli waka,
不行又不是

12. yargiyan i juwe de gemu mangga ohobi,
實在是兩下里全難啊

13. adarame ohode, emu tumen de yooni ojoro arga bahaqi, teni sain
怎麼得萬無一失的計策纔好

14. uttu ofi
因這個上

15. qohome sinde gvnin baime jihe,
特來你這裡討個主意來了

16. age si minde hebexembi kai,
阿哥你和我商量啊

17. bi ainame ainame iqi tamin i jabufi unggiqi,
我要是草草了事的照着答應了去

18. niyaman serengge ai tusa,
要親戚何益呢

19. ere baita iletusaka ai gvnin baharakv sere babi,
這個事情是明明顯顯的有什麼不得主意的去處

20. amaga inenggi urunakv bultahvn tuqinjimbi,
日後必定是要露出來的呀

21. yaburakv oqi,

要是不行

22. sini jabxan,
是你的便易

23. yabuha sehede,
要說是行了

24. wei angga be butuleqi ombi,
掩得住誰的嘴

25. dur sehe manggi, tere erinde,
至於衆論的時候

26. teni mangga de ilinambikai,
那纔難了呢

27. ai oqibe,
總而言之

28. enduringge niyalmai gisun sain, niyalma goro bodorakv oqi, urunakv
hanqi jobolon bi sehebi,
有聖人人無遠慮必有近憂的話呀

29. ere yasa i juleri ajige aisi be urgun seqi ombio,
把這個眼前的小利也算得喜嗎

30. tob seme amaga inenggi amba jobolon i ursan daldaki sehei iletu-
lebumbi,
正是明顯着把日後的大患的根隱藏着

31. jabxan sehei,
總圖便易

32. ufarabumbi kai,
必定是有失的呀

33. aisi biqi, jobolon akv obume muterakv kai,
難保不無有利無害啊

34. mini gvnin ohode,
我的心裡

35. si ume hebexeme gvnire,
你別想着商量

36. kafur seme ashvqi wajiha,
爽爽快快的一捧手就完了

37. aika mini gisun be donjirakv,
要不聽我的話

38. emdubei jequhunjeme lashalarakv oqi,
僅着疑惑着不果斷

39. taha manggi,
到了個絆住的時候了

40. bele baharakv bime,

不但不得米

41. fulhv waliyabure balama,

反把口袋丟了

42. ai gese boqihe tuwabure be gemu boljion akv,

出什麼樣的醜 全定不得呀

43. tere erinde,

那個時候

44. mimbe xame tuwame tafularakv seme ume gasara.

別怨我看着不勸啊

Section 78: An Ungrateful Man

1. sain niyalma sinqi qala jai akv seqina,

說比你徃那們好的人再沒有的呀

2. kemuni angga qi tuheburakv sini guqu be jodorongge,

還不住嘴的提說是你的朋友

3. jaqi nomhon dabanahabi,

太過於老實了

4. tere nantuhvn ai ton bi seme jing dabufi gisurembi,

把那個混帳東西算在那個數兒裡僅着說呀

5. niyalma de baire yandure uquri oqi,

求人的時候

6. musei ai seqi,

喒們怎麼說

7. uthai ai gese gese dahame yabumbi,

就怎麼樣的照着樣兒的行呀

8. ini baita waqihiyame,

他的事情一完了

9. dere be emgeri mahvla nakv,

把臉一抹

10. yaya webe seme herserakv,

任憑是誰全不理了

11. duleke aniya ai hafirabuha

去年不知被什麼逼着了

12. nerginde we inde aika gaji sembiheo,

彼時誰還和他要来着

13. ini qisui inde sain bithe bi,

自己說有好書

319

14. age tuwaki seqi,
阿哥若要瞧

15. bi benebure,
我送去

16. ai wei seme minde angga aljaha,
怎長怎短的許了我了

17. amala baita wajiha seme jondoro ba inu akv oho,
後來事情完了也不提了

18. tuttu ofi,
所以

19. jakan bi dere dokome,
將纔我指着臉說

20. age si minde bumbi sehe bithe, absi oho seme fonjire jakade,
阿哥你給我書怎麼樣了問的上

21. dere emu jergi xahvn emu jergi fulahvn,
臉就一陣白一陣紅的了

22. damu hetu gisun i tookabume gvwa be gisurere dabala,
寡支支吾吾說別的罷咧

23. fuhali karu jabume baharakv ohobi,
總不得答應的話了

24. te biqibe,
即如

25. emu yohi bithe, giyanakv ai hihan,
一套書什麼稀罕

26. buhede, ainambi,
給是怎麼樣的

27. burakv ohode geli ainambi,
不給又是怎麼樣的

28. damu turgun akv niyalma be holtorongge jaqi ubiyada.
但只無緣無故的哄人的 討人嫌

Section 79: A Mean Man

1. sini ere absi,
你这是怎麼說

2. weri ginguleme sinde baimbikai,
人家恭恭敬敬的來求你

3. saqi sambi se,
要是知道就說知道；

320

4. sarkv oqi,
要不知道

5. sarkv seqi wajiha,
說不知道就完了

6. holtofi ainambi,
撒的是什麼謊呢

7. talu de ini baita be tookabuha sehede,
倘要惧了他的事情的時候

8. aimaka si gvnin bifi, imbe tuhebuhe adali,
倒像你有心陷害他的一樣

9. i aika emu usun seshun niyalma oqi,
他要是一個檄檄弄弄的厭惡人

10. bi inu gisurerakv bihe,
我也不說来着

11. tere emu nomhon niyalma jilakan manggi,
他是一個老實可憐的呀

12. fixur seme banjiha mudan be tuwaqi endembio,
看起他那個賴怠樣兒來就知道了

13. gvwa imbe tuwaqi uttu,
別人看他是這樣

14. muse giyan i tafulaqi aqara bade,
喈們理該勸導

15. si elemangga ere gese keike baita be yabuhangge,
你反倒行這個樣的刻薄事情

16. ambula taxarahabi,
大錯了

17. yala mini gvnin de dosiharakv,
實在不入我的意

18. age si dule imbe sarkv,
阿哥你却原來不知道他

19. tede eiterebuhe nikai,
被他哄了啊

20. tere niyalma,
那個人

21. bai oilorgi de mentuhun i gese biqibe,
外面雖像老實

22. dolo ja akv,
心裡卻不平常

23. nini ehe nimequke babe,
他的利害不好處

24. si qendehekv be dahame,
你沒有試過

25. sarkvngge inu giyan,
因此不知道也是應該的

26. arga labdu,
計策多

27. hvbin amba,
圈套大

28. niyalma qi ten gaire mangga,
好與人要實據

29. yaya baita biqi,
凡事將到

30. afanggala gisun i yarume geodebume niyalmai gvnin be muruxeme
baha manggi,
先拿話誆着 把人的心料得了一點規模的時候

31. amala tuwaxame aliyakiyame,
後來纔看着等着

32. sini eden babe hiraqambi,
瞅你的短處

33. majige jaka ba biqi,
料有了一點破綻

34. dahalame dosi nakv,
就跟進去

35. uthai emgeri ura tebumbi,
就給一個湊手不及

36. age si gvnime tuwa,
阿哥你想着瞧

37. ere baita minde hobobuha ba bikai,
這個事情與我有關係啊

38. adarame tondokosaka fere gvnin be inde alaqi ombini,
怎麼把實實在在的心腸告訴他 使得嗎

39. ede mimbe wakaxaqi,
因這個怪我的不是

40. bi sui mangga akv semeo.
我豈不屈嗎

Section 80: A Good Horse

1. udaqi,
要買

2. emu sain morin udaqina,
買一匹好馬啊

3. hvwaitame ujire de inu amtangga,
栓着餵着也有趣兒

4. eiqibe orho turi wajimbikai,
總說是要費草料的呀

5. ere gese alaxan be hvwaitafi ainambi,
拴着這個樣的平常馬作什麼呢

6. age si sarkv,
阿哥你還不知道
Brother, you don't know.

7. sikse gajime jaka,
昨日拿了來

8. bi uthai hoton i tule gamafi qendehe,
我就拿到城外頭試驗了

9. yaluqi ombi,
可以騎得

10. katarara neqin
顛得穩

11. feksirengge tondo,
跑得正

12. niyamniyaqi
要是射馬箭

13. majige dosire milara haqin akv,
一點徃裡踏徃外捌的毛病兒沒有

14. buhi dahame,
隨着膊洛蓋兒

15. galai iqi jabdubumbi,
順着手兒轉動

16. uttu oqi,
要是這樣

17. si dule takarakv nikai,
你原來不認得啊

18. sain morin serengge,
所謂的好馬

19. bethe akdun,
腿子結實

20. on dosombi,
奈得長

21. aba saha de ureshvn bime,
圍場上熟

22. gurgu de mangga,
牲口上親

23. giru sain bime, ildamu,
樣兒好且良善

24. yebken asihata,
俊俏年輕的人

25. kiyab seme jebele ashafi yalumbihede,
擊上一副俏皮撒袋騎上了的時候

26. dere tukiyebufi,
仰着臉兒

27. naqin xongkon i gese ombi,
就像鷹一樣的呀

28. ere ai,
這是什麼

29. se jeke,
老了

30. senqehe gemu labdahvn oho,
嘴唇子全搭拉了

31. bethe ujen,
腿子沉了

32. buldurire mangga,
好打前失

33. sini beye geli laju,
你的身子又重

34. labdu aqarakv,
狠不對當

35. te ainaqi ojoro,
如今可怎麼樣呢

36. emgeri udame jabduha kai,
業已買了麼

37. ainame bikini dabala,
任他有着去罷咧

38. eiqibe

捴而言之

39. minde umai ujen alban akv,
我並沒有什麼重差使

40. geli goro takvran akv,
又沒有遠差遣

41. damu nomhon oqi,
但只老實

42. uthai minde teisu,
就與我對當

43. yafahalara qi ai dalji.
比步行走的如何

Section 81: Bad Temper

1. weri imbe gisurembi kai,
人家說他呢呀

2. sinde ai guwanta,
與你什麼相干

3. ele tafulaqi ele nukqihangge,
越勸越發惱了的

4. xosiki bai,
急躁了罷

5. antaha faqaha manggi,
等客散了的時候

6. jai gisurembi dere,
再說罷咧

7. urunakv ere erinde getukeleki sembio,
一定要這個時候見個明白嗎

8. age sini ere gisun,
阿哥 你這個話

9. fuhali mini gvnin de dosirakv,
捴不入我的意思

10. muse emu jahvdai i niyalma kai,
嗄們是一個船上的人啊

11. ere baita sinde lak seme akv,
這個事情與你也不甚爽利

12. heni majige goiquka ba akv sembio,
說一點關礙沒有嗎

13. imbe leoleqi,

要議論他

14. muse be inu dabuhabi,
也帶着喈們啊

15. si dangname gisurerakv oqi okini dere,
你不替說說就罷了

16. fudarame anan xukin i niyalmai iqi tamin i gisurerengge,
反倒一溜神氣的隨着人家的意思說的

17. ai gvnin,
安什麼心

18. bi yala simbe uruxerakv,
我實在不說你的是

19. tuttu waka,
不是那們

20. gisun biqi elhe nuhan i giyan be baime gisure,
有話慢慢的找着理說是呢

21. xara fanqaha de wajimbio,
生氣就完了嗎

22. si tuwa ubade tehe ele niyalma,
你看這裡坐着的人們

23. gemu sini baita de jihengge,
全爲你的事情來的

24. si qingkai uttu jolhoqome jilidaqi,
你總要這樣掙躍生氣

25. aimaka gvnin bifi webe boxome unggire adali,
倒像有心攆誰的一樣

26. jihe niyalma ai yokto tembi,
來的人有什麼趣兒呢

27. boode yoki seqi,
徃家裡去罷

28. dere de eterakv,
臉上又過不去

29. ubade biki seqi,
在這裡罷

30. si geli ek tak seme nakarakv,
你又威喝的不止

31. tuqiqi dosiqi gemu waka,
出去進來全不是

32. teqi iliqi gemu mangga kai,

坐着站着全是難的呀

33. guquse jai sini boode absi feliyembi jiya.
朋友們再怎麼徃你家來徃走呢

Section 82: Secrets were Leaked

1. jalin i niyalma ejesu akvngge,
世上比你沒記性的人

2. sinqi qala jai akv seqina,
再也沒有了呀

3. qananggi bi adarame sini baru henduhe,
我前日怎麼向你說了

4. ere baita be yaya wede
把這個事情任憑是誰

5. ume serebure seqi,
不要叫知覺了

6. si naranggi firgembuhebi,
你到底漏了風聲了

7. musei weilume hebexehe gisun te algixafi
把喒們瞞着商議的話 如今傳揚出去了

8. baba i niyalma gemu saha kai,
各處的人們全知道了啊

9. qe bahafi donjirakv ainaha,
他們豈沒聽見

10. ese talude yertehe ibagan inenggi xun de maksire balama,
他們倘若惱羞變成怒

11. muse de eljeme iselere oqi saiyvn,
抗拒喒們 好嗎

12. hoqikosaka emu baita be ondohoi,
把這一件好好的事情

13. ere ten de isibuhangge,
弄地到了這個地步

14. waqihiyame si kai,
全是你啊

15. age si mimbe wakaxaqi,
阿哥你怪我

16. bi yala sui mangga,
我實在委屈

17. damu baita emgeri uttu oho,

但只事已至此

18. bi te jayan juxutele, faksalame gisurehe seme,
我如今就分晰着說到嘴酸了

19. si akdambio,
你信嗎

20. ere gvnin be damu abka sakini,
這個心就只天知道罷

21. mini beye biheo, waka biheo,
我的是與不是

22. goidaha manggi, ini qisui getukelebumbi,
久而自明

23. mini gvnin ohode,
我的心裡

24. si gasara be joo,
你也別埋怨

25. ine mene sarkv i gese bisu,
就那們不知道的一樣有着去罷

26. qeni aihara be tuwaki,
看他們怎麼樣

27. oqi,
依了
[They can either] agree,

28. oho,
罷了

29. hon ojorakv dubede,
至於狠不依的時候

30. jai arara be tuwame belheqi,
再酌量着預備

31. inu sitaha sere ba akv.
也不至於晚啊

Section 83: Do not Waste Food

1. sain jaka be hairame malhvxaqi
把好東西稀罕着儉省的時候
2. teni banjire were niyalmai doro,
纔是過日子人的道理呢
3. simbe gisurerakv oqi,
要不說你

4. bi eiqibe ojorakv,

我總是不舒服

5. jeme wajirakv funqehe buda be booi urse de ulebuqi,

吃剩下的飯給家裡的人們吃

6. inu sain kai,

也好啊

7. gvnin qihai waqihiyame ko sangga de doolahangge ainu,

任着意見全倒在洋[陽]溝裡是怎麼樣的

8. sini gvnin de inu elhe sembio,

你心裡也安嗎

9. si damu buda jetere be sara gojime,

你雖然知道吃飯

10. bele jeku i mangga babe sahakvbi,

但只未知米糧的艱難處啊

11. tarire niyalma juwere urse,

耕種與那販運的人們

12. ai gese jobome suilafi,

是怎樣的辛苦勞碌

13. teni ubade isinjiha,

纔到了這裡來了

14. emu belge seme ja de bahangge semeo,

就是一粒是輕易得的嗎

15. tere anggala,

況且

16. muse ai bayan mafa seme,

喒們又是什麼富翁呢

17. erebe jeme,

吃着這個

18. terebe kidume,

想着那個

19. gvniha gvnihai uthai udafi,

想來想去 就買了來

20. waliyan gemin i mamgiyambi,

拋拋撒撒的花費了

21. angga de ai kemun,

嘴有什麼規矩

22. jetere de ai dube,

吃有什麼盡休啊

23. qingkai uttu oqi,

一味的要是這樣的時候

24. hvturi ekiyembumbi, sere anggala,
不但折福啊

25. ai bihe seme wajirakv,
就有什麼不完呢

26. sakdasa i gisun,
有老家兒們說的

27. hairame jeqi jeku i da,
惜食長飽

28. hairame etuqi etuku i da sehebi,
惜衣長暖的話呀

29. sini hvturi giyanakv udu,
你能有多大福啊

30. ere durun i sotaqi,
這樣的拋撒五穀

31. fede,
緊着

32. beyede sui ai isifi,
到了折受的

33. omihon de amqabuha erinde,
受餓的時候

34. aliyaha seme amqaburakv kai.
纔悔之不及呢呀

Section 84: He is Dying

1. juwari forgon de,
夏天的時候

2. kemuni katunjaqi ombihe,
還可以勉強来着

3. bihe bihei
久而久之

4. ulhiyen i nimeku nonggibufi
越發添了病

5. fuhali maktabuhabi,
竟撩倒了

6. erei turgunde
因此

7. booi gubqi buran taran maxan baharakv,

合家全乱乱轟轟的不得主意了

8. sakdasa yali gemu wajiha,
老家兒們全熬的瘦了

9. boo i dolo faqaha sirge i gese ohobi,
家裏就像乱絲一樣了

10. imbe tuwaqi
看起他

11. gebserefi giranggi teile funqehebi,
瘦的寡剩下骨頭了

12. nahan de dedu nakv ergen hebtexembi,
躺在炕上 掙命呢

13. tede bi elhei hanqi ibefi,
那個上我慢慢的到跟前

14. si majige yebeo seme
你好些兒了嗎

15. fonjire jakade,
問時

16. yasa neifi mini gala be jafafi,
睜開眼睛拉着我不放

17. geli jafaxame, ai,
嘆着說

18. ere mini gajiha erun sui,
這也是我作的罪

19. nimeku faquhvn bade dosifi,
病已況了

20. ebsi duleme muterakv be bi endembio,
不能縠脫離 我豈不知嗎

21. nimeku bahaqi ebsi,
自從得病以來

22. ya oktosi de dasabuhakv,
什麼醫生沒治過

23. ai okto omihakv,
什麼要沒吃過

24. yebe ojorolame geli busubuhengge,
將好了 又犯了

25. uthai hesebun,
就是命了

26. ede bi umai koro sere ba akv,

這個我一點兒也沒有委屈處

27. damu ama eme se de oho,
但只父母年老了

28. deote geli ajige,
兄弟們又小

29. jai niyalma hvnqihin giranggi yali gemu mimbe tuwahai bikai,
再親戚與骨肉全不過白看顧着我罷咧

30. bi mangga mujilen i ya emken be lashalame mutere seme,
我就狠着心可離得開誰呢

31. gisun wajinggala
話將完了

32. yasai muke fir seme eyehe,
眼淚直流

33. ai,
唉

34. absi usaquka,
何等的可嘆

35. udu sele wehei gese niyalma sehe seme,
就說是鐵石人心

36. terei gisun de
聽見那個話

37. mujilen efujerakvngge akv.
沒有不動心的呀

Section 85: A Troublemaker

1. ai fusi geli bini,
什麼下賤東西也有呢

2. niyalmai deberen waka,
不是人的崽子

3. ini ama i gese urehe banjihabi,
生活像他阿媽一樣

4. yala ini ama i hvnqihin,
實在是他阿媽的種兒

5. absi tuwaqi, absi ubiyada,
怎麼看怎麼討人嫌啊

6. yaya bade takvrxaqi,
大凡使了去的地方

7. yasa niqu niquxame eiten saburakv,

閉着眼睛 什麼看不見

8. balai qunggvxambi,
混撞啊

9. anggai dolo ulu wala seme,
嘴裡打唔嚕

10. aimaka niyalma be nioboro adali,
倒像戲弄人的一樣

11. we ini gisun be ulhimbi,
誰懂得他的話呢

12. jingkini bade umai baitakv bime,
正經地方狠無用

13. efimbi sere de jergi bakqin akv,
一說玩起來沒有對兒

14. jaka xolo burakv,
一點空兒不給

15. hanqi erxebuqi hono yebe,
叫在跟前服侍着使喚還好

16. majige aljabuha de,
署離了些的時候

17. taji tuwara ba akv,
淘氣的狠不堪

18. fuhali abkai ari,
竟是個天生的惡人

19. terebe gaisu,
拿起那個來

20. erebe sinda,
放下這個去

21. majige andande seme ekisaka banjirakv,
一會兒不閒着

22. kvwak qak seme monioqilambi,
猴兒一樣的跳塌

23. jili nerginde oqi,
一時性子上來了

24. ere lehele i duha be sarabuha de,
把這個雜種的膛開了

25. teni kek sere dabala,
纔稱心入意罷咧

26. duleke manggi,

過去了的時候

27. geli gvniqi ainara jiya,
又想着可怎麼樣呢

28. yargiyan i imbe wambio,
實在的殺他嗎

29. uju de foholon taimin galaqi ai dalji,
第一件火棍雖短倒比手強

30. jai de oqi, booi ujin jui seme
第二件是家生子兒

31. bahara jetere bade,
所得的與吃的去處

32. geli esi seqi ojorakv,
又不由的

33. imbe fulu majige gosimbi.
多疼他些兒

Section 86: I am not Afraid

1. ai guwejihe tatabuhabi,
安的是什麼心腸

2. mimbe weihukelerengge ja akv,
把我輕視的至極了

3. bi sini baru gisun gisureqi teisu akv semeo,
我望你說話不是分內的嗎

4. jime ohode, faksi gisun i mimbe yekerxerengge,
來了就用巧言刻薄我

5. beyebe ai obuhabi,
倒算個什麼

6. dere yasa emu bade fumereme ofi,
常在一處攪混

7. bi damu gisurerakv dabala,
我不過不說罷咧

8. da sekiyen be tuqibuhede,
要把根子說出來的時候

9. geli mimbe fetereku sembi,
又說我刨根子了

10. ini da gaxan,
他的家鄉

11. mini fe susu,

我的住處

12. webe we sarkv,
誰不知道誰的呢

13. niyalma de monjirxaburakv oqi,
不叫人揉搿

14. giyanakv udu goidaha,
能有幾年了

15. akabume te mini baru
受着罪到如今望着我

16. beileqileki sembi,
拿起腔來了

17. ine mene gisun endebuhe seqi,
索性說話說錯了

18. mini dolo hono yebe,
我的心裡還過得去

19. muritai ini gisun be uru arafi,
一定要強着說他的話是

20. ainaha seme waka be alime gaijarakv kai,
任憑怎麼的不認不是

21. tede niyalma esi hvr seqi,
因那個上不由得叫人生氣啊

22. mimbe adarame ja tuwahabi,
怎麼把我看容易了

23. wei fiyanji de ertufi
伏着誰的威勢

24. enenggi teile gala elkime mimbe jio sembi,
今日招呼特意叫我來的呀

25. yala webe we ainambi,
實在誰把誰怎麼樣呢

26. wede we gelembi,
誰怕誰呢

27. meke qeke qendeki seqi,
要試個高低上下

28. mini gvnin de kek sere dabala,
倒狠稱我的心罷咧

29. majige tathvnjaqi,
要是畧畧的遲疑的時候

30. inu haha waka.
也就不是漢子了啊

Section 87: Rainy Days

1. utala inenggi ta ti ta ti seme sirkedeme agahai,
滴滴答答的連霾了這些日子了

2. dolo gemu urehe,
心裡全熟了

3. uba sabdaha,
這裡漏了

4. tuba usihihe,
那裡濕了

5. amgara ba gemu akv ohobi,
睡覺的地方全沒了

6. ere dade,
又搭着

7. wahvn umiyaha suran ai xufarangge,
那個臭蟲虼蚤咬的

8. fuhali hamiqi ojorakv,
狠受不了

9. kurbuxehei tanggv ging tulitele,
翻來覆去的直到亮鐘以後

10. amu isinjirakv,
睡不着

11. yasa eteme niqubu,
把眼睛強閉着

12. geli majige kiriha biqi,
又忍着的上

13. arkan buru bara amu xaburaha,
將將的纔恍恍惚惚的睡着了

14. jing sereme amgara de,
正睡着的時候

15. gaitai wargi amargi hoxo qi
忽聽得西北角上

16. uthai alin ulejehe, na fakqaha adali kunggur seme emgeri guwere jakade,
就像山崩地裂的一樣響的上

17. tar seme dokdoslafi getehe,
我兢兢的驚醒了

18. kejine beye kemuni xurgeme dargime niyalma jaka tuk tuk sembi,
好些工夫身子打顫 心還跳呢

19. yasa neifi tuwaqi,
睜眼一看

20. boo nahan agvra tetun umainahakv,
屋裡炕上一切器具並沒怎麼樣的

21. ekxeme niyalma takvrafi tuwanabuhai,
急忙使人去看

22. adaki boo i fiyasha aga de xekebufi tuheke sembi,
說是隔壁的房山牆被雨湿透倒下來了

23. tere asuki be amu tolgin de donjiha turgunde,
那個聲響 在夢中聽見的上

24. uran ainu tuttu amba bihe.
聲音怎麼那樣的大呢

Section 88: Stay up Late

1. ere udu inenggi baita bifi,
這幾日因爲有事

2. emu siran i juwe dobori yasatabuha turgunde,
一連兩夜熬了眼睛的緣故

3. beye gubqi fakjin akv liyar sembi,
渾身不得主意悉軟的了

4. sikse yamji erinde,
昨日晚上

5. bi uthai amgaki sembihe,
我就要睡覺来着

6. niyaman hvnqihin leksei ubade bisire,
因爲親戚全在這裡的上頭

7. bi ai hendume waliyame amganambi,
我怎麼說撂了睡覺去呢

8. tuttu ofi
因爲那樣

9. katunjara dade geli katunjame,
雖然勉强着又勉强

10. beye udu simen arame teqeqibe,
打着精神坐着

11. yasa esi seqi ojorakv debsehun,
眼睛不由的媽搭下來

12. murhu farhvn ome genembi,
恍恍惚惚的去了

337

13. amala antaha faqame,
後來客們將散了

14. bi emu qirku sindafi,
我就放了一個枕頭

15. etuku nisihai
穿着衣裳

16. uju makta hiri amgaha,
把頭一倒竟自睡熟了

17. jai ging otolo teni getehe,
倒了第二更的時候才醒了

18. tede majige xahvraka ainaha be sarkv,
那個上 也不是涼着了些 或者怎麼樣的了

19. dolo umesi kuxun ping sembi,
心裡狠悵悶

20. beye i gubqi wenjerengge,
渾身發熱

21. uthai tuwa de fiyakvbuha adali,
就像火烤的一樣

22. ere dade xan geli sulhume ofi,
又搭着耳底疼

23. tatabufi jayan ergi gemu suksurekebi,
拉扯的牙花子全腫了

24. jeqi omiqi amtan akv,
吃飯喝茶沒味兒

25. teqibe iliqibe elhe akv,
坐着站着不安

26. bi ere ainqi jeku taksilabuha ayoo seme,
我想這必是存住食了罷

27. emu jemin wasibure okto omire jakade,
吃了一服打藥的時候

28. sain ehe jaka gemu wasinjiha,
把好歹的東西全打下來了

29. tede teni majige sulakan oho.
那個上纔畧畧的鬆閒了些了

Section 89: Court Beads

1. age sini tere erihe be,
阿哥你的那盤朝珠

2. bi gamaki sehei,
我說要拿了去

3. jiduji bahafi gamahakv,
到底沒得拿了去

4. turgun ai seqi
什麼緣故呢

5. jihe dari,
每逢來了

6. si gemu boode akv,
你全不在家

7. simbe aqahakv de,
沒見你的面

8. ai hendume buksuri, sini jaka be gamambi,
怎麼說糊裡糊塗的把你的東西拿了去呢

9. uttu ofi,
所以

10. bi enenggi qohome sinde aqafi alaha manggi,
我今日特來見你告訴了

11. gamaki sembi,
好拿了去

12. tede teherebume,
對着那個置的 387

13. si ai jaka gaji seqi,
你說要什麼

14. bi sini gvnin de aqabume udafi hvlaxaki,
我就照着你的心買了來換啊

15. uthai puseli de unqara sain ningge akv seme,
就是鋪裡賣的沒有好的

16. bi inu urunakv babade ulame baifi sinde bure,
我也必定在各處 轉找了來給你

17. sini gvnin de antaka,
你心裡怎麼樣

18. si kemuni jondofi ainambi,
你還題什麼

---

387 'Teherebume' means 'equivalent or commensurable', corresponding with 置的 (*zhide*). The modern expression is 相稱 (*xiangche*n) or 等值 (*dengzhi*).

19. ine mene gamaha biqi sain bihe,
無論怎麼拿了去也好来着

20. ainahai waliyabumbini,
如何至於丟了呢

21. hairakan bodisu ningge ai yadara,
菩提子的豈少嗎

22. damu tede isirengge umesi komso,
可惜趕得上那個的狠少啊

23. tuttu waka oqi ai,
可不是什麼

24. inenggidari jafaxahai
每日拿着的上

25. gemu siberi daha
汗全浸透的

26. umesi nilgiyan ohobi,
狠光潤了

27. jafaxarakv gvwabsi genembihede,
不拿了徃別處的時候

28. terebe horho de asarambihe,
把他裝在箱子裡来着

29. inu waliyabure giyan ofi,
也是該丟的上

30. manaha biyade be yafan de generede,
去月裡我們徃園裡去的時

31. onggofi bargiyahakv,
忘了沒收起來

32. amasi jifi baiqi,
回來找時

33. aba
那裡有

34. arun durun saburekv oho,
連影兒也不見了

35. wede hvlhabuha be inu sarkv,
也不知道被誰偷了去

36. merkime baiha seme fuhali bahakv.
想着找了個歃捆沒找到

Section 90: A Hot Day

1. enenggi absi nimequke,
今日好利害

2. juwari dosika qi ebsi,
自從立夏以來

3. ujui uju halhvn seqi ombi,
可算得頭一等熱天了啊

4. majige edun akv,
一點風兒沒有

5. ludur sembi,
潮熱的狠

6. eiten agvra tetun gemu gala halame halhvn,
各樣的器具 全燙手的熱

7. ele juhe muke omiqi ele kangkambi,
越喝冰水越渴

8. arga akv ebixefi
沒法兒的上 洗澡去

9. mooi fejile kejine sebderilehe manggi,
在樹底下涼快了許久

10. teni majige tohoroko,
心裡纔畧畧的定了些

11. ere gese hvktame halhvn de
這樣的燥熱

12. weri beye niohuxun,
人家光着身子

13. bai tehede
閒坐着

14. hono halhvn qalirahv sembikai,
還怕受熱中暑呢

15. si ainahabi
你怎麼了

16. uju gidahai hergen ararangge
總低着頭寫字

17. ai sui,
受什麼罪呢

18. ergen haji akv semeo,
不惜命嗎

19. si alban qagan akv,
你沒有差事

20. baisin i jirgame taqiha dabala,
白閒着受受用用的學罷咧

21. duibuleqi hvdai urse okini,
譬如買賣人們

22. haijung sere ujen jaka be damjalafi,
挑着沉重的東西

23. monggon sampi,
伸着脖子

24. ba bade xodome hvlahai
徃各處奔走吻呼[吆喝]

25. nei taran waliyatala arkan
壓的渾身是汗

26. teni tanggv jiha funqere butafi ergen hetumbumbikai,
將將的剩個一百多錢養命

27. mini adali beleningge be jefi,
像我吃着現成的

28. elehun i hergen araki seqi bahambio,
安安靜靜的寫字能彀得嗎

29. tere anggala,
況且

30. tuweri beikuwen,
冬天冷

31. juwari halhun ojorongge,
夏天熱

32. julgeqi ebsi halaqi ojorakv toktoho doro,
自古不移一定的理啊

33. ine mene ekisaka dosobuqi,
要是不論怎麼樣的 靜靜的受去

34. embiqi serguwen ombidere,
也可以涼快罷咧

35. fathaxaha seme ai baita,
煩躁會子何用呢

36. bahafi guweqi ombio.
能彀免得嗎

Section 91: A Rude Man

1. i jidere fonde,
他來的時候

2. bi hono amgaha bihe,

我還睡覺来着

3. sek seme getefi donjiqi,
驚醒了

4. qin i boode niyalma jifi den jilgan i gisun gisurembi,
聽見上屋裡有人高聲說話呢呀

5. we jiheni,
誰來了

6. ai uttu konggolo den,
怎麼這樣的嗓門大

7. ainqi tere usun dakvla jihe aise seme,
大畧是那個討人嫌的來了罷

8. genefi tuwaqi waka oqi ai,
去看時可不是什麼

9. godohon i te nakv,
直梃梃（挺挺）的坐着

10. jing amtanggai leoleme bi,
正有資有味的講論呢

11. jiheqi angga majige mimihakv,
自從以來總沒住嘴

12. uttu tuttu sehei,
怎長怎短的說着

13. juwe erin i buda jefi,
吃了兩頓飯

14. gerhen mukiyetele teni genehe,
直到黃昏 纔去了

15. haha niyalma baita akv de
漢子家沒事的時候

16. weri boode xuntuhuni teme dosombio,
在人家裡坐到日落也受得嗎

17. aibi onggoho xadaha baita be gisurehei,
把那裡忘了乏的事情說的

18. niyalma fehi gemu nimehe,
叫人腦子全疼

19. damu uttu oqi ai baire,
寡要是這樣的還罷了

20. yaya jaka be hono inde sabubuqi ojorakv,
不論什麼東西不可給他看見

21. emgeri yasalabuha sehede,

一說搭上了眼

22. fonjin hese akv nambuha be tuwame,
問也不問 撓着了

23. deleri deleri seme gamambi,
早早的就拿了去

24. yala beye dubentele, damu gaji sere be sambi
實在一輩子寡知道要人家的東西

25. ma sere sere mudan inde fuhali akv seqina,
給人家的遭數兒說是沒有的

26. enteke niyalma duha do
像這樣的五臟

27. absi banjiha be,
怎麼長的

28. bi yargiyan i sarkv,
我實在不知道啊

29. imata si jabxambio,
都是你的便宜

30. si bahambio,
你得嗎

31. abka de yasa bikai,
天有眼睛啊

32. ainahai inde ombini.
未必容他呢

Section 92: You Look Distressed!

1. muse tere guqu ainahabi,
嗒們的那個朋友怎麼樣了

2. ere uquri xenggin hitere nakv munahvn i joboxorongge,
這一向皺着眉愁悶的

3. maka ai turgun bisire be sarkv,
倒像有什麼緣故的樣

4. an i uquri aga labsan inenggi oqi,
素常下雨下雪的天道

5. boode bisire dabala,
在家裡罷咧

6. tereqi tulgiyen murikv bade gemu xudumbikai,
除了那個無緣無故的地方全去到啊

7. baibi boode teme dosombio,

白白的在家裡坐着 也受得嗎

8. ere uquri duka be tuqike akv,
這些日子不出房門

9. boode norohoi tehebi,
總在家裡坐着

10. sikse bi tuwaname genehede,
昨日我去瞧的上

11. tuwaqi qira ai
看那氣色什麼

12. kemuni nenehe adali sembio,
還說像先嗎

13. serebume wasika,
明顯着瘦了

14. tuqire dosire de fuhali teme toktorakv,
出去進來總沒定準

15. ebsi qasi akv seqina,
不知道要怎麼樣的呢

16. tede bi labdu kenehunjeme,
那個上我狠疑惑

17. ere ainahabi ni,
他怎麼了呢

18. teni fonjiki serede,
纔要問

19. ini niyamangga niyalma jio nakv hiyahalabuha,
他的一個親戚去了的上隔開了

20. ara,
哎吆

21. bi bodome bahanaha,
我算着了

22. ainqi tere baita de lahin tafi gvnin farfabuha aise,
大料被那個事情絆住 心全糊塗了罷

23. tuttu seme aga de usihibuhe niyalma silenggi de gelerakv sehe kai,
但有被雨濕的人 不怕露水的話呀

24. seibeni antaka antaka mangga baita be
先前他把什麼樣的難事情

25. i gemu uksa faksa waqihiyaha bade,
全能骰霎時間辦理完結

26. ere giyanakv ai holbobuha seme,

這有什麼關係

27. jing uttu joboxombi.
這樣的愁悶呢

Section 93: Addiction Kills

1. daqi ai etuhun beye,
原先是什麼強壯身子呢

2. tere dade geli ujire be sarkv,
還搭着不知道養法

3. nure boqo de dosifi,
進于酒色

4. balai kokirabure jakade,
混被傷損的過失

5. te nimeku de hvsibufi dembei sirke ohobi,
如今被病包着 瘦的一條了

6. sikse bi tuwanahade,
昨日我瞧去的時候

7. kemuni katunjame qin i boode jifi,
還勉強着來上正屋裡來

8. mini baru age jime joboho kai,
說阿哥勞乏了啊

9. ere gese hvktame halhvn de,
這個樣的燥熱的時候

10. ta seme tuwanjire,
常常的來瞧

11. ton akv jaka benjiburengge,
而且沒遍數的送東西來

12. ambula xadaha,
狠乏了

13. umesi baniha,
着實的費心了

14. inu niyaman hvnqihin i dolo tatabume ofi uttu dabala,
也是親戚裡頭這樣的掛心罷咧

15. halba dalba oqi geli mimbe gvnire mujanggo,
要是不相干的 還想着我嗎

16. bi labdu hukxembi,
我狠感激啊

17. damu hadahai gvnin de ejefi,

不過寡緊記在心裡

18. yebe oho erinde,
等好了的時候

19. jai hengkixeme baniha buki, baili jafaki seme,
再叩謝盛情罷

20. angga de uttu gisureqibe,
嘴裡雖然這樣說着

21. beye serebume katunjame muterakv,
身子顯着勉強不住

22. tuttu ofi,
所以那個上

23. bi age si sure niyalma kai,
我說阿哥你是個明白人啊

24. mini fulu gisurere be baibumbio,
用我多說嗎

25. beyebe saikan ujikini,
把身子好好的養着

26. hvdun yebe okini,
快快好罷

27. xolo de,
有了空兒

28. bi jai tuwanjire
我再來瞧罷

29. sefi amasi jihe.
說了回來了

Section 94: Bond-servants Need Discipline

1. sikse gvwabsi genere jakade,
昨日徃別處去的上

2. fatan ahasi,
臭奴才們

3. uthai qihai balai emu falan daixaha,
就任意鬧了一場

4. bi amasi jihe erinde,
我回來了的時候

5. monio sa jing ge ga seme qurginduhai bi,
猴兒們正還爭嚷喧譁呢

6. tede bi kak seme emgeri

那個上我喀的一聲

7. bilha dasafi dosika biqi,
打掃着嗓子進去的上

8. leksei jilgan nakafi,
一齊住了聲

9. si bi ishunde kvlisitame yasa arafi,
彼此互相作着眼色兒

10. son son i melerjeme yoha,
各自各自畏避了

11. mini jihengge inu goidaha,
我來的也晚了

12. beye inu xadaha turgunde
身子也乏的上

13. umai sehekv,
什麼沒說

14. kirifi amgaha,
忍着睡了覺了

15. eqimari ilifi tuqikede
今日早起起來出去

16. waburu sa gemu jihe,
砍頭的們全來了

17. ahasi meni buqere giyan isika seme,
說奴才們該死

saying that the bond servants all deserve to die.

18. emu teksin godohon i niyakvrafi
一齊的直蹶蹶（撅撅）的跪着

19. bairengge baire
求的求

20. hengkixerengge hengkixere jakade,
磕頭的磕頭的上

21. mini jili teni majige nitaraka,
我的性子纔料料的消了些

22. tede bi suwe ainahabi,
那個上我說你們怎麼了

23. taifin i banjirakv,
不太太平平的過日子

24. yali yoyohoxombio,
肉癢癢了嗎

25. urunakv tantabuha de ai bahambi,

348

一定叫打一頓得甚麼

26. fede ereqi julesi geli ere gese mudan biqi,
好鬆[生]的徃後再有這樣的次數

27. yasai faha guwelke,
提防着眼珠子

28. fita jokjarakv oqi,
要不徃死裡重打的時候

29. gvniqi suwe inu iserakv sehe manggi,
想來你們也不怕啊

30. gemu je sefi genehe.
全喏的一聲 答應了去了

Section 95: A Terrible Person

1. tere kesi akvngge be,
你把那個沒福的

2. si absi tuwahabi,
怎麼看了

3. niyalmai sukv nereqibe,
雖然批的是人皮

4. ulha i duha kai,
確實畜牲的心腸啊

5. jailame yabuha de sain,
躲着走好啊

6. fuhali baita akv de,
於無事的裡頭

7. baita dekdere emu faquhvn da seqina,
生事作亂的頭兒啊

8. gvnin silhingga oforodoro mangga,
心苦善用讒間

9. yala sabuha de saksari,
實在叫他眼睛看見的 就是一個仰面觔斗

10. donjihade dokdori,
聽見了的 就抖露起來

11. qihe use i gese majige baita biqi,
就像蟣子一樣的小事兒

12. ini angga de isinaha sehede,
到了他嘴裡的時候

13. jubexehei fikatala genembi,

說到一個離乎了

14. ubai baita be tubade ulaname,
把這裡的事情告訴那裡去

15. tubai gisun be ubade alanjime,
那裡的話兒告訴這裡來

16. juwe ergide kimun jafabu nakv,
把兩下裡成了仇了

17. i ikiri tatame sidenderi sain niyalma arambi,
他一溜神氣的從中間作好人

18. meni gisun be temgetu akv seqi,
要說我們的話沒憑據

19. si tuwa,
你看

20. ini baru guqulere niyalma akv sere anggala,
不但沒人和他交結

21. fisa jorime toorakv oqi,
若不指着脊背罵

22. uthai ini jabxan,
就是他的便宜

23. ai,
唉

24. nasaquka,
可嘆啊

25. erei ama eme fili fiktu akv,
他的父母無緣無故的

26. ere fusi de uxabufi,
受這個下賤東西拉扯的

27. niyalma de tooburengge,
叫人罵的

28. ai sui.
怎麼樣的一個冤枉呢

Section 96: He Survived!

1. buqere giyan waka oqi,
要不該死

2. ini qisui emu nashvn tuqinjimbi,
自然就出一個機會啊

3. tere emu dobori ujelehe farapi

那一晚上 病的狠昏沉

4. kejine ofi,
遲了許久

5. teni aituha,
纔酥醒過來了

6. angga de bi hvwanggiyarakv,
嘴裡說我無妨

7. suwe gvnin sulakan i sinda seme,
你們把心放的寬寬的

8. niyalma be naqihiyambihe,
不叫人慌来着

9. yala mafai kesi, booi gubqi hvturi,
實在托祖上的恩典 闔家的福上

10. jai inenggi enqu emu oktosi be halafi dasabure jakade,
第二日另請一個醫生來醫治

11. yasa tuwahai emu inenggi emu inenggi qi yebe oho,
眼看着一日比一日好了

12. qananggi bi genefi tuwaqi,
前日我去看了一看

13. da beye bahara unde biqibe,
雖然沒還原

14. qira inu aituha,
氣色也轉過來了

15. yali inu majige nonggiha,
也長了點肉了

16. jing qirku de nikeme tefi,
正靠在枕頭上坐着

17. jaka jeku jeme bi,
吃東西呢

18. tede bi sini jabxan kai,
那個上我說你僥倖啊

19. urgun kai,
大喜啊

20. ere mudan buqehekv biqibe,
這一遭雖然沒死

21. sukv emu jergi kobqiha kai serede,
可脫落一層皮啊

22. mini baru ijarxame injembi,

望着我瞇嘻瞇嘻的笑

23. yala nei tuqifi umesileme dulekebi.
實在可是攥着把汗過來了

Section 97: Obeying the Rules

1. si ai uttu sofin akv,
你怎麼這樣沒定準

2. doronggo yangsanggai teqi,
規規矩矩的坐着

3. we simbe moo xolon sembio,
誰說你是個木頭墩子嗎

4. gisun hese akv oqi,
不說話

5. ya simbe hele hempe akv sembio,
誰說你是個啞巴嗎

6. aimaka wede yobo arara adali,
倒像給誰作笑的一樣

7. erebe neqi manggi geli terebe nungnerengge,
惹惹這個 招招那個

8. ai sebjen babi,
有什麼樂處

9. si sererakv dere,
你不覺罷咧

10. dalbai niyalma gemu dosorakv ohobi,
旁人全受不得啊

11. atanggi biqibe si emu jekxun kequ niyalma be uqarafi,
多嗏你遇見一個狠刻薄的人

12. koro baha manggi,
碰釘子的時候

13. si teni ara, dule uttu nimequke ni sembikai,
你纔說 哎吆原來是這樣的利害啊

14. age sini ahvn i gisun inu,
阿哥你兄長的話對

15. hetu daljakv niyalma uttu gisurere aibi,
要是旁不相干的人 豈肯這樣說嗎

16. efin serengge, beqen i deribun kai,
頑啊是拌嘴的引子啊

17. bihe bihei

352

久而久之

18. ai sain banjinara,

怎麼能骰出（變）好呢

19. eitereqibe,

總而言之

20. ini beye bai hahardaha gojime,

他的身子雖然長大成漢子了

21. se oron unde,

歲數沒到呢

22. muse tere fonqi dulembuhekv nio,

喒們沒從那個時候過過嗎

23. jing efin de amuran erin kai,

正是好頑的時候啊

24. esi uttu oqi,

自然是這樣的

25. ere sidende uttu,

這個時候這樣

26. damu gebungge sefu be solifi bithe be taqibukini,

只有請個有名的先生教書啊

27. doro be urebukini,

演習規矩啊

28. inenggi goidaha manggi,

日子久了

29. qun qun i ulhinjefi,

一歷一歷懂得了

30. emu qimari andande jalan i baita be saha sehede,

一朝要說是知道了世間上的事情的時候

31. ini qisui dasabumbi,

自然就改了

32. hvwaxarakv niyalma ojorakv jalin aiseme jobombi jiya.

何愁不能成人呢

Section 98: Just Let It Out!

1. eiten baita dulembuhekv,

什麼事情沒有經過

2. oliha ten,

怯弱的狠

3. gisun biqi aiseme dolo gingkambi,

有話爲什麼悶在肚裡

4. xuwe genefi,
一直的去了

5. ini baru getuken xetuken i neileme gisureqina,
向他明明白白的徃開裡說啊

6. tere inu niyalma dabala,
他也是人罷咧

7. doro giyan be baime yaburakv mujanggo,
有不遵着道理行的嗎

8. turgun be tuqibume da dube qi aname sume faksalaha de,
把緣故從頭至尾分析明白了的時候

9. simbe ainarahv sembio,
怕把你怎麼樣嗎

10. warahv sembio,
怕殺嗎

11. eiqi jeterahv sembio,
或者怕吃嗎

12. tere anggala,
況且

13. weri tubade umai asuki wei akv bade,
人家那裡並沒什麼聲色

14. afanggala kvlifi fekun waliyabu nakv,
就怕的吞聲失了主意

15. uttu tuttu seme tosorongge,
這們那們逆料預備的

16. aika haha wa bio,
還有個漢子的味兒嗎

17. hvwanggiyarakv,
無妨啊

18. si damu gvnin be sulakan sinda,
你只管把心放寬罷

19. tere unenggi ojorakv,
他要是當真的不依

20. ainaki seqi sinde dere banjimbio,
要說是怎麼樣的給你留臉嗎

21. si uttu tuttu gelehe seme,
你就是這們那們怕了的時候

22. bahafi bolokosaka ukqara aibi,

354

豈能彀乾乾淨淨的脫離了嗎

23. tetele umai mejige akv be tuwaqi,

看起到如今沒有音信來

24. gvniqi aifini hv i da i amala maktafi onggohobi,

想來早已撂在脖子後頭 忘了

25. hon akdarakv oqi,

狠要不信

26. jenduken i mejigele,

悄悄的打聽信去

27. bi akdulafi hvwanggiyarakv obure.

我管保無妨啊

Section 99: Don't Trust the Doctors

1. sini tafularangge sain gisun waka oqi ai,

你勸的可不是好話什麼

2. damu minde emu enqu gvninre babi,

但只我另有心事

3. uennggi okto omiqi aqaqi,

若果應該吃藥

4. bi moo xolon waka kai,

我又不是個木頭墩子

5. jiha menggun be hairame beyebe dasarakv doro bio,

有捨不得銀錢不治自己身子的理嗎

6. adarame seqi,

怎麼說呢

7. qara aniya bi okto de endebufi,

前年我被藥傷着了

8. elekei ergen joqibuha,

差一點沒有傷了命

9. tetele gvnihadari silhi meijembi,

至到如今想起來還膽戰呢

10. te biqibe oktosi sei dorgi de,

既如醫生們裡頭

11. sain ningge fuhali akv seqi,

說是捴沒有好的

12. qe inu sui mangga,

他們也冤屈

13. biqi bi dere,

355

有只有罷

14. damu musei tengkime sarangge umesi tongga,
但只嗏們知道真切的稀少啊

15. tere anggala,
況且

16. nikedeqi ojorongge
靠得的

17. inu talu de emke juwe bisire dabala,
也偶有一兩個罷

18. tereqi funqehengge,
其餘的

19. gemu jiha menggun be butara be sambi,
寡知道爲銀錢啊

20. sini buqere banjire be i bodombio,
你的生死他顧嗎

21. akdarakv ofi,
要不信

22. si qendeme fonjime tuwame geneki,
你試問着瞧

23. okto banin be sahao undeo,
你知道藥性了沒有

24. uthai amban i maname,
就是大方脈兒的

25. niyalma i nimeku be dasambi,
治人的病啊

26. ekxeme saksime sini boode jio nakv,
急急忙忙的来你家裡来

27. sudala jafambi seme,
說是拿脈

28. gala simhun i balai emu jergi bixume,
把手指頭混抹了一會兒

29. ainame ainame emu dasargan ilibu nakv,
草草了事的立了一個方子

30. morin i jiha be gaifi yoha,
要了馬錢去了

31. yebe oqi ini gungge,
好了說是他的功

32. endebuqi sini hesebun seme,

死了是你的命

33. inde fuhali daljakv,
與他毫無相干

34. beye beyei nimeku be endembio,
自己不知道自己的病嗎

35. haqingga okto i baitalabure anggala,
與其用各項的藥材

36. beye ekisaka ujirengge wesihun.
不如自己靜靜的養育爲貴啊

Section 100: Alcohol Kills

1. simbe tuwaqi,
看起你來

2. arki nure de haji,
與燒酒黃酒狠親啊

3. dartai andande seme aljabuqi ojorakv,
一時離不得

4. omihadari urui lalanji heperefi,
每逢喝酒一定要乱醉如泥

5. ilime toktorakv oho manggi teni nakambi,
站不住腳了的時候 纔扳開手

6. sain baita waka kai,
不是好事啊

7. majige targaha de sain,
料戒一戒兒好些

8. sarin yengsi oqi ai hendure,
要是筵席上可怎麼說不喝呢

9. baita sita biqi ainara,
有事故的時候可怎麼樣呢

10. saliha i majige omiha de aibi,
拿着喝些兒有什麼

11. baita akv de baita obume,
無事的時候把他當一件事情

12. hvntahan jafaxahai
拿着盅子不肯放

13. angga qi hokoburakv maktaqi,
稱讚起來

14. ai sain ba banjinara,

有什麼好處

15. ungga dangga de waka baha,
只看見得罪老家兒

16. amba jobolon neqihe,
犯大罪

17. oyonggo baita tookabuha be sabuha dabala,
耽誤要緊的事情罷咧

18. omiha turgunde tenteke bengsen taqiha,
實在沒聽見會喝酒算學了那樣本事

19. erdemu nonggibuha,
長了才學

20. niyalma de kundulebuhe,
叫人恭敬

21. jingkini baita be mutebuhengge be yala donjiha ba inu akv,
成就了正經事情了呀

22. banin be faquhvrara,
乱了性

23. beyebe kokirabure,
傷了身子

24. ehe okto kai,
是不好藥啊

25. qingkai omiqi ombio,
長喝使得嗎

26. akdarakv oqi,
要是不信

27. si bulekuxeme tuwaki,
你照着鏡子看看

28. oforo gemu ibtenehebi,
鼻子全糟了

29. ubu waliyabure niyalma waka kai,
不是撂分兒的人啊

30. inenggi dobori akv,
不分晝夜的

31. uttu bexeme omiqi,
如此徃糟裡喝去

32. Beyebe beye hvdularangge wakao.
不是叫自己快着嗎

358

Section 101: Learning is Difficult

1. age si tuwa,
阿哥你看

2. ai sui biheni,
受什麼罪

3. niyalma uttu tuttu seme sinde jomburengge,
人們這們那們題駁你的

4. inu simbe sain okini,
也是叫你好

5. ehe taqirakv sere gvnin,
不叫你學不好的心啊

6. hvlaha bithe be majige urebuqi
把念的書溫習溫習

7. bahanara de gelembio,
怕會了嗎

8. jingkini bengsen be taqire de umesi mangga bime,
學正經本事狠難

9. ehe demun inde nokai ja,
不好的事情於他狠容易

10. ai haqin i angga hvwajatala gisurehe seme,
任憑怎樣的把嘴說破了

11. i donjiqi ai baire,
他要是聽了求什麼

12. nememe ebi habi nakv,
越發怠兒慢兒的

13. angga mongniohon i dere yasa waliyatambi,
撅着嘴 摺鼻子臉子的上

14. tede bi tuwahai dolo dosorakv,
我看不過

15. fanqafi hiyang seme emgeri esukiyere jakade,
生了氣大聲的呵叱了一頓

16. dere fulara makv,
把臉紅了

17. fudarame mini baru,
反望着我說

18. si mimbe qihalafi ainambi seme,
你尋我的空子作什麼呢

19. yasa muke gelerjembi,

眼淚汪汪的

20. ai hvlhi kesi akv dabala,
何等的糊塗啊沒福的罷咧

21. hendure balama,
可是說的

22. sain okto angga de gosihon,
良藥苦口

23. tondo gisun xan de iqakv sehebi,
忠言逆耳的話呀

24. aika giranggi yali waka oqi,
要不是骨肉

25. bi damu ainame hoxxome urgunjebuqi wajiha kai,
我寡哄着他叫他喜歡就完了啊

26. urunakv inde eimeburengge ai hala.
爲什麼一定要叫他厭煩呢

PART II
THE PRIMERS
THEIR ENGLISH TRANSLATIONS WITH ANNOTATIONS

Chapter 4
Manchu-Chinese Language and Manchu Conventional Expressions - A Book for Illuminating the Qing Language

Preface: A Book for Beginners

1. The Book for enlightening the Qing language,[388]

2. [was] narrated and written by my friend Xeoping.

3. [It is] for teaching in home school.

4. Regarding the Chinese language [which is] put [to] annotate,

5. although[389] [it is] very vulgar and superficial,

6. as for the learners[390] [who] are enlightened to make progress gradually,

7. [it helps to] penetrate from shallow to deep [inside],

8. starting to travel afar from the near, [which is also where] the intention dwells.

9. In addition, in the beginning for the guiding and teaching[391],

10. if it were not for such a clear and obvious text,

11. it would be difficult [for the students] to grasp and to understand[392].

12. Indeed this [is a] training raft[393] for the young learners to cross [the river],

13. and a shortcut[394] to enter the door.

---

[388] The Manchu expression 'Qing wen ki meng' is the transliteration of the Chinese phrase 清文啓蒙 (Qingwen qimeng), which means the 'enlightenment of the Qing language'—i.e. Manchu.

[389] The Manchu expression 'udu...biqibe' means 'although', corresponding with 雖 (sui).

[390] The Manchu expression 'taqire urse' literally means 'learning people', who can be regarded as learners.

[391] The Manchu expression 'yarhvdame taqibure' means 'to guide and to teach', corresponding with 迪 (di), which is a variant of 迪 (di) as in 啓迪 (qidi), enlightenment. .

[392] The Manchu expression 'sara ulhire' derive from sarambi and ulhimbi, which means 'to know and to understand', corresponding with 領會 (linghui).

[393] The Manchu expression 'doobure ada' literally means 'cross-river raft', corresponding with 筏 (fa), with doobure being left out in the Chinese translation.

14. I once witnessed [our] teacher [Xeoping] using this [book] to teach young people;

15. [even] for [those] people [who] are somewhat intelligent[395] and sensible,

16.[it] takes [them] less than a month to learn,

17. [and they] are just able to read and write.

18. Moreover, no one could deny that [their] pronunciation[396] is clear and the strokes of words are [written] properly and decently[397].

19. For anyone [who has] already learned [this book], [they] would not make

mistakes[398] or get confused[399] [any longer].

20. [Hitherto,] the foundation is clearly rectified and the origin is correctly announced[400], [in which] the great intention resides in the first place.

21. Furthermore, its effectiveness[401] is quickly manifested as a miracle.

22. Long ago I [wanted to] get the draft inscribed,

23. [and] make it as a model[402] for the beginners[403], and thus [I] made a request.

24. However, Mister[404] [xeo ping] did not permit, saying [that],

---

[394] The Manchu expression 'doko jurgvn' means a shortcut, corresponding with 捷徑 (jiejing), in which 捷 (jie) is a variant of 捷 (jie).

[395] The correspondence 頴 (ying) is a variant of 穎 (ying), which means smart or clever.

[396] The Manchu expression 'jilgan mudan' means pronunciation, corresponding with 音韻 (yinyun).

[397] The Manchu expression 'tob tondo' means proper and decent, corresponding with 端楷 (duankai).

[398] The Manchu expression 'qalabure' means 'make mistakes', corresponding with 錯誤 (cuowu).

[399] The Manchu expression 'jequhunjere' means 'get confused', which is vaguely expressed in 錯誤 (cuowu).

[400] The original Manchu word is 'segiyen', which must be a spelling error of 'selgiyen' (announcement).

[401] The Manchu word 'gung' is borrowed from the Chinese language, as the 功 (gong) in 功效 (gongxiao) effectiveness.

[402] The Manchu expression 'durun tuwakv' means model, which can be understood as 'a good example' in the context, corresponding with 津梁 (jinliang). 津梁 means 'ferry and bridge', which guide and facilitate people to make achievements in Chinese expression.

[403] The Manchu expression 'teniken taqire urse' means people who just start to learn, which is better translated as 'beginners', corresponding with 初學 (chuxue).

[404] The Manchu expression 'siyan xeng' is borrowed from Chinese, which is identical with 先生 (xiansheng).

25. this book

26. [was designed to] teach my boys[405] at home,

27. [and thus it was] written[406] skillfully[407];

28. the [Chinese] annotations,

29. are all small and unpractical words, which are coarse[408] and vulgar without a decent written style[409].

30. [Therefore,] would it get printed[410] without being ridiculed?

31. Because I repeatedly[411] requested with great effort,

32. finally [I] was able to get a chance to print it.

33. Hereto, regarding the young learners[412],

34. [this book] presumably[413] would become greatly beneficial.

35. A good day of the Spring in the eighth year of Yongzheng [1730]

36. The house owner of Behavior-Loyal Hall, Qeng mingyuwan composed.

Introduction: Reading Thoroughly

1. People who read Manchu books,

2. should definitely know every word clearly,

3. [and it] is not allowed to neglect a little.

4. In this book if [words] are not remembered clearly,

5. on the other books [they] are encountered[414],

---

[405] Mini booi juse literally means 'my home's children', corresponding with 小子 (xiaozi).

[406] The Manchu expression 'gamame' means 'handle or proceed', corresponding with 作 (zuo).

[407] Faksikan i means 'skillfully', corresponding with 設法 (shefa).

[408] The corresponding word 麤 (cu) is a variant of 粗 (cu), coarse, rough, crude.

[409] The Manchu expression 'fiyan akvngge' literally means 'without color', corresponding with 不文 (buwen), not as elegant as the traditional written style.

[410] The Manchu expression 'folobuqi' means to be printed, and the Chinese 梨棗 (lizao) also refers to printing, due to using wood blocks made of pear tree and Chinese-date tree.

[411] The Manchu expression 'dahvn dahvn i' means repeatedly, corresponding with 再三 (zaisan).

[412] The Manchu expression 'ajigan taqire urse' means 'young learners', corresponding with 初學之士 (chuxuezhishi).

[413] The word 'ainqi' (presumable, probably) expresses a hypothetical tone, which is not translated in the Chinese counterpart.

[414] The word 'teisulebuhede' a grammatical form of 'teisulembi' [to encounter] in Manchu. 'bu' indicates a passive form and 'he' past tense. The corresponding Chinese 碰 (peng) is now written as 碰 (peng).

6. then [they] cannot be understood exactly.

7. Not only this,

8. anyone who has a capability in a size of a millet,

9. would claim [that it is] beneficial to themselves.

10. If [learners] don't keep this in mind, is it appropriate?

11. If [they] don't work diligently, is it appropriate?

Section 1: Knowing a Friend

1. Brother's big name has been heard for a long time.

2. [I] just have not [yet] been able to meet [your] honorable face.

3. Today [I am] in great luck.

4. Since [I] get to know [you],

5. Brother, if you do not give up your wish,

6. would visit my home for a little while?

7. What you said is quite[415] true.

8. Of course I will visit [your place].

9. I even think of going to your place for listening to [your] teaching.

10. Is it true that [I] do not want to visit your home?

11. But if [I] visit too often, [there will be] a day that brother feels fed up [with me].

12. What [are you talking about]?

13. I am only afraid that, brother, you are not willing to come.

14. Since [you] are willing to come,

15. [I] rejoice endlessly.

16. [Is there] a reason [of being] fed up?

Section 2: Asking for a Favor

1. Brother, when will you go?

2. [If you] want to go, then [you] say that [you] will go.

3. [If you] will not go, then [you] say that [you] will not go.

4. I only hear that your mouth has purely said [that you will] go,

5. [but I] have never seen that [you] really go [there] for once.

6. In advance if [we] have talked and decisions have been made,

7. other people would just not doubt either.

8. [How could] an unreasonable thing like this exist!

9. If I want to go,

---

[415] The adverb 'quite' corresponds with 狠 (hen), which is an original way to translate 'umesi' (very much). The modern expression is 很 (hen).

10. [it is]my will.
11. If [I] do not want to go,
12. [it is] just my will too.
13. Why would [I] have to tell you?
14. Furthermore, the day before yesterday I went to that place.
15. Combining this matter and the reason of request,
16. [I] have finished talking with him completely[416].
17. Where have you been?
18. Why do you arrive in this [late] time?
19. Is it appropriate [for me] to nag you completely [about it]?

Section 3: Making an Inquiry

1. [Regarding] this matter, except you,
2. other people definitely do not know.
3. If you truly know it clearly,
4. would [you] please tell me to know?
5. I really do not know.
6. If [I] know, then [I] will tell you for sure.
7. But [I] certainly do not know.
8. What can I tell [you]?
9. Could it be that I shall make it up and tell it [to you]?
10. If [I did], you would be able to hear something.
11. Why bother?
12. Forget it.
13. I see that if other people ask you about one thing,
14. you would just from beginning to end,
15. tell [them] one by one.
16. If I ask you for one thing,
17. you would just say that [you] do not know,
18. [or] say that [you] did not hear [it].
19. [You would] just look at me and make excuses hesitatingly.
20. Is it all right to call you a human being?

Section 4: True Friendship

1. Brother, when did you get the promotion?
2. Great joy!

---

[416] 'Completely' corresponds with the Manchu word 'jihengge', which has a Chinese equivalence of 來的 (*lai de*) to emphasize the completion of an action.

3. I have not been able to hear a thing [about it].

4. If [I] did hear,

5. [I] would have come to congratulate [you].

6. Because [I] did not know,

7. therefore [I] did not go to congratulate [you].

8. Brother, do not think less of it.

9. Would [you] please pardon [me]?

10. Brother, why would you say so?

11. We417 are good friends.

12. [We] meet and that will be fine.

13. Why must [we] uphold the empty courtesy?

14. Friends' way of interacting

15. [is] just [to] keep each other in their hearts,

16. and this is the [real] friendship.

17. That kind of affection is all fake.

18. Regarding the empty manners, some people

19. even though are very straightforward,

20. but if [you] expect him to consult a confidential thing,

21. [they] would just superficially agree [to help].

22. If it is like that,

23. what fun [is it]?

Section 5: Being Occupied by Work

1. Yesterday where did you go?

2. I sent someone to invite and take you [to my place].

3. Your family's servants said you were not at home but went somewhere else.

4. I reckon418 that you

5. must have come to my home.

6. [I] waited for a day [until] the sun went down,

7. [but] you surprisingly did not come.

8. In vain [I] waited for one day.

9. [I] wanted to go for another thing,

10. but fearing that you would come.

---

417 The Manchu word 'muse', as a first-person plural pronoun 'we', includes both the speaker and listener in the context.

418 The corresponding word in Manchu is 'bodoqi', in which 'qi' is a hypothetical tone. The original form is 'bodombi' [to calculate, to reckon]. The Chinese word 筭 (*suan*) is a variant form of 算 (*suan*).

11. Very much [I] worried [about you].

12. Brother, you are wrong about this.

13. Who does not have an inconvenient matter?

14. [Is it] only about visiting people's home?

15. Moreover, my body is [buried] in official work [so I don't] have free time.

16. If [I] go to manage other people's private matters,

17. how can [I] have free time?

Section 6: Setting Your Heart at Rest

1. [Regarding] the matter I entrusted you,

2. have you talked to him?

3. Does it look possible in his opinion?

4. I talked to him.

5. His words [are that]

6. if [it] is one person's matter,

7. it would have been easy.

8. Because it concerns many people's matter,

9. [it is] very difficult.

10. Slowly proceed,

11. [and] do not rush.

12. I furthermore ask when exactly [I] can get a firm message.

13. His words [are that once he] gets the message,

14. [he] would have [it] delivered to you [and] that will be all.

15. Why [do you] ask repeatedly?

16. I look at his situation,

17. [seeing that] he is not a person that causes things to be delayed.

18. You just set your heart at rest.

19. Your thing will be accomplished and that's it.

20. Is there any doubt about it?

Section 7: A Solid Word

1. Where on earth do you want me to go?

2. Suddenly [you] want this way,

3. [and] suddenly [you] want that way.

4. [There is] no certainty.

5. If [there is] a solid word,

6. [it would be] easy [for] other people to follow and carry on.

7. How come there are such people who change [their] mouths so frequently!

8. [It is you who] said that you would go by yourself.

9. Who [else] made you go?

10. Up to now,

11. [speaking of] the people who do not want to go,

12. is it appropriate to force [them] to go?

13. However, as people say,

14. a bystander sees [the problem] clearly,

15. [but] one himself sees [it] hazily.

16. [For] anything [that you] do not desire for yourself,

17. do not impose [it] on the others.

18. Presumably there will be no such a place [where you] cannot do [things].

Section 8: Trying to Make an Accomplishment

1. One of my things

2. seems impossible to carry out.

3. Brother, if you sympathize [me],

4. go, speak on my behalf and make it.

5. I definitely will not betray brother's great generosity.

6. Certainly [I] will repay your top-important kindness.

7. All of these are ordinary things.

8. You just go and talk by yourself.

9. Is there a place where [you need to] ask people for help?

10. Even [you] say so,

11. nowadays [we] must agree beforehand.

12. If at the moment [he] said [he] can make [it],

13. in the future [he] cannot, what would happen?

14. Now [he] said it could not be done,

15. what would happen if it is accomplished in the future?

16. Speaking of the way [things should be done],

17. I certainly would try my best to work on[419] it.

18. If by any chance your thing is accomplished,

19. you do not rejoice;

20. if your thing can not be accomplished,

---

[419] The Manchu word 'faxxambi' means 'to work hard on something', while the Chinese counterpart of '巴結' (bajie) could lead to 'flattering', especially in the modern context. So a modern translation can be 努力去做 (nuliquzuo).

21. you do not get annoyed either.
22. If [you agree] so,[420]
23. I will go on your behalf to proceed.

Section 9: Being a Good Friend

1. Brother, what I have advised
2. is for your benefits,
3. fearing that [you] will learn bad things.
4. If it seems reasonable,
5. you just follow and carry on.
6. If it doesn't conforms to reasons,
7. just stop it.
8. Because of you
9. I would just say so.
10. If it were other people,
11. I would not have said so.
12. Isn't that so?
13. Because you, brother, are a friend [who] knew [my] heart,
14. so [I] advise you this way.
15. If for the common friends,
16. after they have known people's faults,
17. not only do [they] not persuade,
18. but also laugh at [you].
19. [I] have heard that faithful words offend the ears
20. but benefit the behaviors;
21. good medicine is bitter for the mouth,
22. [but] good for the illness.
23. Among friends a good person like you, brother,
24. how many are there?

Section 10: Which One is Good?

1. If this one cannot be considered good,
2. compared with this, what are the defects for the good ones?
3. If [you] do not say this is good,
4. what else can be considered good?

---

[420] The Manchu word 'uttu', means 'so' or 'this', corresponding with 這們 (*zhemen*) .
A modern Chinese expression is 這麼 (*zheme*).

5. Because you have not seen the very good ones,

6. then [you] consider this as good.

7. If [you] have seen one better than this,

8. [you] would say that is good,

9. [and] will not consider this good.

10. Speaking of the good things,

11. [they are] different than anyone.

12. Not only do we say good,

13. all people see [it] and no one will dislike [it].

14. Only by that one can call [it] a good thing.

15. If the good and bad things cannot be distinguished,

16. is it appropriate to consider them all good?

Section 11: Seeking Something

1. From the tone of his words I hear that,

2. seemingly [he] is seeking something from you.

3. What things is he seeking from me?

4. I do not have anything worth seeking.

5. Thinking that it must be that you definitely have something.

6. He therefore says so and seeks [from you].

7. [He] is not short of anything, [then] what [would he] seek?

8. But once he said [that he] seeks from you,

9. you just give [it] to him.

10. This is [a] strange [thing] to say.

11. If I have something,

12. [I] would just give [it] to him.

13. [But] I certainly do not have [it].

14. What can I give?

15. Isn't that I buy and give [it] to him?

16. It would not work this way.

17. I am still in a hurry, looking for [it] everywhere.

18. Instead [he] seeks [it] from me!

19. This is so out of reason!

20. [We shall] think [and] understand mutually,

21. [and] that is friendship.

22. Is it appropriate to harm others but benefit oneself?

23. That would not be appropriate.

24. According to my idea,

25. if he does not open his mouth to seek from you, that will be fine.

26. Hypothetically when [he] seeks from you,

27. give [and] deal with him with all [you] have.

28. That's the way it is.

Section 12: Contending for Something

1. If [it] is supposed to be yours,
2. you will definitely obtain [it].
3. For what are you contending?
4. [Is it because you believe that] you will get what you contend for,
5. [and] you do not get [it] if you don't contend?
6. If [it] is supposed to be yours,
7. even though you do not contend, [you] still get [it].
8. If [it] is not supposed to be yours,
9. even though you contend, you will not get [it].
10. Just as people say,
11. [If you] let people watch over the mountains,[421]
12. the watchman will watch over his house [by the way].[422]
13. According to my opinion,
14. rather than fighting against people for the insignificant things,
15. [you'd better] show some respect.
16. No matter what,
17. There is a natural reason,
18. [which] does not work by forcing people to do so.

Section 13: Want It or Not?

1. If you want to have [it],
2. then take [it].
3. Now if [you] do not want [it],
4. [and] when other people get [it],
5. please do not think less of it.
6. When that moment comes,
7. you would be sorry and cannot make up to it.
8. Even though [you] say that [you] want to have it, but [you] cannot.
9. It does not matter.
10. This has already become mine.
11. Who dares to come and take away the things I occupied?
12. If it seems like you cherish it very much,

---

[421] The counterpart in Chinese means 'it is not stupid to give precedence to the other people'.
[422] The counterpart in Chinese means '[you] would get extra benefits afterwards'.

13. then forget about it.

14. If [you] are willing to give,

15. it would be interesting to ask for [it].

16. [If you] are not willing to [give],

17. what fun [even though I] got [it]?

Section 14: A Trustworthy Man

1. You talk to him.

2. Whether [he] gives or not?

3. If seemingly [he] gives,

4. people would also expect to have it.

5. The day before yesterday [he] said [he would] give, [but he] did not;

6. yesterday [he] said [he would] give [but] again [he] did not.

7. It is fine that you do not give,

8. but just give [me] a firm message,

9. [so that people] will feel a little better.

10. Merely [he] postpones it day after day,

11. [and] it turns out [that he] is deceiving people on purpose.

12. What matters whether [he] gives or not?

13. If there is a decisive word,

14. people will have no grounds to complain.

15. But [he] only talks through his mouth,

16. without thinking whether he could realize his words later on.

17. Can this be considered as a trustworthy man?

Section 15: An Official Business

1. This is all official business,

2. which cannot be compared with private affairs.

3. If it is a private affair,

4. it could be done in casual ways[423].

5. Regarding the official business, if [we] do not keep it in mind [but act effortlessly],

6. it will not be easy when things went wrong.

7. Who will take the responsibility?

8. Will you take the responsibility?

---

[423] The Manchu expression 'ainame ainame', which means 'carelessly or casually', corresponding with 胡里瑪里 (*huli mali*) in the original translation. The modern expression is 隨隨便便 (*suisui bianbian*).

9. Do [I] take the responsibility?
10. Or didn't [anyone] tell you?
11. Or didn't you hear it?
12. Or don't you want to hear about it?
13. It is well said that
14. [it is fine] to fill your mouth [with food],
15. but not with words [you cannot actualize].
16. Is it appropriate to be reckless?

Section 16: To Go or Not to Go?

1. If you go to meet him,
2. meet me [first] and then [we] go together.
3. I will wait at home.
4. Remember that seriously.
5. Do not forget these words of mine.
6. We are not able to meet you.
7. Your home lives very far.
8. What time will that be [when] we reach your home?
9. On the contrary, our traveling will be delayed.
10. Secondly,
11. in our heart, we are not afraid of going a long way round,
12. but because [you] say that you will go but actually not,
13. [but] again [you] say that you will go.
14. [You] just repeatedly afflict[424] people,
15. and [you] do not have an affirmative word.
16. Who can endure such a troublesome situation?

Section 17: Growing into a Good Person

1. He was born that way!
2. How could [he] change!
3. Nonsense!
4. [Even though] this is [his] nature.
5. Is that not changeable?
6. Even the holy people still need to amend [their] mistakes,
7. not to mention the ordinary ones.

---

[424]The word 'akabumbi' means 'to afflict or torture'. The corresponding Chinese 勒捎 (leken) is an original translation. The modern expression is 折磨 (zhemo) or 折騰 (zheteng).

8. Because [he] behaves according to his own will,

9. then [he] learns [to behave] despicably[425],

10. and has become a person without improvements.

11. If [he] only follows his own insights,

12. how far can [he] reach?

13. It is better to approach the learned people,

14. to seek his knowledge and experience,

15. and to take after and carry out his behaviors.

16. Only through that way, one can grow into a good person.

17. If one behaves carelessly[426] like this,

18. what is the point?

Section 18: Being Straightforward

1. Repeatedly[427] [people] say that you have done that thing,

2. [but] you would not admit.

3. Instead [you] shift the responsibility to the irrelevant people.

4. Whether [it is] true

5. or false,

6. eventually [the fact] cannot be covered.

7. It naturally appears.

8. [You] shed responsibility to the others,

9. then would [you] get away?

10. Would [you] be exempted?

11. Until now,

12. since you would not admit,

13. other people will come and say that indeed you did that thing;

14. at that moment it is impossible [for you] to move on,

15. either to move backward.

16. [You] can only open your eyes wide [but nothing else you can do].

17. Even [you] argue skillfully,

18. can you answer capably?

---

[425] The Manchu word 'usun', which means 'despicable or abominable', corresponding with 厭 (*yan*).

[426] The phrase 'hvluri malari' means 'to do things carelessly', corresponding with 哈里哈賬 (*hali hazhang*). The modern Chinese expressions are 敷衍了事 (*fuyan liaoshi*) or 馬馬虎虎 (*mama huhu*).

[427] The Manchu word 'lalanji' means 'repeatedly' in the context. However, the Chinese transliteration of '拉累的' (*laleide*) is a made-up word, which makes little sense here.

19. Frankly [you'd better] tell them a way [to solve the problem],

20. [and] people would have something to consider.

21. Some ambiguous words,

22. will not help.

Section 19: A Talented Man

1. Do not be deceived by his coarse manners.

2. [he has] a clear mind inside.

3. Isn't that so?

4. I look at him [and believe that he] is a delicate and talented[428] person.

5. Everything can be handled efficiently [by him].

6. Every word [he says] is brilliant.

7. There is no such a place [where he] cannot do all sorts of things.

8. If [we] look from this aspect,

9. people should not be judged by their appearance,

10. [and] the sea water cannot be measured by bushel, as a saying goes.

11. [It is] not empty words.

12. Hence one would say that it is up to people who want to work hard or not.

13. Since [you] want to work hard,

14. Is there any kind of hard thing which cannot be accomplished?

Section 20: Individual Matters

1. [I] heard that you were able to get out of that difficult situation.

2. I am really happy [for you].

3. [When I] first heard the words,

4. [I] have been suspicious[429] of [what I heard].

5. Later when [people] discussed in a bustle,

6. I then believed.

7. Indeed a lucky person like you,

8. certainly would not fall into such an unlucky place.

9. But you got an idea [to get away from the trouble] beforehand,

10. how could people know that?

11. Other people worried very much about you.

---

[428] The Manchu expression 'giltukan yebken' means 'delicate and talented', corresponding with 秀氣敏捷 (*xiuqi minjie*).

[429] The Manchu words 'buru bara' mean 'dim and faint', which has a Chinese equivalence of 恍恍惚惚 (*huanghuang huhu*).

12. All this happens because you, brother, usually get along with friends[430].
13. Therefore, [friends] are concerned about[431] you sincerely.
14. If there are no benefits [of doing that],
15. who would come and pay attention?
16. Moreover, do not rejoice for what [you] gain,
17. [and] do not say regretful [words when you] lose.
18. These are all individual matters,
19. and naturally there is a fixed reason [to deal with them].
20. There is nothing strange about it.

Section 21: Being Thankful

1. I totally know brother's great kindness.
2. [You helped me] with all [your] heart,
3. Is there a reason that I do not feel and think of thankfulness?
4. At the moment I cannot repay [you],
5. [but] in the future [I will] definitely work hard to return the favor.
6. However, whatever I say right now, please keep in mind[432].
7. Absolutely [I] will never forget.
8. Brother, why are you saying so?
9. Isn't anyone a friend?
10. Speaking of the days [in the future], [they] are more than the leaves of trees.
11. There is no such a place where [we] cannot meet in the world.
12. Why do [you] have to follow [the path leading] to nowhere?
13. Is it appropriate to expect [all people to] repay [you]?
14. Brother, you are thinking too much of it,
15. [and] being too cautious.

Section 22: Being Content

1. How come you do not know of being content?

---

[430] The Manchu word 'habqihiyan' means 'warmhearted, harmonious, or getting along with people', but the Chinese counterpart 和抄 (hechao) makes little sense in the context.
[431] The Manchu word 'gvnin de tebure' means 'caring about someone', so the word '垫' (dian) in '诚心垫着' (chengxin dianzhe) could be another word '惦' (dian), which means 'to remember, to care about'.
[432] The Manchu expression 'hadahai ejefi' means 'to remember carefully', corresponding with 緊記 (jinji). The modern expression is 謹記 (jinji).

2. It is hopeless[433] if all people behave like you.

3. It is better to obtain a little rather than a lot;

4. [and] to possess it right now is better than to obtain a little.

5. If [you] bite off more than [you] could chew,

6. it would be useless.

7. Even though [my situation] is worse than [some people whose status is] above [me],

8. comparing with [the people] under [me], [I] am better off.

9. If [you] just move forward by all means,

10. [but] do not look backward, is it appropriate?

Section 23: Great Concern

1. You are supposed to work hard on that thing.

2. [Why are you] so sloppy?

3. That thing has critical and great concern [with other matters],

4. [and we] should be very careful [to deal with it].

5. [We are] not allowed to disclose it randomly to people.

6. Is there any certainty for such a thing?

7. [I] would not say this if [there is] no need to take precautions.

8. If you are doubly careful,

9. [and] doubly cautious,

10. and [you] will not break the rules and system,

11. [and] when you make up a serious mind to do it,

12. [I] believe [you will] stay patient regarding everything.

13. [I] just voluntarily remind you with all I know.

14. [As for] where and how to conduct [the details],

15. it is your decision to make.

Section 24: A Burdensome Matter

1. For anything it would be good to finish it once for all.

2. If it takes a second time,

3. it would result in something unexpected.

4. [People] might as well regret when things are done,

5. [but] it is no better than being prepared [and] cautious in the beginning.

6. This matter can be considered as [being finished] smoothly,

7. and there was no places [where we encountered] trouble.

8. [We] were able to finish it crisply.

---

433 The Manchu word 'joo' means 'no longer to give consideration to something'.

9. There is no need to ask again and again.

10. [There are things] you do not know.

11. [To accomplish] this matter, it definitely takes a second time.

12. How do [I] say this?

13. If [you] look at the big picture,

14. [You will know that] it is a burdensome matter.

15. If [you] cannot perceive the essential causes,

16. in the future [the problems] will definitely go as far as to stand out.

Section 25: To Know It Exactly

1. Some people [may] say it this way,

2. [and] some people may say it that way.

3. It is reasonable to believe this is all empty.

4. [But that is] not necessarily true.

5. Now which one should [I] believe?

6. Which one should [I] listen to?

7. Instead, [my] heart is disturbed.

8. The aspects of this thing, [such as] benefits, farm, success and failure,

9. cannot be determined at all.

10. Now how can [I] do it well?

11. If [I] pretend not to know,

12. do not say that it is inappropriate to dress up truth as falsehood.

13. It is improper to take the fake as the genuine.

14. It is improper to take the right thing as the wrong.

15. It is also inappropriate to do it conversely.

16. In a word,

17. surely [it is necessary to distinguish] the right, wrong, true and false [things].

18. [We] should know [the situation] exactly.

19. [and] that would be fine.

20. Is it appropriate to encounter[434] the problems and then speak some confusing words?

Section 26: An Obvious Thing

1. You can just do it at your discretion.

---

[434] The Manchu expression 'nambuhai nambuhai' means 'encounter...then...', corresponding with '撈把住' (*laobazhu*). A modern expression is 遇到 (*yudao*)......就 (*jiu*) ......

2. Do not ask for instructions.

3. This is just an obvious thing.

4. Surely [it] will not get entangled and delayed.

5. If there is any place where there is a flaw,

6. [I am] afraid that people might consider it as a reason [to make trouble].

7. There is no such an eccentric stipulation.

8. Do it in decent ways,

9. and that would be fine.

10. There is no need to hesitate[435].

11. Just when [you] encounter something,

12. do not underestimate [the difficulties].

13. Think thoroughly first.

14. When [you] do it again,

15. usually there will be easy things,

16. [and you] may not necessarily suffer from losses.

Section 27: Keep Your Words

1. Do all these words come out from your heart?

2. Or [you] simply say it by speculation?

3. The thing [you did] is just like to plug your ears while stealing a bell.

4. It will not help [you] get anywhere.

5. You say that [you] cannot accept [the consequences];

6. compared with you, he can accept less.

7. The day before yesterday [I] repeatedly said that you [need to] undertake it.

8. Today as soon as [you] came, [you] changed your mouth.

9. Is this other people's fault,

10. [or] your own fault?

11. Even so, what [is that]?

12. You undertake [the work] and work [it] out in a higher level.

13. [It would be hard] for people to meet such a high expectation this way.[436]

14. [They] would not like it.

---

[435] The Manchu expression 'tathvnjara' means 'hesitating', corresponding with 遊疑 (youyi). The modern expression is 猶豫 (*youyu*) or 遲疑 (*chiyi*).

[436] The Chinese counterpart means 'there is no such a way of forcing people to make promises'.

Section 28: A Predetermined Principle

1. Cheer up[437], young men!
2. [If you] lose such a good opportunity,
3. do [you] still hope to get a second chance like this?
4. Timing is important,
5. [and] working hard is also important.
6. When I look at you,
7. sometimes [you] are impatient,
8. [and] sometimes [you] are too relaxed[438].
9. The words you said are true,
10. but you only know one aspect, not the other.
11. Everything naturally has a predetermined principle.
12. If [you] are supposed to get it,
13. [you] will encounter it unintentionally;
14. If [you] are not supposed to get it,
15. even though [you] try every effort but it will not work.

Section 29: A Fixed Conclusion

1. It seems like [I] know you, brother.
2. Somewhere [I] met you, so your face looks familiar.
3. Today is my lucky day to see you again.
4. Anyway [I] have to stay at one place with you so [I] can often hear brother's teaching.
5. That is really my luck.
6. How can [I] explain the reasons?
7. Stay close to good people,
8. and gradually [you] will become good.
9. Approach the bad people,
10. [and] as time passes, [you] are involved with the bad people.
11. This is a fixed conclusion.
12. Is it definite to say that it takes many days [in order to] recognize the good and bad people?

---

[437] The Manchu expression 'majige fede' is the Manchu expression of encouraging people, corresponding with 上緊些 (*shangjinxie*).
[438] The Manchu expression 'elehun dabahabi' means ' being too relaxed', corresponding with 過於皮鬆 (*guoyu pisong*). The modern expression is 過於鬆懈 (*guoyu songxie*).

13. In a moment [we can] also tell the difference [between the good and bad].

Section 30: A Bitter Memory

1. Why do [you] mention the thing [which] has already gone?
2. Every time [when you] mentioned it, I felt ashamed and bitter.
3. If a man has something,
4. do it loudly and clearly,
5. and act it in open and straightforward ways.
6. That is the right way.
7. When people entrust [you] to do something,
8. but [you] can not accomplish their assignment;
9. instead [you] play both sides as a 'good man',
10. [and] only [want to] divert your problems to [the other] people.
11. However [you] boast behind people's back,
12. but cannot settle disputes in front of people.
13. How could [we] consider this kind of people capable?

Section 31: To Pay Respect

1. [Today I] pay respect to brother specially.
2. I, your younger brother, mail [this] letter respectfully.
3. Is brother's noble body good?
4. Are [your] family members all good?
5. Since [I] said farewell to you, brother,
6. [I] wanted to send regards by mails.
7. Because [I] did not have a convenient person,
8. so I was not able to mail the letters.
9. I, your younger brother, was in the middle of thinking of you,
10. and suddenly brother's letter arrived.
11. I was really overjoyed and embarrassed.
12. Needless to say, the two brothers of us live in two places being far apart,
13. [but] our minds and hearts are not separated by the space.
14. Even so,
15. from now on when there is a convenient time,
16. please send letters of [your] safety [from your] place, brother.
17. I, your younger brother, am gratified to hear.
18. As for me and the others, [we] are all good because of brother's blessings.
19. I sincerely send a letter for this.

Section 32: School Education

1. Recently, has your master come often?

2. [Yes, he has] come.

3. [He]comes once everyday.

4. If so,

5. what does [he] teach you [when he] comes everyday?

6. The teaching of our master

7. is just the usual words in front of eyes,

8. and some coarse languages for questions and answers.

9. But there are no difficult words which are unusual.

10. Brother, it is unreasonable for you to learn these stuff.

11. Why don't [you] let him teach the Four Books[439]?

12. [Why] don't you learn translation?

13. What is the point of learning these coarse words all year long[440]?

14. What brother said is very correct.

15. What [you] taught is very reasonable.

16. Even so,

17. brother, you only know your personal situation,

18. [but] not ours.

19. If we are all clever and sensible like brother, you,

20. needless to say about learning the Four Books,

21. even the Five Scriptures and [the work of] Pre-Qin Scholars[441],

22. should all be read.

23. Is it appropriate to compare our capability with brother's?

24. The days we have spent on learning are few,

25. and what [we] have mastered is little.

26. Moreover, our mouths are dull.

---

[439] The Manchu expression 'syxu i bithe' means 'the Four Books' of Confucian classics, which are The Great Learning 大學 (*daxue*), The Doctrine of the Mean 中庸 (*zhongyong*), The Analects of Confucius 論語 (*lunyu*), and Mencius 孟子 (*mengzi*).

[440] The Manchu expression 'aniya hvsime' means 'a whole year', corresponding with 成年甲 (*chengnianjia*). '甲' (*jia*) is just helping word which bears no meaning in the Chinese context.

[441] The Manchu expression 'sunja nomun' means the Five Scriptures, which are The Book of Songs 詩經 (*shijing*), The Book of History 書經 (*shujing*), The Books of Changes 易經 (*yijing*), The Book of Rites 禮記 (*liji*), and The Spring and Autumn Annals 春秋 (*chunqiu*). 'geren dz i bithe' refers to the works written by the Pre-Qin philosophers, which were differentiated from the Confucians' in scholarly tradition.

27. If there are five or six sentences in a row,

28. then [we] cannot speak them out.

29. If [I] spoke that way, [I] would often stammer[442].

30. But as people say,

31. [we] have not yet learned to crawl,

32. can [we] learn to walk?

Section 33: Being Ill

1. The night before yesterday [[I] slightly caught a cold.

2. These two days [I] feel very uncomfortable.

3. What [I] ate cannot be digested,

4. [and I] do not feel good either [when] sitting or standing.

5. [I] feel weak all over,

6. but can only lie down slantingly[443] [on the brick bed].

7. Last night [I] stewed some ginger soup[444],

8. drank it and then sweat some.

9. Today my body then [felt] a little relaxed.

10. So [I see].

11. [Almost everyone] has been like this recently.

12. In these days even my body

13. is not every comfortable either.

14. Inside [I] feel bloated and uneasy.

15. [I] cannot taste the flavor [when I] eat and drink.

16. [My] body feels like being puffed up in the air, and my feet feel like stepping on bales of

17. cotton.

18. [I] almost tumbled over.

19. [There is] not much [I] can do but to struggle through it.

20. [I] believe it is all because of the plague[445] in this unfortunate year.

---

[442] The Manchu expression 'urui tanjambi' means 'often stammer', while the Chinese translation is 'surely stammer'. The modern expression for 打登兒 (*dadeng'er*) is 結巴 (*jieba*).

[443] The Manchu expression 'gvwaidame deduki' means 'lie down slantingly', corresponding with 歪蒯倒着 (*waikuai daozhe*). The modern expression is 斜躺着 (*xietangzhe*).

[444] The Manchu expression 'furgisu i muke' means 'boiled ginger soup' (*shengjiang tang* 生薑湯), which is a Chinese medicine to help people prevent or recover from a cold.

[445] The Manchu expression 'geri sukdun' literally means 'pathogenic air', corresponding with 時氣 (*shiqi*), which actually means the prevalent epidemic pathogens.

Section 34: A Difficult Time

1. Nowadays I feel very difficult to make a living.
2. There are many mouths [to be fed] in [my] family,
3. and [I] am in [my] servants' debt.
4. Expenses are many,
5. [but] income is little.
6. Neither do [I] have business.
7. Even though [I] told people,
8. [they] do not believe.
9. On the contrary they said that I purposely pretended that way.
10. Brother, you say that you live a hard life,
11. [but] my sufferings of being cold and hungry,
12. to whom [can I] tell?
13. Nowadays nine out of ten families are struggling to make a living.
14. Which family can live abundantly and richly?
15. However people say,
16. every family [prays to] goddess of mercy[446],
17. [and] every place [people pray to] the merciful Buddha[447].

Section 35: Grass Has Ears

1. Brother, why do you argue in such a sophisticated way?
2. Do [we] have to match the mouths[448]?
3. There must be some evidence[449] [against you]
4. Therefore people discuss [you] that way.
5. Why won't they accuse me?
6. For whatever [we] do,
7. [we] can only deceive people,
8. but the Upper Heaven can not be deceived.
9. A popular saying:
10. [when you] talk on the road,
11. there are people listening in the grass.

---

[446] The Manchus have adopted the Chinese pronunciations of 觀世音 (*guanshiyin*), which is a Buddhist goddess of mercy.

[447] The Manchu expression 'o'mi'to'fo' is similar to 阿彌陀佛 (*e'mi' tuo'fo*), which is shortened as 彌陀 (mi'tuo), referring to one of the highest figures in the Buddhist belief.

[448] The Manchu expression 'angga aqabuki' means 'to verify testimonies'.

[449] The Manchu word 'muru' means 'the appearance, look'.

12. If the wind does not blow,
13. do tree leaves move?

Section 36: Don't be So Polite

1. Brother, who else will [you] give [your] seat to?
2. Please go up and sit in the middle.
3. Ask them to give a little space to us.
4. We also sit.
5. What this brother said is correct.
6. Brother, you just sit facing the entrance.
7. This brother, please sit next to [the one facing the entrance].
8. Brother, please do not decline.
9. Please just take the seat next the other brothers.
10. I just sit opposite.
11. Anyway, everyone please take a seat and eat.
12. What are you so polite for?
13. This is not a grand banquet.
14. There is no such a thing as seat of honor or inferior.

Section 37: What is True?

1. Brother, please do not listen to other people's words.
2. He said it was me that let out the secret.
3. Presumably I did say it;
4. in front of whose front did [I] say?
5. There must be a witness.
6. If he said that [I] killed people,
7. [would you] agree that I killed someone?
8. Brother, please do not agonize people for no reasons.
9. There is a clear sky above [our] heads!
10. As the old people say,
11. what [you] see with [your] eyes is true,
12. [and] what [you] hear with [your] ears is false.

Section 38: Time Flies

1. Time flies very quickly!
2. Imperceptibly it is another year.
3. The first month [of the lunar year] has arrived.
4. In the Heavenly grace, [I] have gained another year.
5. Days and months flash by quickly like a weaver's shuttle, which urges people to get old.

6. When I was young,

7. [I] also love and expect the festivals [to come].

8. Nowadays because of the age,

9. not only is the heart longing for [the festivals] gone,

10. just when I heard about the festivals and holidays,

11. [my] head would hurt!

Section 39: Cannot Promise

1. Here I have a thing,

2. [and] I come especially to ask brother for a favor.

3. [When] thinking of our old friendship,

4. and taking my matter

5. please surely pass the message and talk to the lord.

6. Yes.

7. I go and try my best to talk and see [what happens].

8. If he agrees, you do not get excited;

9. If he does not agree,

10. Brother, [you] do not complain.

11. I just interact with him on an ordinary term.

12. There is no place where we are alike in temperament.

13. Whether this matter can be accomplished or not,

14. I cannot guarantee either.

Section 40: Expecting for a Reply

1. [Your] foolish brother, I, respectfully send a letter.

2. During that time, [I] was not able to see you.

3. Because time goes by quickly into a trance,

4. [every thing] happened just like a few years ago.

5. [I] wish [I could] visit your noble home in person,

6. [but] thinking of that [you] might not be able to meet me.

7. [My] virtuous brother, [you] are a good person,

8. [everything] will definitely go well with you.

9. Needless to say.

10. In the past because you are fond of me,

11. [regarding] the thing [I] asked from you,

12. [you] said [you] would give it to me.

13. Up to now, [you] have not yet delivered [it].

14. It must be that the people of your noble home do not have time.

15. It might disturb you for delivering it,

16. [so] I would rather send our little servant to get it.

17. My virtuous brother, please send and give it [to me] soon.

18. I wait and expect it [while] leaning on the door frame.

19. Whether [you] can give it or not, please write a letter and send it back [to me].

Section 41: Interview for Work

1. Brother, which banner are you from?

2. I am from the Plain Yellow Banner.

3. Do you belong to a Superintendent Commander of the Imperial Household Department[450]?

4. Or do you belong to a company[451]?

5. I belong to a company.

6. Whose company do you belong to?

7. I belong to Qangxeo's company.

8. What is your surname?

9. [My] surname is Jeo.

10. What is [your] first name?

11. [My] first name is Fengxengge.

12. Whose son [are you]?

13. A son of Gingguji, who is a first-class Imperial Guard.

14. How old?

15. Nineteen years old.

16. What [animal] year were you born in?

17. In the dragon year.

18. [Do you] belong to any lineage[452]?

19. No.

20. [Or the answer could be] Yes. I belong to a lineage.

21. Whose lineage?

22. Regimental Commander[453] Bayantu's lineage.

---

[450] The Manchu expression 'hontoho' is a Superintendent Commander (*guanling* 管領) in basic level of the Imperial Household Department (*neiwufu* 內務府).

[451] The Manchu expression 'niru' (company) is a basic fighting community of the Eight Banners, which usually contains 300 soldiers.

[452] The Manchu expression 'mukvn' means a lineage, which corresponds with 戶中 (*huzhong*).

[453] The Manchu expression 'jalan i janggin' means 'regimental Commander, corresponding with *Canling* (參領) in the Han Chinese translation, which is a third-grade military officer under the Banner system.

23. Do you have older and younger brothers?
24. I have both.
25. What official department is your older brother in?
26. My older brother is a blue-feather official[454].
27. How old is your younger brother?
28. Only six years old.
29. Still young.
30. When [is his] birthday?
31. The twenty fifth day of the first month of the lunar year.
32. Where is your home located?
33. I live in front of the Drum Tower, the side where the sun comes up.
34. What is Huri Ama, the Vice Director of Ministry of War, to you?
35. [He is] my [cousin] brother .
36. What is his father to you?
37. [He is] my uncle.
38. Biological uncle[455] [your father's younger brother]?
39. Yes.
40. Biological uncle.
41. Are you able to shoot from stance and from horseback?
42. [I] can shoot [from stance].
43. [I] am not able to shoot from horseback.
44. Why don't you learn to shoot from horseback?
45. Because [I] do not have a horse, therefore, [I] have not yet learned.
46. Let me see you draw a bow.
47. Yes.
48. Ah!
49. I can not even pull the string off the pads[456].
50. [It is] too hard [to pull the bowstring]!
51. In that case,
52. Put down the bow.
53. Let's see if you can read the chronicles.
54. Yes.
55. For how many years have you been reading the books?

---

[454] For the Qing government officials whose rank is lower than the sixth grade (with the sixth included), they wear a dyed blue feather on their hats. The feather is from the tail of a brown eared pheasant.
[455] The Manchu word 'banjiha' means 'birth'.
[456] The Manchu expression 'beri i tebke' are the pads fixed on the bow to stabilize the string.

56. I have read for three years.
57. [Have you] expounded the Confucian Books?
58. Not yet.
59. Yes, I have expounded.
60. Can you expound any book?
61. Some books I can,
62. [and] some books I cannot.
63. As for some details,
64. I cannot [expound].
65. At which master's school are you reading books?
66. I read at Master Jao's school.
67. Where does this Master Jao live?
68. [He lives] opposite to the house where I live.
69. [It turns out] that big house is his house!
70. What is the alternative name of Master Jao?
71. [He is] called Jooli Ama.
72. What is his official position now?
73. Originally [he] was an academician of the Imperial Academy.
74. Because of [his] physical disability,
75. [he] resigned from [the position of] academician.
76. How is [his ability of expounding] the books?
77. [He is] good.
78. Powerful without rivals.
79. Translating and expounding the books,
80. writing, shooting from a stance and horseback, there is nothing he cannot do.
81. Is [he] strict with [his] disciples?
82. Brother, please do not mention this.
83. As soon as the little children hear his voice,
84. [they] are frightened out of [their] wits.
85. Are you also afraid of him?
86. Ah! What are these words for?
87. [Your] master is just like [your] father.
88. If [you] are not afraid of [your] master,
89. who else are [you] afraid of?
90. How is his livelihood?
91. [He] just makes a living by keeping his old property.
92. Besides of this, I do not know where else he makes [income].
93. How many disciples are studying with him now?
94. [I] suppose the current [number] has reached one hundred now.
95. Did you take the examination last year?

96. [I] took the examination.

97. Because [I] was poor in reading and writing,

98. I did not get a name.

99. That is the reason in the first place.

100. Just now I asked you many questions,

101. and that was to test your abilities.

102. In my opinion, your learning is good enough.

103. Tomorrow I will tell the superior ministers,

104. and will definitely send your name [to them].

105. Either [they let you] take the examination again,

106. or maybe [you] will be employed directly and either could happen.

107. Within these days,

108. regarding your shooting skills from a stance and horseback,

109. [you] still practice as usual,

110. [and you] still learn to read and write as before.

111. Stay at home.

112. Do not go to other places.

113. Keep an eye on the messenger[457] who runs quickly like flying.

114. Do not miss [the good news].

115. Yes. I understood.

Section 42: Borrow Books

1. Brother, where are you going?

2. At other places [I] have something to do.

3. Brother, let's go.

4. Stop by my home.

5. Not now.

6. Today I have an urgent thing and do not have time.

7. [I] drop by another day.

8. Compared with the past, your heart has changed greatly.

9. We formerly talked to each other freely without any inhibition.

10. [We] visit [each other] innumerably.

11. There are so many days that you do not even come to my door.

12. [Now we] meet and you [are] so cold.

13. Has anyone done something to you?

14. [There is something] you do not know.

---

[457] The Manchu expression 'selgiyere' means 'delivering the official message', corresponding with 傳去 (*chuanqu*).

15. It is not [because] I do not want to come.
16. Just because of the family's difficulties,
17. [I am] busy everyday,
18. and I do not have time [to visit you].
19. What am I supposed to do?
20. Brother, it is not because of your family's difficult situation.
21. [I] think it must be that [you] prioritize the benefits, [so you] distance [your] good friends.
22. [You] think of [everything] except of me.
23. Brother, what words are you saying?
24. Regarding our friendship,
25. how can other people's [friendship] compare with [ours]?
26. Why do you say these words?
27. That's it.
28. If my work got delayed today,
29. let it be delayed.
30. I stop going,
31. but to visit your home.
32. If I did not go [to work],
33. would you still blame me?
34. Brother, if you act this way,
35. this is real friendship.
36. Where is the big boy?
37. Take the horse.
38. Yes.
39. Take this horse to the back yard and tie it.
40. Do not tie it at the doorway.
41. Beware of the bad people.
42. Hang the rein on the saddle.
43. Lift up the apron.
44. Yes.
45. Brother, let's go.
46. Go inside.
47. Brother, go up the heated brick bed.
48. I go up.
49. Brother, this side is good.
50. Here is also good.
51. Go up a little.
52. This way is quite comfortable.
53. Where is the big boy?
54. What are you doing outside?

55. I am here to tie the horse.
56. The beheaded [servant] should have finished tying the horse and come here.
57. He has been tying the horse for too long.
58. How come there is such a dead servant?
59. Fill the tobacco [into the pipe] and bring it over.
60. You go inside and tell [the other servants to]
61. warm up the tea and bring it here.
62. Put more milk inside.
63. Make it thick.
64. Do not make it too clear[light].
65. Yes.
66. Is your mother alright?
67. Yes.
68. How is your wife?
69. Fine.
70. How are the children?
71. Fine.
72. Ah!
73. Where is the big boy?
74. Why hasn't he brought the tea?
75. [I am] bringing [it].
76. Brother, please take some.
77. Brother, you take some too.
78. There is no such a rule.
79. Brother, you take first.
80. I take some first.
81. Brother, I would spare kowtow.
82. You are being too polite.
83. [What I give you] is just a bowl of simple tea and you are talking about [thanking me with]
84. kowtow.
85. Brother, I hear
86. [people] say that you go to school reading books. Is that true?
87. Yes.
88. Every time our Company Commander[458] saw me,
89. and told me to work as an official clerk.

---

[458] The Manchu expression 'nirui janggin' means a Company Commander, which is a military officer that leads three hundred soldiers.

90. I think that even though [I] know a few words in Manchu books,

91. but I do not know the sentences/words in chunks.

92. I should read books for another few months,

93. and then go to work,

94. It wouldn't be late.

95. So on the thirteenth of last month,

96. I went to school again.

97. How could you hear that?

98. The day before yesterday brother Jooli i Ama came to my house,

99. and I asked about you from him.

100. When he told me,

101. I then got to know.

102. Brother, do you have Manchu books?

103. Please lend [me] a few copies.

104. I transcribe [it] and read.

105. When I finished, I will just send it back to you.

106. I do not have books.

107. I look for them at [my] friends'.

108. After I get them, [I] will send someone to deliver it to you.

109. This is the way that brother cherishes me.

110. Brother, since you study very seriously.

111. is it appropriate for me not to find a few books for you to transcribe?

112. That's it!

113. I will not borrow books from the others.

114. Brother, you do not need to seek from the others.

115. I already said that I will search and send them to you.

116. Yes.

117. Brother, I am leaving.

118. Eat food and then go.

119. How come you are so busy?

120. Food can be prepared [soon] and then served.

121. That is fine.

122. I am really busy with something.

123. A friend called me to consult something.

124. He is waiting at home.

125. If I do not go,

126. how could he not blame me?

127. Really?

128. How can this be wrong?

129. There is nothing worth lying about.

130. If it is true,

131. I will not keep you.
132. But when you are free, please come and sit.
133. [I] will come again.
134. Brother, please go inside [back to your home].
135. One or two days later,
136. I will visit you again.

Section 43: Visiting a Friend

1. Is brother good [how are you]?
2. Fine.
3. Brother, is your body good?
4. Good.
5. Where have you been recently?
6. [I] did not even see you.
7. I just wanted to visit you,
8. [but] suddenly I got involved with a small thing.
9. Therefore, [I] was not able to come.
10. The day before yesterday I just finished the matter.
11. Yesterday [I] got some free time and wanted to come,
12. and it started to rain.
13. Brother, as you know,
14. I do not have either a raincoat nor a fur coat.
15. Neither have [I] a horse.
16. The road was muddy.
17. Because of that,
18. I was not able to come.
19. Since today it is sunny,
20. I travel on foot.
21. Especially [I] come to see you, brother.
22. Ah, it is far away.
23. Thank brother for taking the trouble to see me.
24. How could I deserve such [an honor]?
25. Really I am deeply grateful.
26. Please do not mention that.
27. Brother, I sat at home alone and got bored beyond endurance.
28. Your arrival has just met my expectation.
29. So the heart which longs to see brother,
30. also has become cheerful.
31. Since we, older and younger brothers, got together today,
32. there is no such a rule to let you go with an empty [stomach].
33. A cup of weak wine will be prepared.

34. The two of us have a drink together.
35. Sit and have a little chat.
36. Brother, since you cherish me this much,
37. I will not decline [your hospitality].
38. Definitely [I] will meet brother's expectation.
39. Just disturbing you for no reasons,
40. is not appropriate.
41. You are welcome.
42. Where is Kesitu?
43. [I] ordered [him] to prepare the drink and food, and deliver them over.
44. Yes.
45. Kesitu, why didn't you sweep the floor?
46. [You] did not dust the table either.
47. For what purpose did you stay at home?
48. I have already swept,
49. [But] the wind blows all the time.
50. Besides, there is no curtain hanging on the door.
51. That is why it is dirty.
52. [You] are such a beheaded servant who doesn't know courtesy!
53. How could [you] contradict [me]!
54. Check the wine immediately.
55. Yes.
56. Brother, we in this moment
57. first move the table to the yard and sit there.
58. This room is very hot.
59. Indeed very much.
60. If we move outside,
61. it is good to [stay] under the Chinese-scholar-tree[459],
62. [and] it is comfortable to enjoy the shade there.
63. It is not good there.
64. There are many worms on the tree [and they are] ceaselessly dropping.
65. It is not as good as [the place] under the eaves in the backyard.
66. In that case, the backyard would be fine.
67. Generally speaking,
68. it is cooler in the yard than in the room.
69. Certainly.
70. Moreover, the room is narrow,

---

[459] The Manchu expression 'singgeri xan i moo' literally means a 'mouse-ear's tree'.

71. [and] people are many [cramping in it].

72. [If I] sit for a long time, [my] head gets dizzy and [my] heart gets disordered.

73. My nature cannot stand the heat either.

74. Brother, it is the season of late spring.

75. Everything[460] starts to grow.

76. It is a good season for traveling in the mountains and looking at the waters.

77. This little study and the yard of mine,

78. even though are not a famous garden nor a scenic spot,

79. [it is] not different than the mountains and forests.

80. It is the right place for people like us to live in solitude.

81. Exactly.

82. Ah!

83. Because [We] were only making idle talks,

84. [I] forgot to encourage you for a drink.

85. Serve the wine, big boy.

86. Brother, please drink one cup.

87. I drank it.

88. This wine is strong and formidable.

89. I only drank one cup and got drunk.

90. What are you talking about?

91. [We] just raised the cups,

92. which had not touched the mouth yet.

93. Is it reasonable to say [you] are drunk?

94. You are good at lying.

95. I am not lying.

96. I naturally cannot drink.

97. Because brother cherishes me so much.

98. so [I] just drank one cup.

99. If [I am at] other places,

100. definitely [I] will not drink.

101. Brother, if [you] don't believe,

102. [you] can ask the people of [my] house.

103. I do not believe any of your words.

104. I do not care whether you can drink or can not.

---

[460] The Manchu expression 'tumen jaka' literally means 'ten thousand things', which corresponds well with the Chinese counterpart of 萬物 (*wanwu*).

105. You just finish the three cups of my wine,
106. I will spare you.
107. Wine is not poison.
108. Are you afraid of being poisoned?
109. Forget it.
110. It wouldn't matter.
111. [Though] these three cups of wine
112. would make [me] drunk to death,
113. I drink.
114. Brother, please look.
115. I drank it all.
116. It is getting late outside.
117. I should go.
118. Brother, sleep over here.
119. Tomorrow [you] go.
120. I can't.
121. Tomorrow I have some business at home.
122. It is inappropriate not to go.
123. If it isn't because of this,
124. I would stay at your home for a night.
125. Brother, if you got some time,
126. please come to my home for one time.
127. Definitely I will go.
128. Thank[461] you very much.
129. You are welcome.
130. What did you eat?
131. And [you] say thanks?
132. Yes. Brother, [I am sorry to let] you go [with] empty [hands].

Section 44: A Banquet

1. Outside, a person calls at the door.
2. Who is that?
3. I cannot recognize.
4. Eljitu, you go out and have a look.
5. Yes.

---

[461] The Manchu expression 'baniha' means 'thanked', corresponding with 生受 (shengshou), which is a traditional way of saying 'thanks'.

6. Outside a person, sitting on the horse, said [he] looks for brother to tell some words.

7. Didn't you ask what [he wanted] to tell?

8. I did ask.

9. He said after he met brother, [he] would tell.

10. In that case, I go and have a look.

11. Ah, brother, you have come.

12. Where are you from?

13. All over [your] body is covered by dust.

14. Brother, please come in.

15. No.

16. I won't go in.

17. [I] will leave as soon as [I] tell you the words.

18. How could [you] be so busy?

19. At another place a friend is waiting for me.

20. [I] do not have time.

21. How could that be?

22. Even though [you] have a friend at another place,

23. for the moment, come into my home, and have a cup of light tea and then go.

24. How do [you] like [it in] your heart?

25. If I could go inside,

26. [I] would have already gone inside.

27. Would [I] wait for your modest invitation?

28. Furthermore, brother respects me so much,

29. [and] don't I really know such a truth?

30. It is true that [you] do not have time.

31. Brother, today if you do not come into my house,

32. I am really discontented with you.

33. For the moment I ask you,

34. you must invite me in; what stuff do you have to feed me?

35. [We are] a poor family.

36. What good stuff do we have?

37. Prepare a bowl of vegetarian meal[462] to feed you.

38. Except this, [we do not have] other stuff.

39. If there are piglet meat and goose meat,

---

[462] The Manchu expression 'untuhun buda' means 'a regular meal without meat', corresponding with 空飯 (*kongfan*) which means a vegetarian meal.

40. I would go inside and eat.

41. If not, I wouldn't go.

42. I am not used to eat vegetarian meal since childhood.

43. Brother, you just come in.

44. Is there such a custom that treats you with vegetarian meal?

45. Even though [you want to] eat piglet meat and goose meat,

46. it is pretty easy.

47. There are no difficulties.

48. There is [food] ready-made.

49. If so, you can go ahead.

50. How could that be?

51. This is my home.

52. Is it appropriate for me to go first?

53. Where is Eljitu?

54. Spread out the cotton-padded mattress.

55. Add more charcoal to the fire pan.

56. Blend some milk tea.

57. Fill the tobacco in and send it here.

58. Yes.

59. Is the old grandpa at home?

60. [He is] not at home.

61. Where did he go?

62. He went to a friend's home today to redeem vows and eat meat.

63. If so, when grandpa returns,

64. please give my best to him.

65. Yes.

66. Brother, let's put away the idle talk.

67. Do you drink liquor,

68. or rice wine?

69. Whatever [you have] is good.

70. [Tell them] to prepare the food and dishes immediately.

71. I am still waiting to eat.

72. Bring the wine and dishes first.

73. Tell [them] to be quick.

74. Brother, please take the honorable seat.

75. The brick bed over there is chilled to the bones, [which is] not good for sitting.

76. Move a little over there.

77. It is their decision to sit.

78. Let it be.

79. Brother, you go inside to urge the dishes [to be cooked faster].

80. Whether it is boiled or fried,

81. [or] whichever is ready-made,

82. bring them for us to eat.

83. [Otherwise,] do you want to keep them at home for yourselves to eat?

84. Brother, sit quietly and do not talk nonsense.

85. If [you] act so rashly and wildly,

86. won't people laugh at you?

87. Eljitu, pour some wine.

88. This cup of wine,

89. is from me to respect you.

90. You must finish it.

91. Why are you doing this?

92. Do you only know me?

93. [You] should propose a toast to the other brothers.

94. Do not push me.

95. I am the kind of person who will not stop until [I get] drunk.

96. Brothers, please drink a few cups.

97. Why are you being so polite?

98. You are the host.

99. If you do not eat,

100. the guests will not drink either.

101. Why don't I eat?

102. Of course [I] eat.

103. Since you have come here.

104. wherever [you] are supposed to eat,

105. just eat until [you are] full.

106. Wherever [you] are supposed to drink,

107. just drink until you are drunk.

108. That would be fine.

109. You just sit there humbly for no purposes,

110. [and] modestly do not drink at all.

111. [You don't] even touch the chopsticks.

112. Must be that my wine is not strong,

113. [and] vegetable and dishes have no flavor?

114. It is not necessary for you to encourage us[463], brother.

115. We are all eating and drinking here.

---

[463] This Manchu word 'be' means 'we' as a first-person plural pronoun, which does not include the host who was serving the others in the banquet.

116. Where is Eljitu?

117. Please give the horse-keepers wine to drink and food to eat.

118. Ah! Do not give wine to my servants to drink.

119. They are not good at drinking.

120. Just in case they are drunk,

121. How could [they] follow us?

122. Please set your heart at rest.

123. It doesn't matter.

124. I just will not let them drink too much.

125. Brother, you originally were the person who is good at drinking.

126. What is wrong today?

127. [You] don't even drink.

128. You do not know that

129. I drank some beforehand.

130. Otherwise,

131. even though you let me drink for a day until sunset,

132. I will not get tired of that.

133. Speaking of eating food,

134. I am really no match for you.

135. Speaking of drinking wine,

136. you are far behind me.

137. Even though you say that,

138. if you drink that way,

139. not only did the food get held up,

140. but in the future when you get old,

141. you will definitely get hurt.

142. What I advised you is all good words.

143. It is up to you to believe it or not.

144. It is all because brother cherishes me,

145. then you would suggest me this way.

146. If [you] do not care about me,

147. for sure you will not advise me with such hearty words.

148. But I am used to drinking,

149. [and] I cannot quit in such a short time.

150. That's not what I meant.

151. It would be fine that you do not drink too much.

152. It is not good [for you] to quit completely.

153. Let me ask you again.

154. After drinking, on the second day morning when [you] get up, are you nauseous or not?

155. [I] am nauseous so much that I cannot even look at it.

156. If so,

157. that is because of the wine.

Section 45: An Ungrateful Person

1. Brother, if you do not mention this ungrateful person,

2. I will not get angry.

3. Once you mentioned him,

4. my anger just goes up to block my throat.

5. During those few years,

6. Even the threshold of our home was kicked broken by him [because of his frequent visit].

7. If there was nothing to wear,

8. from my body, I would take off [the coat] to dress him.

9. If he had nothing for daily usage,

10. he would take my silver money to use.

11. If there was nothing to eat,

12. [he] would fill the big sack with rice and then carry it home.

13. If there is a poor thing that occurs,

14. [he] would come to me to beg for help.

15. Brother, you know me very much.

16. When he is begging,

17. my heart calms down.

18. Even though I do not have [what he wants],

19. I would borrow from friends to meet his [needs].

20. Honestly nothing of mine did he not eat,

21. and nothing did he not take.

22. [I would say that] only my inner-side meat[464] did I not slice for him to eat.

Section 46: Qingming Festival

1. The scene has been bustling recently.

2. Because it is the Cold Food day[465],

---

[464] The Manchu word 'doko' means 'inner side or the inside surface', corresponding with 腿班裡 (*tuibanli*) .

[465] The Manchu word 'hangsi' comes from the Chinese 寒食 (*hanshi*), which literally means 'cold food'. In the Western Han dynasty, a book named New Thesis(xinlun 新論) records that in the Spring and Autumn Period, Jie Zi Tui (介子推) helped Chong Er (重耳) regain his throne, and then Jie went away as a hermit in the Mian Mountain (綿山). In order to recruit Jie again, Chong Er burned the mountain to force him out,

404

3. countless people come out from the city to visit the graves.

4. One can see that carriages, sedans, horses and mules travel endlessly.

5. There are [some people who] offer food and pour some wine,

6. and [some people] add soil [to the graves] and burn paper money.

7. People who hold the graves to cry, cry together.

8. People who sit in a circle under the tree for a drink, drink together.

9. Honestly, [your] heart gets broken [when you] see people grieve,

10. [and you] would say that it is happy to live when you see people who are happy.

11. From this perspective [we] can see that

12. people in the world raise children

13. all for the things [such as offering the sacrifices] in one hundred years.

Section 47: Lie to Me

1. Brother, you are not trustworthy.

2. The day before yesterday you said you would come but didn't come.

3. It is fine that the day before yesterday [you] did not have time,

4. but what was wrong yesterday?

5. Your are supposed to come.

6. Why didn't you come either?

7. Today you say [you will come] tomorrow ,

8. [and] tomorrow you say [you will come] the day after tomorrow.

9. You always say either today or tomorrow.

10. Are you deceiving people everyday?

11. Brother, it is not appropriate [to do] so.

12. Do not behave like this from now on.

13. It is fine that you lie once or twice.

14. If you lie often,

15. will there be people who trust your words?

Section 48: An Honest Man

1. If you say that person is arrogant[466],

---

but Jie died in fire. To remember Jie, Chong Er honored his memorial day as the Cold Food Day, ordering people not to cook with fire but eat cold food. In the Qing dynasty, the Cold Food Day was just one day before the Tomb Sweeping Day, therefore, people treated them as one festival.

[466] The Manchu expression 'ambaki' means 'arrogant or proud', corresponding with 大道 (dadao), whose meaning has shifted into 'a big road' in modern context.

2. [you] really have misunderstood him.
3. [He is] a first-grade honest person.
4. He would not even speak carelessly in front of people.
5. If [he] has a word, [he] will say a word.
6. His nature is just like that.
7. If people do not know him,
8. [they would] say that he pretends[467] to be like that.
9. Because you have not been with him in a place,
10. [so you] do not know his behaviors.
11. I have been interacting with him.
12. Not only do I know his personality,
13. I know [him] exactly including all the places [he] lived.

Section 49: A High Expectation

1. Brother, you are very troublesome.
2. [I] give [you] this, [but] you will not take;
3. [I] give [you] that, [but] you say [it is] not good.
4. If [I] send you something big,
5. you would say it is too big;
6. If [I] send you something small,
7. you would say that it is too small.
8. It is not acceptable this way.
9. It is not acceptable that way.
10. I do not know how
11. to meet brother's expectation.
12. What you want to get must be in a certain pattern.
13. Where can people find it?

Section 50: A Foolish Man

1. Brother, you are very foolish.
2. If you have money,
3. [you] should use money to deal with people.
4. If [you] do not have money,
5. [I would] say, use nice words to soothe and implore.
6. If so,
7. that would be fine.

---

[467] The Manchu expression 'durun arambi' means 'to fake a manner', corresponding with 捏款 (*niekuan*), which is another way to say 造作 (*zaozuo*) in modern context..

8. People's white silver was taken and loaned [to you].

9. The capital and profit were not returned at all,

10. but [you] blame others for urging [you] to return.

11. Is that appropriate?

12. This is the person who made up mind to borrow money but will not return.

13. If all people [behave like] these brutal and unreasonable rascals[468],

14. who else dares to lend money for interest?

15. On one side you [borrow] for the cause of using silver;

16. On the other side, [some of you lend it out] for the purpose of profit-making.

17. Why do you involve us as the innocent guarantors?

18. This man also calls for me;

19. that man also calls for me.

20. In the first place [I] vouched for you,

21. because [I have a] good heart.

22. Who has took or received food and drinks from you?

Section 51: A Wordy Man

1. Brother, why do you have so many words?

2. Every time you come, [your] mouth speaks carelessly and endlessly.

3. Don't you get sick of that? Isn't your mouth getting tired?

4. What [you] said is still those old words.

5. Who would listen [even though you] tell repeatedly?

6. Old brother, do not blame me for these straight words.

7. You are not aware of it yourself.

8. When other people hear,

9. [your] words are garrulous.

10. You are bewildered[469] in such a [young] age.

11. When [you] get older,

12. how could [you] administrate [your] family property and manage the affairs?

The first month of the Opalescent-White Snake [twenty-sixth] Year in the Qianlong's reign [1761] , spring season.

---

[468] The Manchu expression 'etuhuxere guwangguxara' means brutal and unreasonable, corresponding with 強賭光棍 (*qiangdu guang'gun*).

[469] The Manchu expression 'oiboko' means 'getting confused because of age', corresponding with 老悖回 (*lao bei hui*).

Chapter 5
Book of Essential Elements
of Manchu Language

Foreword : The Root of Manchu People

1. Manchu language

2. is the root and head[470] for all the Manchu lineages.

3. It is unacceptable for anyone who cannot master it.

4. How do [I] say it?

5. We[471] are fortunate to live in a prosperous age, [and] as distinguished[472] Manchu people,

6. if [we] cannot speak Manchu language,

7. every time when people met and asked [us in Manchu language],

8. [our] mouths would just open and eyes would just roll [but nothing else we can do].

9. Compared to this, [is there anything more] shameful?

10. Compared to this, is there [anything] more annoying?

11. Regarding this, needless to say that people laugh and make fun of [us],

12. [we] even have given up our own identity.

13. Isn't that a pity?

14. [I] have seen some people speaking Manchu language,

15. obviously [they] could have spoken the words but as it happened [they] could not.

16. Suddenly they stopped, and up to when they could remember,

17. [their] faces had already turned red very much.

18. There are no other reasons,

19. all because in normal times [they] did not study diligently and did not practice speaking.

---

[470] The Manchu expression 'fulehe da' (root and head) was translated as 根本 (*gen-ben*), which literally means "root and body" in Chinese.

[471] The Manchu expression 'muse' is the Manchu word for 'we' as a first-person plural pronoun, which includes the listeners and readers in the context. The other Manchu word for 'we' is 'be', which only refers to the speaker[s], but does not include the listeners and readers. Thus it is obvious that this book was written for the Manchus due to the employment of 'muse', which implies that both the author and readers are Manchus.

[472] The Manchu expression of 'ayan suwayan' literally means 'big yellow', which refers to the noble social status in the East Asian culture.

20. Moreover [there are some] ridiculous people,

21. [and their] Manchu language is still shadow-less,

22. but [they started to] learn translation first.

23. Aren't such people [different than the one who] wants to go to the Yue land[473] [in the

24. south]but their carriage goes back [to the north],

25. [and also different than the ones who] boil the sands for food?

26. No matter how proficient their Han Chinese language is,

27. [when they] use brushes [to write],

28. [their] Manchu language is in shortage and crippled,

29. which cannot match the edge of fur,

30. and cannot make a complete expression.

31. Even though people say that they have learned up to the old age,

32. [they] cannot avoid becoming into incapable scholars with bad names.

33. Roughly speaking, it is just like building a house.

34. If [you] do not have beams, pillars, tiles, bricks and things like that,

35. but only call the craftsmen in,

36. what [can they] work with?

37. [They would] just fold their hands and look on.

38. There is no way that the house can be built!

39. If we have looked this way,

40. before people learn to translate,

41. they should know that it is important to learn Manchu language [well] first.

42. But Manchu books are very large in quantity.

43. For people who just [start to] learn,

44. [if they want] to read completely,

45. when [can they reach] the end from the head[474]?

46. Therefore,

47. I take some free time from work.

48. With the traditional words of the old generations,

49. [and] with what I have learned and remembered,

50. [I] have collected them one sentence by another.

51. All together [I] have accumulated one hundred sections,

52. [and I] teach them to the children of my lineage.

---

[473] The Manchu expression is 'yuwei gurun', which is 'the Yue's land'.
[474] The Manchu expression 'dube da' literally means 'the end and the head', when implies 'to finish something' in the context.

410

53. The book's name is called 'The Essential Elements of Manchu Language'.

54. Inside this book,

55. [there are] directions and rules [learners should] fall into and comply with,

56. [also there are] all kinds of methods to speak Manchu.

57. Even though [this book] does not cover [everything] completely.

58. [However,] the big structure before eyes [which] should be used [as] the most important

59. [elements] is all prepared.

60. If learners can really concentrate their minds consistently,

61. [and] repeatedly practice,

62. after a long time, [learners] will be able to apply [the rules] according to their will.

63. No matter how [you] say [it],

64. there are no words which could not be created accordingly.

65. Why would you worry that [you] are not able to do it?

66. But this book's words are too many,

67. and [I] hope that people who read [this book] will not spend too much energy transcribing it.

68. So [I] hand it to the craftsmen for engraving.

69. For friends who like Manchu language as we do,

70. [we] would share [this common interest].

71. Though it has little benefit to the insightful scholars,

72. for the beginners,

73. it is not necessarily helpless.

Some Basic Rules of Pronunciations

1. Now to help the young learners who just begin to learn Manchu language,

2. they should know a few sentences clearly,

3. so it would be convenient to explain and practice.

4. When speaking Manchu, the word 'i' and the word 'ni' must be distinguished as in reading.

5. This is very important for speaking [Manchu],

6. [and learners] should know this.

7. Within the twelve syllabaries[heads],

8. only under the fourth syllabary,

9. it is supposed to write the word 'i'.

10. Although it is written as 'i',

11. it reads as 'ni', [and] is spoken as 'ni'.

12. For example, as the 'i' in emperor's grace and country's fortune in reading and speaking[475].

13. Taking this point and generalizing it,

14. under the fourth syllabary,

15. any [syllable] which should be written as 'i',

16. is written as 'i',

17. [but] read as 'ni' and spoken as 'ni'.

18. All [similar cases] follow this rule.

19. Under the fifth syllabary,

20. when 'i' is supposed to be written,

21. it is written as 'ni',

22. and also read and spoken as 'ni'.

23. For example, the 'i' in Chieftain's gate keepers and duke's subordinate officials is read andspoken as 'ni'.[476]

24. Taking this point and generalizing it,

25. under the fifth syllabary,

26. when 'i' is supposed to be written,

27. it is all written as 'ni',

28. read and spoken as 'ni'.

29. All [similar cases] follow this rule.

30. Except for the fourth and fifth syllabaries,

31. under the rest ten syllabaries,

32. when 'i' is supposed to be written,

33. all is written as 'i',

34. read as 'i',

35. [and] spoken as 'i'.

36. Under the words such as year, day, night, spring, summer, autumn, and winter,

37. or the word 'arrived',

38. or the word 'encountered' [and] all the other similar sentences,

39. 'de' is used; besides,

40. for the other sentences which do not have words like 'arrived' and 'encountered',

41. the word 'de' is not used.

42. For example,

---

[475] The Manchu word 'i' functions as the possessive word in-between ejen (emperor, lord) and kesi (grace).

[476] Here, instead of 'i', 'ni' is used as the possessive word because of the previous syllable is a postnasal sound, such as 'ang' and 'ung'.

43. [people] wait until that year, that day and that night,
44. and then inspect and conduct.
45. When encountering words like that spring, that summer, that autumn and that winter,
46. then [people] discuss and make a firm decision;
47. just under the words such as year, day, night, spring, summer, autumn, and winter,
48. the word 'de' is used.
49. If there are no words such as 'arrived' and 'encountered',
50. but to directly connect what follows in the passage to continue the writing,
51. 'de' is not used.
52. For example, when referring to the admitted candidates in the imperial examinations at the provincial level in the Alpha-Horse year,
53. [and] the admitted candidates in the highest imperial examinations in the Beta-Goat year,
54. [and] the first day of a certain year and certain month,
55. [and] submitted a memorial,
56. [and received] the current day's imperial order,
57. [and the emperor's reply] I knew [it],
58. [and by the emperor himself] agreed.
59. [and] for this matter [I] submitted a memorial respectfully,
60. [and] submitted an official document for this matter, with similar writings and speakings,
61. [and] in all such conditions, under the words such as year and day,
62. 'de' is not used.
63. Regarding the currently ongoing format,
64. the Book of Politics, translated and produced according to the Emperor's edict, says,
65. on the first day of January,
66. [the Emperor Xun] received his emperor-ship at the Emperor Wen Zu [Yao's ancestral] Temple.
67. Such words can be found in the Records of Xun.
68. The Book of Poem, translated and produced according to the Emperor's edict, says,
69. during the day [people] cut the twitch-grass,
70. and during the night [people] make the grass into ropes.
71. Such words can be found in the chapters of the Bin Country's Poems.
72. In the Book of The Sacred Teachings for General Illumination, it says,
73. what [the emperor] worries is that,
74. [even] when the crops are abundant in a good-harvest year,

75. [people] may not think of gathering [the crops] and storing [them] up;

76. when the silk and cloth are plentifully obtained,

77. [people] may spend extravagantly on the [daily] usage,

78. [including] their defects of being thriftless and not hardworking.

79. Such words aim at the emphasis of lands and mulberry [farm and textile],

80. so people have ample clothes and food.

81. Moreover [the emperor] said,

82. you, soldiers and people should scrutinize and speculate in the deep night,

83. so that my expectation can be met accordingly.

84. The purpose of such words is that the taxation on the crops and money can be collected without force and compression.

85. In the book of The Ancient Prose as a Profound Dictionary produced by the Emperor's Edict, it says,

86. hunting [the non-pregnant animals] selectively in spring,

87. hunting in the fields [for the animals that damage the crops] in summer,

88. hunting for kill in autumn,

89. and enclosing [the animals] for hunting in winter,

90. are all military maneuver in leisure times.

91. All these words can be found in the chapter of 'Zang Xi Bo Remonstrated Lu Yin Gong from Going to Watch Fishing'.

92. In the above few chapters,

93. under the words such as year, day, night, spring, summer, autumn, winter and cause,

94. 'de' is not used on a solid basis.

95. Within this Manchu language, there are many empty words, such as 'be', 'me', 'qi' and 'fi'.

96. are not discussed here intentionally.

97. [We] only take a few words such as 'i', 'ni', and 'de' as examples,

98. to imitate the ongoing rules and patterns;

99. moreover, to cite from the classics and teachings, and to elaborate repeatedly.

100. What intentions do [we] have here?

101. Specifically [I want to explain these rules] clearly, obviously, brightly and understandably,

102. so that all people know them.

103. There is no need to gabble repeatedly.

104. [For the things people] cannot notice and take for granted,

105. and the things that are easily confused, [I] point them out one by one,

106. so that learners can be equipped to select and apply.

107. Generally speaking, I just offer all my inadequate understandings,

108. for the reasons of correcting the mistakes and inconsistencies,

109. also to supplement the prejudices,

110. and also start to remedy the malpractice.

111. Besides, the confused usage of 'i' and 'ni' is circulating [widely],

112. and people do not think of making corrections.

113. Especially this is a defect of [misusing] Manchu language.

114. When a beautiful jade has a small flaw,

115. it cannot be called an intact jade.

116. If there are flaws in people's Manchu language,

117. it would impossible to expect them to be proficient [in this language].

118. Since they are able to use Manchu language,

119. but if they do not work hard to perfect it,

120. it is such a pity.

121. Honestly if [people] realize the relevant importance [of learning],

122. read this book repeatedly and think it over,

123. [and] remember it consciously,

124. keep it in mind and examine it from time to time,

125. correct the mistakes and the inconsistencies;

126. after studying hard for a long time,

127. [they] will improve gradually.

128. Not only can [they] be spared from being ridiculed for being unskilled in language,

129. but can [they] gain a reputation of being proficient and flawless.

130. Isn't that really good?

131. On the left side, at the end of the seventy-second letters under the sixth syllabary,

132. there are two dots attached;

133. and within the same syllabary, there are forty letters which do not have dots.

134. All of these relate to Manchu language,

135. [learners] should write these twenty words from time to time.

136. [But] it is still difficult for them to remember.

137. Therefore, [I] composed a song, [which contains] six sentences with seven words [in each sentence],

138. [if learners can] remember this [song] adeptly,

139. [they] will be able to discern without making mistakes.

140. The seven-word-six-sentence song goes as,

141. if a sentence begins with 'e' and ends with 'fu',

142. then 'ne', 'se', 'de', 'le', 'me' and 'qe' are the same;

143. the combinations of 'be', 'pe', 'je' and 'ye' are similar to 'hv ';

144. sentences that end with 'ke' and 'ku' will all make sense.

145. plus 'fe', there will be twenty words

146. whose appearances all look like a bow, without two dots attached.

Section 1: The Most Important Thing

1. hear that now you are learning Manchu books.

2. Very good.

3. Manchu language,

4. is our most important thing,

5. [which] is like the Han Chinese language in each place.

6. Is it acceptable that [we] cannot use it?

7. Isn't that so?

8. I have learned the Han Chinese books for over ten years,

9. [but] up to now, the end and the head[477] have not even showed up.

10. Furthermore, if [I] do not read Manchu books,

11. [and] do not learn how to translate,

12. and that will cause both of them to be delayed.

13. Therefore,

14. on one hand, I

15. come to visit brother [you];

16. moreover,

17. I have something to ask [my] old brother [you for help].

18. [It is] just difficult to open the mouth.

19. What is that?

20. If [you] have words,

21. just say;

22. if [it is] something that I can do,

23. [Will I] refuse in front of you?

24. What I am asking is,

25. if brother you cherishes [me],

26. even though you are tired,

27. in [your] free time,

28. please compile a few chapters of Manchu language,

---

[477] The Manchu expression 'dube da' literally means 'the end and the head', corresponding with 頭緒 (*touxu*). This sentence could be understood as 'I have no clues of what I have read'.

29. [and] please teach me to read.
30. If [your] younger brother, I, can have some achievements,
31. that is all [because of] your kindness.
32. Absolutely [I] will not forget your favor.
33. Definitely [I] will repay you abundantly.
34. Why[478] would you say so?
35. Are you a stranger?
36. [I am afraid that] you do not want to learn.
37. Since [you] want to learn,
38. I eagerly expect you to become a [successful] person.
39. As for repaying [me],
40. what words [are those]?
41. Is it all right to say this among us?
42. Even [you] say so,
43. I appreciate sincerely without ending.
44. Just give thanks with kowtow.
45. What are you talking about?

Section 2: Concentrate on Learning

1. Brother, [regarding] your Manchu language,
2. in what free time did you learn?
3. Your pronunciation is made good and clear.
4. How could my Manchu language be worth speaking of?
5. Brother, [you] cherishes me, [so you] overpraise [me].
6. One of my friends' Manchu language is good,
7. clear and quick,
8. without any Han Chinese accent,
9. and very skilled.
10. Furthermore, his ears are old[479].
11. That can be called 'being proficient'.
12. Compared with you, how is he?
13. How could I be compared with him!
14. Totally [I am] not his opponent.
15. [We are] separated like the heaven and the earth.

---

[478] The Manchu expression 'ainu' means 'why', corresponding with 什麼 (shenme). A modern expression is 怎麼 (zenme).

[479] 'Xan geli fe' literally means 'ears are old', which implies the person has heard many old expressions.

16. What reason is that?

17. His learning is deep,

18. [and] his capabilities are many.

19. [He] is fond of reading.

20. Up to now even [his] mouth never stops reading.

21. [He] reads [in a way that his] hands never leave the books.

22. To catch up with him,

23. is really difficult.

24. Brother, are such words of yours not mistaken a little?

25. [People] say that being consistent, even mountains can be penetrated.

26. He has learned to be capable.

27. [He] was not born to be capable.

28. Where can't we do better than he does?

29. No matter how proficient and capable he is,

30. we just make up our mind,

31. and concentrate our hearts on learning;

32. even though we cannot reach his level,

33. definitely [it] will not be far away.

Section 3: Your are Making Progress!

1. You are a person who can [read] the Han Chinese books!

2. It would be very easy for you to learn the translation.

3. Just concentrate your mind without stopping,

4. and learn sequentially;

5. within two or three years,

6. the end and the beginning will naturally show.

7. If you learn in a way like exposing it to the sun for one day and then cool it for ten days,

8. even though you read books for twenty years,

9. it would be difficult to learn anything.

10. Brother, please look at my translation,

11. and modify a little.

12. Your learning is much progressed.

13. Every sentence is smooth,

14. and words are written clearly.

15. Completely there are no any flaws[480].

16. If [you] take exams, you would be able to get [a name easily].

Section 4: To Attend an Exam

1. This time when [you] took the translation exam,

2. did you hand over your name or not?

3. If you are able to take the exam,

4. it would be certainly good.

5. But I am afraid that the Cultivated Talents will not be allowed to take the examination.

6. Whose rule is that?

7. Any person in the Eight Banners, like you, is allowed to take the exam.

8. Is there a reason why only you cannot take the exam?

9. Moreover, even the [poor] students[481] from the free schools are allowed.

10. Needless to say a Cultivated Talent [like you].

11. Because [we] are allowed to take the exam,

12. your younger brother, I, grabs this moment to read Manchu books.

13. Quickly register your name.

14. Do not miss the opportunity!

Section 5: Practice Makes Perfect

1. Your Manchu oral language is taking a good shape.

2. Where are [you leading this conversation] to?

3. Even though I can understand what people said,

4. I, myself, still cannot speak well enough.

5. Needless to say, I cannot speak as those who speak in chunks.

6. If [people] say four or five sentences in a row, I cannot even keep up.

7. Besides,

8. there is something strange;

9. before [I] speak,

10. I am only afraid of making mistakes[482], [so in order] not to make mistakes[483],

---

[480] The Manchu expression 'qilqin' means 'flaws', such as grammatical errors. The Chinese expression of 乞星 (*qixing*) is a transliteration of Manchu word 'qilqin'.

[481] The Manchu expression 'jurgangga taqikvi juse' (*yixuesheng* 義學生) are the poor students who were not able to join the official schools. Usually these students were financially supported by gentries so they were exempted from paying tuition.

11. I cannot speak decisively but hesitatingly.
12. [In a way] like this, how[484] could I speak?
13. I am downhearted.
14. Thinking of that, in whatever way I learn,
15. that would just be [my little] capability.
16. Where can [I] improve?
17. This is all because you have not practiced [enough].
18. Let me teach you [something].
19. Do not care who he is,
20. If you see [him], chase [him] for [engaging] conversations,
21. and then [you] seek to read with teachers who are good at books;
22. you stay close and speak with friends who are good at Manchu language.
23. If [you] read everyday,
24. [you] would remember those sentences.
25. [If you] speak all the time,
26. [your] tongue would stay practiced.
27. If you learn this way,
28. at most two or three years,
29. [your] mouth would naturally speak fluently as [you] wish.
30. Why would [you] worry that [you] could not do that?

Section 6: Receiving a Guest

1. Where have you been?
2. I have gone to a relative's house here.
3. At your convenience please visit my house and sit for a while.
4. Brother, do you live here?
5. Yes.
6. Recently [I] moved here.
7. If so,
8. how far would it be between [the two places] where we live?
9. If [I] knew, wouldn't [I] have come to visit you already?
10. Brother, [please] go [ahead].
11. What are you doing?

---

[482] The Manchu expression 'taxaraburahv' means 'to be afraid of causing mistakes'.
[483] The Manchu expression 'alaburahv' means 'to be afraid of making mistakes'.
[484] How (仔麼 *zime*) is the equivalence of Manchu 'adarame', which is 怎麼 (*zenme*) in modern Chinese language.

12. This is at my house.
13. Brother, please sit up there.
14. Here is comfortable.
15. You sit that way.
16. How do I sit?
17. Good.
18. [I] have already sat.
19. Here is a place [I] can lean upon.
20. Where are the family servants?
21. Bring the fire.
22. Brother, I do not smoke[485].
23. [I] have oral ulcer.
24. If so,
25. Bring some tea.
26. Brother, please drink some tea.
27. Wow!
28. Very hot!
29. If it is hot,
30. [let the servant] cool it a little.
31. It does not matter.
32. Just cool it a little.
33. Yes.
34. [Go and] check the meal.
35. Tell them to quickly bring [some food] that is already made,
36. Don't do that.
37. Brother, please don't.
38. I still need to go somewhere else.
39. So what?
40. The ready-made food is not prepared for you [on purpose].
41. Eat a little and then go.
42. That would not be necessary.
43. Once I recognize your house,
44. another day I especially come,
45. [and] we will sit and talk for a whole day.

---

[485] The Manchu expression 'dambagu omirakv' literally means '(I) do not drink to-bacco', while the Chinese counterpart is '(I) do not eat tobacco'.

Section 7: Going to School

1. Brother, you pass by here everyday.
2. Where are you going after all?
3. I go and read books.
4. Don't you read Manchu books?
5. Yes.
6. Nowadays what books are you reading?
7. No other books.
8. Just bits and pieces in front of eyes.
9. Other than that, [we] just [read] the Essential Elements of Manchu Language.
10. [Did your teacher also] teach you the standard Manchu script in print style or not?
11. Now daytime is short.
12. There is no time for writing words.
13. After these days, when the daylight gets longer,
14. not only [will the teacher] let us write words,
15. but also order us to translate.
16. Brother, in order to [find a place] to read books,
17. [I] really poke [my] head [everywhere].
18. Is there any place [I] didn't look for?
19. The surrounding of our place,
20. really has no Manchu schools.
21. Thinking of the place where you study,
22. what standard [do they have]?
23. Sometimes[486] I also want to read books[487].
24. Could you talk [to someone] on my behalf?
25. Brother, regarding the person that teaches us, who do you think [he] is?
26. Is [he] a teacher?
27. No.
28. [He] is a cousin of my lineage.
29. All the people [he is] teaching,
30. are the children of our family,

---

[486] The Manchu expression 'atanggi biqibe' means 'when or what time', corresponding with 多咱 (*duozan*).

[487] The Manchu expression 'bithe hvlanaki' (去念書 *qu nianshu*) actually means 'go to school'.

422

31. and some relatives [of my lineage].
32. There are no other people.
33. How do I say this?
34. My brother goes to the government office everyday.
35. He doesn't have time.
36. Because we go and implore in mornings and evenings,
37. [so he] has no choice.
38. [He] has spared time to teach us.
39. Otherwise,
40. if brother, you, wants to go [to school and] read books,
41. that would be a good thing.
42. [I would have] spoken on your behalf,
43. Would it cost me anything?

Section 8: A Successful Man

1. That brother,
2. is our old neighbor.
3. A child [we] watch him growing.
4. How many years have passed?
5. Now we hear that [he] has become really outstanding, [and] has become a government official.
6. In the beginning I half believed and half doubted.
7. Later [I] asked my friends.
8. Indeed, looking from this respect,
9. [when] there is a will, things can be accomplished after all.
10. As a saying goes, it is not about the age,
11. [and it] is not false.
12. Brother's words are true.
13. Even so,
14. it is also because his older generations' endless good blessings,
15. and then such a successful child was brought up.
16. [He] is honest and kindhearted,
17. [and he is] good at asking questions and learning,
18. [and also good at] shooting form a stance and horseback,
19. [including] every capability a man [should know].
20. [He] has learned so much and this does not correspond with his [young] age.
21. Usually at home,
22. he just reads books.
23. [Regarding] bad places, he would not take one step in.
24. Moreover, about the official business,

25. he is respectful and careful with
26. the places he knows,
27. and he never gets near those [bad] places.
28. This thing [matches] well with the [words] that families who accumulate virtues
29. definitely have extra blessings.

Section 9: Bumping into a Friend

1. Brother, you are riding [a horse to come here].
2. I am hiding from you.
3. [You are] tired and why would you come down [from the horse]?
4. What words are you talking about?
5. If [I] didn't see [you],
6. what would happen?
7. I just saw you from far away.
8. Is there a reason to ride and pass by [without greetings]?
9. Brother, don't you come in and take a seat?
10. That is right!
11. We haven't met for quite a long time.
12. I shall go inside and sit for a little while.
13. Wow!
14. [You] have planted many kinds of trees and flowers,
15. [and you] have kept many goldfish.
16. The rockeries are piled up in a good way.
17. The creative mind is very ingenious.
18. In every layer there is a design.
19. This study is quite clean.
20. In whatever way [you] look,
21. in whatever way it is pleasant.
22. It is a right place where we should read books.
23. But what [I] hate is that
24. I do not have any friends.
25. I study books alone.
26. Very lonely.
27. How difficult is that?
28. If you do not get fed up,
29. I make a company for you, how about that?
30. If so,
31. that would benefit me well.
32. I would worry that you will not come even when [I] invite [you].
33. If you really come,

34. It is my luck.
35. Is there a reason [that I get tired] of you?

Section 10: Reading is the Key

1. For people who live in this world,
2. the most important [thing] is to study.
3. Reading the books,
4. is to understand the morals and principles.
5. If the morals and principles can be learned clearly,
6. at home the older generations would be treated with filial piety;
7. [the person] would also exert his efforts to serve the country as an official.
8. Everything would be accomplished naturally.
9. Up to now,
10. indeed if [you] have learned some abilities;
11. no matter where [you] go,
12. not only do people respect you,
13. but also will you walk with pride.
14. There is a kind of people,
15. who do not read books,
16. do not work on [his] personal characters,
17. but only speculate and secure personal gains, and consider flattering other people as a capability.
18. [I] wouldn't know what is going on in his heart.
19. I really feel ashamed and regret for him.
20. For people of this kind,
21. not only [do they] bring disgrace to himself and damage his personal characters,
22. but also would people insult his parents.
23. Brother, you just look and think of this,
24. [How could] parents' grace upon the children be repaid by one in ten thousand.
25. [That kind of people] did not bring glory or honor [to their parents],
26. On the contrary, they caused [their parents] to be cursed.
27. He is just something without future.
28. When [you] think of this thoroughly, as a person,
29. how could [you] not read books,
30. not to nurture [your] personal character?

Section 11: Where Did You Go?

1. Yesterday whose house did you go to?
2. You came so late.
3. I went to see a friend of mine.
4. They live far away
5. in a section close to the bottom of the western city wall.
6. Besides, they gave me supper to eat.
7. That is why I was late.
8. I have a word to consult with you.
9. Quite a few times I sent people to invite you.
10. People at your home said that
11. you went out by a carriage.
12. As for where you went,
13. no words were left.
14. In [my] estimation,
15. the places you visited are very limited.
16. [The places you visited are] nothing but our few friends' houses.
17. [You] would definitely visit my place.
18. However, [I waited until] the sun set down,
19. [but you] did not come.
20. [I] waited for one day in vain.
21. Yes.
22. Before brother's family people arrived,
23. I had gone out of the door already.
24. After I returned,
25. [my] family people told [me that]
26. brother, you sent people
27. to call me two or three times in a row.
28. At that time I wanted to come,
29. [but] the sky was turning dark,
30. and [I am afraid that] the barriers would be closed,
31. so I just came today.

Section 12: Just Work Harder

1. People who work as a government official,
2. only look at the favorable opportunities of each own.
3. If the fortune is ordinary,
4. either way is not working smoothly.
5. Everything will soon be accomplished in front of [your] eyes,
6. but get obstructed by people deliberately.

7. New problems crop up unexpectedly.

8. There is a good luck.

9. When people have the luck,

10. things really happen in accordance with what [you] have planed in mind.

11. There is nothing which is not going smoothly as [you] wish.

12. People just get promoted exceedingly in front of your eyes.

13. Brother, didn't you say that?

14. In my heart [I] did not think so.

15. People only care [whether you] work hard[488] or not.

16. If [the officials] just behave like statues which just consume tax revenues and salaries,

17. but do not work all year long,

18. they should just be removed from office.

19. How could [they] expect to be promoted?

20. It is important to work hard on the official business.

21. Harmony should be prioritized among the friends.

22. It is not good [if they] cannot get along [with each other].

23. Do not implicate[489] other people when there are things happening.

24. Anything [we] encounter,

25. bend our body to work on [it],

26. [and] march forward courageously.

27. Definitely there will be something good for you.

28. Is there any reason [you] won't get promoted?

Section 13: Eating Meat

1. Brother, why did you come [so late]?

2. I have been waiting [for you],

3. [and] nearly did not take any nap.

4. I tell you [that]

5. we were just about to depart,

6. coming to your home.

7. Suddenly we met a piece of decayed meat which is abominable.

8. His words were endless and pointless,

---

[488] The Manchu expression 'faxxara' means 'to work hard', corresponding with 作爲 (*zuowei*). A modern translation is 努力做事 (*nuli zuoshi*).

[489] The Manchu expression 'guqihiyererakv' means 'will not implicate', corresponding with 不攀 (*bupan*). A modern translation can be 不牽涉 (*bu qianshe*).

9. [talking about] this and that.

10. [He just] couldn't finish easily.

11. When [there are] no things [to do],

12. what hurts if [he] nags?

13. If [I] just let him tell [his stories],

14. I am afraid that [I will] keep you waiting.

15. Therefore, I had no choice.

16. [but said] we had some business [to do],

17. [and] tomorrow I would talk [to him] again.

18. I just cut his words off.

19. Otherwise I would have already come and sat [until we are] tired.

20. Who is there?

21. Set the table quickly.

22. I think the lords must be hungry.

23. Food and such things should be neat and tidy.

24. Brother, how could you say this?

25. If there is meat which can be cut [into pieces][490], it would be fine.

26. What are the delicacies for?

27. Do you consider us as guests?

28. [What I offer is] just a kind of snack.

29. What good things can [we] have?

30. Brothers, please eat some food [along with the snack].

31. You have prepared so abundantly[491].

32. We[492] surely eat.

33. If [we] are not full, [we would] not put down the chopsticks.

34. If so, there is nothing [we can say].

35. [Thank you for] cherishing [us as your] younger brothers.

Section 14: Shooting An Arrow

1. Speaking of shooting from a stance,

2. it is an important thing for us [as] the Manchus.

3. Though it is easy to watch,

---

[490] The Manchu expression 'faitaha yali' means meat boiled for religious rituals. People would just cut it into pieces and eat directly.

[491] The Manchu expression 'ambarame dagilahabi' means 'have prepared abundantly', corresponding with 盛設 (shengshe).

[492] The Manchu word 'be' means 'we' as a plural pronoun in English, which refers to the speaker along with the other guests because the host was going to prepare the meal or receive guests.

4. it is difficult to master the essentials.
5. Nowadays [people] draw the bow regardless of day and night,
6. there are even people who sleep while holding the bows.
7. [As for the ones who] reached [the level of being] extremely skillful,
8. [and] become famous, how many [would there be]?
9. Where is the difficult part?
10. The body should be straightened up.
11. There should be no bad habits nor strange-looking.
12. Keep shoulders horizontally,
13. while being at ease.
14. The bow should be strong,
15. so that arrows will shoot powerfully,
16. and each arrow hits the target when counting.
17. That would be excellent!
18. Brother, you please look at my shooting from a stance.
19. Compared with the past, is there any progress or not?
20. If there is any place disagreeable [to your eyes],
21. please set it right.
22. There is nothing [I] can say about your shooting from a stance.
23. Sooner or later, [you can] depend on your thumb
24. and put a peacock tail on your headgear.
25. [Your] gesture looks good,
26. and very skillful,
27. [and your] release is very clean.
28. If people can all become like you,
29. What else would [I] expect?
30. Only the bow is a little soft,
31. so the string is a little loose after a full draw.
32. [and] it cannot stabilize well.
33. [Please] remember these a few places [where you need to improve].
34. Say, if [you] can make changes [according to my suggestion],
35. no matter where [you] go and shoot from a stance,
36. surely you will be above the ordinary.
37. How could [you] be suppressed?

Section 15: A Frank Person

1. You are such a good person whose stories can be told without ending.
2. There are no impurities inside you.
3. Just your mouth is too straightforward.
4. If you knew people's rightness and mistakes,
5. you would not keep [it as a secret] a little.

6. You would just speak directly.

7. Even though there is a reason to correct mistakes among the friends,

8. giving advice depends on whether [you] get along with each other or not.

9. [People] just say that friends are similar to each other,

10. [but] that doesn't necessarily work out.

11. [Regarding] this [one] section of words [we just said],

12. can't you say that [they are] out of good intentions?

13. Inside his heart [he is] very uncomfortable,

14. [and] he stared blankly [and said],

15. Ah!

16. Be careful!

17. [I] suspect that I am being framed for the unpredictable[493] reasons !

18. Brother's words [which you just said],

19. actually are a good medicine to cure me.

20. In my heart, I am convinced.

21. There is where I fell ill.

22. Don't I know that?

23. But [every time] when [I] encounter such things,

24. my mouth cannot help getting itchy.

25. Talking to the people with whom you are not supposed to talk, is called an indiscreet remark.

26. From today let me reinforce the changes.

27. If this happens again,

28. if I talk excessively,

29. brother, please spit on my face.

30. I am willing to accept sweetly.

Section 16: A Difficult Friendship

1. You really got along well [with each other].

2. What happened now?

3. How come [he] does not even come to step on your door sill?

4. I do not know.

5. If there is a place where [I] offended him,

6. it would make sense.

7. Actually there is nothing happened.

---

[493] The Manchu expression 'boljon akv' (*buce* 不測) means something unpredictable, which was not translated in the Chinese counterpart.

8. We interacted in a good condition.

9. Suddenly, one sentence went wrong.

10. He was annoyed and then decisively would not interact [with me].

11. It is fine that we do not visit each other.

12. [but] behind my back he would just defame me for no reasons.

13. [He did] that ruthlessly,

14. [When he] met all the friends who I know well,

15. [He would] take [me] as a subject for ridicule, and simply spread slanders.

16. Recently my son got married,

17. [and] I still have considerations for his feelings,

18. [so I] invited him to come.

19. [He] did not even send a dog [to my son's wedding].

20. All I have met

21. is such a friend like that.

22. How could I make friends with him?

23. Didn't I say that, this person's words and behaviors are false and exaggerating,

24. and should not be trusted?

25. Did you pay attention to [what I said] at that time?

26. [Just then] you really did not like me [for what I said].

27. [We can] only recognize people's face,

28. [How could we] know their hearts directly and thoroughly?

29. [How could we] not discern the good and bad [people],

30. without exception, say that they are all good friends?

Section 17: A Stingy Friend

1. Recently,

2. where are you busy running about?

3. Occasionally please visit my place for a while.

4. How come I cannot see your face?

5. Long ago I wanted to see you.

6. Unexpectedly I got entangled by an irrelevant thing,

7. and got involved actually.

8. Being kept busy everyday, how could I have time?

9. If it were not for today, I wouldn't get free.

10. I just made an excuse and said that [I] have something urgent and important,

11. [and then they] let me go.

12. [You] just came in a good time.

13. I just felt suffocated.

14. Thinking of that you do not have any important thing [to do],
15. we can sit and talk for a day.
16. Eat some ready-made food and then go.
17. I would not cook food in addition.
18. If [I] come too often,
19. I would bother you [too much], brother.
20. I have no peace in my heart.
21. Therefore, I don't dare to come very often.
22. How could you consider [me] as a stranger?
23. When did we make distinctions between you and me?
24. If a few days passed and [you still] did not come,
25. I still would prepare some stuff,
26. [and] specially invite you.
27. [It is] just a ready-made vegetarian meal,
28. Is it worth talking about it?
29. Furthermore, regarding your things,
30. what didn't I eat?
31. Looking at this [situation],
32. apparently [you do not hope] me to come to your home anymore.

Section 18: Encountering a Stubborn Man

1. In my opinion, originally regarding this thing of yours,
2. [you] can talk to him,
3. and that would be very easy.
4. Who expected that there was such an annoying man, who has a stubborn face and clenching his teeth[494]?
5. Therefore, it took a lot of heart [energy] to [deal with it].
6. [I] told him about what we have discussed.
7. [He] felt dishonored by this,
8. [and] considered my words as a reversed winnowing fan[495].
9. So I got angry,
10. and the temper rose up to [my] neck.
11. [I] would do whatever [I can],
12. and my heart is full [of intentions] to offend him.

---

[494] The Manchu expression 'jayan qira fangnai ojorakv' literally means 'teeth and face stubbornly would not', which means 'he wouldn't agree to help'.
[495] The Manchu expression 'fudasihvn i fiyo' means 'a reversed winnowing fan', corresponding with '乖謬之談 (*guaimiu zhitan*). Using a winnowing fan upside down is an absurd thing.

432

13. But later [I gave it a second] thought.
14. [I] questioned myself, [saying]
15. you are wrong.
16. [I] came here not for my own matters,
17. [but] for [my] friend!
18. Just tolerate him a little.
19. What would that cost?
20. So I just put up with his insult and scolding,
21. and did not make a sound,
22. [but] accept it peacefully.
23. I sat for a long time.
24. Looking at his situation,
25. [I] appealed for sympathy slowly according to his idea.
26. He just nodded his head.
27. You, please look and think,
28. if my temperament is a little more impatient,
29. wouldn't your thing be sabotaged?

Section 19: A Good Rain

1. Yesterday I got up early,
2. and it was very dark in the room.
3. I thought it was not very bright yet [outside].
4. [I] went out to the yard and looked up,
5. [and] it turned out that it was very cloudy.
6. [I] washed my face and just was about to leave for the government office.
7. the raindrops thinly scattered.
8. I waited for a while,
9. [but] quickly it rained loudly.
10. And then I sat for a while.
11. After a time period for drinking a cup of tea,
12. suddenly the sky cracked open and the thunder rumbled once.
13. It started a heavy downpour.
14. I thought it was a rainstorm for a period of time,
15. [and] I would set out after the rain passed.
16. Unexpectedly it kept showering to the night,
17. through the night, to the dawn, but did not stop.
18. Up to today's mealtime,
19. then hazily the sun light can be seen.
20. It is such a good rain that is in time.

21. Presumably there is no land anywhere which is not soaked.

22. How come the crops will not be harvested in autumn?

Section 20: A Role Model

1. Didn't you inquire about that brother?

2. Speaking of him,

3. [he is like] an awl in a bag.

4. No matter when, [he] will definitely rise [his] head above the others.

5. What is the reason for that?

6. [He] was born to be steady and calm, and [he] learned a lot.

7. When [he] walks, [he] is a good example; when [he] acts, [he] establishes rules.

8. Regarding the official business,

9. [He] does it with a single mind.

10. What about at home?

11. [He] lives wholeheartedly.

12. Truly [he] does not have a single problem.

13. [He] is filial in front of [his] parents.

14. [He] is warmhearted among the brothers.

15. Besides, among the friends,

16. [he] is very protective.

17. Anyone who asked him for a favor,

18. if [he] does not agree, that's it;

19. if [he] nods his head,

20. definitely [he] would bend his body and rack [his] brain on your behalf.

21. [He] wouldn't stop if [he] can not accomplish.

22. Therefore,

23. [there is no such a person] who does not respect him.

24. [There is no such a person] who does not want to stay close to him.

25. As a saying goes, the Heaven helps good people.

26. For a person like this,

27. how could he be born for nothing and accomplish nothing?

28. The Heaven definitely sends blessings down [upon him].

Section 21: A Harsh Discipline

1. This morning [I called] them to recite books.

2. They performed worse one after another.

3. They just hum and hum but cannot answer.

4. They stumble and make a lot of clicking sounds.

5. At that moment I asked them to stop.
6. Listen to my words.
7. Since you are reading Manchu books,
8. you should learn with a single mind.
9. If you just make up a number like this,
10. [and] pursue an empty fame,
11. when can [you] reach the end?
12. Indeed, not only do you waste your days and months idly,
13. but also do I exert my strength for nothing.
14. Isn't that you hold up your own [success],
15. or, it is me that causes your success to be delayed?
16. You are robust and big men.
17. [As I] speak to you again and again,
18. [but you would] just hear it in [your] ears,
19. [and] discard it in [your] heart.
20. [Your] face is thick-skinned.
21. The words out of my mouth are bitter,
22. [but] do not think that I talk too much.
23. Do not say that [I] am picking a quarrel[496].
24. Nowadays I serve at the government in person.
25. When I have some free time,
26. how nice it would be if I just take some rest!
27. But being stuck with you,
28. [I] talk in this way and that way,
29. for what?
30. Because in the first place, [we] are bones and flesh.
31. [My] purpose is to make you distinguished [from the ordinary];
32. [My] intention is to make you into a useful person.
33. So [this is] what [I get in return]?
34. For what I am supposed to teach with my heart,
35. it would be fine that [I] just teach according to conventional rules.
36. It is your decision to listen or not.
37. What [else] could I do?

---

[496] The Manchu expression 'fiktu baimbi' means to 'pick a quarrel', corresponding with 尋趁 (*xunchen*). A modern expression is 找茬 (*zhaocha*).

Section 22: To Protect our Manchu Reputation

1. No[497]!
2. How could you say so?
3. [You] are well fed everyday.
4. [Look at] the time [you] spent on playing the Chinese lute and the three-stringed instrument!
5. Would [you] call that a government business?
6. Do you still want to earn a name [to serve in the government]?
7. Or do you want to live a life depending on these [musical instruments]?
8. We were lucky because of [our] Manchu [identity].
9. What we eat is official rice,
10. [and] what we use is official silver.
11. [In our] whole family, what we put on our heads and step under our feet,
12. is all acquired through [our] Master's grace.
13. [You] are not learning abilities,
14. [you] don't work hard as an official to serve [at government] either,
15. but only concentrate on learning these [musical instruments].
16. [You] have disdained [our] Manchu reputation!
17. Rather than wasting your useful mind on these useless things,
18. you should read books!
19. People who learn [to sing] songs,
20. can only stand behind the doors.
21. People who learn to become scholars,
22. can sit in opposite.
23. There is a saying,
24. no matter how superior level [you] have reached [in music career],
25. [you] can only make [a toy] for people to amuse with.
26. [You] cannot be spared from getting a humble and lowly name!
27. When [you] come to decent and official occasions,
28. can the thing such as playing instrument be called a capability?
29. [If you say that] there is no evidence [to support] my words,
30. [which] cannot be trusted;
31. Among the high officials and ministers,

---

[497] From the context, this word must imply a message, which is 'what you are doing is wrong'.

32. if there is anyone who has an origin in playing the musical instruments,
33. now you can tell it out loud.

Section 23: Being Promoted!

1. Brother, good news!
2. It says that [you] have been appointed and dispatched as a Company Commander.
3. Yes!
4. Yesterday when selecting the officials,
5. I was appointed as the first candidate[498].
6. Who is the second candidate[499]?
7. I cannot recognize [him].
8. A vanguard leader of ten soldiers.
9. Does he have soldiers or not?
10. No.
11. [He] only has [some men] for hunting.
12. I have already thought it thoroughly for you.
13. A peacock tail is prepared for [you] to wear.
14. How could I be counted as outstanding?
15. There are many people who are better than I am.
16. How could [I] expect to get the position for sure?
17. By the blessings of my grandfather,
18. probably I can get it when there is a good luck.
19. What are you talking about?
20. What generation were you [born] in?
21. [You were born] many years ago.
22. Regarding the old [age],
23. the friends who interacted with you all have became high ministers.
24. Even the young generations who were selected after you,
25. all succeeded you.
26. Speaking of military service,
27. [you] fought a war and got wounded.
28. Furthermore,

---

[498] The Manchu expression 'qohoho' has an equivalence as 拟正 (*nizheng*), which means the first candidate for the emperor to appoint an official.
[499] The Manchu expression 'adabuhangge' has an equivalence as 拟陪 (*nipei*), which means the second candidate for the emperor to appoint an official.

29. Now [you] are a military officer among the top fifteen shooters[500].

30. You tell [me], who can succeed you in your banner?

31. I knew it.

32. You might be afraid that [I] come to drink your wine for celebration.

33. [Therefore,] you said this [in a low profile] on purpose.

34. What are you talking about?

35. If [I] truly got the position,

36. needless to say wine,

37. I [would] invite you [for a banquet] according to your expectation.

38. Just kidding.

39. I am supposed to congratulate you.

40. Instead [I] will eat your stuff.

41. Is that appropriate?

Section 24: Some Strange Visitors

1. Has anyone come here today?

2. [As soon as] brother [you] left the door,

3. immediately two people came to visit.

4. They said that brother [you] had been promoted,

5. [and] especially [they] come to congratulate you.

6. Who went out to answer the door?

7. I stood at the outside of the door,

8. I [said] my older brother is not at home.

9. [So I invited] the lords to come inside and have a seat.

10. Decisively [they] did not come in,

11. [but] returned later on.

12. What kind of people are they?

13. How do [they] look like?

14. A fat man,

15. [who is] a little bit taller[501] than brother [you];

16. his body looks well-balanced,

17. [with] full beard,

18. [and] panther eyes.

---

[500] The Manchu expression 'tofohon mangga' 十五善射 (*shiwu shanshe*) is a military officer who is able to shoot with a strong bow of fifteen drawing-force units (十五力 *shiwu li*). There are also fifteen positions assigned for these good shooters in every banner.

[501] The Manchu expression 'dekdehun' means 'a little taller', corresponding with 略 猛 (*lüemeng*). A modern translation is 略高 (*lüegao*).

19. [His face is] purple.
20. The other one looks very funny.
21. [He is] so dirty that [I] cannot even look at [him].
22. [He] is one-eyed,
23. and [the one eye] looks sideways.
24. [His] face is full of smallpox.
25. His beard is back-rolling.
26. He looks at me in a [funny] way.
27. When he talked,
28. I nearly laughed with a sound of 'busa'[502].
29. About that fat man,
30. I knew him.
31. Who is the other man?
32. I asked their surnames.
33. They both left me a note written with their official positions.
34. I bring them for you to look at.
35. Ah!
36. Where did this evil creature come from?
37. You'd better not say that
38. [he is] not good-looking.
39. [You] have despised [him].
40. Even though his physical appearance is crooked,
41. he writes well,
42. [and he] is intelligent on the inside[503].
43. Speaking of him,
44. who doesn't know?
45. He has became famous already.
46. In the past, [he] was famous for trouble-making[504]!

Section 25: Looking for a Friend

1. The two of us,
2. got along in the first place.

---

[502] The Manchu expression literally means 'I nearly laughed with a sound of busa', and the Chinese counterpart means 'I nearly did not laugh out loud'.
[503] The Manchu expression literally means 'there is something inside', corresponding with 內囊 (neinang), whichfunctions like 內秀 (neixiu), being intelligent without seeming so.
[504] The Manchu expression 'koikaxambihe' (攪渾 jiaohun) means creating a disturbance, which can be translated as 鬧事 (naoshi) in modern context.

3. Now we have several kinds of relationships.

4. For many years we have not seen [each other].

5. I came back from where I conducted military service,

6. and then I wanted to find him,

7. talking about how much I missed him.

8. Unexpectedly I was involved by some matters,

9. [and] did not find time.

10. Yesterday I dropped by his home and asked [about him].

11. [He] moved away long ago.

12. It says that [he] lives at the corner of a small street on the west side of the city wall.

13. I went to have a look according to what I was told.

14. A very remote place.

15. The door was closed.

16. I called [for people] to open the door,

17. [but] there was no one to answer.

18. Then [I] knocked at the door, and called for a while.

19. An old woman stumbled and fumbled out,

20. [saying that] my master was not at home

21. [and he] went to somewhere else.

22. I said, after your master comes back, please tell him

23. that I have come to visit.

24. [Her] ears were muffled,

25. [and she] did not hear [me] at all.

26. Therefore, I had no choice,

27. [but] found a brush and an ink-stone from a small shop in their neighborhood,

28. [and] wrote down the words about my visit and left [the note] there.

Section 26: Happy New Year!

1. Brother, Happy New Year!

2. Yes.

3. Likewise!

4. Brother, please sit.

5. What are you doing?

6. I want to kowtow for the new year ceremony.

7. What are you talking about?

8. You are my older brother!

9. Shouldn't I kowtow to you?

10. Well.

11. [I wish that you will] get a promotion in official ranks,

12. to raise more sons,
13. [and] to live a rich life.
14. Brother, please stand up and sit up there.
15. The boiled dumplings are available for you to eat a few.
16. I ate at home and then came out.
17. How could [you] eat that full?
18. The young people even ate just now,
19. [and] soon they would be hungry [again]!
20. Maybe you just feel embarrassed.
21. Seriously,
22. do I need to pretend at brother's home?
23. [I] do not dare to lie.
24. Well.
25. That is fine.
26. Make some tea and bring [it here].
27. Brother, I do not drink tea.
28. Why?
29. I still need to go to other places.
30. [There are] many homes [I] am supposed to visit.
31. [If I] am tired and forget [to visit],
32. when I get there finally,
33. people would think too much of that.
34. Brother, please just eat,
35. and do not show me out.
36. [Otherwise] the flavor of [the food] would be taken out.
37. What are you saying?
38. Is there such a custom [that I] do not walk you to the door?
39. Well.
40. [You must have] got tired.
41. [You] came for nothing,
42. [and you did not] even drink some tea.
43. After [you] get home, please say that [I] sent [my] good wishes.

Section 27: Don't Fall into Buddhism!

1. As for doing good things,
2. we are talking about filial piety, respecting one's older brother, loyalty, faithfulness and so on;
3. not about offering to the Buddha and supernatural beings, nor feeding the Buddhist monks
4. and Taoist priests.
5. Taking the evil doers for an example,

6. no matter how [they] become a vegetarian, mending the road or building a bridge,

7. how could [they] be freed from their sins?

8. Even the Buddha and the supernatural beings would not send blessings!

9. [As for] the vegetarian people will ascend to the heaven,

10. and those who kill living creatures will come across the hell,

11. all such words

12. are the excuses of the Buddhist monks and Taoist priests to make a living.

13. If they do not use these and those terrifying words to deceive people

14. for the purpose of [making them] follow Buddhism;

15. [and if they just] close the temple's door,

16. maintain [their] vegetarian diet quietly,

17. and read [their] scriptures,

18. there would be no food [for them] to eat, nor clothes to wear.

19. Who would feed them?

20. [Would they] drink wind for a living?

Section 28: A Respectable Leader

1. [That] respectful old minister's capabilities are quick and resolute.

2. Any matter that comes into [his hands] would be conducted properly and logically.

3. Furthermore, he is clear in his heart,

4. [and] he knows people well.

5. Whether good or bad things cannot be hidden from his eyes.

6. He unusually cherishes the young and brilliant people who are diligent in the official work.

7. When there is a chance for promotion,

8. he would just promote and recommend.

9. For anyone who is sly and lazy at official business,

10. making people see their good behaviors on purpose,

11. [or] attempting to be lucky,

12. that is planning to lose their heads in front of him.

13. If [these kinds of people] happened to be caught[505] [by him],

14. there is no such a rule to let them go easily.

15. Even though it is said so,

---

[505] The Manchu expression of 'nambuha' means 'it happens to be caught or seen', corresponding with the Chinese counterpart 捞把着 (*laobazhao*).

16. everyday brothers look upon me with [their] eager eyes,
17. expecting to grow up to be useful people [by my recommendation].
18. If [I] do not recommend the ones who should be recommended,
19. and do not restrain the ones who should be restrained,
20. how could the good people be encouraged,
21. [and] the evil ones be punished?
22. [Your were] born with a straight mind and a fast mouth.
23. [The way you] speak and handle things is correct and upright.
24. People all admire and lose their hearts [to you].
25. [We should] advise and encourage each other,
26. to make great efforts and press forward!

Section 29: A Good Old Man

1. This person who has caught up with the old time,
2. is widely different.
3. [He is] affectionate and warmhearted when seeing people.
4. When sitting at one place,
5. discussing books and learning,
6. he likes [these things] very much.
7. Continuously [he] would talk for a day,
8. but will not get tired.
9. He would guide people where they need guidance,
10. [and] would teach people where they need to be taught,
11. [by] quoting the ancient things [as examples].
12. Compared to the current people,
13. he is guiding the young generations to good places by kind words.
14. He is also very kindhearted,
15. [and] very protective.
16. When [he] saw people's sufferings,
17. [he] would be worried as if encountering [the problems] himself.
18. Definitely he would try his best to help and look after [people].
19. Surely this is an old man who is clean, dignified, and well-blessed.
20. Therefore,
21. if I don't visit him every a few days,
22. [I] would feel sorry in [my] heart.
23. As the saying goes,
24. if one man is blessed,
25. the whole family would be extended with the luck.
26. This family's property is prosperous,
27. [and their] sons and grandchildren are thriving.
28. This is a good reward to the old person's behaviors!

Section 30: The Right Way of Eating Meat

1. Yesterday [I] ate the meat that was offered to ancestors,
2. [and] that would be [good] enough.
3. Why do you deliver the Lights-out Meat[506] [to me]?
4. Just now [I] still wanted to invite brother [you] to come,
5. [But,] brother, you know
6. what [I] have or don't have.
7. Only these few servants
8. kill pigs,
9. and clean the internal organs.
10. Is there a place that does not occupy hands?
11. Because of that, [I] did not send people to invite [you].
12. I clearly know that you cannot spare a person [to invite me].
13. Would [I] wait [for you to send someone to] invite?
14. Therefore,
15. I met a few friends,
16. and came to eat big meat [pork][507].
17. [I am] still afraid that [we] could be late.
18. Unexpectedly we made it easily.
19. Well.
20. Brothers, we shall not exhaust the host's mind.
21. We sit and eat in the order of age.
22. Brothers, please eat some meat.
23. Shall we boil the meat in broth[508] to eat?
24. Ah!
25. What are you saying?
26. Wrong.
27. Did we have such a rule originally?
28. This meat
29. is a blessing from the ancestors!

---

[506] A legend says that 'tuibuhe yali' (*bei deng rou* 背灯肉) is the meat offered to the goddess of Wanli Mother (*wanli mama* 万历妈妈) in darkness. Wanli Mother's name is Xi Lan (喜兰), who was a concubine of Li Chengliang (李成梁). Li was the Regional Commander of the Liaodong province in the Late Ming dynasty while Nurhaqi served Li as a slave. Xi Lan set Nurhaqi free in secret, and Li removed her clothes and killed her. In order to honor Xi Lan, Nurhaqi commanded his people to offer her a sacrifice in darkness.

[507] The Manchu expression 'amba yali' (*darou* 大肉) means pork in this context.

[508] The Manchu expression 'barafi' (*maotang* 沏湯) means 'to boil the meat in broth'.

30. Is it appropriate to persuade [people to eat]?

31. Moreover, [regarding] the guests who come and leave.

32. there is no such a custom to receive or see them out.

33. You just give precedence to each other in such a manner;

34. doesn't it violate something?

Section 31: Brotherhood

1. Older and younger brothers

2. are born by the same mother.

3. In childhood,

4. they eat together,

5. play together,

6. and make no distinctions between one another.

7. How intimate they were and how kind they were!

8. The reason they became distant after they grew up,

9. is probably because of the instigating words of their wives and concubines.

10. They fight for family properties,

11. or they have listened to the dissenting words of other people[509].

12. They reserve selfish motives respectively,

13. [and] generate very much [resentment].

14. How could I explain [this]?

15. They have listened to these slanderous talks everyday,

16. and their hearts are filled up [with such things].

17. For a moment when they cannot endure each other,

18. they would go as far as to quarrel and fight.

19. They become like enemies.

20. Think and look [this way].

21. If properties are gone,

22. [you] can set them up again;

23. If women are lost, [you] can marry again.

24. Among the older and younger brothers,

25. if one gets hurt,

26. it would be like [you] have lost one hand or foot.

27. How could you get [it] back?

28. Occasionally [if you are] unfortunate,

---

[509] The Manchu expression 'hetu niyalma' means 'other people', corresponding with 傍人 (*bangren*). A modern translation is 旁人 (*pangren*).

29. running into an accident,
30. the older and younger brothers are still closely connected.
31. They would risk their life to find a way for rescue.
32. Other people would be afraid of being involved,
33. or [they would just] get busy hiding away.
34. [Would they] make an effort for you?
35. Looking this way,
36. there are no blessings [as great as] older and younger brothers.
37. Why wouldn't people think of this thoroughly?

Section 32: Raising Children to Take Care of Parents

1. Raising children
2. originally is to be prepared for the old time.
3. As for the sons,
4. [they] should think of their parents' grace of hard working to bring [them] up.
5. Before their parents grow old, they should take the moment
6. to dress [them] with good clothes,
7. to serve[510] them with good food,
8. [and] to make them happy by a pleasant face and peaceful words.
9. If [children] do not care what [the parents] eat and wear,
10. do not ask [if they are] cold or hungry,
11. but treat them like strangers,
12. that would make the old people sad and stuffy.
13. After they pass away,
14. no matter how hard [the children] cry,
15. what is the point?
16. Even though the crying is out of a sincere heart,
17. who would believe?
18. [Their crying] is nothing but out of fear that people might ridicule.
19. It is just pretending.
20. Even though [children] offer all kinds of sweet and delicious stuff as sacrifices [for the dead],
21. who has seen the spirits enjoy [the food]?
22. [Offering sacrifice] is just for the living people to make excuses.
23. What would the deceased people get?

---

[510] The Manchu expression 'alibume' means 'to serve', corresponding with 事奉 (*shifeng*). A modern expression is 侍奉 (*shifeng*).

24. Unthinkably, some children say that their parents were old
25. and become confused,
26. so they create a disturbance to force [family members] live apart [from one another].
27. When words come to this point,
28. people cannot help
29. signing and getting resentful.
30. Such people,
31. will not be tolerated by the heaven and earth;
32. [and] will be hated by the ghosts and the supernatural beings.
33. How could they end up well?
34. [If you don't believe,] just look quietly.
35. How could such things exist in the long run?
36. In a moment of blinking eyes,
37. his children would follow his example to behave.

Section 33: A Greedy Man

1. What is the strange thing that [you] cannot get?
2. Every time [we] met,
3. [you] just bothered [me].
4. [You kept] asking [people] for that.
5. It is a very indecent [behavior]!
6. People might feel embarrassed,
7. [and] also gave you a lot [which you asked for].
8. [But] you do not feel satisfied in your heart,
9. [and] try to get it all by force.
10. What reason is that?
11. It is a sympathy to give it to you,
12. [and] it is still reasonable if they do not give [at all].
13. On the contrary you lose your temper and blame people.
14. That would be absolutely wrong.
15. For example, it is your stuff.
16. [and] people love it;
17. Don't you love it?
18. [However,] you completely cannot decide [where it should go],
19. [and] people completely take it away.
20. How do you feel in your heart?
21. Because it was me yesterday,
22. you lost your temper, and I just endured.
23. Except for me,
24. would anyone else

25. tolerate you?

26. Remember my words.

27. It is good to change [your behaviors].

28. A moment ago if you just had no capabilities[511] [to make a living],

29. that would explain [why you behaved that way],

30. because your purpose was for something to eat and wear.

31. [But] you just wanted to take extra advantages by unfair means.

32. What was that?

33. Behind you, wouldn't people say that you are shortsighted?

Section 34: Why Did I Help?

1. Who is willing to mind his business?

2. I am a person who sits at home in a good condition.

3. From where did he inquire and find me indirectly[512]?

4. I can recognize that person.

5. He came here many times in a row,

6. to me saying that, brother, regarding this matter I have to depend on you.

7. Even though you are tired,

8. but please cherish and speak for me.

9. Would he let me go by following me behind [like this]?

10. My face [heart] has been soft all the time.

11. You know this very well.

12. People feel anxious and beg me by kneeling down and kowtow.

13. How embarrassed if [I] let him go back without any satisfaction?

14. Because [I] cannot make any excuse,

15. so I agreed.

16. [I] told it to a friend clearly and thoroughly.

17. Unexpectedly, this is not a matter of him alone.

18. Many people are involved and his elbow is impeded, so this friend did not promise to help.

19. Therefore, I still cannot say anything without looking at the situation.

20. Later I gave it a second thought.

21. Forget about it.

---

[511] The Manchu expression 'enqehen' means 'capability', corresponding with 能奈 (*nengnai*). A modern translation is 能耐 (*nengnai*).

[512] The Manchu expression 'ulan ulan i' means 'indirectly', corresponding with 灣轉 (*wanzhuan*), which is 婉轉 (*wanzhuan*) in modern Chinese.

22. Looking at this situation,

23. [I] cannot redeem [it].

24. Is there such a reason of forcing people to make promises by fixing eyes on them?

25. Therefore,

26. I came back to tell him a message.

27. On the contrary he blamed me for being an obstacle,

28. [and] showed me [an angry] face.

29. Very sad![513]

30. If [I] knew that,

31. why did I speak [for him] for no reasons at all?

Section 35: An Awkward Situation

1. Brother, you refuse in such a strong way,

2. I feel horrified endlessly.

3. [You might have] said I came late.

4. Why do [you] behave this way?

5. Or because of something else?

6. Usually [we] interact on a frequent term.

7. Today is a good day of an old friend [like you],

8. instead if I do not come,

9. how could that be counted as a friend?

10. Indeed I did not know why.

11. If I really knew,

12. I should have come beforehand.

13. With me, there will not be too many people,

14. [and if] without me, there will not be less of them.

15. It would be good if I just receive the guests for you.

16. There must be many good things given by the honored relatives and lineage relatives[514].

17. What else would you need?

18. Presumably you cannot eat them all.

19. This little thing from me must not be worth mentioning at all.

20. However, it is still a [little] piece of my heart!

---

[513]In this context, the Manchu word 'koro' means sad. 慚心 (*kuixjin*) means 'a guilty conscience' in modern Chinese language.

[514] The Manchu expression 'hvnqihin' (lineage relatives) are people who bear the same family name. So 宗親 (*zongqin*) should be added into the Chinese parallel.

21. I wouldn't say that [you] must invite the older generations to eat it.
22. But [if you] just taste a little,
23. that would be considered as cherishing me.
24. That is all I want for coming here.
25. You just do not accept [my present],
26. [but] I am still sitting here.
27. Or shall I go back?
28. Indeed that makes me feel awkward!

Section 36: Reading the Right Books!

1. If [you] read books, [you] should read the Comprehensive Mirror[515],
2. [Your] learning would grow,
3. [You] would remember the things from the past,
4. [and] follow the example of the good ones,
5. [but] the bad ones would be taken as avoidance.
6. It benefits both [your] body and mind!
7. As for the novels,
8. are all groundless words made up by people.
9. Even though [you] read thousands of them,
10. is that useful?
11. Some people even read [the novels] to the others shamelessly.
12. During the time of such a country [dynasty],
13. with whom [they] fought a few times;
14. that person chopped with a sword;
15. this one blocked it out with a spear;
16. this person charged with a spear,
17. that one defended with a sword.
18. If they were defeated,
19. what they invited,
20. would come through clouds,
21. and go through fog.
22. They are all supernatural beings who are capable of sorcery,
23. cutting grass and changing it to horses,
24. [or] throwing the beans out and changing them into people.
25. Obviously these are lies.

---

[515] The Manchu expression 'fafu buleku' refers to Comprehensive Mirror in Aid of Governance (*zizhitongjian* 資治通鑑), which was combined by Sima Guang (1019-1086 AD) and published in 1084.

26. [But] the muddled people take them as true,
27. being confused and listening with great interest.
28. If knowledgeable and capable people saw this,
29. not only would [they] laugh,
30. but also would [they] be sick of this.
31. Why do people spend time on this [novel-reading thing]?

Section 37: Living a Simple life

1. Brother, have you heard of this?
2. From beginning to end, his words
3. were mocking me,
4. [and] making fun of me.[516]
5. I am not exaggerating.
6. Speaking of him,
7. [he] was a kid just now.
8. How many days could he have wet the bed[517]?
9. Seriously these are not the things they could understand.
10. New clothes
11. are supposed to wear in the occasion of [important] matters.
12. What I wear [right now] is just for the usual days.
13. What's wrong with the old [clothes]?
14. What's wrong with the broken [ones]?
15. If [a person] does not have capabilities as a real man does,
16. that is shameful.
17. To wear [new clothes] or not,
18. why does it matter?
19. Nowadays,
20. though I do not wear good clothes,
21. I have peace in my heart.
22. How do I put this?
23. I do not need to beg people [for anything],
24. [and] I am not in debt.
25. There is nothing of being shameful and anxious about.

---

[516] The Manchu word 'yekerxembi' means 'to make fun of someone', and the Chinese translation 說穿的曹少 (*shuo chuande zao*) literally means 'saying that [I] wear terribly'. The original Chinese character is made of a 曹 and a 少, which could bear a similar meaning with 糟(*zao, terrible*).
[517] The Manchu expression 'siteku' means 'wetting the bed or urinating sperms', corresponding with 溺精 (*niaojing*).

26. As for the young people like them,

27. I do not even look at [them] with the corner of my eyes.

28. [They] only know wearing the magnificent clothes,

29. and pretend to be decent.

30. Do they know how to become as capable as a real man?

31. That kind of appearance is nothing but being wrapped in silk and satin.

32. How miraculous is that?

33. Only the very low and humble

34. people who do not have eyes,

35. [but] talk nonsense in sleep,

36. would say that he is decent and respectable,

37. and would look up at him.

38. I would call him a rack for hanging the clothes!

Section 38: An Irresponsible Servant

1. Have [you] got that book?

2. I haven't got it.

3. Did you send someone?

4. Why hasn't he arrived yet?

5. [I] sent someone to get it.

6. First, we ordered him to go.

7. Would he ask us about it?

8. [His] spirit was low,

9. [and he was] wasting time,

10. All he wanted is to delay.

11. Later [he heard that] it was your words,

12. then he left in a hurry.

13. Does one set [of these books] contain four?

14. He went in a great rush,

15. [and] only took three [of them].

16. He left one out.

17. You should go back quickly.

18. Otherwise be careful,

19. When brother [your master] comes back,

20. you should be prepared to be sorry.

21. On the contrary, he said that what we told him is confusing and unclear.

22. He went back while complaining a lot.

23. Up to now he hasn't returned.

24. [I] shall send someone to meet him.

25. [I] am afraid [he] went on a diversion.
26. What a sly and lazy man [he is]!
27. Definitely he has gone to a busy place to play.
28. It is inappropriate if [I] do not discipline him strictly.
29. When he comes,
30. [I shall] tie him up and beat [his] buttocks severely.
31. That would be good.
32. Otherwise,
33. [he] would be intolerable if [I] spoil [him].

Section 39: To Help a Friend

1. Brother, I need to entrust you with something.
2. But it is hard to open [my] mouth.
3. What reason is that?
4. There are too many times I have implored.
5. But if I don't ask you,
6. except for you,
7. nobody would be capable of making my things happen.
8. Therefore I come to trouble you.
9. Didn't you come for that thing?
10. Yes.
11. How did brother [you] know that?
12. This morning your brother told me.
13. Before the lunch time[518],
14. I went there once.
15. Suddenly [what I] encountered is that he was not at home.
16. When it just turned into midday,
17. I went back again.
18. Before I reached his living room,
19. I heard the sound of laughing.
20. I wet and broke the paper on [his] window.
21. From the hole I looked inside:
22. this person pours some wine for that man,
23. [and] that man returns a cup to this person.
24. [They] mingle together and eat happily.
25. [I] wanted to go inside.

---

[518] The Manchu expression 'osohon budai erin' (*xiaofanshi* 小飯時) means the time period before lunch.

26. Because there are many friends [I] do not know in person,

27. what would happen if [I] disturb their mood of drinking?

28. So I withdrew my body and went out.

29. His family servants saw [me] and wanted to tell [their master],

30. I immediately waved hands to stop [them].

31. You do not hurry.

32. I will go back tomorrow in the early dark morning[519].

33. It would be fine to talk to him properly.

Section 40: Traveling Faraway

1. Haven't you set out?

2. Sooner or later [I shall] leave.

3. Bat-horse, luggage and bundles are all organized and ready.

4. [I] am still short of some silver for traveling expenses.

5. It is easy to catch a tiger,

6. but it is hard to ask people for help.

7. I begin to believe [such words] today.

8. Regardless of [my] dignity,

9. I borrowed money everywhere,

10. But still I did not get it.

11. There are no other choices.

12. I came to [you] brother.

13. Either silver,

14. or pawns,

15. please help me a little.

16. When I return,

17. the capital and interest will be calculated and paid back.

18. Fortunately you came early.

19. If you are late slightly,

20. you won't make it.

21. Just now I got some silver from a village,

22. and [I] haven't used [it].

23. You take half of it to use.

24. After drinking some tea,

25. [I] will measure it for you.

26. Isn't this your first time to travel?

---

[519] The Manchu expression 'farhvn' means darkness, corresponding with 黑早 (*heiz-ao*), which means the early morning when it is still dark.

27. Yes.

28. Here are some words to tell you.

29. A principle for going on a long journey,

30. is to maintain harmonious relationships among friends.

31. What comes next is

32. not to distinguish the government officials to see who is inside or outside [of your network],

33. [but] cherish them equally.

34. Then you will have some connections to earn silver and make money.

35. It is important to respect people's dignity.

36. Do not grow long hands [to steal or take bribery].

37. If [you did] so,

38. it will implicate your name and reputation.

39. Brother, what you remind me,

40. is words like gold and jade.

41. I get [them] through [my] lungs like a string and tie a knot in [my] liver[520] so [I] remember [them].

Section 41: A Good Harvest

1. Brother, when did [you] arrive here from that village?

2. I have been here for quite a few days.

3. [I] totally did not hear that brother [you] had come here.

4. If I heard,

5. [I] would have come to visit you.

6. We lived in different directions,

7. and [we have] government official status.

8. It is reasonable that we haven't heard about each other.

9. Where is your land?

10. Across the river, [there is] a place which belongs to Ba Jeo.

11. Isn't it Huen River?

12. Yes, [it is] Huen River.

13. How are the crops over there this year?

14. Good.

15. Very abundant.

16. [People have] harvested a lot.

---

[520] The Manchu expression 'ufuhu de ulime fahvn de falime' means 'to pull the thread through the lungs and tie a knot in the liver'. 牢託肘腸 (*laotuo zhouchang*) means 'to commit something firmly to the elbows and intestines'.

17. First [people said the crops] were waterlogged.
18. Then [they said] there was a drought.
19. It is all rumors,
20. [which are] not trustworthy.
21. It is not necessary to say something else.
22. Black beans are really cheap.
23. One liter [of black beans] is only worth a dozen coins.
24. It hasn't been like this for a few years recently.
25. Really?
26. Truly.
27. Brother, if [you] still need to send family people [to buy black beans],
28. please buy a few *dan*[521] of black beans for me.
29. [As for] how much silver would that cost after conversion,
30. please calculate and tell me.
31. I will send the silver to [you] brother, according to the original price.
32. Yes.
33. There are quite a few horses tied at your home.
34. [You] should buy [a lot of black beans].
35. Rather than buying with an expensive price at our place,
36. [I would rather] buy from that place and get it with a price several-times cheaper.

Section 42: A Sight-seeing

1. Days ago a few of us
2. [went for] a so-called sight-seeing.
3. Unexpectedly [we] suffered.
4. [We] went out of town,
5. [and] did not take the regular road,
6. [but] took a roundabout way leading to nowhere.
7. [We] asked for directions along the way.
8. As soon as we arrived at the irrigation gate,
9. [we] took the boat.
10. talked to each other,
11. [and] drank some wine.
12. [Finally we] arrived at the Dung Gao garden.
13. When [we] came back to the irrigation gate again,
14. the sun had already set to the west horizon.

---

[521] One *dan* equals 62.5 kilograms.

15. As soon as [we] finished supper,
16. I said, brothers, [we] should go.
17. All of our servants walk on foot,[522]
18. [and they] fall far behind.
19. [So we] sat in a row [to wait],
20. [and] did not move at all.
21. Later when the sun was about to set,
22. we then got on the horses, and hurried back.
23. [When we] just arrived at the pass,
24. hazily [we] saw the moonlight.
25. People who came out of the city,
26. told us to hurry.
27. Because one gate wing was already closed.
28. [I] felt more anxious in heart,
29. [and] urged the horse by whip to catch up with one breath.
30. [I] caught up with the end [of the line].
31. [Even though] we just came inside [the gate] at the right time,
32. family servants fell far behind,
33. [and they] were stopped outside of the pass.
34. Indeed [we] went out with great interest,
35. [but] came back with a sad heart.

Section 43: A Condescending Man

1. I went to the government office, and just came back.
2. From afar a group of people roared.
3. [A man] rode a horse coming [to me],
4. When [he] came close,
5. [I] carefully looked at [him].
6. It was someone from our old neighborhood.
7. What he wears and rides is magnificent:
8. a fat horse and light warm fur clothes;
9. good looking with an imposing appearance.
10. [He] became very fat.
11. When [he] saw me,
12. [he] didn't even greet [me].
13. [He] turned his face away,

---

[522] From the context, this sentence should mean 'we all have servants who walk on foot'.

14. [and] passed by while looking at the sky.
15. At that time I wanted to call him for a stop,
16. and to humiliate [him] squarely.
17. Later [I] gave a second thought,
18. Why would [I] do that?
19. [If] he took notice of me,
20. would I have some decency?
21. He just deceived other people.
22. Brother, didn't you know?
23. Three years ago,
24. in our place,
25. who was him?
26. [He] was extremely poor[523].
27. [He] rose up and ate in the morning,
28. [then he] planned what to eat in the evening.
29. All day long [he] was like a ghost.
30. [His] stomach was hungry,
31. [and] in every place [he] did whatever [he] could [to find something valuable].
32. Even [he] found a string of grass,
33. [and] that would be precious[524].
34. [He] would visit our home two or three times a day,
35. either asking for this,
36. or looking for that.
37. Is there anything of mine didn't [he] eat?
38. Even the chopsticks were sucked broken[525].
39. Nowadays [he] does not need to ask people for help.
40. [He] changed over night and forgot the old [friends].
41. I am not trying to lift myself up.
42. Who would care his nasty behaviors[526] [and look at him] in the eyes?

---

[523] The Manchu expression 'fungsan yadahvn' means 'extremely poor' in the context, which corresponds with the Chinese expression of 腥氣 (*xingqi,* the smell of fish or meat).

[524] The Manchu expression 'hihan' means 'rare or precious', corresponding with 希罕 (*xihan*). The modern characters are 稀罕 (*xihan*).

[525] The Manchu expression 'manaha' means 'broken', corresponding with 明 (*ming*). A modern translation can be 破 (*po*).

[526] The Manchu expression 'nantuhun' means 'nasty behaviors', corresponding with 行次 (*xingci*). A modern translation could be 行爲 (*xingwei*).

Section 44: A Beautiful Snow Scene

1. It was cold last night.
2. In my dream [I] felt frozen and woke up,
3. When it turned bright,
4. I got up in a hurry.
5. [I] opened the door [and] looked [outside].
6. It turned out to be the big white snow.
7. After eating some food,
8. when it was close to the midday,
9. the floating snow flakes became bigger.
10. I thought there was nothing going on.
11. At least one person needs to come,
12. to sit and talk [with me].
13. My family servants came in and told that people are coming.
14. I felt refreshed inside.
15. One side [I] told people to prepare wine and dishes;
16. on the other side [I] lit a bowl of roaring fire.
17. [and] invited brothers immediately.
18. Wine and dishes are already prepared,
19. [and] brought here so [we] drank slowly.
20. [We] lift up the door curtain and looked outside.
21. The scenery of snow
22. is more elegant than anything else.
23. The heavy snow fluffs.
24. Everything between the sky and earth,
25. was all turned into white.
26. [We] became happier while looking at this,
27. [and] discussed some truth of correcting the wrongs into right.
28. After eating supper,
29. [we] lit the light,
30. [and] dispersed away.

Section 45: Don't Mess with Him

1. Look at you!
2. [You are] merely a mouth.
3. [Your] appearance looks clever,
4. [but] your inside is not bright.
5. If he does not offend you,
6. that would be your luck.
7. Why did you irritate him?

8. [You] never listened to the good words.

9. In the past [you] seemed like being bewitched.

10. Finally [you] went there stubbornly.

11. [You were] insulted [in a way of] being exposed [to people].

12. That trouble-maker, who do you think he is?

13. [He] is not an easy [person to irritate].

14. [He] is an infamous merciless man!

15. When [did] he show mercy to people?

16. It is fine if you have nothing to do with him.

17. If there is anything in [his] way,

18. [he] spares no feelings to anyone!

19. [He] would accumulate strength to win the arguments,

20. and [he] wouldn't stop until [he] gains some advantages.

21. Isn't that so?

22. To the end [you] woke up the tiger who had been lying down,

23. [so your] nose got knocked[527],

24. [and you] came back being disappointed.

25. What fun is that?

26. It says that people who have a crutch will not fall,

27. and people who are famous do not make [stupid] mistakes.

28. [If] you really knew it in person,

29. where would you go ?

30. No matter how,

31. I am quite a few years older than you,

32. If there is something [you] are supposed to do,

33. even though you don't care much in your heart,

34. I would urge you to do it.

35. Is there a reason [I] would stop you?

Section 46: Dealing with a Drunk

1. Who expected him to speak this and that?

2. [I] was forced by his words to speak so!

3. Even other people can be deceived,

4. how can you be concealed?

5. From the new year up to now,

---

[527] The Manchu expression 'kangsiri foribufi' literally means 'nose gets knocked/beaten', and the Chinese expression 碰了釘子 (*pengle dingzi*) means 'bumped against a nail'.

6. did he accomplish any official business?

7. Today [I] drank some wine there.

8. As soon as [I] came back,

9. Ah!

10. Why didn't I see you until now!

11. Even so,

12. I did not delay any thing.[528]

13. Every month I did the official work for you.

14. On the contrary I became the one to blame.

15. Hearing these words,

16. my anger rose up to the neck.

17. Whatever [you] say today,

18. [we] will settle down tomorrow.

19. Brother, why did you argue with him in this way?

20. He's used to joking that way.

21. How come you didn't know?

22. It must be that

23. [he] went crazy after drinking.

24. Please just pretend that [you] didn't see and didn't hear.

25. What do you say?

26. Brother, you don't know.

27. [He] is a person that believes the easy thing is easy, and the difficult thing is difficult.[529]

28. If you leave room [for him], he would be happy.

29. Frankly you said that I was joking[530] and didn't notice that I offended people by careless words.

30. Some people might let it go,

31. but [few people would] say it seriously with an angry face.

32. Who would deal with him that way?

33. Brother, please don't be mad.

34. I will take this alcoholic man to a remote place,

---

[528] The Manchu word 'tookan' means 'delay', corresponding with 脱空 (tuokong), which means 'to deceive' in traditional Chinese literature.

[529] In the traditional Chinese way of recording years, months and days, 丁 (ding) is one of the Heavenly Stems 天干 (tian'gan) and 卯 (mao) belongs to the Earthly Branches 地支 (dizhi). 丁是丁卯是卯 (ding shi ding mao shi mao) usually means taking things seriously, but in this context they imply someone is stubborn.

[530] The Manchu expression 'yobodombi herqun akv' means making jests without noticing what happens, corresponding with 頑不覺 (wan bujue).

35. gouging his eyes out,

36. and humiliating him,

37. to give vent to your anger[531]!

Section 47: A Cheater

1. When [I] met him in the beginning,

2. [I] considered him as a warmhearted and straightforward man.

3. His appearance is impressive,

4. with a good mouth and sharp teeth.

5. [I] envied by just looking at him.

6. [I] was even thinking of how to make friends with him.

7. [I also] praised him without stopping [my] mouth.

8. Later on [we] interacted,

9. mingling at one place,

10. [and I] carefully observed the things he did.

11. It turned out that [he] is not an honest man.

12. [He] employs trickery and resorts to deception.

13. Where can [we] find out what is true or false about him?

14. [He] is sinister on the inside,

15. and will not lead people on a good path.

16. [His] mouth says that it is good for you,

17. [but] behind [your] back [he] would frame [you] up in an uneasy way.

18. If [you] fall into his traps, [you] fall down flat on [your] back.

19. Up to now, are there only a few people harmed by his hands?

20. [You] cannot count [them] by wiggling [your] fingers.

21. Therefore, when friends mentioned him,

22. all said that [he] is horrifying!

23. There is no one who doesn't have a headache.

24. Panther's color is on the skin,

25. and people's color is on the inside.

26. That is especially for this kind of person.

27. Indeed it is my good luck.

28. If I didn't pay attention to distance him,

29. wouldn't I fall into his trap?

---

[531] The Manchus have adopted 氣 (*qi*) to refer to 'anger'.

Section 48: A Stupid Man

1. Human is said to be more honorable than all things.
2. To be a human,
3. if [he] cannot distinguish the good from the bad,
4. [and] cannot tell what is right or wrong,
5. how is that different than animals?
6. Just like the way of maintaining friendship,
7. you and I should respect each other.
8. Isn't that good?
9. Frequently [if some people] act outrageously and offend others,
10. [and they] do not look at the face and buttocks,
11. [but only] run wild and swear with a dirty mouth,
12. can that be counted as a capability?
13. How could that be!
14. Look at his strange appearance
15. [with] a big belly puffed up!
16. Totally a fathead!
17. [He] also pretends to be a knowledgeable person.
18. [and] that makes people's flesh feel creepy[532]!
19. [He] seems like a dog [that is] barking.
20. People feel tired and no longer want to listen.
21. If [he] has a little piece of human heart,
22. [he] would have a little consciousness.
23. But [he] does not have any sense of shame;
24. [he] feels like someone is praising him,
25. [so he] feels more excited.
26. How could I say this?
27. His father was a real man who has done things right[533] in his life.
28. Somehow [he] committed sins,
29. and raised such a tramp.
30. Pathetic!
31. [He is] wasted.
32. His fortune was all taken away by his father's ghost.

---

[532] The Manchu expression 'yali madabumbi' literally means 'to make flesh swell', corresponding with 肉麻 (rouma).
[533] The Manchu expression 'yabumbihe' means 'have done things correctly', corresponding with 行走 (xingzou). A modern translation could be 正經做事 (zhengjing zuoshi).

33. That is the end of his [life].

34. It wouldn't be possible [for him] to be promoted [as a government official].

Section 49: Abiding the Law

1. Among us,

2. are you a stranger?

3. Look at me!

4. [I would just] come in directly.

5. Why did [you] need [my gatekeepers] to deliver a message [to me]?

6. [You] have already arrived at [my] door,

7. but then [you] turned away.

8. Are [you] angry because the family servants said I was not at home?

9. How could that happen?

10. If [you] don't tell me the reason,

11. how could [I] know?

12. Recently,

13. That group of our brothers,

14. made a partnership,

15. [and] opened up a place for playing money.

16. [They] just came to [me],

17. swearing and making oath,

18. to make me come definitely.

19. I am not free. Don't you know that?

20. [I] have official business from now and then.

21. How could [I] make a firm decision?

22. Moreover, the law and prohibition are very strict.

23. If occasionally there is an accident,

24. where could [I] put [my] face?

25. Therefore, if [they] are angry, so be it!

26. Finally I didn't go,

27. [and I] told my family people that

28. no matter who come and look for me,

29. answering that [I] am not home.

30. [We] didn't expected that you came here.

31. The ignorant servants

32. answered in the same way.

33. [and] sent [you] away.

34. Then [they] came in and told me.

35. So I sent people to chase you immediately.

36. [But they] said [that they] didn't catch up with [you].

37. I am really disappointed inside.

38. [I] do not know what to do.

Section 50: Visiting the Grave

1. The day before yesterday, did you visit the grave in the graveyard?

2. Yes.

3. Why did [you] come back today?

4. It is very far apart.

5. Because [I] cannot make a round trip within one day,

6. so [I] rested two nights there.

7. On the first day, [I] set out when the city gate just opened.

8. [I] traveled until it turned dark and then [I] arrived.

9. Yesterday [I] offered food as a sacrifice.

10. Another night passed.

11. Today when it was dawning,

12. [I] just set out and came back.

13. On the road except for eating meals,

14. [I] did not take any rest.

15. [I] just made it back when the city gate was closed.

16. Brother [you] buried [your ancestors] in a far place.

17. It is a good thing.

18. If the children have no capabilities,

19. it is difficult [for them] to visit the graves.

20. How can [I] say this?

21. There is no space in the old graveyard.

22. People who looked at the location of the tomb,

23. all said that it was a good place.

24. Therefore [we] made it into a graveyard.

25. Generally speaking,

26. if we have [money],

27. [we would do it] in a having-money way.

28. If [we] don't have,

29. [we do it in a way of] having no [money].

30. No matter how poor and bitter,[534]

31. [we must] visit the graveyard,

32. to offer a cup of wine as a memorial ceremony.

---

[534] 'Hafirahvn suilashvn' means 'poor and bitter', while 窄累 (*zhailei*) means 'narrow and tired'. A modern translation can be 穷困 (*qiongkun*).

33. When it comes to the children,
34. what matters is that they are outstanding or not.
35. If [people] raised a son who makes no progress,
36. even [he] lives in the graveyard himself,
37. [he] won't burn a piece of paper money [as an offering to the dead].

Section 51: Being Caught in a Rain

1. Ah!
2. Where are [you] going in such a big rain?
3. Go inside quickly.
4. One friend of mine passed away,
5. [I] came to attend [his] funeral.
6. This morning it was cloudy.
7. Even though it might rain,
8. when the midday came,
9. it turned bright and clear.
10. One the way back I walked and looked around,
11. the dense clouds spread one piece by another.
12. Regarding that, I said to the family people,
13. this weather is not right.
14. Walk faster.
15. If not,
16. we will be caught in the rain for sure.
17. While [we] were talking,
18. it started to rain quickly.
19. Brother, as you say,
20. in such a wilderness,
21. where could we hide?
22. There was not enough time [for us] to wear the raincoats and fur clothing.
23. We were soaked wet all over.
24. It doesn't matter.
25. There is my clothes.
26. Take them out for you to change.
27. It is getting late.
28. You go back to city tomorrow.
29. In our remote and secluded garden,
30. though there is no good stuff [to eat],
31. there are still a few piglets and geese raised at home.
32. Let's slaughter one or two to feed you.
33. Why are you talking about eating?

34. In this way [we] find a good place to rest,
35. [and] this is [our] luck!
36. Otherwise,
37. if [we] do not walk in the rain,
38. is there any other choices?

Chapter 6
The Continuously Compiled
Essential Elements of Manchu Language Book
with Chinese Words Combined

Section 52 : Go Hunting

1. For the first time I went hunting,
2. [and I] was riding a horse.
3. It galloped steadily,
4. [and it] ran fast.
5. [I] carried a quiver,
6. just relieved the hunting encirclement and walked.
7. [Suddenly] a gazelle ran out of the grass.
8. I urged the horse,
9. drew the bow,
10. [and] shot an [arrow].
11. [I] missed[535] [the target] a little.
12. When [my] hand returned to get [another] arrow,
13. the gazelle waggled its tail.
14. In no time,
15. it ran over a hill,
16. [and] went away up to[536] the hillside which faces the sun[537].
17. [I] followed [its] tail and chased after [it],
18. went over the hill and came down from the hill's back.
19. Over there I spurred the horse, got closer [to it] and shot another [arrow],
20. [but the arrow] went over its head.
21. I didn't expect that a deer ran over here from the front side,
22. [and it] just ran over the hill, coming towards [me].
23. [It] was directly hit by the arrow I shot out,

---

[535] The Manchu expression 'amariha' means 'fell behind', or 'was late'. From the context, it implies that the hunter did not hit the target.

[536] The Manchu word 'iqi' means 'toward', corresponding with 徃 (*wang*), which is a variant form of 往 (*wang*).

[537] The Manchu expression 'alin antu' (*shanyang* 山阳) is the mountain side that faces the sun.

24. [and] fell over, making a sound 'kub'.

25. Indeed it sounds like a joke,

26. [but] it is a good luck.

27. The one I caught up with was released,

28. instead [I] caught an unexpected one[538].

29. If [I] tell [it] to people who did not know,

30. it sounds like a lie which was told [seriously] by opening [my] eyes.

Section 53: Gambling

1. Ah! What happened to you?

2. For how many months we haven't seen [each other]?

3. How fast [time flies]!

4. [Your] beard has turned white,

5. [and you] have got an old looking.

6. Brother, please do not blame my mouth for being straightforward.

7. I heard that

8. you nowadays are addicted to playing[539] money [gambling],

9. [and you] owed a lot of debts[540].

10. If true,

11. it is not a joke!

12. It would be good if you have some restraints.

13. All these words are shadow-less and made up by people.

14. If you don't believe [me],

15. [you] can inquire carefully.

16. What words are that?

17. Don't you know the things done by yourself?

18. Look, all friends are discussing you.

19. [So] you must have done something.

20. Regarding playing money, what is the end[541]?

---

[538] The Manchu expression 'murakvngge' is a variant form of 'murambi' (*chui lushao* 吹鹿哨), which means that hunters blow a whistle to mimic the bleating of a stag, so the females will be attracted nearby for mating. Hunters would take the opportunity to hunt. 'Murakvngge' (*mei shao de* 没哨的) means that a hunter got a deer which he did not whistle for.

[539] The word 'efire' means 'to play', corresponding with 頑 (*wan*). The modern character is 玩 (*wan*).

[540] The Manchu expression 'bekdun araha' means 'owed debts', corresponding with 作賬 (*zuozhang*). The modern translation is 欠債 (*qianzhai*).

21. If [you] got involved deeply,

22. what would [you] save?

23. At the end, even though you do not commit crimes and sins,

24. when the family properties are exhausted, you won't have much left either.

25. Then [you] would stop.

26. Things like this, what we heard with ears[542] and saw with eyes,

27. even though are not many,

28. at least[543] [there are] more than one hundred cases.

29. You and I, we are friends who have known and seen [each other for a long time].

30. If [I] know but do not persuade,

31. [merely] saying 'who cares'[544];

32. [how could you] say that [we] get along [with each other]?

33. If there are no such things,

34. that is fine.

35. [But] why would I make inquiries [if there are no such things]?

Section 54: A Terrible Weather

1. Yesterday there was no wind at all.[545]

2. It was a sunny day.

3. Suddenly it changed, and the yellow[546] sun light became gloomy,

4. Regarding this, I [said] it was not right[547].

5. The big wind was blowing [and] coming!

6. Before the wind prevails,[548]

---

[541] The Manchu expression 'dube' means 'the end' or 'the termination', corresponding with 了手 (liaoshou). A modern translation could be 終了(zhongliao) or 停住 (tingzhu).

[542] The Manchu expression 'xan' means 'ears', corresponding with 耳躲 (erduo), which is written as 耳朵 (erduo) in modern Chinese texts.

[543] The Manchu expression 'absi' means 'at least', corresponding with 只少 (zhishao) . A modern expression is 至少 (zhishao).

[544] The Manchu word 'guwanta' has similar pronunciations with the Chinese 管他 (guanta), which means 'who concerns or cares'.

[545] The Manchu expression 'su akv' (wanquan meiyou 完全没有) means 'not at all'.

[546] The Manchu expression 'sohon' means 'yellow', which is a little different than the corresponding translation of 清清亮亮的 (qingqing liangliang de, clear and bright).

[547] The Manchu expression 'faijume' means 'to feel strange or inappropriate'.

7. let's take off.

8. [So we] scattered respectively.

9. As soon as [I] reached home,

10. the big wind howled[549] and blew fiercely.

11. The tree branches swayed in the wind, tossing around and making noises.

12. [The wind] sounded so ugly,

13. whistling all the time.

14. [When] blowing to the midnight,

15. [the wind] calmed down a little[550].

16. This morning when [I] came here,

17. [I saw] people who walked on the roads and streets,[551]

18. could not stand steadily at all.

19. They ran [while] making noises of 'ho' and 'ha'.

20. If I came with the wind,

21. it would be just right.

22. [But I] went against the wind,

23. [and] my face was hurt, feeling like being poked by needles.

24. [My] finger tips were frozen [and I] did not even have the strength to hold the whip.

25. Before a spit reaches the ground,

26. [it] would freeze,

27. fall and break into pieces.

28. How cold is that!

29. Since [I] was born,

30. who has experienced such a cold weather?

Section 55: Kung Fu Fighting

1. You don't know [that]

2. this is all because of his young age of being hot-blooded[552], vigorous and strong.[553]

---

[548] There is no a correspondent word for 乘着 (*chengzhe*, seize the moment) in the parallel Manchu text. 乘着 is now written as 趁着 (*chenzhe*).

[549] The Manchu expression 'hoo' sounds similar to 嗥 (*hao*), which means 'to roar or howl'.

[550] The Manchu expression 'majige' means 'a little', corresponding with 料料 (*liaoliao*). A modern expression is 略微 (*lüe wei*).

[551] The Manchu expression 'giyai' bears a similar sound with 街 (*jie*, street).

3. After encountering a few failures,

4. his impulses[554] would naturally disappear.

5. Where did [I] know?

6. In the past I very much loved creating a disturbance.

7. With one of my cousins from the same lineage[555],

8. we practiced [martial arts] everyday.

9. My cousin was very good at lance.

10. [I would say that] even a dozen people

11. can not come near him.

12. [Even a capable person] like this

13. met a worthy opponent later on.

14. A man from a village came to [my] uncle's home.

15. His leg was crippled.

16. [People] said [he]was capable of using a sword.

17. The two of them met at one place,

18. [and] wanted to compare abilities.

19. Either of them took their weapons.

20. Did my cousin ever consider him [as an opponent] in [his] eyes?

21. [My brother] did not even give precedence [to him],

22. [but] waved[556] [his] lance,

23. [and] pricked[557] towards [the man's] heart[558] once.

24. That lame person was not panicked at all,

25. [but] slowly knocked the lance with [his] sword.

26. Once in order to avoid being chopped,[559]

27. the head of lance was broken into two pieces.

28. When [my brother] was just about to pull the lance back,

---

[552] The Manchu expression 'aenggi sukdun' literally correspond with the Chinese notion of 血氣 (*xueqi*) which can be understood as 'hot-blooded and vigorous'.

[553] 過失 (*guoshi*, fault or mistake) only appeared in the Chinese text. The parallel Manchu word is 'haran', which means 'cause or reason'(*yuanyin* 原因).

[554] The Manchu expression 'amtan' means 'spirit, interest or mood', corresponding with 高興 (*gaoxing*, happiness). A modern expression would be 興致 (*xingzhi*).

[555] The Manchu expression 'mukvn' means lineage, corresponding with 戶中 (*hu-zhong*).

[556] The Manchu expression 'dargiyafi' has derived from the original verb 'dargiyam-bi', which means 'to raise or to wave'.

[557] The Manchu expression 'gidalaha' has derived from 'gidambi', which sounds similar to 擊打 (*jida*).

[558] The Manchu expression 'niyaman jaka' (*xinwo* 心窩) means 'the pit of the stom-ach/heart'.

[559] Originally there is no Chinese translation corresponding to this Manchu sentence.

29. the sword was already put on [his] neck.
30. When [he] was just about to jump away,
31. [his] neck was entwined by the sword.
32. [The sword] swayed[560] and immediately threw[561] at [his neck],
33. [and my cousin] went backward quite a few steps,
34. [and] fell with a loud sound.
35. Since then, [my brother's] buoyant spirits were interrupted,
36. [and he] didn't learn anymore.
37. Looking from this perspective,
38. it is a big [world] under the heaven.
39. Is there short of capable people?

Section 56: A Beautiful Scenery

1. The day before yesterday we went to the western mountain,
2. [and the trip] was very pleasant.
3. Needless to say the sight-seeing during the daytime,
4. when the night came,
5. it became happier.
6. A few of us ate supper,
7. [and] took a boat.
8. Soon after,
9. the moon rose high.
10. The moon light was shining,
11. just like the sun light in the daytime.
12. [We] paddled the boat slowly,
13. [and] went with the wind.
14. We turned around the pointed end of the mountain range[562] and saw that
15. the colors of sky and river cannot be distinguished, and the big water[563] stretches endlessly.
16. It may well be said as green mountains and clear water.

---

[560] The Manchu expression 'lasihime' has deviated from 'lasihimbi' (*huiwu* 揮舞), which means 'to sway or to swing'.
[561] The Manchu expression 'fahara' has derived from 'fahambi' (*zhi* 擲), which means 'to throw'.
[562] The Manchu expression 'alin i oforo' literally means 'a mountain's nose', which is a little different than 山嘴子 (*shanzuizi*), a mountain's mouth.
[563] The Manchu expression 'hvwai seme' means 'a large water body', which is different than its Chinese parallel 幽静匪常 (*youjing feichang*, extraordinarily quiet).

17. [We] paddled the boat deep into the reeds.

18. The sudden strokes[564] of [temple] bell reached our ears through the wind and at that moment,

19. thousands of our thoughts

20. were washed in the water,[565]

21. [and] there was nothing left unclean.

22. [People] may say that the supernatural beings transcend the world,

23. [but their] happiness is nothing more than this.

24. Therefore,

25. [we] drank happily with each other,

26. without noticing that the sky has turned bright.

27. For anyone who lives in the world,

28. how many times can [we come across][566] such a bright moon and a beautiful scenery?

29. Isn't that a pity if [we] just let them slip away?[567]

Section 57: Caught a Cold

1. How are you?

2. Your face turned really pale,

3. [and you] become thin like this.

4. Brother, you don't know that

5. these days [I have been] digging the sewer [and] the smell was horrible.

6. Besides, the weather suddenly turned cold and immediately it became hot,

7. [which] was not stable at all.

8. Therefore,

9. people cannot take care of their bodies as usual.

10. The day before yesterday during the mealtime,

11. it was very cool.

12. Suddenly it became very hot, so people could not stand but became agitated.

---

[564] The Manchu expression 'yang seme' is the sound of bells, corresponding with 喈喈的 (jiejie de).

[565] The Manchu expression 'muke de oboho' means 'have washed in water', which is slightly different than its Chinese counterpart 付與流水 (fuyu liushui, to give it to the running water).

[566] The word 遇見 (yujian) appears in the Chinese translation, not in the Manchu text.

[567] The Manchu expression 'untuhuri dulembumbi' can be translated as '徒然放過' (turan fang'guo), which did not appear in the original Chinese text.

13. [My] whole body was covered by sweat,
14. [and I] took off the gown to cool off.
15. Because [I] drank a bowl of cold tea,
16. immediately [I] had a headache[568].
17. [My] nose was stuffy[569],
18. [and my] throat was hoarse.
19. [My head] dizzy dizzy[570] [feeling like] the whole body was sitting in the cloud[571].
20. You are not the only one.
21. My body is not comfortable either.
22. [I] am too tired to move.
23. Fortunately the things [I] ate and drank yesterday were all vomited out.
24. Otherwise [I] cannot even manage to [come] today.
25. I teach you a good method.
26. Just empty your stomach,
27. eat less,
28. [and] do not eat or drink much.
29. If [you maintain] that way,
30. even though you caught a cold,
31. it wouldn't hurt much.

Section 58: Being Haunted

1. How is the house opposite yours?
2. Why do you ask that?
3. One of my lineage cousins said [he wanted to] buy.
4. That house is not good to live.
5. It is very ominous.
6. In the beginning one of my lineage brothers bought it.
7. From the seven gate rooms

---

[568] According to the Manchu context and the corresponding Chinese translation, there should be a missing Manchu word 'uju' (head).

[569] The Manchu expression 'wanggiyanaha' (齉 *nang*) means nasal obstruction due to a common cold.

[570] The Manchu expression 'hvi' sounds similar to 昏 (*hun*), which means dizzy or dazed.

[571] The Manchu expression 'tugi de tehe' means 'sitting or living in the cloud', which is a little different than the Chinese translation of 渾身發冷 (*hunshen faleng*, feeling cold all over).

8. to the five rooms behind the principal ones,

9. [they] were all comfortable and clean.

10. When my brother's son took [them] over,

11. [because] the wing-rooms on the two sides were all decayed[572] and pulled down,

12. [and therefore they] were rebuilt.

13. Suddenly they were haunted.

14. In the beginning it was [just] causing a little disturbance and that was fine.

15. As time passed,

16. [the ghosts even] made sounds in the daylight, and could be seen [with eyes].

17. The women at home frequently said that [they] encountered with ghosts and got scared,

18. and their life was disturbed.

19. Shamanistic ritual was futile[573],

20. [and] exorcism[574] was useless.

21. Because of that

22. [they] did not have other choices,

23. but sold it with a cheap price.

24. Brother, do you know [that]?

25. This is all because of bad luck.

26. It had nothing to do with the house.

27. With good luck,

28. even though there were demons and ghosts,

29. they would just stay away.

30. How could they hurt people?

31. Furthermore,

32. this brother of mine is very timid.

33. It would be fine that I tell him the real reason of making inquiries.

34. Whether to buy or not,

35. it is his decision to make.

---

[572] The original Chinese word for 'sangsaraka' [rotted, decomposed] is a character made up of 曹 and 少, which could be a variant of 糙 (*cao*, coarse) or 糟 (*zao*, terrible).

[573] The Manchu expression 'mekele' means 'futile or useless', corresponding with 是個白 (*shi ge bai*). The modern expression is 枉然 (*wangran*) or 無用 (*wuyong*).

[574] The Manchu expression 'fudexeqi' is a ritual performed by shamans to cast out demons, corresponding with 送幣 (*songbi*), which literally means 'to send paper money'. An alternative translation is 跳神送祟 (*tiaoshen songhui*).

Section 59: A Fortune Teller

1. Brother, have you heard [of that]?
2. Recently outside the city wall, there came a man who can tell fortune from the Eight Characters of the birth time[575].
3. That is extraordinarily good!
4. I heard people say
5. that man was totally born like a supernatural being.[576]
6. Regarding all the things in our past,
7. it seems like someone has told him already.
8. [He] was able to calculate and find out.
9. A good many of our people went to [him],
10. in a row, [and] continuously filled up his place.
11. Since there is such a miraculous man,
12. [and] when there is time[577], our older and younger brothers should also visit [him].
13. I already knew [it],
14. because these days our friends clustered in groups and went there.
15. The day before yesterday I also went there,
16. and showed him with the Eight Characters of my birth.
17. Which years my father and mother [were born in],
18. the number of brothers,
19. the names of women,
20. the time when [I] acquired the official rank,
21. [and] each thing was reckoned correctly.
22. Nothing was mistaken.
23. The bygone was calculated right,
24. but the future things
25. will not necessarily happen according to what he said.
26. Even so,
27. is there a place we did not spend some money?
28. Anyway,
29. you do not have many things [to do].

---

[575] The Manchu expression 'jakvn hergen tuwara niyalma' means 'a person who looks at the Eight Characters', which is slightly different than 算命的 (*suanmingde*) that is usually translated as a fortune-teller).
[576] The Manchu word 'banjihabi' (to be born) was not translated in the corresponding Chinese text.
[577] The Manchu expression 'atanggi' means 'when', corresponding with 多喒 (*duozan*) which is 什麼時候 (*shenme shihou*) in modern Chinese language.

30. Rather than sitting at home with no purposes,

31. you'd better just go to amuse yourself.

32. [I] hope that [you] will just consider it as a way to divert the mind from boredom.

33. Does such a thing matter?

Section 60: A Silly Man

1. [Looking at] his behaviors,

2. [you] do not know what [he] will do.

3. When [I] first saw him,

4. [he] was quiet at the side.

5. Now you see that people could not even look at him.

6. [He] was exceedingly crude[578].

7. He babbled and gabbled in front of people,

8. [and] he did not even know to answer each question successively.

9. He was timid,

10. and did not understand how to advance and retreat.

11. Even [he] was awake, [he] seemed asleep.

12. [He] could barely be considered as a man.

13. How could [he] live such a bewildered life?

14. You get along with each other.

15. [You] are supposed to give directions to him.

16. Brother, because you have not known each other for long,

17. [you] have not yet understood [him] thoroughly.

18. There are things even funnier than this.

19. When [you] sit together and talk with each other,

20. [and] while [you] are talking about this matter,

21. suddenly [he] would discuss[579] that thing.

22. Otherwise [he] would droop his mouth,

23. [pretending to be dead] without life and breath.

24. He would not move [his] eyeballs,

25. [but] looking at you straightforwardly.

26. Suddenly [he] would let out silly words which has no beginning and ending,

---

[578] The Manchu expression 'albatu' means 'being rude', corresponding with 粗村 (cucun). The modern expression is 粗野 (cuye).

[579] The Manchu expression 'gvninafi leolembi' means 'to mention or discuss', corresponding with 題起 (tiqi). The modern words are 提起 (tiqi).

27. [and] people would laugh so hard that [their] intestines get broken.
28. The day before yesterday [he] came to visit me.
29. On the way back [he] did not walk straight ahead,
30. [but] turned [his] back and walked backward out.
31. At that moment I said, brother, be careful of the door sill!
32. Before [I] could finish [my] words,
33. his feet had been tripped and [he] fell down with his face towards the sky.
34. I went forward immediately,
35. helped [him] get up with all [my] strength,
36. [and] then cleaned [him] up.
37. At first I advised [him] innumerable times.
38. [but later] saw that [he] did not show any interest in changing [himself].
39. [He] will never grow into a useful person.
40. Why would [I] exhaust [my] mouth to talk to [him]?

Section 61: An Alcoholic

1. Brother, please look,
2. [he] has crossed the line[580].
3. [He] was so drunk that [he] could not even stand firm.
4. I asked him whether you have told him that thing or not,
5. [but] [he] was shaking,
6. looking at me straightforwardly and waving hands.
7. [He] is not either deaf nor mute[581].
8. Why couldn't [he] answer [me]?
9. How come there is such [a man] that makes people angry?
10. Today if [I] don't beat him severely,
11. I would swear to do so [in the future].
12. Brother, please don't [do that].
13. Probably he forgot and didn't go.
14. Didn't he know that this was his mistake?
15. Because of this, [he] was scared and have no words to answer.
16. Today [you] meet me here,

---

580 The Manchu expression 'isika' means 'to cross the line or to go too far', corresponding with 分了 (fenle). The modern expression is 過分 (guofen).
581 The Manchu expression 'hele' means 'mute', corresponding with 啞叭 (yaba). The modern words are 啞巴 (yaba).

17. [and] look at my face,
18. please spare [him] this time.
19. From now on,
20. [he must] quit drinking and stay away from wine.
21. Say it the other way round,
22. it is easy to rid a donkey,
23. [and] it is easy to oppress the underlings.
24. [But] you are the master [who] has grabbed their queues[582]!
25. Where else can [he] go to plead for [his wrong behaviors][583]?
26. If [he] can change, change;
27. If [he] can't change,
28. [and] still get [himself] wasted to such a mess,
29. [then] the punishment is up to brother.
30. Even I ran into [this situation] again,
31. it would be hard [for me] to intercede [for him].
32. Brother, how could you know this?
33. He was born to be a worthless soul.
34. With regard to drinking wine,
35. he would rather die [than letting it go].[584]
36. [He] loves [wine] more than his father's blood.
37. [Even we] spare him this time,
38. would [he] make changes?
39. Hereafter, [he] would sober for only one or two days.
40. Afterwards,
41. [He] would drink as usual.

Section 62: Raising Children

1. Brother, which one is this son?
2. This is my youngest son[585].
3. Has [he] got smallpox already?

---

[582] The Manchu expression 'sonqoho jafaha' means 'grabbed the queue, corresponding with 摸着頭頂 (*muozhe touding*). A modern translation is 抓着辮子 (*zhuazhe bianzi*).

[583] The Manchu expression 'ukqambi' (to plead for one's guilt) was not translated in the Chinese parallel sentence.

[584] The Manchu sentence only says 'just die'. The Chinese expression of 也不肯放 (*ye buken fang*) was added by the original translator to makes more sentence in the context.

[585] The Manchu expression 'fiyanggv' (*laoda'er* 老搭兒) means the youngest child who usually was born when the parents were old.

4. Not yet.

5. They are brothers born in a row.

6. Nine [of them] were born and nine survived.

7. Brother, I am not joking.

8. Sister-in-law is proficient[586]!

9. [She] is good at raising children.

10. [I] would say [she] is a goddess of [delivering] children.

11. You are such a person with all sorts of blessings.

12. It may not be blessings.

13. They are inherent sins.

14. The older ones are better.

15. The younger ones mingle together everyday, crying, hollering and talking.

16. [I] can no longer bear [their] chattering.

17. [I] have suffered[587] too much inside.

18. People in the world are all like this.

19. People who have many children

20. would be weary and make complaints.

21. People like us who love children very much, want even just one, [but] where [can we get it]?

22. [It] is hard to [predict] the [will of] heaven.

23. If your beloved son did not die,

24. [he] must be nine or ten years old.

25. [He was] a very good son.

26. Up to now [when we] mention [him] every time,[588]

27. I grieve[589] and miss [him] on your behalf.

28. His appearance,

29. words,

30. are quite different than the other children.

31. [He looked] heroic after dressing up.

32. When [he] met people,

---

[586] From the context, 'mergen' (*hao shouduan* 好手段) means she is good at raising children.

[587] The Manchu expression 'urehebi' means 'sad or heart-broken', corresponding with 熟了 (*shule*, well-cooked). The modern words are 傷心 (*shangxin*).

[588] The expression of 從心裡 (*cong xin li*, from the bottom of heart) is the original translation, which does not correspond well with 'jongko dari' (mention every time).

[589] The Manchu expression 'nasame' means 'to grieve', which was not translated in the Chinese counterpart.

33. [he] would stand upright;
34. slowly [he] would move forward and give regards.
35. His small mouth is so adorable.
36. What words couldn't [he] say?
37. If [you] ask him one thing,
38. it seems like that someone has already taught him [what to say].
39. From beginning to end,
40. [he] could elaborate all the details.
41. If [you] have one child like that,
42. it is worth ten.
43. Why would people raise those useless ones?

Section 63: A Fur Coat

1. Did you buy this sable upper garment at the shop?
2. Not at the shop.
3. At the temple.
4. How much is it in silver?
5. You make an estimation, please.
6. No matter what,
7. it would be worth sixty taels of silver.
8. [I started to bargain] from thirty taels,
9. added up to forty taels,
10. [and the merchant] sold [it].
11. How could the price be so low?
12. In the past,
13. such [a clothes] generally could make eighty taels of silver.
14. The color [is] dark,
15. the fur [is] thick,
16. the technique is delicate,
17. [and] the edges are cut clean.
18. Moreover, the lining satin is thick[590].
19. The new designs are in fashion.
20. It is really worth [buying].
21. I remember
22. brother, you also have one.
23. How could that one of mine be counted?

---

[590] The Manchu expression 'jiramin' means 'thick', corresponding with 狠好 (hen-hao), which should be 很厚 (henhou).

24. It is just a name.

25. The fur is worn,

26. [and] the glaze[591] is gone.

27. [So I] cannot wear the inside out.

28. After [you] receive the salary,

29. [you] should buy a good one.

30. Young people like you,

31. are the ones that move upward.

32. In the occasions as government office or gathering,

33. [you should] wear decently.

34. That is reasonable.

35. What appearance do I need?

36. That moment has gone.

37. Staying warm would be just fine.

38. Even I wore some thing good,

39. [I] would lose shape,

40. [and] also feel uncomfortable.

41. Moreover,

42. it does not match my military work.

43. No matter how old or broken [the clothes are],

44. [they would] fit me well instead.

Section 64: A Funeral Affair

1. Who passed away[592] at their house?

2. The day before yesterday I passed by there,

3. [and I] saw people wearing white mourning dresses at the house.

4. Because I was in a hurry to take over a shift,

5. [I] didn't ask.

6. Recently his uncles died.

7. Is that his real uncle?

8. Yes.

9. Have you expressed your condolences[593] for such a misfortune or not?

---

[591] The Manchu expression 'simen' means the secretion on the fur, such as grease, corresponding with 火力 (*huoli*, fire power). The modern translation could be 光澤 (*guangze*), which is a good color maintained by grease.

[592] The Manchu expression 'akv oho' is an indirect way to say someone died. A polite translation is 去世 (*qushi*). The original 死了 (*si le*, died), which is too direct and impolite.

10. Yesterday there was a religious rite for reading scriptures,
11. [and] I was there all day.
12. When will [they] hold a funeral?
13. [I] heard it will be at the end of the month.
14. Where is their graveyard?
15. It is close to ours.
16. If so,
17. It is a long way.
18. About forty [Chinese] miles[594].
19. During this period of time,
20. [if you] ran into him again,
21. please give condolences [on my behalf].
22. After I get off work,
23. [I] will join you to pay a visit.
24. Before [they] carry the coffin out,
25. give me a message.
26. Even though I cannot walk it to the end,
27. [I] would walk them out of town.
28. Though [we] did not interact usually,
29. [he] was warmhearted every time [when he] saw me.
30. Speaking of people [who] live in the world,
31. which one is not a friend?
32. For people who encountered such things,
33. even we visit in person,
34. presumably no one would say that [we] fawn upon the rich and powerful.

Section 65: Making Clothes

1. Aren't these clothes for [your] son-in-law?
2. Yes.
3. What are these people doing here?
4. They are the hired craftsmen.
5. Sad.
6. Our old way is all gone.
7. In the old time,

---

[593] The Manchu expression 'jobolon de aqambi' means to 'express condolences', corresponding with 道惱 (*daonao*). A modern translation is 弔唁 (*diaoyan*).
[594] A Chinese mile is half of a kilometer.

8. Even the teen-aged children

9. could make a complete clothes,

10. padding with cotton,

11. lining with cloth.

12. When turning it over,

13. you sew the front [of the garment],

14. [and] I make a shape[595].

15. This person would make the waist,

16. [and] that person would make a collar.

17. [Someone would] burn pleats on the sleeves,

18. [and someone] would sew the buttons on.

19. No more than one or two days

20. [the whole gown] would be finished.

21. Besides,

22. even hats were made at home.

23. If [you] pay someone to do the work,

24. or [you] buy clothes to wear,

25. people would laugh at [you] from the nostrils.

26. Though brother's words are reasonable,

27. but you are only aware of one aspect but ignorant of the other.

28. How could you compare that [old] time with this [present] time?

29. Moreover, the wedding day is near.

30. If [you] count by fingers,

31. It would be exact ten days.

32. This period of time

33. will not give [us] a moment [to rest].

34. People must catch up day and night.

35. Catching up or not,

36. either is possible.

37. If [people] rigidly adhere to[596] the old rules,

38. [instead] let the roe deer run away,[597]

39. [and] cause delay with eyes wide open,

40. what fun is that?

---

[595] The Manchu expression 'jurgan goqimbi' means 'to make a shape or to draw the lines', corresponding with 行 (*xing*).

[596] The Manchu expression 'memereme' means 'to rigidly adhere to', corresponding with 拘擬 (ju ni). The modern words are 拘泥 (*ju ni*).

[597] The Manchu expression 'gio turibuhe' means 'to let the roe deer run away', which is different than 旗杆底下誤了操 (*qigan dixia wu le cao*), to delay the drills under the flagpole.

Section 66: Being Frugal

1. Humans cannot live more than one hundred years old.
2. This is so called 'the temporary life itself is really like a dream'.
3. How often can [a person] takes pleasure in it?
4. The sun and moon pass by like a weaver's shuttle.
5. In a trance,[598] the hair on head has turned white,
6. [and people] become useless in every place.
7. [They] would just look at the lower jaws of [their] sons and children,
8. [and] spend the rest of life.
9. What fun is that?
10. Moreover, when muscles and bones become stiff,
11. [they would] be out of shape [even they wear new clothes]
12. [and] cannot discern the taste of food [when they] eat.
13. What is the use of living?
14. Now seizing the moment before getting old,
15. if people do not eat or wear [well],
16. why do [they] clench the money and silver so tightly?
17. You are too frugal.[599]
18. You calculate every expense,
19. [and] it would be enough to take pleasure [in doing so].
20. It is inappropriate to be too [frugal].
21. Do you say so because you know me?
22. Or do you just guess[600] so without knowing me?
23. If I have some [money to spend],
24. I should be happy.
25. But [I] am not like some other rich people who have ways of making profits.
26. How could I be happy?
27. Or shall I borrow money to buy clothes?
28. Or [shall I] sell house [for money] to eat well?

---

[598] The Manchu expression 'geri fari' means 'in a trance or absent-minded', which is translated as 一仰一合 (*yiyang yihe*), in a moment of raising and lowering one's head, time flies away quickly.
[599] The Manchu expression 'dababume mamgiyafakv' literally means 'excessively not luxurious', corresponding with 不過費 (*bu guofei*). A modern expression can be 很節儉 (*hen jiejian*, very frugal).
[600] The Manchu expression 'bai tubixeme' means 'to guess, to speculate, corresponding with 約模 (*yuemo*), which is expressed as 揣摩 (*chuaimo*) or 猜測 (*caice*) in modern Chinese language.

29. If I live according to your words,
30. recklessly spend all the money,
31. [It] would be good [if I] fell over and then die .
32. If [I] did not die,
33. yearning for life,
34. how can I live at that time?
35. If [I] stretch hands to beg from you,
36. you would not even modestly decline[601].

Section 67: To be Reliable

1. All people must be faithful,
2. [and] human minds would be genuinely convinced.
3. [Things are postponed] from today to tomorrow,
4. [and] from tomorrow,
5. again to the day after tomorrow.
6. [If the responsibility] is evaded continuously[602] in this way and that way.
7. When is the end?
8. After you agree,
9. [and] then [you] change [your] words.
10. It is this way in the morning,
11. [and] that way in the evening.
12. How could people trust your words?
13. [If you] put things off in this way,
14. not only are [you] not decisive[603],
15. but when do you tell people something solid in advance,
16. people's hearts are tired,
17. and they wouldn't expect much.
18. [I am] not [that kind of person]!
19. Is it true that at some place or about something I break my promises?
20. Now you pointed out.
21. Before[604] [knowing] what [really happened],

---

[601] The Manchu expression 'anabumbini' means ' to modestly decline', corresponding with 給 (gei), which is more accurate than 謙讓(qianrang, to decline) in this context.
[602] The Manchu expression 'anatahai' means 'to evade one's responsibility continuously', corresponding with 支悟 (zhiwu). A modern expression is 推卸 (tuixie).
[603] The Manchu expression 'kengse lasha' means 'resolute and decisive', corresponding with 簡斷 (jianduan). A modern translation can be 果斷 (guoduan).

22. [you] just ruin [my] reputation this way.
23. Such a thing is totally groundless[605].
24. Why are [you] worried for me?
25. When you encounter something,
26. you should think over and over.
27. When [you] have an idea,
28. then [you] criticize people,
29. people would be convinced.
30. You do not know clearly.
31. It is correct to blame me totally?
32. Furthermore,
33. it is my decision to go,
34. [and] it is also my decision not to go.
35. What are you urging me for?
36. I was born this way of being firm and unyielding!
37. Before the things are totally clarified,
38. you just grab me and make complaints,
39. For whatever reason, I would not allow this to happen.
40. How do [I] say this?
41. [and] that would leave [you] as a laughing stock.
42. [and you] will become into a subject for ridicule.
43. I didn't learn these things in childhood.
44. If he trusts [me], [let's] wait to [see what happens].
45. If not,
46. let him go somewhere else to ask people for help.
47. Who told him to stop and wait [for something else]?

Section 68: A Ghost

1. These days,
2. because [weather] is suffocating and hot,
3. windows were propped up,
4. [I] slept in an inner room[606].

---

[604] The Manchu expression 'onggolo' means 'before, in advance', which was not translated in the Chinese counterpart. 什麼什麼的裡頭 (*shenme shenme de litou*) literally means 'what what inside', which is not an accurate translation.
[605] The Manchu expression 'oron unde' means 'shadow-less', corresponding with 沒影兒 (*meiying'er*). A modern expression can be 無根據的 (*wu genju de*).
[606] The Manchu expression 'dorgi giyalan' means 'an innter room', corresponding with 外間 (*waijian*, an outer room), which could be a wrong translation.

5. Last night when it was midnight,

6. I turned over to face inside and slept.

7. In the ears [I] heard a sound.

8. With tiredness [I] opened [my] eyes to look;

9. a monster was standing in front of [my] head!

10. [Its] face looked like a piece of white paper,

11. [and] its eyes were bleeding.

12. The body was white,

13. [and] its hair was fluffy.

14. He was jumping on the ground!

15. When suddenly seeing that,

16. I was greatly shocked.

17. Ah!

18. This could be the ghost!

19. [I] wanted to see what he is going to do,

20. [so I] narrowed my eyes into slits to look.

21. Unexpectedly [he] jumped for while,

22. then opened the trunks,

23. [and] took out a lot of clothes.

24. Putting [the clothes] in the armpits,

25. [he] was going to jump out of the window.

26. Suddenly I understood what was happening.

27. Thinking of that,

28. if it were a ghost,

29. why would he take the clothes?

30. [I] stood up,

31. [and] took out the broadsword.

32. Before [he] could react,

33. [I] chopped him with the back of the sword solidly.

34. [He] cried,

35. [and] fell on the ground with a sound 'aro'.

36. I called upon the family people,

37. [and] lit a lamp to look.

38. It was funny.

39. It turned out to be a burglar.

40. He played ghost to scare people [so he could steal]!

Section 69: A Marriage Interview

1. Being destined to meet,

2. we are here to seek a marriage alliance.

3. This son of mine

4. does not have capabilities which are outstanding above others.
5. But regarding drinking, gambling,
6. mingling with the bad rebellious people,
7. [and] other things like running wild,
8. he does not have [such problems].
9. Lords, if [you] are not offended,
10. please give some good words.
11. Son, you come forward.
12. Let's kowtow and beg the lords for help.
13. My lords, please do not refuse.
14. Listen to my words.
15. We are all old relatives,
16. [which] are like bones and flesh.
17. Who don't know each other?
18. Speaking of husband and wife,
19. [their] fate is destined,
20. [and it] is not up to people.
21. [It is difficult to] raise children.
22. In person [we] look at [them] growing up into a couple,
23. [and] that is all parents want for laboring and taking pains.
24. Even so,
25. the first thing is that
26. I have older generations
27. [who] haven't seen this son.
28. The second thing is that
29. the madams [who] have come
30. also can take a look at my silly daughter[607].
31. Indeed,
32. the lords' words are particularly brilliant.
33. Please pass these words onto our madams who have come here.
34. When they take a look at the girl,
35. please also call the young man inside.
36. Let the madams take a look [at the young man].
37. If their minds fit each other well[608],

---

[607] The Manchu expression 'mentuhun sargan' means 'a silly daughter', corresponding with 醜女兒 (*chou nü'er*, an ugly daughter), which is different than the Manchu expression.
[608] The Manchu expression 'gvnin de aqahame' means 'to agree in opinion/mind', corresponding with 合式 (*heshi*). The modern words are 合適 (*heshi*, to fit well).

38. and then [they] kowtow.

39. It wouldn't be late.

Section 70: Bad Marriage

1. Would you say that they are husband and wife by the first marriage?

2. [The woman] was remarried.

3. This female has jeopardized several husbands.

4. [She] was born with a good appearance.

5. [Her] needlework is also fine.

6. [She] only has one shortcoming,

7. [which] was very jealous.

8. [Her] husband has turned into the age of fifty,

9. [but] has no children.

10. When [he] mentioned about getting a concubine or gaining another woman,

11. she would disagree by lying down[609] [rolling on the ground],

12. saying [she] would hang herself,

13. [and] would kill herself.

14. She would by all means make disturbances to terrify [people].

15. [The husband] was intimidated so much that [he] acted like a turtle.

16. [He] was so terrified by the woman

17. that [he] cannot display his power at all.

18. [He] couldn't do anything to her.

19. [He] can only swallow the humiliation silently,

20. like a dead person.

21. When [you] look at this,

22. there are no perfect things in the world.

23. There is a man in our place.

24. Recently [he used] five hundred taels of silver,

25. bought a woman [and] took her in.

26. He treated her like the armpit hair[610],

27. [and] loves [her] dearly this much and that much.

28. Whatever [she] says,

29. [he] would not disobey at all.

---

[609] The Manchu expression 'dedufi' means 'lying down', corresponding with 橫倘 (*heng tang*). The modern words are 橫躺 (*heng tang*).

[610] The Manchu expression 'oho' i funiyehe' literally means 'armpit's hair', which is a metaphor of treasure(*baobei* 寶貝).

30. This immoral bond servant[611]

31. was carried on the head [by him].

32. On the contrary, he treated his wife as an animal and lowered her status to a male bond servant or a female servant[612],

33. beating her everyday so [she] hanged [herself].

34. People of her parents' home sued [the husband],

35. [and the case] has not yet been finished up to now.

36. This trouble-making woman,

37. [and] that ferocious man,

38. are just right for each other.

39. Why the Heaven did not make them into a husband and a wife?

Section 71: Getting into Trouble

1. Our sinister stuff [a close friend/relative],

2. incurred a big trouble.

3. What happened?

4. [He] beat and killed someone.

5. For what reasons?

6. For no reasons at all!

7. [People said] one of their neighbors[613]

8. peed beside[614] his door.

9. [Our man] did not even ask,

10. but wrestled him on the ground, striding[615] and sitting on him,

11. [and] hitting on his face and eyes.

12. In the beginning [when our man was] hitting, [the person] still yelled and swore back.

13. Later on [our man] kept beating,

14. the person did not even make a sound.

15. People who surrounded and looked

---

[611] The Manchu expression 'hayan' (immoral) was not translated in the Chinese counterpart.

[612] The Manchu expression 'nehv' (female servants) was not translated in the Chinese counterpart.

[613] The Manchu expression 'adaki' means 'neighbor', corresponding with 街房 (jiefang). The modern expression is 街坊 (jiefang).

[614] The Manchu expression 'dalbade' means 'side or near', corresponding with 傍邊 (pangbian). The modern expression is 旁邊 (pangbian).

[615] The Manchu expression 'aktalame tefi' (striding and sitting) was not translated in the Chinese text.

16. knew the situation had gone badly.

17. When he stopped beating [the person],

18. [he] found that [the person] had already stopped breathing.

19. So the armored[616] foot soldiers arrested and took him away.

20. The family people of the dead person all came,

21. [and] demolished the heat-able brick bed[617] of his home.

22. Furniture and utensils were all destroyed,

23. [and] even the tiles on the roof were uncovered.

24. The voice of shouting can be heard from two or three [Chinese] miles away.

25. Yesterday [I] went to the Ministry [of Penalty],

26. [and] heard that [he] was tortured.

27. Brother, didn't you hear that?

28. The evil people are revenged with evil.

29. This is caused by himself.

30. Does it involve other people?

Section 72: Real Friends

1. Speaking of making friends,

2. [people] can learn from Guan Zhong and Bao Shu in the old time.

3. These two people

4. one day went to the bright wilderness,

5. [and] saw on the roadside

6. [where] there lies a gold bar[618].

7. [They] gave precedence to each other,

8. [and] either wanted to take it [first].

9. Finally [they] left [it] behind and went away.

10. [They] saw a farmer,

11. pointed at [the gold bar] and said,

12. there is a gold bar

13. [and] you go and get it!

14. That farmer immediately went to get it.

---

[616] The Manchu expression 'uksin' (armor) was not translated in the corresponding Chinese text.
[617] The Manchu expression 'nahan' (the heat-able brick bed) did not appear in the corresponding Chinese text. The Manchu text says that people destroyed the brick bed, while the Chinese text says people created a hideous mess at the man's house.
[618] The Manchu expression 'aisin i xoge' means 'a gold bar', corresponding with (*jinkezi* 金錁子). The modern words are 金條 (*jintiao*).

15. [He] didn't see the gold,
16. [but] saw a two-headed snake.
17. The farmer was greatly surprised,
18. [and] chopped the snake into two pieces with [his] hoe.
19. [The farmer] came back and made a noise, [saying]
20. do I have any grudge against you?
21. Why did you fool me with a two-headed snake for the gold bar?
22. [You] almost got me killed!
23. The two people did not believe,
24. [and] went together to have a look.
25. It was still the gold bar,
26. [but] chopped into two pieces on the ground.
27. Guan Zhong and Bao Shu each took half of it.
28. [But] that farmer
29. went back with empty hands.
30. The principle for people to make friends in the old time is just like this.
31. This is close to the unofficial history.
32. To the people who scramble for profit,
33. [Guan Zhong and Bao Shu] can really make a [good] example.

Section 73: A Dirty Old Man

1. These days our place is bustling with people.
2. So many women went to the temple to burn incense.
3. One [was] more beautiful than another.
4. There were some [women] who were like fairies coming down from the ninth heaven[619],
5. [with] beautiful face,
6. [and] white skin.
7. [They have] black eyebrows which are long and thin,
8. [and their] bright eyes were just like the autumn water.
9. [Their] soft and slim bodies were trembling,
10. just like the willow trees in springtime.
11. Once [they] moved steps,
12. the jades and agates were jingling clearly.
13. Every move would release the fragrance of orchid and musk,

---

[619] The Manchu expression 'uyun dabkvri' means 'nine layers', corresponding with 九天 (*jiutian*). In traditional Chinese belief, the number nine is the greatest single number, which refers to the ultimate limit.

14. [and] the scent wafted in gusts.
15. [Look at] your [nasty] appearance!
16. Even though [you] said [you came] to see the young people,
17. is it appropriate if [you] do not know how to behave?
18. Of course not!
19. If I don't criticize you,
20. [you] wouldn't be able to restrain[620] [yourself].
21. It is such a pity that a human skin
22. was wrapped on you!
23. [You] are closer to the age of sixty,
24. [and would you] call that young?
25. Dirt has reached [your] neck,
26. [and] only the scalp can be seen.
27. [You] squinted [your] eyes,
28. [and only] in the crowd of women,
29. [you] sneak around, dodged, and pretended to be a decent man.
30. How can [I] tell [you]?
31. If people behind [your] back
32. discuss your wife in this way and that,
33. what would you say in your heart?
34. The good act will be well rewarded,
35. [and] the evil will be paid with the evil.
36. The retribution of good and evil is like the shadow follows the form.
37. In such an old age,
38. you do not even accumulate a little virtue,
39. but insisted [you] did dishonorable things like feeding on stool.
40. Nowadays the law of heaven is quite low[621],
41. How am [I] worried about you!

Section 74: Spring Outing

1. This is the end of spring.
2. I sat quietly at home.

---

[620] The Manchu expression 'dosorakv' means 'cannot control oneself or cannot endure', corresponding with 受不得 (*shoubude*). A modern translation can be 忍不住 (*renbuzhu*).

[621] The Manchu expression 'abka fangkala' (sky is low) means the imperial punishment is imminent. There is a Chinese common phrase '天高皇帝遠' (*tian'gao huangdi yuan*) which says the imperial law cannot reach remote places where the sky is high.

3. How depressed [I am]!

4. Yesterday my younger brother came to call [me],

5. [and] invited me to the outside of town for a sight-seeing.

6. [So we] went out from the side door,

7. got to the open field and had a look.

8. How lovely was the spring scenery!

9. Along the riversides,

10. peach flowers are red,

11. willow branches are soft and swaying,

12. birds are tweeting,

13. tree leaves are green,

14. spring wind is blowing,

15. [and] the smell of grass is vigorous.

16. There are boats in the river,

17. [and] trees on the riverbanks.

18. People are playing [music instruments] and singing on the boats,

19. [and the boats] come and go continuously.

20. [People] walk under the trees to look at the flowers,

21. in groups of four and five.

22. Regarding that,

23. there are people waking on the narrow winding trail [and] looking for a creek for fishing.

24. Really pleasant!

25. Deep in the forest,

26. there are people relaxing in a cool place,

27. [and] drinking wine.

28. That is very interesting.

29. Moreover, in the region following the line of [the river],

30. flower gardens are all good,

31. [and] the big temples are also clean.

32. Therefore,

33. We tried our best to stroll for a day.

34. As things should be,

35. [I] was supposed to invite you.

36. The reason I did not send you a message,

37. is not to leave you out on purpose,

38. but because there are people who do not get along with you.

Section 75: A Prodigal Son

1. I hear that

2. our greedy brother has become really poor.

3. [His life] is extremely difficult.
4. [His] dress is shabby like a beggar.
5. He cuddled up[622] in a heap on the bare brick bed, shivering.
6. He was under a shabby quilt.
7. He deserved it. The beheaded one!
8. Didn't [he] set his feet down into all the luck[623]?
9. What hardship did he not suffer last year?
10. What kind of hard time did he not experience?
11. If he had a little human heart,
12. [he] would repent.
13. As the saying goes,
14. if [you] chase after the rich,
15. [you] will become bare feet.
16. Suffering from such hardships,
17. what mood would [he] have [to say],
18. wine is sturdy[624] here,
19. [and] food is delicious there.
20. [How could he] join the rich people to stroll around?
21. When I encounter the cold seasons,
22. [I] would check on [him] again!
23. Now [he] is really suffering.
24. Even so,
25. or whatever [you say],
26. will you watch him die?
27. In my heart [I really think],
28. we should raise [money] together and help him, and that is good.
29. Silver will not be helpful.
30. How do I say this?
31. Don't you know his problems?
32. Presumably when [money] comes into [his] hands,
33. [he] would eat them up,
34. [and] then [he] becomes poor as usual.

---

[622] The Manchu expression 'xoyohoi' means 'to curl up', corresponding with 咕推 (gutui), and the modern expression is 蜷縮 (quansuo).
[623] The Manchu expression 'wasihvn bethe gaiha' means 'setting one's feet down into', corresponding with 四達運氣 (sida yunqi), which is a sarcastic expression to translate the Manchu text.
[624] The Manchu expression 'tumin' means 'sturdy', corresponding with 豔 (yan). Another expression is 釅 (yan, the strong taste of tea or wine).

35. What would be left?

36. We might just simply buy a suit of clothes for him,

37. [and] that would be beneficial.

Section 76: A Sparrow

1. I tell you a joke.
2. Just now I sat here alone.
3. A sparrow sat on the window pillar.
4. In the sunlight,
5. the bird pecked and jumped.
6. At the moment I did not make a sound.
7. Slowly I walked near it.
8. Suddenly I caught it,
9. [but my fingers] broke through the window paper.
10. [I] caught and looked at [it].
11. It was a sparrow.
12. When I changed hands,
13. it flew away with a sound 'pu'.
14. Immediately [I] closed the door to catch it,
15. [and] I almost caught it.
16. [but it] went away again.
17. Here and there [I] was going to catch it,
18. [but] the little children heard that a sparrow was caught.
19. They yelled and ran here, stumbling along the way.
20. [We] pounced to chase after it,
21. [tried to] catch it,
22. [and we] caught it with a hat.
23. Later I said there are even people who buy the animals and set them free.
24. For no reasons,
25. why would we catch it?
26. Let it go!
27. [The little children] preferred to die than to agree,
28. Putting a long [face, they] said [they must] have [it].
29. Finally [I] gave [it] to [them].
30. Then [they] rejoiced, jumped and went away.

Section 77: A Dilemma

1. How is your thing?

2. I am still thinking[625] about it.

3. [I] am going to proceed,

4. [but] it seems like impossible [because] something was involved.

5. [If I] give up halfway,

6. It is a pity.

7. It is like something comes into [your] mouth,

8. [but you] cannot eat it,

9. [and have to] give [it] to other people without compensation.

10. [I] can neither proceed,

11. nor give it up.

12. [I] am really caught in a dilemma.

13. [I] must find a strategy which will not fail under all circumstances.

14. Because of this,

15. [I] come to you for ideas.

16. Brother, [I am glad that] you consult with me.

17. [But] if I carelessly agree to help according to your wish,

18. what benefits [do you have me] as a relative?

19. Obviously somewhere this thing [is wrong so it] cannot be helped with an idea.

20. If I do help, in the future [the problem] will definitely become visible.

21. If [you] stop [here],

22. [it would be] your luck.

23. If [you] proceed,

24. whose mouth can [you] muffle?

25. When public opinions are divergent, [and] by then,

26. that would be really difficult [to calm down].

27. In a word,

28. as the sage said, one has no long-term considerations, [he] will definitely find trouble right at hand.

29. Regarding this small benefit that lays before [your] eyes, would [you] call it a happy event?

30. Obviously [you] are covering up a tendency which might turn into a huge disaster in the future.

---

[625] The Manchu expression 'gvnin baibumbikai' means 'thinking about something', corresponding with 犯着思想呢 (*fanzhe sixiang ne*). A modern translation can be 正在思考 (*zhengzai sikao*).

31. Doing things in irregular ways
32. will lead to failures.
33. Even there are benefits, [you] cannot guarantee no harm will occur.
34. In my heart,
35. you do not expect to consult with me,
36. [and then] briskly shake it off [and hope] it will be fine.
37. If you do not listen to my words,
38. merely feel uncertain [and] cannot make firm decisions;
39. [and] when [you] get stuck,
40. not only do [you] not get the rice,
41. but also lose the bag.
42. It is still unknown that what kind of disgrace will appear .
43. When that comes,
44. do not blame me for simply watching without advising.

Section 78: An Ungrateful Man

1. Say, there are no people better than you!
2. [There is someone] who ceaselessly says that [he] is your friend.
3. [You] are too well-behaved.
4. Regarding that unreasonable fellow, who does [he] think [he] is?
5. When [he] asked people for a favor,
6. whatever we said,
7. [he] would follow and act accordingly.
8. [But] when his things were finished,
9. [he would] put on a [stern] face,
10. [and] ignore whoever [comes to him].
11. Last year somehow he was in a harsh situation.
12. At the moment no one asked him [for anything],
13. [he] said he had a good book.
14. [He said,] brother, if [you] want to look at it,
15. I will deliver it to [you].
16. [He] promised me thus and thus.
17. Later on when [his] things were done, he no longer mentioned it.
18. Therefore,
19. just now I said to him face to face.
20. When I asked him, brother, how is the book you [promised to] give,
21. [his] face turned from white to red now and then.
22. He spoke something else with hesitation.
23. He cannot give any firm answers.
24. Up to now,
25. who cares about a set of books?

26. What happens if he gives,

27. [and] what happens if not?

28. [I] feel disgusted because [he] deceived people for no reasons.

Section 79: A Mean Man

1. Why are you doing this?

2. Respectfully people beg you for help.

3. If you know, you should say so;

4. If [you] don't know,

5. [then you should] say [you] don't know and that's it.

6. Why are you lying about it?

7. Accidentally if you delayed his thing,

8. it might seem that you frame him up on purpose.

9. If he is an abominable[626] person,

10. I won't say anything.

11. He is an honest man, very pathetic.

12. [You] would know it from his sloppy[627] appearance.

13. If other people look down on him,

14. we shall persuade them not to.

15. On the contrary you are doing such a mean thing,

16. [and] that is really wrong.

17. That is really not my intention.

18. Brother, you don't know him in the first place.

19. [and that is why you] are deceived by him.

20. That person,

21. though his appearance looks honest,

22. his heart is not simple.

23. He has some bad and horrible deficiencies,

24. [which] you haven't encountered yet.

25. It is reasonable that [you] don't know him.

26. [He] has many strategies,

27. [and] large traps.

28. [He] is good at asking people for evidence.

---

[626] The Manchu expression 'usun seshun' means 'offensive and abominable', corresponding with 檓檓弄弄 (huihui nongnong), in which 檓 (hui) originally was written as 扌(a hand) and 毁 (hui, to destroy).

[627] The Manchu expression 'fixur' means 'petty and sloppy', corresponding with 賴怠 (laidai). A similar modern expression is 窩囊 (wo'nang) or 邋遢 (lata).

29. No matter what happens,
30. [he would] deceive people with good words first, and [wait until he] could read your thoughts;
31. and then [he] would wait and see.
32. Looking[628] at your shortcomings,
33. when you show some weak points,
34. [he] would immediately follow up,
35. [and] beat [you] by surprise[629].
36. Brother, please think and look.
37. Does this thing concern me?
38. Is it appropriate to tell him honestly from [my] heart?
39. If [people] blame me for this,
40. am I being treated fairly?

Section 80: A Good Horse

1. [If] you buy,
2. buy a good horse!
3. It would be fun to keep and feed it.
4. Anyway it costs grass and beans [to feed it].
5. Why do you keep such an ordinary horse?
6. Brother, you don't know.
7. Yesterday I got it,
8. [and] I took it to the outside of town for testing[630].
9. It was good for riding.
10. It trotted steadily,
11. [and] ran squarely.
12. [If you] shoot from the horseback,
13. there were no problems such as stepping inside or outside.
14. Following [the movements of its] knee caps[631],
15. [I] could move [my] hands smoothly.

---

[628] The Manchu expression 'hiraqambi', means 'to cast a look at', corresponding with 瞅 (chou), which is a variant form of 䁘 (chou).

[629] The Manchu expression 'ura tebumbi' means 'to suddenly attack someone', corresponding with 湊手不及 (coushou buji). The modern expression is 措手不及 (cuoshou buji).

[630] The Manchu expression 'qendehe' means 'to test, corresponding with 試驗 (shiyan). 騐 (yan) is a variant form of 驗 (yan).

[631] The Manchu expression 'buhi' means 'knee caps', corresponding with 膊洛蓋兒 (boluo gai'er). The modern expression is 膝蓋 (xigai).

16. If so,

17. you don't know horses in the first place.

18. A good horse,

19. has strong hooves,

20. [and it] is able to bear[632] [a long] way,

21. [and it] is familiar with the hunting grounds.

22. [Also it] can get along with other animals.

23. The appearance should be good and [it can] act quickly.

24. The talented young man

25. equips himself with a suitable quiver and rides [the horse],

26. raising [his] face,

27. [and he would] look like an eagle!

28. What is this?

29. It is old.[633]

30. The lips are drooping,

31. [and] legs are heavy.

32. It stumbles very often,

33. [and] your body is heavy.

34. So [you and the horse] don't fit each other well.

35. What would [you] do now?

36. Have you already bought [it]?

37. [I] would let it go that way.

38. Generally speaking,

39. I do not have any important work,

40. neither any assignment [which is] far away.

41. As long as it is easy to control,

42. [and] that would fit me well.

43. How is it in comparison with walking?

Section 81: Bad Temper

1. People are talking about him!

2. Why did it concern[634] you?

---

[632] The Manchu expression 'dosombi' means 'to endure or to persevere', corresponding with 奈 (nai). The modern character is 耐 (nai).

[633] The Manchu expression 'se jeke' literally means 'the age has been eaten', which implies that the horse teeth have been worn out due to years of grinding grass.

[634] The Manchu expression 'guwanta' (concern, relation) could have derived from the Chinese word 管他 (guanta). Or 'ta' is a Manchu ending for the plural form, and 'guwan' has derived from the Chinese word 管 (guan).

3. The more [we] persuade [you], the angrier [you] are.

4. [You] are impatient.

5. After the guests leave,

6. [we] will discuss about it.

7. Why would [you] clarify it right now?

8. Brother, your words

9. do not agree with what I meant.

10. We are the people on the same boat.

11. This thing also makes you uncomfortable.

12. Could [you] say there is no impediments at all?

13. If [we] discuss him,

14. we will be involved too.

15. I wouldn't mind that you did not intercede [for me],

16. on the contrary, [you] just followed other people's minds to speak.

17. What heart [did you have]?

18. Indeed I can not agree with you.[635]

19. It is not like that.

20. If [you] have a word, slowly find a reason and say it.

21. Will it be done by getting angry?

22. Please look at the people [who] sit here.

23. They all come because of your thing.

24. [But] arbitrarily you become hopping mad[636] like this,

25. it seems like that you want to drive someone away.

26. What fun is it for the people who have come?

27. If [they] go home,

28. their faces wouldn't get by [because their feelings were hurt by you].

29. If [they] stay here,

30. you wouldn't stop rebuking [others].

31. It is wrong either to go out or come in,

32. [and] it is difficult to either stand or sit.

33. How could friends come to visit your home again?

---

[635] The Manchu expression 'simbe uruxerakv' means 'cannot agree with you', corresponding with 不說你的是 (*bu shuo ni de shi*).

[636] The Manchu expression 'jolhoqome' (*zhengyao* 挣躍) means 'hopping around because of anger'.

Section 82: Secrets were Leaked

1. Is there anyone who has a poorer memory?
2. Compared with you, there is not.
3. The day before yesterday, how did I say to you?
4. Regarding this matter, no matter who [they are]
5. do not let [them] know.
6. Finally you leaked out the secret.
7. What we discussed in secret is now spread out.
8. Everywhere people know it.
9. Haven't they heard that?
10. Instead if they get angry [like] monsters dancing in the daylight[637],
11. [and] resist us, would that be good?
12. Such a good thing has been messed up,
13. [and] gets into such a situation,
14. [this is] all because of you!
15. Brother, you blame me,
16. [and] indeed I feel misjudged.
17. But things have gone this far,
18. [and] even now I can analyze[638] this until my teeth get sour[639],
19. would you believe that?
20. Only the Heaven knows this heart [of mine].
21. Whether I am right or wrong,
22. it will become clear as time passes by.
23. In my heart [I really say that],
24. you, please don't complain,
25. [I] would keep it in a way that is unknown to the others.
26. [Let's] see what they can do about it?
27. [They can either] agree,
28. [or] let it go.
29. When [they] really cannot yield,
30. [we] can think again and get prepared.
31. It wouldn't be late by then.

---

[637] The Manchu expression 'ibagan inenggi xun de maksire balama' means 'the monsters dance in the daylight', which was not translated in the Chinese counter-part.

[638] The Manchu expression 'faksalame' means 'to analyze', corresponding with 分晰 (fenxi). The modern expression is 分析 (fenxi).

[639] The Manchu counterpart is 'jayan juxutele' (teeth get sour), while 嘴酸 (zuisuan, mouth gets sour) is the Chinese expression.

Section 83: Do not Waste Food

1. If [you] cherish and save the good stuff,
2. that is the right way for people to live their life.
3. If [I] don't say anything about you,
4. I wouldn't feel good.
5. The unfinished food could be given to family people to eat,
6. [and] it is good [to do so]!
7. Why did you pour[640] it down the entrance[641] of the uncovered drain arbitrarily?
8. Do you have peace in heart?
9. Even you know [the need of] eating food,
10. [but you] have no idea of the difficulty [to get] rice and food!
11. The people who cultivate and transport
12. are really hard-working.
13. Then [the food] arrives here.
14. Is it easy to get just one grain?
15. Besides,
16. what kind of rich people are we?
17. Eating this
18. and thinking of that,
19. [we] buy things [without] thinking over and over again.
20. [We] are extravagantly throwing money away.
21. Are there any rules for mouth?
22. What is the end of eating?
23. If [we] keep [wasting food] this way,
24. not only do [we] lose [our] blessings,
25. what else wouldn't be exhausted?
26. Just like the old people's words,
27. If [we] eat frugally, food will be enough[642];
28. if [we] wear frugally, clothes will be plenty.
29. How much blessing can you have,

---

[640] The Manchu expression 'doolahangge' (pouring, dumping) has a similar sound with 倒 (dao).

[641] The Manchu expression 'ko sangga' means the entrance of the drain. The word 'entrance' did not appear in the Chinese translation. 陽溝 (yang'gou) is an traditional expression for the uncovered drain, which is different than the covered one (yin'gou 陰溝).

[642] From the context, 'i da' means 'an adequate supply', which corresponds with the Chinese word 長 (chang) in the long run.

30. if you throw [food] away like this?

31. Save it,

32. [otherwise] when the difficult time[643] comes,

33. [and] when [you] suffer from starvation,

34. there would be no time [for you] to regret!

Section 84: He is Dying

1. In the summertime,

2. [He] could still manage [to live normally].

3. As time passed,

4. the illness became worse.

5. Finally [he] dropped down.

6. Because of this,

7. the whole family is in a noisy disorder and cannot make up one mind.

8. The older people have lost weight,

9. [and] the family is like a mess.

10. Looking at him,

11. he has become into a mere bag of bones,

12. lying on the brick bed and struggling to live.

13. At that time I slowly approached him, [asking,]

14. are you feeling better?

15. When [I] asked,

16. [he] opened his eyes and grabbed my hand,

17. sighing,

18. this is the punishment [for] the sin I have committed.

19. The disease has spread to the disordered places[644].

20. Can't I know that [I] cannot get over it?

21. Since the moment I was ill,

22. What kind of doctor didn't [try to] cure [me]?

23. What kind of medicine didn't [I] eat?

24. I was nearly recovered, and then it returned.

25. This is [my] fate.

26. Regarding this, I do not feel unfair at all.

---

[643] The Manchu word 'sui' sounds like 罪 (*zui*), which has a meaning of suffering. The original translation 折受 (*zheshou*) means 'difficult times' in the context.

[644] The Manchu expression 'faquhun bade' literally means 'disordered places', corresponding with 况了 (*kuangle*). An alternative Chinese expression is 病入膏肓 (*bingru gaohuang*), which means the illness has spread into the vital organs, which can no longer be cured.

27. But my parents are old,

28. [and] brothers are young.

29. Besides, relatives, family, bones and flesh all look after me [in vain][645].

30. How could I harden [my] heart and leave them behind?

31. [His] words are finished,

32. [and] tears were running down.

33. Ah!

34. How pitiable!

35. Even if some people are made of iron and stone,

36. hearing these words,

37. [their] hearts cannot remain undisturbed.

Section 85: A Troublemaker

1. What kind of filthy stuff!

2. He is not a human descendant.

3. [He] lives his life like his father does.

4. He is a real seed of his father.

5. No matter how [you] look at him, [you] feel disgusted.

6. No matter where [I] send him,

7. [he] closes his eyes and sees nothing.

8. [He] dashes around madly,

9. [and his] mouth screams aloud,

10. as if he is teasing people.

11. Who understands his words?

12. He is useless in the formal occasions,

13. [and] has no opponents when [he] plays.

14. [He] won't give [you] a moment for rest.

15. [He] is good when [you] keep him nearby for service,

16. [But] when [you] leave [him] alone,

17. [he] is so naughty that [you] cannot watch [him].

18. Totally [he] was born to be a trouble-maker[646].

19. [He] picks this up,

20. [and] puts that down.

---

[645] 白 (*bai*, in vain) appears in the Chinese text, but not in Manchu. However, 白 makes more sense in the context.

[646] The Manchu expression 'ari' means a mischievous child who is difficult to control, corresponding with 惡人 (*e'ren*). A modern translation can be 淘氣包 (*taoqibao*).

21. No moments stay quietly.

22. He jumps amok like a monkey.

23. If [I] lost [my] temper,

24. [I] would cut this bastard's bowels out,

25. [and] that would satisfy [me].

26. When [that angry moment] passed,

27. what would [I] think?

28. Do [I] really [want to] kill him?

29. First, a short poking bar is better than[647] [bare] hands;

30. second, [he] was born as a family servant[648].

31. Whatever he gets and eats,

32. is not up to [him].

33. [I] shall sympathize him more.

Section 86: I am not Afraid

1. What intention is that?

2. I am extremely despised.

3. Isn't it reasonable that I am talking to you?

4. As soon as [I] come, [he] uses artful words to embarrass me.

5. What is that for?

6. [We] used to mingle together,

7. so I just won't tell [people about his past].

8. If I uncover his [secrets from the] bottom,

9. [he] would blame me for exposing his root.

10. [Regarding] his hometown,

11. [and] my old birth place,

12. who doesn't know?

13. [He] thought people can do nothing at about it.[649]

14. For how long did that last?

15. [He] has been suffering, but now to me,

16. [he even dares to] make grand gestures.

17. If [he] just said something wrong,

---

[647] The Manchu expression 'qi ai dalji' means 'better than', which corresponds with 比…強 (bi … qiang).

[648] The Manchu expession 'booi ujin jui' (jia sheng zi'er 家生子兒) means a child born by the family servants, therefore, the child was born to be a bond servant.

[649] The Manchu expression 'monjirxambi' means 'to rub one's hands together', corresponding with 揉捔 (rouken). 'monjirxaburakv' means 'one can do nothing but rub his/her hands together(wukenaihe 無可奈何)'.

18. I wouldn't mind in my heart.
19. [But he] must insist that his words are right,
20. [and] no matter what, [he] wouldn't admit his fault.
21. Because of that, [I] cannot help being angry.
22. [He thought] I am easy to deal with.
23. Backing up by someone's power,
24. today he waved his hands[650] to get me here on purpose.
25. Indeed who knows what would happen?
26. Who is afraid of that?
27. If [we] contest and see who is better,
28. that would go as I wish.
29. If [any one] hesitates a little,
30. [he] is not a real man.

Section 87: Rainy Days

1. Tick tack, it has been raining for quite a few days.
2. [My] heart has been totally broken[boiled].
3. It is dripping water here,
4. it is wet over there,
5. [and I] do not even have a [dry] place to sleep.
6. Moreover,
7. [I] was bitten by bedbugs and fleas,
8. [and that was] much intolerable.
9. I tossed over and over until the one hundred bells[651] [rang],
10. [and I] still couldn't sleep.
11. [I] managed to close my eyes,
12. [and] tolerated [all the problems].
13. In a daze, [I] was going to fall asleep.
14. During the sleep,
15. suddenly in the northwest corner,
16. the loud noise was like a landslide and ground fracturing.
17. [I] woke up in a fright,
18. [and] for a long time [my] body was still trembling and [my] heart was still pounding fast.

---

[650] The Manchu expression 'gala elkime' means 'waving one's hands', corresponding with 招呼 (*zhaohu*).

[651] The Manchu expression 'tanggv ging' literally means 'one hundred bells', which indicates the dawn has come. The original Chinese equivalence is 亮鍾 (*liangzhong*), which means 'bright bell'.

19. [I] opened my eyes for a look.

20. In the room and on the brick bed nothing was wrong.

21. Immediately I sent people to look around.

22. [They] said the head wall of the next door was soaked by rainwater and fell down.

23. [Speaking of] the reason for the loud noise which [I] heard in dream,

24. how did it make such a loud noise?

Section 88: Stay up Late

1. These days things are happening,

2. [and] because [I] have stayed up late two nights in a row,

3. [my] whole body has no strength [but feels] weak.[652]

4. Last night,

5. I was going to sleep,

6. [but] because all the relatives were here,

7. how could I leave them alone and go to sleep?

8. Therefore,

9. [even though I] managed to [stay awake] again and again,

10. [and] maintained [my] spirit to sit,

11. [but my] eyes couldn't help dropping down[653].

12. [Finally I] dozed off in a trance.

13. Later guests were about to leave,

14. [and] I laid down a pillow [for myself].

15. With clothes on,

16. [I] put my head down [on the pillow and] slept soundly.

17. I woke up at the second strike[654].

18. At that moment, without knowing whether being cold or something else,

19. [I] felt suffocated inside.

20. [My] whole body heated up,

21. [and I] felt like being burned by fire.

22. Moreover, the bottom part of [my] ears ached,

---

[652] The Manchu expression 'fakjin' means 'a support or something to fall back on', corresponding with 主意 (*zhuyi*). The modern translation is 憑藉 (*pingjie*) or 依靠 (*yikao*).

[653] The Manchu expression 'debsehun' means 'drop down', corresponding with 媽搭下來 (*mada xialai*). A modern expression can be 搭拉下來 (*dala xiala*).

[654] 'jai ging' (*di'er geng* 第二更) is a traditional way to indicate the time period between nine to eleven o'clock in the evening.

23. [which] caused [my] gums to swell.
24. Eating and drinking became tasteless,
25. [and I felt] uneasy whether sitting or standing.
26. I thought it must be the reason of indigestion.
27. After taking a dose of arthritics[655],
28. the good and bad things all came down [out of body].
29. At that moment I slightly felt easier.

Section 89: Court Beads

1. Brother, about that court beads of yours,
2. I said [I] was going to take it.
3. In the end [I] didn't take it.
4. For what reasons?
5. Every time [I] came,
6. you were not at home.
7. Without seeing your face,
8. How could [I] take your stuff ambiguously?
9. Therefore,
10. today I especially come to see you and tell [you in person],
11. [so I] can take it.
12. According to its value,
13. whatever you say,
14. I would buy according to your idea for an exchange.
15. If there are no good ones in the shops,
16. I would find it through many places and give it to you.
17. What is your opinion now?
18. Why do you mention[656] it?
19. It would be fine if you just take it [even without compensation].
20. It wouldn't lead to losing [it].
21. Are [people] short of the seeds of bod-hi trees?
22. But very few can be comparable to the ones [I lost]!
23. Isn't that so?
24. Everyday [I] took [it with me],
25. [and it] was soaked by sweat.

---

655 The Manchu words 'wasibure okto' literally means a 'make-things-go-down medicine'. The correspondent Chinese 打藥 (dayao) is now expressed as 瀉藥 (xieyao).
656 The Manchu expression 'jondofi' means 'to mention, corresponding with 題 (ti).
The modern translation is 提 (ti).

26. So [it] was smooth and glowing.
27. If [I] didn't take it somewhere else,
28. [I] would keep it in a box.
29. [It] was supposed to be lost.
30. Last month we went to a garden,
31. [I] forgot to put [it] away.
32. When [I] came back to look for [it],
33. Where [is it]?
34. [I] couldn't even see its shadow.
35. [I] do not know who took it.
36. [I] recalled and searched, but didn't find it in the end.

Section 90: A Hot Day

1. Today it is horrible.
2. Since the beginning of summer,
3. it would make the hottest day.
4. There is no wind at all,
5. [and] it is very humid.
6. All kinds of utensils are hand-burning hot.
7. The more cold water [I] drink, the thirstier [I] become.
8. There is no other choices, but only to take a shower.
9. I cooled myself off under a tree for a long time,
10. [and] calmed down a little.
11. In such a dry and hot weather,
12. people even expose their bodies,
13. sitting at leisure,
14. [and] still worry about heatstroke.
15. What is happening to you?
16. You have been lowering your head and writing words.
17. What hardship is that?
18. Don't [you] cherish [your] life?
19. You do not have any official duty,
20. [and you can just] learn [something] comfortably.
21. Take the merchants for an example.
22. [They] carry heavy things,
23. [and] stretch their necks,
24. walking around and crying out for customers.
25. [They work] until [they] are totally covered by sweat,

26. [and they] can make one hundred coins just to keep alive.
27. For [people] like me, [I] just eat whatever is ready,
28. how could [I complain because I just] write the words quietly?[657]
29. Moreover,
30. winter is cold,
31. summer is hot,
32. [and] this is a firm and unshakable truth since the ancient time.
33. No matter what happens and [I just] endure quietly,
34. [and that] would cool [myself] off.
35. Would it help by being agitated?
36. Would it exempt [me] from [feeling hot]?

Section 91: A Rude Man

1. When he came,
2. I was still sleeping.
3. I was startled,
4. hearing that someone was talking loudly in the principal room.
5. Who has come?
6. How come the voice[658] is so loud?
7. Probably that abominable person has come.
8. What was there when [I] went to check?
9. [He] was sitting there upright,
10. discussing [something] with great interest[659].
11. [His] mouth hasn't stopped since [he] came here,
12. talking about this and that.
13. After eating two meals,
14. [he] didn't leave until sunset.
15. Even when a man has nothing else to do,
16. how could he sit at other people's home until sunset?
17. [He] talked about the forgetful and tiring things[660],

---

[657] The Manchu expression 'bahambio' means 'how could that be counted as', corresponding with 能彀得嗎 (*neng gou de zhao ma*). From the context, the speaker means writing is nothing in comparison to the vendors who walked around in such a hot day.
[658] The Manchu word 'konggolo' is a bird's craw [crop), which was translated as 嗓門 (*sangmen*, throat or voice) correspondingly.
[659] The Manchu expression 'amtanggai' means 'cheerfully', corresponding with 有資有味 (*youziyouwei*). The modern words are 有滋有味 (*youziyouwei*).

515

18. [and that] caused people a headache.
19. If [he stopped] here, that would be fine.
20. Whatever [you] have, [you] cannot let him see.
21. If [he] laid his eyes on [it],
22. [he] wouldn't even ask but took it immediately[661] [when he] saw it.
23. He would even take it earlier [before you notice].
24. Indeed in his life, he only knows taking stuff from other people.
25. There is not even one time that he gives something to people.
26. [Regarding] such a person's intestines and [other] organs,
27. how did he grow [them that way]?
28. I sincerely do not know.
29. [Even though] it is all your fortune,
30. would you take it [all for granted]?
31. The Heaven has eyes,
32. [and] will not necessarily put up with him!

Section 92: You Look Distressed!

1. How is that friend of ours?
2. Recently he has been frowning and gloomy,
3. [and] seemingly there are some unknown reasons.
4. Say, if it rains or snows,
5. [he can] just stay at home.
6. Except for that, even the far places should be visited.
7. Sitting at home without doing anything, how could [he] bear that?
8. These days [he] hasn't gone out of the door,
9. [but] only sat at home.
10. Yesterday I visited him,
11. [and] looked at [his] face.
12. Could [I] say he just looks like before?
13. Obviously he has lost weight.
14. [He] went out and came in irregularly,
15. [and no one] knows what was happening.
16. I was confused about that.
17. What was he doing?

---

[660] The Manchu expression 'onggoho xadaha baita' can be understand as 'things that are easily forgotten and tiring'. The Chinese literal translation of 忘了乏的 (wangle fade) must be a traditional expression.
[661] The Manchu expression 'nambuha' means 'took away immediately', corresponding with 撓着了 (naozhaole). The modern expression is 拿走 (nazou).

18. When [I] was about to ask,

19. [I] was interrupted by one of his relatives.

20. Ah!

21. I was able to figure it out.

22. Probably [he] was entangled by that thing and his heart was muddled.

23. Once people are caught in the rain, they are no longer afraid of dew-drops.

24. No matter what difficult things he had before,

25. if he could finish them instantly,

26. how could [he] be involved now?

27. [He] wouldn't be so distressed like this!

Section 93: Addiction Kills

1. What kind of strong body [he] had before?

2. Besides, [he] does not know how to look after it.

3. He is addicted to wine and women.

4. Without any control, [his health] has been damaged.

5. Now [he] is entrapped by diseases, which have become severe[662].

6. Yesterday when I visited [him],

7. [he] still could manage to come to the principal room,

8. saying to me, brother, you must be exhausted for coming here;

9. in such a dry and hot weather,

10. you come to visit [me] very often,

11. [and] countless times you delivered things to me,

12. [so] you must be tired;

13. [I] thank [you] very much;

14. only among the relatives, people would care about each other like this;

15. if for the irrelevant[663] people, who would remember me?

16. I really appreciate that!

17. [I] can only remember it firmly[664] in [my] heart.

18. When [I] get better,

---

[662] The Manchu expression 'dembei sirke ohobi' means 'the illness has become severe', corresponding with 瘦的一條了 (*shoude yitiao le*). An alternative translation can be 病得很嚴重了(*bingde hen yanzhong le*).

[663] The Manchu expression 'halba dalba' must be an old Manchu expression. 'halba' means scapula, and 'dalba' means 'side or flank'. Therefore, 'halba dalba' could refer to the people who are not centrally important.

[664] The Manchu expression 'hadahai ejefi' is to keep something firmly in mind, which was translated as 緊記 (*jinji*). The modern Chinese expression is 謹記 (*jinji*).

19. I will kowtow and give thanks to [your] great kindness.
20. Even [his] mouth could say so,
21. [his] body seems that [he] barely could hold up.
22. Therefore,
23. I said, brother, you are a sensible man.
24. Need I say more?
25. Take care of your body
26. [and] recover soon.
27. In free time,
28. [I] will come to visit [you] again.
29. [I] said so [and then] came back.

Section 94: Bond-servants Need Discipline

1. Yesterday [I] went somewhere else.
2. The coarse bond-servants
3. just arbitrarily caused a disturbance.
4. When I returned,
5. the monkeys were still arguing and yelling.
6. At that moment I made a loud sound,
7. cleared my throat and went inside.
8. All the noises stopped at the same time.
9. They winked at each other
10. [and] went away out of fear.
11. It was late when I came home,
12. [and my] body was tired.
13. I didn't say anything,
14. [and just] endured and slept.
15. This morning I got up and went out,
16. The beheaded all came [to me],
17. saying that the bond servants all deserve to die.
18. They knelt down straightaway in a row.
19. Some were begging,
20. [and] some just made a kowtow [to me].
21. My anger was slightly soothed.
22. At that moment I asked what happened to you all,
23. [and] why don't you live in peace,
24. [and] is your flesh itching?
25. Do [I] have to beat [you] or do something else?
26. Be careful [and] if this happens again in the future,
27. [and your] eye balls should look around cautiously.
28. If [I] don't beat [you] to death,

29. presumably you are not afraid.

30. [They] all responded with a 'yes' and went away.

Section 95: A Terrible Person

1. Regarding that [man who] has no luck,

2. how do you look at [him]?

3. Even though he takes on a human skin,

4. [inside of him] is really a beast's bowel!

5. It is good for [people] to walk around and avoid [him].

6. When there is a peaceful moment,

7. [I] would say that [he] is a defiant leader that disturbs things!

8. [His] heart is full of jealousy[665], and [he] is good at sowing dissension among [people].

9. When [his] eyes look at [you], [you would] fall over with [your] face towards the sky.

10. Whatever [he] hears, [he] will stir it up.

11. Even the small things which are like lice nits[666],

12. when [they] come into his mouth,

13. [he] would slander[667] behind back and make it far away[668] from what is normal.

14. [He would] spread the things from here to there,

15. tell the words from there to here.

16. [and] breed enmity between the two sides.

17. He acted like a good person, swaying between them back and forth.

18. If [he] says that our words are unproven,

19. please look at that

20. not only do few people make friends with him,

21. [but] if [they] do not point at [his] back and swear at [him],

22. that would be his luck.

23. Ah!

24. How pathetic!

---

[665] The Manchu expression 'gvnin silhingga' means 'a jealous heart', corresponding with 心苦 (*xinku*, a bitter heart). A modern translation can be 心裏妒忌 (*xinli duji*).

[666] The Manchu expression 'qihe use' literally means 'lice, larva or nits', which was translated as 虮子 (*jizi*) in the Chinese parallel.

[667] The Manchu expression 'jubexehei' means 'slandering behind back', corresponding with 說到 (*shuodao*). An alternative expression could be 誹謗 (*feibang*).

[668] The Manchu expression 'fikatala genembi' means 'to go a long way round', corresponding with 離乎 (*lihu*). An alternative translation can be 離奇 (*liqi*).

25. For no reason at all, his father and mother
26. were implicated by this shameless [son];
27. [and they] were cursed by people.
28. How unjust is that?

Section 96: He Survived!

1. If [he] is not supposed to die,
2. naturally there will be a chance [for him to live].
3. That evening, he was severely sick.
4. After a long time,
5. [he] regained consciousness.
6. His mouth said 'I am fine',
7. [and] 'you put your heart at ease',
8. [and] 'tell people not to panic'.
9. Thanks to the grace of ancestors and the blessings upon [his] family,
10. the next day [they] invited another doctor to heal [him].
11. Soon [he] is getting better day after day.
12. The day before yesterday I went to visit [him].
13. Though [he] hasn't recovered completely,
14. The color of [his] face has turned better,
15. [and he] has gained some weight.
16. He was leaning against a pillow,
17. [and] eating something.
18. At the moment I said you are lucky!
19. Congratulations!
20. Even though this time [you] didn't die,
21. [you] have shed a layer of skin.
22. [He] looked at me, smiling faintly[669].
23. Indeed he made it with a lot of sweat.

Section 97: Obeying the Rules

1. Why can't you sit still,
2. [and] remain orderly while sitting there?
3. Would anyone call you a wood stump?
4. If [you] don't talk,
5. would [not] anyone call you mute?[670]

---

[669] The Manchu expression 'ijarxame' has an equivalence as '眯嘻眯嘻' (*mixi mixi*), in which '眯' was written as a 耳 and 密. A modern translation is 笑眯眯 (*xiaomimi*).

6. It seems like [you are trying to] make fun of[671] someone.

7. [You] tease this one and provoke that one.

8. What fun is that?

9. You can't feel it,

10. [but] others couldn't stand it.

11. Maybe sometimes you will encounter a mean man,

12. get [yourself] into trouble,[672]

13. [and] you will say, 'ah! how scary is that'!

14. Brother, your words are correct.

15. If [you] are an indifferent person, would [you] say so?

16. Teasing [people] is the trigger for quarrel!

17. As time passes [and he develops this as a habit],

18. how could [he] become better?

19. All in all,

20. [even] his body has grown into a man,

21. [his] age is not there yet!

22. Haven't we gone through that period?

23. It is a time of being playful!

24. Naturally [people grow up] this way.

25. When [they] behave like this,

26. [we] can only invite a famous teacher to teach [him] books [about courtesy],

27. [so he would] practice [obeying] the rules!

28. As days go by,

29. gradually[673] [they would] understand.

30. One day when [they] understand the things in the world,

31. [they] naturally change [into better people].

32. Why do [you] worry that [they] cannot become useful people?

Section 98: Just Let It Out!

1. [He] hasn't experienced any thing yet,

2. [and] he is very timid.

---

[670] The Manchu expression 'akv' (not) did not appear in the Chinese counterpart, which makes more sense without it.

[671] The Manchu expression 'yobo arara' means 'to make fun of', corresponding with 作笑 (*zuoxiao*). A modern translation is 戲弄 (*xi'nong*).

[672] The Manchu expression 'koro baha' [ran into trouble) originally was translated as 碰釘子 (*peng dingzi*), which is a metaphor of 'bumping one's head against a nail'.

[673] The Manchu expression 'qun qun i' means 'gradually, corresponding with 一歷一歷 (*yili yili*). The modern translation is 逐漸地 (*zhujian de*).

3. If [you] have words [to say], why do [you] hold them back inside?

4. [You] should go [to him] directly,

5. [and] explain to him as clearly as possible.

6. He is also a person.

7. Would he not act according to the rules?

8. When you analyze and break it down from beginning to end,

9. what could [he] do to you?

10. Would [he] kill [you]?

11. Or would [he] eat [you] up?

12. Moreover,

13. [He] has not made a sound over there.

14. Nothing happened yet, [but][674] you got scared[675] and lost your ideas[676].

15. [You] take precautions over here and there.

16. Is that a man's behavior?

17. Don't worry!

18. You just lay your heart at ease.

19. If he really does not agree,

20. do [you] think [he] would spare your feelings?

21. Even you are scared this much or that much,

22. do [you] think [you] could get away in a clean way?

23. Up to now there is still no messages coming through,

24. [so] presumably he has already thrown [your thing] behind [his] neck, and forgot it.

25. If [you] don't really trust [what I said],

26. [you can] inquire about it in secret.

27. I guarantee there is no harm.

Section 99: Don't Trust the Doctors

1. Regarding what you advised, isn't it good words?

2. But [I] have another thing on [my] mind.

3. If [I] really need to take medicine,

4. I am not a wood stump.

---

[674] The Manchu expression 'afanggala' means 'nothing happens yet, but'.

[675] The Manchu expression 'kvlifi' means 'being intimidated', which was translated as 怕的 (*pade*).

[676] The Manchu expression 'fekun waliyabu' is a common phrase, which means 'being smitten with fear' (喪膽 *sangdan*).

5. Is there a reason that [I] cherish money so much that [I] won't spend it on my body?

6. How do I say this?

7. The year before last I was hurt by the [wrong] medicine,

8. [and I] almost lost [my] life.

9. Up to now [every time when I] remember this, [I] still tremble with fear[677].

10. Nowadays[678] among the doctors,

11. if [I] say there are no good ones ever[679],

12. [I] would judge them wrongly.

13. Even there are some [good doctors]

14. but we only know very few.

15. Moreover,

16. the trustworthy ones,

17. are only one or two.

18. The rest of them

19. only know about making silver and money!

20. Does he care whether you die or live?

21. If [you] don't believe [me],

22. You go, try, ask and look.

23. Haven't you known the nature of medicine?

24. It is just the incompetent medicine[680].

25. [A doctor's purpose is supposed to] cure people's diseases.

26. In a hurry [the doctor] came to your home,

27. [and] claimed to take [your] pulse,

28. [but actually he just] put his fingers [on your wrist] and rubbed casually.

29. [The doctor] just finished the work carelessly, gave [me] a prescription,

---

[677] The Manchu expression 'silhi meijembi' (gallbladder breaks or fractures) is metaphor to describe 'tremble because of fear'. The parallel Chinese 膽戰 (danzhan) is also written as 膽顫 (danchan).

[678] The Manchu expression 'te biqibe' means 'nowadays', corresponding with 既如 (jiru), which is 如今 (rujin) in modern Chinese.

[679] The Manchu expression 'fuhali' means 'ever or always, corresponding with 搃 (zong), which is a variant form of 總 (zong).

[680] The Manchu expression 'amban i maname' is a Manchu common phrase for 'being confused and careless', which was translated as '大方脈兒' (dafang mai'er) of the time. The modern expression is 糊塗 (hutu) or 馬虎 (mahu).

30. charged the horse fee[681] and left.
31. If [you] are cured, that is his credit.
32. If you die, that is your fate,
33. [which] has nothing to do with him.
34. Don't [I] know my own illness myself?
35. Rather using all sorts of medicine,
36. it is better that [I] just take care of myself quietly.

Section 100: Alcohol Kills

1. Look at you!
2. [You] are so intimate with liquor and yellow wine.
3. [You] can't even leave them for a moment.
4. Every time [you] drink, [you] would by all means become as drunk as a jelly-fish[682].
5. [You] wouldn't let the [cups] go until [you] cannot stand up.
6. That is not a good thing.
7. It is good to quit.
8. If in a banquet, how could [you] not drink?
9. How could [you] avoid [drinking] if there are some [important] things?
10. What matters if you just take some and drink [in such occasions]?
11. When there are no things, [you] still consider drinking as an important thing,
12. grabbing the cup [and refusing to let it go].
13. From [your] mouth endless praises come out.
14. What good is that?
15. [You] will only offend the older generations[683],
16. commit big crimes,
17. [and] delay important things.
18. Indeed [I] never heard that drinking can be considered as learning an ability,
19. growing intelligence,

---

[681] The Manchu expression 'morin i jiha' (horse's money) is a fee charged for visiting a patient.

[682] The Manchu expression 'lalanji heperefi' (*luan zui ru ni* 乱醉如泥) could be a common phrase for describing a person's body which is as soft as mud due to a high level of drunkenness. The modern Chinese expression is 爛醉如泥 (*lan zui ru ni*).

[683] The Manchu expression 'ungga dangga' means 'the older generations', corresponding with 老家兒 (*laojia'er*). A modern translation is 長輩 (*zhangbei*).

20. earning people's respect,
21. [and] accomplishing real business!
22. [It will only] disturb [your] nature,
23. [and] hurt your body.
24. It is a bad medicine!
25. It is appropriate if you drink in the long term?
26. If [you] don't trust [me],
27. you look in the mirror.
28. [Your] nose is rotten.
29. [You] are not a person that damages[684] yourself.
30. Without noticing day and night,
31. [you] just drink and immerse[685] [yourself in alcohol].
32. Isn't that [killing] yourself quickly[686]?

Section 101: Learning is Difficult

1. Brother, please look.
2. What hardship are [you] suffering from?
3. People remind[687] you here and there,
4. [and] that is for your benefit.
5. [Their] purpose is to prevent [you] from learning bad things,
6. [and to remind you] to review what [you] have read.
7. Are [you] afraid of learning something?
8. It is difficult to learn something decent,
9. [but] very easy for him to learn the bad things.
10. No matter how [you] talk [to him], even [you] damage [your] mouth [by talking too much],
11. if he really listened, and what else would [you] want?
12. But he just became sluggish and inert,
13. pouting his mouth, and hanging down his face and eyes.
14. I couldn't watch and tolerate[688] it in my heart anymore;

---

[684] The Manchu expression 'ubu waliyabure' literally means 'doubly discard', which was translated as 撂分兒 (liao fen'er) in the first place. A modern translation could be 反覆作踐 (fanfu zuojian).

[685] 'To immerse, soak' corresponds with bexeme (wang zaoli 徃糟裡). A modern expression could be 泡在酒裏 (paozai jiuli).

[686] The original expression 'hvdularangge' (being quick or fast) was translated as 快着 (kuaizhe), which is an indirect way to say 'die quickly'.

[687] 'To reminder' corresponds with jomburengge (tibo 題駁). A modern translation is 提醒 (tixing).

15. [I] got mad and denounced him in a loud voice.
16. [His] face turned red.
17. Instead [he] looked at me, [saying,]
18. why are you picking up my weaknesses?
19. [His] eyes got watery.
20. How confused and unlucky [he seems]!
21. But as [people] say,
22. good medicine tastes bitter in mouth,
23. [and] faithful words offend the ears!
24. If [we] are not bones and flesh,
25. I would just delude him and make him happy.
26. Why must I make him irritated?

---

[688] The Manchu expression 'dolo dosorakv' means 'cannot tolerate something in heart', which was translated in the Chinese counterpart.

Epilogue

History does not equate with the past. Essentially, historical books are personal perceptions of historians, whose thoughts are often affected by external factors. Therefore, readers should develop a capability of critical thinking, to read historical documents according to their own judgments, rather than being manipulated by primary and secondary sources.

In a context of China's late imperial history, most people would assume a past solely written in the Chinese characters. This book offers a Manchu perspective to disclose amounts of historical events composed in the Manchu language, which has been ignoredfor a long time. Not only some particular phenomena do we observe, but also the Manchu culture displayed by the Manchu-speaking people: how they interacted with one another and with people of different cultures.

Since Yongzheng's reign (r. 1723-1732), these Manchu primers were widely distributed as textbooks for the banner people to study their first language that functioned as the state language across the vast Qing empire. Language is a soft power that manifests the persuasive dominance over the ethnic boundaries, being conducted by the ruling elites that centers around the Manchus. Furthermore, millions of Manchu documents were produced since the Manchu script was created in 1599. The idea of interpreting the Qing history based on Manchu chronicles has been well accepted in the academia. Thus, this book will serve as a crutch for researchers to master a basic capability of reading Manchu documents for greater purposes.

Furthermore, interdisciplinary studies have developed into a trend of academic research. In terms of history, It is closely involved with philosophy, linguistics, arts, religion, literature and even natural science. It is impossible to draw a distinctive line between these subjects as they inevitably share more and more research themes and methods, which aim to interpret human activities that have happened and are still happening. This book is accordingly presented as a platform for integrating linguistics, history, literature and anthropology into one domain, for better knowing what actually happened in East Asia.

These three Manchu manuscripts served as major textbooks in the Qing dynasty for banner-men to learn Manchu as their first language. Various themes are included in these books as topics for conversations between banner-men, ranging from Manchu language learning, attending translation examination, martial practice, family life and all sorts of social norms.

For linguists, this book surely offers a Manchu angle to examine Mandarin, the modern Chinese language, whose pronunciation has been largely shaped by the Manchus of the Qing dynasty. From the original document of qingwen kimeng, one can see that many Chinese characters were aligned with Manchu alphabetical letters, which regulate new ways of pronouncing the Chinese characters. This phenomenon indicates the beginning of the formation of the current Standardized Chinese Language with regard to phonetics.

For historians, these Manchu primers enlarge the view of looking into the past via Manchu communities, and thus scholars are better equipped to reinterpret the history of late imperial China from a Manchu perspective, rather than a fixed Han Chinese Confucian angle. Joot Fujun, who presumably was the author of *Oyonggo One* and its *Oyonggo Two*, served as a grand minister and military commander-in-chief for a long time, both in inner court and frontier regions. As a banner-man, Fujun endorsed the distribution of these books with insights into preserving the language and maintaining its identity.

For Manchu literature studies, these primers provide plentiful literary works for research and recreational purpose. Social customs, descriptions of natural scenery, stories of individual and family life frequently appear throughout theses primers. The Manchu literature is a grand treasury and little research has been devoted to exploring this field.

For anthropological studies, this book offers primary sources for researchers to look into the banner society that existed between the early and late Qing periods. Abundant materials are available for anthropologists to interpret the Manchu people's behaviors and thoughts, in comparison to the Chinese of the Qing dynasty and the Manchu people who live in modern times. The Manchu customs went through significant transformations since their unification of China proper and the evidence of their cultural heritage remains in their writings.

For all academic researchers, these Manchu primers serve as a convenient tool to enhance our Manchu language competence, not just for reading the Manchu documents, but also for speaking the Manchu language itself. It takes a long time to be proficient in any language, but as Joot Fujun said, as long as we study hard on a daily basis (*kiqeme genehei inenggi goidaha manggi*), our language capability will grow naturally (*ulhiyen i elhun de isinafi*); not only will we be exempted from being ridiculed for incompetence in a language (*gisun ede narhvn akv sere basuqun qi guweqi ojoro teile akv*), but also we will be praised for being proficient and unimpaired (*umesi urehe bime qilqin akv sere maktaqun bahaqi ombi*). It is a long way to go. Since we cannot achieve the goal in one day, we had better start right now!

Bibliography

Traditional Works in Eastern Asian Languages:

Dongyi kaolüe 東夷考略 (Evidential Research upon the Eastern Barbarians) composed by Mao Ruizheng 茅瑞徵 (circa 1601), collected in *Qing ruguanqian shiliao   xuanji yi* 清入關前史料選輯 1 (Compilation of Selected Historical Materials before the Qing Entered the Passes), vol. 1, compiled by Pan Zhe 潘喆 et al., edition Beijing: Zhongguo renmin daxue chubanshe, 1984.

Dorgi yamun asaraha manju hergen i fe dangse a.k.a., *Neige cangben Manwen laodang*   內閣藏本滿文老檔 (The Version of Manchu Old Archives Stored by the Grand Secretariat), compiled by Wu Yuanfeng 吳元豐 (b. 1956) et al., edition Shenyang: Liaoning minzu chubanshe, 2009.

27. *Douzhen yiguan* 痘疹一貫 (Same Principle for Treating Small Pox and Herpes), Sun   Feiran 孫斐然 (?-?),edition Beijing: Jingdu yongkuizhai keben, 1717.

28. *Jiang Liangqi* 蔣良騏(b. 1723-1790), Donghua lu 東華錄 (The Record of Donghua Gate), edition Beijing: Zhonghua shuju, 1980.

Jinshi 金史 (History of Jin)*,* Tuotuo et al, edition Beijing: Zhonghua shuju, 1975.

Manwen yuandang 滿文原檔 (The Original Manchu Archives), Dijiuce 第九冊 (Book 9), edited by Feng Mingzhu 馮明珠, edition Taioei: Guoli gugong bowuyuan, Taibei, 2005.

Mingdai Man Meng shiliao 明代滿蒙史料 (Manchu-Mongol Historical Materials of the Ming Dynasty), Lichao shilu chao 李朝實錄抄, di yi ce 第一冊, edition Tokyo: Wenhai chubanshe youxian gongsi yinxing 文海出版社有限公司印行, 1953.

Qingchu shiliao congkan diqi zhong 清初史料叢刊第七種 (The First Compilation of Early Qing Historical Materials), *chaoxian lichao shilu zhong de nüzhen shiliao xuanbian* 朝鮮李朝實錄中的女真史料選編, Wang Zhonghan jilu 王鍾翰輯錄, edition Shenyang: Liaoning daxue chubanshe 遼寧大學出版社, 1978.

Qingshigao 清史稿 (A Draft Qing History), di er ce 第二冊, Zhao Erxun deng zhuan 趙　爾巽等撰, edition Beijing: Zhonghua shuju 中華書局, 1977.

Qingshilu 清實錄 (The Qing Veritable Records), vol. 1, *Manzhou shilu,* edition Beijing: Zhonghua shuju, 1986.

29. *Qingshi liezhuan* 清史列传 (Biographies of Qing History), edited by Wang Zhonghan 王　钟翰, edition Beijing: Zhonghua shuju, 1987.
30.
31. *Taizong wen huangdi shilu* 太宗文皇帝實錄 (The Veritable Records of Taizong Wen Emperor), excerpted from *Qingshilu* 清實錄 (The Qing Veritable Records), vol. 2, edition Beijing: Zhonghua shuju, 1986.

32. *Yuanshi* 元史 (History of Yuan), Song Lian 宋濂 et al., Liezhuan dishiyi 列傳第十一, collected in *Chizaotang Sikuquanshu huiyao* 摛藻堂四庫全书薈要 (Compendiums of Complete Four Categories of Literature at Chizaotang), edition Taipei: Taiwan shijie shuju, 1985.

Secondary Sources
in Western and Eastern Languages:

Crossley, Pamela Kyle (1999), *A translucent mirror: history and identity in Qing imperial ideology,* University of California Press, Berkeley and Los Angeles, California.

Elliott, Mark C. (2001), The Manchu Way: The Eight Banners and Ethnic Identity in Late Imperial China, Stanford University Press, Stanford California.

Hucker, Charles O (1988), *A Dictionary of Official Titles in Imperial China,* Taiwan Edition, Southern Materials Center, INC, Taipei.

Kiyohiko Sugiyama (2010), The Qing Empire in the Central Eurasian Context: Its   Structure of Rule as Seen from the Eight Banner System, Collected in   Comparative Imperiology (2010) , edited by Matsuzato Kimitaka, Slavic Research Center, Hokkaido University, Sapporo.

Kihohiko Sugiyama (2015), *The Formation of the Qing Empire and the Eight Banner System,* the University of Nagoya Press, Nagoya.

Meilan Zhang and Jin Qi (2017), "The Decline of Manchu in Its Contact with Late Qing Chinese-A Case Study of Several Editions of *Qingwen Zhiyao,*" in Dan Xu and Hui Li (eds.), *Languages and Genes in North-western China and Adjacent Regions,* Springer, Singapore.

Meng Sen 孟森 (1992), *Manzhou kaiguo shi* 滿洲開國史 (History of Founding the Manchu State)*,* Shanghai guji chubanshe.

33. Rawski, Evelyn S. (1996), "Presidential Address: Reenvisioning the Qing: The Significance of the Qing Period in Chinese History", *The Journal of Asian Studies*, 55.4: 829-850.

34. Saarela, Martin Soderblom (2015), *Manchu and the Study of Language in China (1607-1911),* PhD dissertation, Chieftainton University, New Jersey.

35. Takashi Takegoshi 竹越孝 (2015), *Ichi hyaku Jō Kiyofumi yubi yō taishō tekisuto* 『一百　條』・『清文指要』対照テキスト古代文字資料館発行, published by Ancient　　　Character Museum, 149: 18.

36. Von Ranke, Leopold (1855), Geschichiten der romanischen und ger-manischen Voelker von 1494-1514, Saemtliche Werke vol.33, Leipzig.
37. Wylie Alexander (1855), Translation of the Ts'ing wan k'e mung, a Chinese Grammar of the Manchu Tartar Language with Introductory Notes on Manchu Literature, London Mission Press, Shanghai.

38. Zhang Huake 張華克 (2005), Qingwenzhiyao jiedu 清文指要解讀 (Guidance of   Essential Elements of Manchu Language), Wenshizhe chuabanshe 文史哲出版社, Taipei.

39. Zhang Meilan 張美蘭 (2016), "Cong *Qingwen zhiyao* manhan wen-ben yongci de bianhua   kan manwen tezheng de xiaoshi 從《清文指要》滿漢文本用詞的變化看滿文   特徵的消失 (Observing the Disappearance of Manchu-language Features Based   upon Word Changes in Manchu-Chinese Texts of *Qingwen zhiyao*)" *Zhongguo yuwen* 中國語文 (Chinese Language and Literature), 2016.5: 566-577.